RICHARD BEATON is Assistant Professor
of New Testament at Fuller Theological
Seminary in the School of Theology. He is a
member of the Catholic Biblical Association
and the Society of Biblical Literature.

ISAIAH'S CHRIST IN MATTHEW'S GOSPEL

Matthew's Jesus is typically described as the humble, compassionate messiah. This book argues that this is, however, only half the story. Matthew's theologically rich quotation of Isaiah 42.1–4, traditionally considered one of the four servant songs, underscores that manifest in Jesus' powerful message and deeds, particularly his healings and inclusion of the marginalized, is the justice that was thought to accompany the arrival of the Kingdom of God. The study explores modifications to the text-form of the Isaianic citations, their relationship to the surrounding context, and the rhetorical force of the final form. It argues that the quotations are bi-referential, functioning on both a narrative and theological level, and also explores the issues surrounding the troublesome 'extraneous' content. It arrives at the conclusion that this citation was central to Matthew's understanding of Jesus' life and mission. In sum, this study offers a fresh exploration of Matthew's high, ethical christology.

RICHARD BEATON is Assistant Professor of New Testament at Fuller Theological Seminary in the School of Theology. He is a member of the Catholic Biblical Association and the Society of Biblical Literature.

SOCIETY FOR NEW TESTAMENT STUDIES
MONOGRAPH SERIES
General Editor: Richard Bauckham

123
ISAIAH'S CHRIST IN MATTHEW'S GOSPEL

Isaiah's Christ in Matthew's Gospel

RICHARD BEATON

Fuller Theological Seminary, California

CAMBRIDGE
UNIVERSITY PRESS

PUBLISHED BY THE PRESS SYNDICATE OF THE UNIVERSITY OF CAMBRIDGE
The Pitt Building, Trumpington Street, Cambridge CB2 1RP, United Kingdom

CAMBRIDGE UNIVERSITY PRESS
The Edinburgh Building, Cambridge, CB2 2RU, UK
40 West 20th Street, New York, NY 10011-4211, USA
477 Williamstown Road, Port Melbourne, VIC 3207, Australia
Ruiz de Alarcón 13, 28014 Madrid, Spain
Dock House, The Waterfront, Cape Town 8001, South Africa

http://www.cambridge.org

© Richard Beaton 2002

First published 2002

Printed in the United Kingdom at the University Press, Cambridge

Typeface Times 10/12 pt   *System* LATEX 2$_\varepsilon$ [TB]

A catalogue record for this book is available from the British Library

Library of Congress cataloguing in publication data

Beaton, Richard.
Isaiah's Christ in Matthew's Gospel / Richard Beaton.
    p.   cm. (Society for New Testament Studies monograph series; 123)
Includes bibliographical references and indexes.
ISBN 0 521 81888 5 (hardback)
1. Jesus Christ – History of doctrines – Early church, c. 30-600.   2. Bible. N.T.
Matthew – Relation to Isaiah.   3. Bible. O.T. Isaiah – Relation to Matthew.   I. Title.
II. Monograph series (Society for New Testament Studies); 123.
BT198.B33   2002
226.2′06 – dc21   2002067096 CIP

ISBN 0 521 81888 5 hardback

BT
198
.B33
2002

CONTENTS

PREFACE

In the midst of the process of research and writing, one increasingly appreciates the privilege of higher education, the value of a learning community and the efforts of those people who make contributions to one's growth and development. During the preparation of my doctoral dissertation, which was submitted to the University of Cambridge in January of 1999 and forms the basis of this book, there were several people to whom I would like to express my gratitude for graciously giving of their valuable time and resources, offering encouragement along the way. Dr Gordon Fee first suggested the topic of study while I was still at Regent College. Professors Morna Hooker and William Horbury offered patient and invaluable instruction. Dr Markus Bockmuehl kindly read numerous papers related to my topic. I also want to thank Professors Graham Stanton, Peter Stuhlmacher, Ulrich Luz and Donald Hagner for their rigorous discussion and hospitality. To my wise and careful supervisor, Dr Ivor H. Jones, I am especially indebted. His breadth of learning, painstaking attention to detail and engaging discussion made our forays into Matthean studies both challenging and enjoyable. Finally, I am grateful to the editor of this series, Professor Richard Bauckham, for including this volume and for his insightful comments on the manuscript.

Thanks also go to the staff and fellows of Selwyn College and to the staff and frequenters of Tyndale House. Additionally, to Markus and Celia Bockmuehl, Bruce Longenecker and Mike Thompson; the evenings together, peripatetic cultural excursions, and the like somehow made the Kingdom of God more tangible in Cambridge. Financial assistance was given by the Bethune-Baker and Hort Memorial funds and Selwyn College. The generous support of the Wabash Center and the Alexander von Humboldt Stiftung have allowed for the completion of the manuscript.

Finally, without the benefaction and encouragement of our families this project would never have seen the light of day. To Mr and Mrs Clarence

Beaton, Dr and Mrs W. Dawson Durden and the now late Mr Sharp Queener, I owe a debt that cannot be repaid. To my beloved wife Catherine, who endured too many years of student life and evenings apart, I dedicate this book.

ABBREVIATIONS

Abbreviations for biblical books, Qumran literature, Old Testament pseudepigrapha, rabbinic literature and other ancient literature follow the standard forms and are generally cited according to their own conventions, which should be clear (see *The SBL Handbook of Style*, pp. 121–52). New Testament quotations are from Nestle–Aland[27] (= UBS[4]) or the New Revised Standard Version (unless otherwise specified).

AB	Anchor Bible
ABD	*Anchor Bible Dictionary*. Edited by D. N. Freedman. 6 vols. New York, 1992
ABRL	Anchor Bible Reference Library
AJSL	*American Journal of Semitic Languages and Literature*
AnBib	Analecta biblica
ANRW	*Aufstieg und Niedergang der römischen Welt*. Edited by H. Temporini and W. Haase. Berlin, 1972–
ANTC	Abingdon New Testament Commentaries
AusBR	*Australian Biblical Review*
BAGD	Bauer, W., W. F. Arndt, F. W. Gingrich and F. W. Danker, *Greek–English Lexicon of the New Testament and Other Early Christian Literature*. 2nd edn. Chicago, 1979
BASOR	*Bulletin of the American Schools of Oriental Research*
BDB	Brown, F., S. R. Driver and C. A. Briggs, *A Hebrew and English Lexicon of the Old Testament*. Oxford, 1907
BDF	Blass, F., A. Debrunner and R. W. Funk, *A Greek Grammar of the New Testament and Other Early Christian Literature*. Chicago, 1961
BETL	Bibliotheca ephemeridum theologicarum lovaniensium
BEvT	Beiträge zur evangelischen Theologie
BHT	Beiträge zur historischen Theologie
Bib	*Biblica*

BJRL	*Bulletin of the John Rylands University Library of Manchester*
BKAT	Biblischer Kommentar: Altes Testament
BNTC	Black's New Testament Commentaries
BR	*Biblical Research*
BWANT	Beiträge zur Wissenschaft vom Alten und Neuen Testament
BZ	*Biblische Zeitschrift*
CBQ	*Catholic Biblical Quarterly*
CBQMS	The Catholic Biblical Quarterly, Monograph Series
CRINT	Compendia rerum iudaicarum ad novum testamentum
CSEL	Corpus scriptorum ecclesiasticorum latinorum
DJD	Discoveries in the Judaean Desert
DSS	*Dead Sea Scrolls*
EBC	The Expositor's Bible Commentary
EDNT	*Exegetical Dictionary of the New Testament.* Edited by H. Balz and G. Schneider. Grand Rapids, 1990–3
EKKNT	Evangelisch-katholischer Kommentar zum Neuen Testament
EpRev	*Epworth Review*
ErFor	Erträge der Forschung
ET	English Translation
ETL	*Ephemerides theologicae lovanienses*
EvQ	*Evangelical Quarterly*
ExpTim	*The Expository Times*
FRLANT	Forschungen zur Religion und Literatur des Alten und Neuen Testaments
GKC	*Gesenius' Hebrew Grammar.* Edited by E. Kautzsch. Translated by A. E. Cowley. 2nd edn. Oxford, 1910
HDB	*A Dictionary of the Bible.* Edited by J. Hastings. 5 vols. Edinburgh, 1898–1904
HKAT	Handkommentar zum Alten Testament
HTKNT	Herders theologischer Kommentar zum Neuen Testament
HTR	*Harvard Theological Review*
HTS	Harvard Theological Studies
HUCA	*Hebrew Union College Annual*
IBS	*Irish Biblical Studies*
ICC	International Critical Commentary
IDB	*Interpreter's Dictionary of the Bible.* Edited by G. A. Buttrick. 4 vols. Nashville, 1962

ITQ	*Irish Theological Quarterly*
JBL	*Journal of Biblical Literature*
JJS	*Journal of Jewish Studies*
JPT	*Journal of Pentecostal Theology*
JSJ	*Journal for the Study of Judaism in the Persian, Hellenistic and Roman Period*
JSNT	*Journal for the Study of the New Testament*
JSNTSup	Journal for the Study of the New Testament, Supplement Series
JSOT	*Journal for the Study of the Old Testament*
JSOTSup	Journal for the Study of the Old Testament, Supplement Series
JSS	*Journal of Semitic Studies*
JTS	*Journal of Theological Studies*
LCL	Loeb Classical Library
LSJ	Liddell, H. G., R. Scott and H. S. Jones, *A Greek–English Lexicon*. 9th edn with revised supplement. Oxford, 1996
LXX	The Septuagint
MajT	The Majority Text (= the Byzantine text-type)
MeyerK	Meyer, H. A. W., *Kritisch-exegetischer Kommentar über das Neue Testament*
MM	Moulton, J. H. and G. Milligan, *The Vocabulary of the Greek Testament Illustrated from the Papyri and Other Non-literary Sources*. London, 1930
MS(S)	Manuscript(s)
MT	Masoretic Text
MVEOL	Mededelingen en verhandelingen van het Vooraziatisch-Egyptisch Genootschap 'Ex Oriente Lux'
NA[27]	Nestle, E. and K. Aland, *Novum Testamentum Graece* (27th edn)
NCBC	New Century Bible Commentary
NIGTC	New International Greek Testament Commentary
NovT	*Novum Testamentum*
NovTSup	Novum Testamentum, Supplements
NPNF	Nicene and Post-Nicene Fathers
NRSV	New Revised Standard Version
NTAbh	Neutestamentliche Abhandlungen
NTD	Das Neue Testament Deutsch
NTL	New Testament Library
NTS	*New Testament Studies*

OL	Old Latin
PGM	*Papyri graecae magicae: Die griechischen Zauberpapyri.* Edited by K. Preizendanz. Berlin, 1928
RB	*Revue biblique*
ResQ	*Restoration Quarterly*
RevQ	*Revue de Qumrân*
SAB	*Sitzungsberichte der königlich Preussischen Akademie der Wissenschaften zu Berlin*
SANT	Studien zum Alten und Neuen Testament
SBLDS	Society of Biblical Literature, Dissertation Series
SBLMS	Society of Biblical Literature, Monograph Series
SBLSCS	Society of Biblical Literature, Septuagint and Cognate Studies Series
SBT	Studies in Biblical Theology
SC	Sources chrétiennes
SJLA	Studies in Judaism in Late Antiquity
SJT	*Scottish Journal of Theology*
SNTSMS	Society for New Testament Studies Monograph Series
SNTU	Studien zum Neuen Testament und seiner Umwelt
SPB	Studia post-Biblica
ST	*Studia theologica*
STDJ	Studies on the Texts of the Desert of Judah
Str-B	Strack, H. L. and P. Billerbeck, *Kommentar zum Neuen Testament aus Talmud und Midrasch.* Munich: C. H. Beck, 1922
SUNT	Studien zur Umwelt des Neuen Testaments
SVTP	Studia in veteris testamenti pseudepigrapha
TDNT	*Theological Dictionary of the New Testament.* Edited by G. Kittel and G. Friedrich. Translated by G. W. Bromiley. 10 vols. Grand Rapids, 1964–76
TDOT	*Theological Dictionary of the Old Testament.* Edited by G. J. Botterweck and H. Ringgren. Translated by J. T. Willis, G. W. Bromiley and D. E. Green. 8 vols. Grand Rapids, 1974–
THKNT	Theologischer Handkommentar zum Neuen Testament
TNTC	The Tyndale New Testament Commentaries
TSAJ	Texte und Studien zum antiken Judentum
TZ	*Theologische Zeitschrift*
UBS[4]	United Bible Societies Greek New Testament (4th edn)
VT	*Vetus Testamentum*

VTSup	Vetus Testamentum, Supplements
WBC	Word Biblical Commentary
WUNT	Wissenschaftliche Untersuchungen zum Neuen Testament
ZAW	*Zeitschrift für die alttestamentliche Wissenschaft*
ZNW	*Zeitschrift für die neutestamentliche Wissenschaft*

1

INTRODUCTION

Ensconced in Maimonides' *Commentary of the Mishnah Tractate Sanhedrin* between comments concerning the fundamental tenets of the Jewish faith and his well-known thirteen fundamental principles is a brief section on the days of the messiah. Somewhat surprisingly, Maimonides (AD 1135–1204) cites Isa. 42.4a to validate the proposition that following an extended reign the messiah will die. A translation reads as follows:

> And the Messiah will die, and his son will reign in his stead and then his grandson. God has already predicted his death in the verse,
> 'He shall not fail nor be crushed,
> till[1] he have set the right in the earth.'[2]

Maimonides' usage provides but one, albeit late, example of Jewish messianic exegesis of Isa. 42.1–4. That he would appeal to this text in support of his understanding of the days of the messiah is not unexpected given its long history of usage within Jewish messianic thought.[3] What is rather unusual, however, is that he would cite Isa. 42.4a to validate the messiah's death.

Engaging in a messianic exegesis of his own nearly a millennium before, the author of the Gospel of Matthew also cites Isa. 42.1–4; however, in Matthew's version of the text in 12.18–21, the reference to weakness and perhaps even death found in Isa. 42.4a is absent. This line of text has been excised from Matthew's version of Isa. 42.4a (Matt. 12.20b) and an unknown piece of text inserted in its place (see the passages below). Despite Maimonides' and Matthew's common interest in the messiah, their

---

[1] Maimonides has understood עַד in a temporal sense, thus subordinating the messiah's death, when he would 'fail' and 'be crushed', to the establishment of 'the right in the earth'.

[2] *Maimonides' Commentary on the Mishnah Tractate Sanhedrin*, translated by F. Rosner, New York: Sepher-Hermon Press, 1981, p. 148.

[3] Evidence of a pre-Christian messianic reading does exist. The Targums seem to contain early material that reads the passage messianically. See the discussions in chapters 3 and 5.

handlings of Isaiah's text contrast markedly. Separated by a considerable span of time and evincing no reliable evidence of direct traditional links, these treatments give rise to the surprising judgment that the Jewish interpretation focuses upon the messiah's frailty while the early Christian interpretation, as presented in Matthew's text, seemingly disregards this emphasis.[4] This omission from Matthew is rather curious given the widely held view that a 'suffering servant' motif is implicit in Matthew's usage in 12.18–21 and undergirds a thoroughgoing motif of weakness and lowliness that is traditionally considered fundamental to Matthew's portrait of Jesus.[5] Such a presentation of these thematic elements appears to overstate Matthew's intended emphasis.

Herein lies the problem: if Matthew's text-form does not support the traditional presentation of a meek and lowly Jesus, then Matthew's portrait of Jesus may be more complex than is otherwise thought. Such a proposition, however, raises a host of issues concerning Matthew's presentation of Jesus and the role of the OT quotations in framing that portrait and, in particular, his use of the formula quotations, of which Isa. 42.1–4 in 12.18–21 is but one. Although the process of determining the function of Isa. 42.1–4 and its influence upon Matthew's portrait of Jesus, the Christ, within Matthew's narrative may be beset with obstacles, a careful investigation of this topic has the potential to make a substantial contribution to our understanding of his richly textured and high christology.

When the two passages are placed beside each other, the differences become more pronounced.[6]

Isaiah 42.1–4	Matthew 12.18–21
[1]Here is my servant, whom I uphold,	[18]'Here is my servant, whom I have chosen,
my chosen, in whom my soul delights;	my beloved, with whom my soul is well pleased.
I have put my spirit upon him;	I will put my Spirit upon him,
he will bring forth justice to the nations.	and he will proclaim justice to the Gentiles.

---

[4] In Matthew's version, Isa. 42.4a is not the only verse to undergo modification and be stripped of an allusion to weakness. God's sustainment of the servant also is excised from the text of Isa. 42.1a. See chapter 5.

[5] R. T. France, *Jesus and the Old Testament: His Application of the Old Testament Passages to Himself and His Mission*, London: Tyndale Press, 1971, pp. 124–5.

[6] Both passages are taken from the NRSV translation.

[2]He will not cry or lift up his voice,	[19]He will not wrangle or cry aloud,
or make it heard in the street;	nor will anyone hear his voice in the streets.
[3]a bruised reed he will not break, and	[20]He will not break a bruised reed
a dimly burning wick he will not quench;	or quench a smouldering wick
he will faithfully bring forth justice.	
[4]He will not grow faint or be crushed	
until he has established justice in the earth;	until he brings justice to victory.
and the coastlands wait for his teaching.	[21]And in his name the Gentiles will hope.'

Thesis

Views on the importance of Isa. 42.1–4 to Matthew as a whole range from the grand assessment, that the entire book of Matthew may swing on it, to the more modest which categorizes it as an example of simplistic 'prediction-fulfilment', or proof-texting, to validate merely a single event in the life of Jesus of Nazareth.[7] Recent scholarship has tended to focus upon its role in Matthew's depiction of Jesus the messiah. G. Barth's statement is illustrative of this tendency: 'By means of the quotation in 12,18–21 Matthew has especially underlined the humility and lowliness of Jesus ... in which he proves himself the servant of God of Isa. 42.'[8] Although Barth has touched upon a significant aspect of Matthew's usage of the citation, his position has not received universal assent. J. Neyrey counters that such a portrait of Jesus does not necessarily square with the one the reader meets in the pericope immediately following the citation, for in 12.22ff. an apologetic component is present in Matthew's account of Jesus' conflict with the Pharisees that is somehow foreign to Barth's

[7] C. F. D. Moule, 'Fulfilment-Words in the New Testament: Use and Abuse', *NTS* 14 (1967–8): 297–8. See also M. D. Hooker, *Jesus and the Servant: The Influence of the Servant Concept of Deutero-Isaiah in the New Testament*, London: SPCK, 1959, p. 84, and B. Lindars, *New Testament Apologetic: The Doctrinal Significance of the Old Testament Quotations*, London: SCM Press, 1961, p. 151.

[8] 'Matthew's Understanding of the Law', in *Tradition and Interpretation in Matthew*, edited by G. Bornkamm, G. Barth and H. J. Held, NTL, London: SCM Press, 1963, p. 128 (also cited by J. H. Neyrey, 'The Thematic Use of Isaiah 42,1–4 in Matthew 12', *Bib* 63 (1982): 457).

characterization.[9] W. Rothfuchs points to the correlation between the majesty and power manifest in Jesus' miracles and the servant texts with which the miracles are associated (Matt. 8.17 and 12.18–21).[10] R. Schnackenburg, in an attempt to maintain *Hoheit und Niedrigkeit im Bild Jesu*, argues that one must preserve a connection between the present lowliness of the servant and his future victory.[11] The wide variety of opinions concerning this text might lead a person to agree with C. Torrey's assessment, 'This [Matt. 12.18–21] is one of the best examples of Matthew's way of quoting scripture. It has not been correctly explained hitherto, nor has its significance been perceived.'[12]

If Isa. 42.1–4 were a straightforward affirmation of the humble servant, one might expect that this text would have played a more prominent role in the church's liturgy, art or music. Yet J. Sawyer, in his recent work *The Fifth Gospel*, which catalogues the uses of passages from Isaiah throughout church history, observes that the text rarely, if ever, appears.[13] It seems that the usage of this 'servant' text represents an early development in Christian thought that has unfortunately been either forgotten or little explored. While this quotation, and the ideas associated with it, may have suffered poor visibility in the succeeding eras of Christian history, I will argue that the image of the servant presented through Matthew's anomalous text-form is central to his overall portrayal of Jesus and, ultimately, to his profound christology.

The aim of this book, then, is to explore Matthew's use of Isa. 42.1–4. It is hoped that such an endeavour will divulge a more comprehensive understanding of its role in the Gospel, the results of which may then be extrapolated to explain the role of other OT usages as well. It will be argued that in 12.18–21 Matthew employs a redactionally nuanced quotation of Isa. 42.1–4,[14] a quotation already in use in Jewish and early Christian traditions. Furthermore, he does so in order to capture aspects

---

[9] 'Thematic Use', 457–9.

[10] *Die Erfüllungszitate des Matthäus-Evangeliums: Eine biblisch-theologische Untersuchung*, BWANT 88, Stuttgart: Kohlhammer, 1969, p. 129.

[11] ' "Siehe da mein Knecht, den ich erwählt habe..." (Mt 12,18): Zur Heiltätigkeit Jesu im Matthäusevangelium', in *Salz der Erde–Licht der Welt: Exegetische Studien zum Matthäusevangelium. Festschrift für Anton Vögtle zum 80. Geburtstag*, edited by L. Oberlinner and P. Fiedler, Stuttgart: Katholisches Bibelwerk, 1991, p. 221.

[12] *Documents of the Primitive Church*, New York: Harper & Brothers Publishers, 1941, p. 64.

[13] *The Fifth Gospel: Isaiah in the History of Christianity*, Cambridge: Cambridge University Press, 1996, p. 243. Note, however, that along with Isa. 11.1–2 and 61.1–3, 42.1–4 does appear in the latest Catholic *Lectionary*, p. 889, to validate the actions of the messiah (so Sawyer, *Fifth Gospel*, p. 80 n. 75).

[14] Whether Matthew is himself responsible for the translation is a key question.

of Jesus' character, identity, and mission that are integral to his portrayal of Jesus. Here he presents Jesus as the enigmatic Davidic messiah, who is surrounded by increasing hostility evidenced in his interactions with various people and groups in Matt. 11–13. The primary link between the quotation and its context is to be found in a developed contradistinction between injustice and justice. The Pharisees' concern for strict adherence to halakhah, their unjust treatment of the people and concomitant failure as religious leaders are set against Jesus' own concept of observance of the Law together with the justice evidenced in his care for the people as Davidic messiah.

To validate this thesis, it will be argued that Matthew's usage of this formula quotation, and others, is bi-referential.[15] In other words, the quotation contributes to the meaning of Matthew's story on two levels. First, it possesses significance on the narrative, or linear, level and validates previous elements recounted in the life and ministry of Jesus. On a second level, its usage is fundamentally theological, that is, the passage is employed in light of the realities presented by the teachings and deeds of Jesus of Nazareth, the rejected messiah of Israel.

Problems

Previous studies of Matthew's use of the Old Testament have been broad ranging, usually devoting a few pages to a particular citation and offering a brief analysis along with comments upon what 'prompted' the citation; hermeneutical issues are rarely broached.[16] The great value of such

---

[15] This language is similar to that employed by others on this topic; for example, D. Kupp, *Matthew's Emmanuel: Divine Presence and God's People in the First Gospel*, SNTSMS 90, Cambridge: Cambridge University Press, 1996, p. 168, speaks of 'surface congruity' and 'deeper motifs'.

[16] K. Stendahl, *The School of St Matthew and Its Use of the Old Testament*, 1st Sigler Press edn, Ramsey: Sigler, 1991; R. H. Gundry, *The Use of the Old Testament in St Matthew's Gospel: With Special Reference to the Messianic Hope*, NovTSup 18, Leiden: Brill, 1967; Lindars, *New Testament Apologetic*. The studies of R. S. McConnell, *Law and Prophecy in Matthew's Gospel: The Authority and Use of the Old Testament in the Gospel of St Matthew*, Basel: Friedrich Reinhardt, 1969, Rothfuchs, *Erfüllungszitate*, and G. M. Soares Prabhu, *The Formula Quotations in the Infancy Narrative of Matthew: An Enquiry into the Tradition History of Mt 1–2*, AnBib 63, Rome: Biblica Institute Press, 1976, all focus upon the theological usages of the citations; however, due to the breadth of material covered, they offer only minimal comments upon a given passage. Several notable exceptions are Kupp, *Matthew's Emmanuel*, M. Knowles, *Jeremiah in Matthew's Gospel: The Rejected Prophet Motif in Matthean Redaction*, JSNTSup 68, Sheffield: Sheffield Academic Press, 1993, and J. Miler, *Les citations d'accomplissement dans l'évangile de Matthieu: quand Dieu se rend présent en toute humanité*, AnBib 140, Rome: Editrice Pontifico Istituto Biblico, 1999. See the fine general studies and evaluations in F. van Segbroeck, 'Les

syntheses lies in their capacity to enable one to grasp the overall tendencies of an author. In this work, I have chosen a slightly different tack.
It primarily seeks to consider in depth one troublesome quotation, Isa.
42.1–4 in Matt. 12.18–21, in order to determine its function within its
surrounding context. In an age when studies are increasingly focusing
upon minutiae, the limited scope of such an investigation may need to be
defended.

Matthew's use of Isa. 42.1–4 confronts the investigator with a host of
challenges that demands a more extensive, thorough and nuanced study.
First, as with many of Matthew's distinctive formula quotations, Isa. 42.1–
4 possesses idiosyncrasies in its text-form which appear to support christological and ecclesiological themes fundamental to the Gospel and its
portrait of Jesus.[17] Whether Matthew is personally responsible for these
textual adjustments has not been immediately obvious to many; however,
a thorough assessment of the mixed text-form has provided the common
jumping-off point in a study of this nature. As a result, the text-form is

citations d'accomplissement dans l'évangile selon Saint Matthieu d'après trois ouvrages
récents', in *L'évangile selon Matthieu: rédaction et théologie*, edited by M. Didier, BETL
29, Gembloux: Duculot, 1972, pp. 107–30; G. N. Stanton, *A Gospel for a New People:
Studies in Matthew*, Louisville, KY: Westminster/John Knox, 1993, pp. 346–63; R. Pesch,
'Der Gottessohn im matthäischen Evangelienprolog (Mt 1–2). Beobachtungen zu den
Zitationsformeln der Reflexionszitate', *Bib* 48 (1967): 395–420; 'Eine alttestamentliche
Ausführungsformel im Matthäus-Evangelium: Redaktionsgeschichtliche und exegetische
Beobachtungen', *BZ* 10 (1966): 220–45; 'Eine alttestamentliche Ausführungsformel im
Matthäus-Evangelium (Schlub)', *BZ* 11 (1967): 79–95; J. M. van Cangh, 'La bible de
Matthieu: les citations d'accomplissement', *ETL* 6 (1975): 205–11; A. Baumstark, 'Die
Zitate des Matthäus-Evangeliums aus dem Zwölfprophetenbuch', *Bib* 37 (1956): 296–313;
R. T. France, *Matthew: Evangelist and Teacher*, London: Paternoster, 1989, pp. 171–84;
and the excursuses in U. Luz, *Matthew 1–7: A Commentary*, translated by W. C. Linss,
Continental Commentaries, Minneapolis: Augsburg, 1989, pp. 156–64, and W. D. Davies
and D. Allison, *A Critical and Exegetical Commentary on the Gospel according to Saint
Matthew*, 3 vols, ICC, Edinburgh: T. & T. Clark, 1997, vol. III, pp. 573–7.

[17] The studies on Matthew's use of the Old Testament, already an extended list, continue
to multiply with the recent works on specific passages by L. Lybaek, 'Matthew's Use of
Hosea 6,6', in *The Scriptures in the Gospels*, edited by C. M. Tuckett, BETL 131, Leuven:
Leuven University Press, 1997, pp. 491–9; M. J. J. Menken, 'The Source of the Quotation
from Isaiah 53:4 in Matthew 8:17', *NovT* 39 (1997): 313–27; 'The Quotation from Isaiah
42,1–4 in Matthew 12,18–21: Its Text Form', *ETL* 75 (1999): 32–52; D. P. Senior, 'The
Lure of the Formula Quotations: Re-Assessing Matthew's Use of the Old Testament with
the Passion Narrative as a Test Case', in *The Scriptures in the Gospels*, edited by Tuckett,
pp. 89–115; W. Weren, 'Quotations from Isaiah and Matthew's Christology (Mt 1,23 and
4,15–16)', in *Studies in the Book of Isaiah: Festschrift Willem A. M. Beuken*, edited by J. van
Ruiten and M. Vervenne, BETL 132, Leuven: Leuven University Press, 1997, pp. 447–65;
'The Use of Isaiah 5,1–7 in the Parable of the Tenants (Mark 12,1–12; Matthew 21,33–46)',
Bib 79 (1998): 1–26; A. M. Leske, 'Isaiah and Matthew: The Prophetic Influence in the
First Gospel; A Report on Current Research', in *Jesus and the Suffering Servant: Isaiah
53 and Christian Origins*, edited by W. Bellinger and W. Farmer, Harrisburg: Trinity Press
International, 1998, pp. 152–69.

perhaps the most exhaustively explored area in analyses of Matthew's OT usage.[18] Nevertheless, a comprehensive theory of Matthew's text-form(s) has thus far eluded investigators.[19] This is not unexpected given the tenuous strands of evidence by which textual theories have often been strung together. One may find assistance in understanding Matthew's text-form in the more recent discoveries of texts at Khirbet Qumran, Masada, Wadi Murabbaʿat and Naḥal Ḥever, which have challenged many of the theories concerning the development of the text-form that previously dominated the academic landscape.

Second, closely related to Matthew's text-form is the matter regarding whether a relationship exists between the adjusted text-form and its context. Doubt continues to be expressed about the assertions that Matthew himself adapted/redacted the citations in light of his theological agenda and that these changes reflect the content of the narrative into which the quotations are inserted. Third, Isa. 42.1–4 is the longest of the OT quotations in Matthew, but at first glance very little of the citation appears to relate to the surrounding context. This would mean that much of the citation is essentially irrelevant and raises the troubling question why a conscientious redactor like Matthew would have haphazardly included such an extensive amount of superfluous material. It remains incumbent upon those who presuppose greater significance in the superfluous elements to explain their presence.[20] A fourth difficulty concerns Matthew's

[18] This is an ancient discussion which has received much attention. See the following on 12.18–21 (= Isa. 42.1–4): P. Kahle, *The Cairo Geniza*, 2nd edn, Oxford: Clarendon, 1959, pp. 249–52; Lindars, *New Testament Apologetic*, pp. 144–52; E. Nestle, 'Matthew xii.19–Isaiah xlii.2', *ExpTim* 20 (1908–9): 92–3, 189; W. C. Allen, 'The Old Testament Quotations in St Matthew and St Mark', *ExpTim* 12 (1900–1): 281–3; 'Matthew xii. 19–Isaiah xlii. 2', *ExpTim* 20 (1908–9): 140–1; T. Stephenson, 'The Old Testament Quotations Peculiar to Matthew', *JTS* 20 (1918): 227–9; N. Hillyer, 'Matthew's Use of the Old Testament', *EvQ* 36 (1964): 12–26; J. Grindel, 'Matthew 12,18–21', *CBQ* 29 (1967): 110–15; Stendahl, *School*, pp. 108–15; and Gundry, *Use of the Old Testament*, pp. 110–16.

[19] One might simply compare the comments by D. S. New, *Old Testament Quotations in the Synoptic Gospels and the Two-Document Hypothesis*, SBLSCS 37, Atlanta: Scholars, 1993, p. 121, who asserts that Matthew's Bible was the LXX, with those by Davies and Allison, *Matthew*, I.52, who concur with the judgment that Matthew knew and translated directly from Hebrew.

[20] The literature on 12.18–21 is extensive. In addition to the short discussions scattered throughout various books and articles, the passage has received focused attention from Stendahl, *School*, pp. 108–15; Gundry, *Use of the Old Testament*, pp. 110–16; Neyrey, 'Thematic Use', 457–73; O. L. Cope, *Matthew: A Scribe Trained for the Kingdom of Heaven*, CBQMS 5, Washington: The Catholic Biblical Association of America, 1976, pp. 32–52; and Schnackenburg, 'Siehe da mein Knecht', pp. 203–22. Recently, there has been a spate of short studies on other quotations in Matthew. For example, see Weren, 'Quotations from Isaiah', pp. 447–65; 'Jesus' Entry into Jerusalem: Mt 21,1–17 in the Light of the Hebrew Bible and the Septuagint', in *The Scriptures in the Gospels*, edited by Tuckett,

insertion of Isa. 42.1–4 into what is perhaps the most thematically diverse and complicated context in the Gospel, chs. 11–13.[21] Fifth, there is evidence that the quotation was part of both Jewish and early Christian exegetical traditions. It seems to have been interpreted messianically prior to the emergence of Christianity. Finally, taking a page from literary theory, the rhetorical function of the final form of the citation poses an intriguing challenge. The grammatical and linguistic adjustments in Matthew's peculiar text-form create a new set of associations and distinctive meanings, affecting the rhetorical force of the citation within its context. Although this particular emphasis has been little explored, it may prove to be the most promising.[22] When taken all together, these various issues warrant a more exhaustive analysis that may shed light upon the role of this formula citation within Matthew's narrative and thought world.

Guiding presuppositions and assumptions

Essential to the process of understanding a biblical text is an awareness of the assumptions that one personally brings to both the book and the interpretative task. What is particularly difficult about Matthean studies is that numerous 'introductory matters' remain unresolved. Scholarship has, however, arrived at many reasonable and informed conclusions that offer a place to begin. Rather than taking the space to argue each position at length, I will simply state the assumptions central to this study, most of which have now generally become accepted views in Matthean scholarship.

Fundamental to the study is the question of the author's nationality and literary abilities. Although a segment of twentieth-century commentators have posited gentile authorship,[23] the evidence seems to support the

---

pp. 117–41; Menken, 'Isaiah 53:4 in Matthew 8:17', 313–27; Lybaek, 'Hosea 6,6', pp. 491–9; M. Hasitschka, 'Die Verwendung der Schrift in Mt 4,1–11', in *The Scriptures in the Gospels*, edited by Tuckett, pp. 487–90; and S. Graham, 'A Strange Salvation: Intertextual Allusion in Mt 27,39–43', in *The Scriptures in the Gospels*, edited by Tuckett, pp. 501–11.

[21] D. J. Verseput, *The Rejection of the Humble Messianic King: A Study of the Composition of Matthew 11–12*, Frankfurt: Peter Lang, 1986, pp. 1–2.

[22] L. Hartman, 'Scriptural Exegesis in the Gospel of St Matthew and the Problem of Communication', in *L'évangile selon Matthieu: rédaction et théologie*, edited by M. Didier, BETL 29, Gembloux: Duculot, 1972, pp. 131–52, examines the rhetorical force of the citations.

[23] K. W. Clark, 'The Gentile Bias in Matthew', *JBL* 66 (1947): 165–8; W. Trilling, *Das wahre Israel: Studien zur Theologie des Matthäus-Evangeliums*, Munich: Kösel, 1964, pp. 219–24; P. Nepper-Christensen, *Das Matthäusevangelium – ein jüdenchristliches Evangelium?*, Acta Theologica Danica 1, Aarhus: Universitetsforlaget, 1958, pp. 202–7;

historic position that Matthew was Jewish and wrote within a Jewish framework for a primarily Jewish audience.[24] While it is difficult to say whether he knew Hebrew well, he does appear to have been 'an intellectual'.[25] His work, as evinced in the Gospel, suggests a thoughtful, reflective author who took great care with his sources and yet also adjusted them to create the grand composition of the Gospel.[26] It appears that Matthew was written in the latter half of the first century, probably between AD 70 and 85 .[27] The Gospel's Jewish content and the thematic development of conflict with the Pharisees seem to indicate a location of composition in either northern Palestine or southern Syria. Although Antioch is a possibility,[28] serious questions remain regarding its feasibility. Another contentious issue concerns whether Matthew's Gospel represents a community that was still connected to its parent body Judaism (*intra muros*)[29] or had recently undergone a painful separation (*extra muros*).[30] However

G. Strecker, *Der Weg der Gerichtigkeit: Untersuchung zur Theologie des Matthäus*, FRLANT 82, Göttingen: Vandenhoeck & Ruprecht, 1962, pp. 15–35.

[24] Reasons for this conclusion include Matthew's use of the Old Testament and particularly the formula quotations (so D. A. Hagner, 'The *Sitz im Leben* of the Gospel of Matthew', in *Treasures Old and New: Recent Contributions to Matthean Studies*, edited by D. R. Bauer and M. A. Powell, SBL Symposium Series, Atlanta: Scholars, 1996, p. 45) and the close similarity his argumentation bears to rabbinic debate (see, for example, M. Bockmuehl, 'Matthew 5:32; 19:9 in the Light of Pre-Rabbinic Halakhah', *NTS* 35 (1989): 291–5; and, most recently, P. Luomanen, '*Corpus Mixtum* – An Appropriate Description of Matthew's Community?' *JBL* 117 (1998): 478–9).

[25] Davies and Allison, *Matthew*, I.133; see also E. von Dobschütz, 'Rabbi and Catechist', in *The Interpretation of Matthew*, translated by R. Morgan, edited by G. N. Stanton, 2nd edn, Edinburgh: T. & T. Clark, 1995, pp. 27–38. The majority of scholarship has concurred on this throughout history. See Papias (Eusebius, *HE* 3.39) and Irenaeus (Eusebius, *HE* 5.8.2).

[26] See most recently the provocative discussion by I. H. Jones, *The Matthean Parables: A Literary and Historical Commentary*, NovTSup 80, Leiden: Brill, 1995, pp. 16ff.; also G. N. Stanton, 'Matthew as a Creative Interpreter of the Sayings of Jesus', in *Das Evangelium und die Evangelien*, edited by P. Stuhlmacher, Tübingen: J. C. B. Mohr, 1983, pp. 273–87; and D. Senior, 'A Case Study in Matthean Creativity: Matthew 27:3–10', *BR* 19 (1974): 23–36.

[27] The case for a date after AD 70 relies upon Matthean dependence upon Mark and especially Matt. 22.1–10, which appears to contain a reference to the destruction of Jerusalem. Davies and Allison, *Matthew*, I.132–3, add 28.19 to the equation and argue that its theological sophistication would demand a date between AD 85 and 100.

[28] See most recently D. C. Sim, *The Gospel of Matthew and Christian Judaism: The Historical Setting of the Matthean Community*, Edinburgh: T. & T. Clark, 1998, pp. 53–62.

[29] G. D. Kilpatrick, *The Origins of the Gospel according to St Matthew*, Oxford: Oxford University Press, 1946, p. 122; G. Bornkamm, 'End Expectation and the Church in Matthew', in *Tradition and Interpretation in Matthew*, edited by Bornkamm, Barth and Held, p. 22 n. 1; most recently, A. J. Saldarini, *Matthew's Christian-Jewish Community*, Chicago: University of Chicago Press, 1994, pp. 2–4, 84–7, and J. A. Overman, *Matthew's Gospel and Formative Judaism: The Social World of the Matthean Community*, Minneapolis: Fortress, 1990, pp. 4–5.

[30] Stendahl, *School*, p. xiii; G. N. Stanton, 'The Origin and Purpose of Matthew's Gospel:

one decides, the Gospel reflects a running conflict with the parent body. Finally, while acknowledging that the textual situation was perhaps more complex than has otherwise been suggested, this work presupposes Marcan priority throughout and assumes that Matthew also had access to the sources known as Q and M.[31]

Limitations

The primary limitation of this work is that it will not directly address or interact with OT scholarship concerning the so-called 'servant songs'. Several considerations have led to this restriction. First, the predominant interest of OT critical scholarship has been to locate the historical identity of the servant figure, thus rendering moot any application of the text in the first century AD.[32] Second, Matthew's understanding of the text does not represent the concerns of critical OT scholarship. This is no doubt a reflection of the increasing difficulty of squaring historical research of the Hebrew Bible with first-century studies.[33] Third, the source-critical concerns behind Duhm's programmatic agenda which argued that the 'servant songs' were originally lifted from one source and later inserted into Isaiah are of little import for a study of Matthew, for whom there existed neither Deutero- nor Trito-Isaiah.[34] Thus, it would be anachronistic to speak of Deutero-Isaiah, the role of the 'servant' in the theology

---

Matthean Scholarship from 1945–1980', in *ANRW* II.25.3, Berlin: de Gruyter, 1983, p. 1915; B. Gerhardsson, 'Sacrificial Service and Atonement in the Gospel of Matthew', in *Reconciliation and Hope: New Testament Essays on Atonement and Eschatology Presented to L. L. Morris on his 60th Birthday*, edited by Robert Banks, Exeter: Paternoster, 1974, p. 27.

[31] The recent rise in support for the Griesbach hypothesis is evidence that the issue of Matthean sources is more convoluted than the simplistic affirmation that Matthew used Mark, Q and the source M (most recently argued by W. R. Farmer, *The Synoptic Problem: A Critical Analysis*, Dillsboro: North Carolina Press, 1976). See, for example, the exploration of Matt. 18 in Jones, *Matthean Parables*, pp. 16–30.

[32] Note the final footnote in T. N. D. Mettinger's essay *A Farewell to the Servant Songs: A Critical Examination of an Exegetical Axiom*, translated by F. H. Cryer, Lund: CWK Gleerup, 1983, p. 46 n. 83, where the author offers two restrained comments on the servant in early Christianity. First, motifs similar to the christological usage in the Gospels are used of the church in Acts 13.46–7 ('I have set you to be a light to the gentiles'); and second, 'language and imagery used of Israel' in the Old Testament are frequently applied to Jesus in the New Testament.

[33] F. Watson, *Text and Truth: Redefining Biblical Theology*, Grand Rapids: Eerdmans, 1997, pp. 4–6.

[34] B. Duhm, *Das Buch Jesaia: Übersetzt und Erklärt von Bernhard Duhm*, HKAT III/1, Göttingen: Vandenhoeck & Ruprecht, 1922, pp. 284–7; 339–43; 351–4; 365–78. Already in the second century BC, Jesus ben Sira, author of Ecclesiasticus, presented Isaiah as a book composed by one author (48.24).

of Deutero-Isaiah, or salvation in Deutero-Isaiah. Such designations would have been incomprehensible to the author of Matthew, who cited freely from the entire book under the name of the prophet Isaiah.[35] Instead, the focus will be upon early Jewish and NT perceptions of the text.

Method

As this study presents an attempt to determine Matthew's use of the citation, a variety of methods commend themselves. Efforts to penetrate the various layers present in Matthew's use of the Old Testament confront several interrelated problems. Prior discussions on his use of the Old Testament, particularly those concerning his formula quotations, have focused primarily upon his distinctive text-form. It has been assumed that a comparison of Matthew's text-form with the known sources (Mark and Q) and major textual traditions would reveal Matthean interests. This, of course, presupposes that the points where Matthew's quotations differ from known textual traditions find their origin in Matthew.

Two related issues are pertinent here. First, to demonstrate conclusively that Matthew made adjustments to the text, one must be able to establish the base text from which he worked, a task not easily accomplished. In their quest, authors have resorted to detailed comparisons with other texts. This method is essentially that of redaction criticism, which, while remaining an effective tool, depends upon the assurance that one is working with the same source(s) Matthew used.[36] With regard to the citations, however, determining a standardized OT text or group of texts upon which Matthew may have drawn has proved elusive.[37] Without such texts with which one may compare Matthew's text-form, it becomes difficult to ascertain what is or is not the result of Matthean composition.[38] Thus,

---

[35] Modern studies in Isaiah, however, ought not to be considered completely out of bounds. There is much valuable material in the presentations of Isaiah upon which I shall draw.

[36] For a history of redaction criticism and critical evaluation, see Stanton, *Gospel for a New People*, pp. 23–53, who, on p. 24, notes what he labels the three pillars of redaction criticism: (1) the sources which Matthew drew upon were Mark, Q and the so-called M material; (2) the changes made by Matthew reflect his theological concerns; and (3) these adjustments reveal the concerns within his own community. See also Jones, *Matthean Parables*, pp. 1–55, for a detailed critique and refinement of the linguistic and syntactical assumptions upon which the method functions. This is to be compared to the earlier and more optimistic introduction by N. Perrin, *What is Redaction Criticism?*, Philadelphia: Fortress, 1969, pp. 64–79.

[37] The earlier studies of Stendahl, *School*, and Gundry, *Use of the Old Testament*, were too hopeful with regard to the OT text. See the discussion in chapter 2.

[38] Regarding Mark and Q, Jones, *Matthean Parables*, p. 16, observes that 'it has become

a general overview of the state of research on text-forms in the Second Temple period may assist in evaluating Matthew's aberrant text.[39]

A second issue of method concerns the need to establish criteria by which one may detect the possible interrelationships between the distinctive quotation and the Matthean context. This is a complicated matter that depends in part upon whether the textual peculiarities originate from earlier Jewish traditions or early Christian usage. If there is evidence that the alterations do not derive from another Hebrew, Greek or Aramaic *Vorlage*, then the postulate that Matthew may be responsible for them seems reasonable, unless of course Matthew was working with, or was dependent upon, a group of scholars. Several criteria have been employed in order to determine whether Matthew's peculiar text-form is related to the context and his broader theological interests. The presence of Matthean vocabulary is one element that may be observed. Another approach, which is more difficult to control, involves matching the thematic and theological elements from the citation with those throughout the Gospel. R. E. Brown rightly observes that this method is susceptible to a degree of circularity.[40] U. Eco raises a similar point when he proposes that many 'smart readers' will pick up references and allusions not intended by the 'empirical author'.[41] The challenge is to determine the thematic and theological parallels between the quotations and the Gospel intended by the empirical author, not those discerned according to the insights of 'perceptive' readers.

An additional component in the grouping of methods that will guide this study is the delineation of the usage of the quotation in Jewish and Christian tradition contemporaneous with Matthew. This is an important exercise as it establishes a possible basis for Matthew's thought world. Finally, a method rarely applied to the formula quotations will be used to investigate the final form of Isa. 42.1–4 and its rhetorical impact. The presence of anomalies in Matthew's text-form and their attendant grammatical and terminological relationships allow for a rhetorical force that

increasingly difficult to determine the sources and the text of the sources which Matthew may have used'.

[39] Stanton, *Gospel for a New People*, pp. 349–53, suggests that this area is one of the most promising for Matthean studies. The recent discoveries of textual manuscripts and fragments of significant texts have led to a more sophisticated and informed perspective of the transmission and use of texts that will no doubt give rise to more learned theories concerning Matthew's use of the Old Testament than those of thirty years ago.

[40] *The Birth of the Messiah: A Commentary on the Infancy Narratives in Matthew and Luke*, New York: Doubleday, 1977, p. 104.

[41] *Interpretation and Overinterpretation: With Richard Rorty, Jonathan Culler and Christine Brooke-Rose*, edited by Stefan Collini, Cambridge: Cambridge University Press, 1992, pp. 82–3.

is distinct from other versions of Isa. 42.1–4 and more suited to Matthew's narrative and theological concerns. Thus, exploring Matthew's use of Isa. 42.1–4 is a complex affair. The search must also extend to the intermediate and remote contexts in addition to the immediate one. Furthermore, the inclusion of a narrative-critical element may assist in determining whether the citation transcends the context to serve Matthew's overall presentation of Jesus and his concomitant christology.

Procedure

The procedure that will be followed is relatively straightforward. Chapter 2 will consist of the traditional presentation of the history of research of topics relevant to the argument. In particular, the emphases and approaches of prior generations of scholars will be reviewed in the hope that a more comprehensive perspective may be tendered and a way forward plotted. Chapter 3 will seek to establish a historical background for the study in two areas. First, an updated overview of the state of the text-form in the period prior to AD 70 will be offered. Second, an attempt will be made to locate the use of the text and ideas of Isa. 42.1–4 in the Second Temple period in order to establish a historical context and framework for Matthew's usage. This will allow the study to move cautiously forward with a greater awareness of where both continuity and discontinuity exist. Chapter 4 will endeavour to explore in greater detail the possible relationship between text-form and usage in the context of other Isaianic citations in Matthew. The study will investigate the usages of Isa. 7.14 in Matt. 1.23, Isa. 8.23b–9.1 in 4.15–16, and Isa. 53.4 in 8.17 in the hope of determining not only the relationship between text-form and usage but also whether the 'superfluous content' of the citations bears any relationship to Matthean interests. Building upon the work of the previous chapters, chapter 5 will offer a detailed analysis of the use of Isa. 42.1–4 in 12.18–21, explicating its text-form and relationship to immediate and more remote contexts. Chapter 6 will consider the possible christological import of Isa. 42.1–4, with particular attention paid to the contrast between the compassionate servant and the aggressive polemicist. Chapter 7 will form the conclusion.

With this as the overall strategy, I now move to an overview of scholarship's attempt to wrestle with the question of Matthew's use of the Old Testament and the so-called formula citations.

2

HISTORY OF RESEARCH

The composition, interpretation and redeployment of texts, otherwise known as intertextuality, is, as M. Fishbane has persuasively demonstrated,[1] an ancient practice. A perusal of the sacred and non-sacred early Jewish texts will introduce the modern reader to this prolonged discourse that has been conducted over a period spanning many centuries as each generation of authors interpreted and applied authoritative texts in an attempt to address contemporaneous situations.[2] In addition to the explicit discussions about the meaning of the texts evidenced in the commentary found in Qumran *pesher* and in the rabbis, there is the residue, or deposit, that is extant in the text and translations themselves, such as the MT, LXX and Targums. As M. Black reminds us, 'problems of translation, interpretation and text are inextricably inter-connected: there is no translation that is not an interpretation and questions of text are basic to all

---

[1] *Biblical Interpretation in Ancient Israel*, Oxford: Clarendon, 1985. Fishbane distinguishes between three types of exegesis: Legal (pp. 91–231); Aggadic (pp. 281–408); and Mantological (pp. 443–505). See also his 'Use, Authority and Interpretation of Mikra at Qumran', in *Mikra: Text Translation, Reading and Interpretation of the Hebrew Bible in Ancient Judaism and Early Christianity,* edited by M. J. Mulder, CRINT 2.1, Assen and Maastricht: Van Gorcum; Philadelphia: Fortress, 1988, pp. 339–77. Helpful introductions to Jewish exegesis include G. Vermes' study 'Bible and Midrash: Early Old Testament Exegesis', in *Cambridge History of the Bible*, vol. I: *From the Beginnings to Jerome,* edited by P. C. Ackroyd and C. F. Evans, Cambridge: Cambridge University Press, 1970, pp. 199–231, and G. J. Brooke, *Exegesis at Qumran: 4Florilegium in Its Jewish Context,* JSOTSup 29, Sheffield: JSOT Press, 1985, pp. 1–45.

[2] See J. Culler, *The Pursuit of Signs: Semiotics, Literature, Deconstruction,* London: Routledge & Kegan Paul, 1981, pp. 100–2. The emphasis in studies on intertextuality upon the reader rather than the author is not completely foreign to historical biblical studies. Every author, particularly Matthew, was a reader of texts prior to their compositional activity (M. Worton and J. Still, eds., *Intertextuality: Theories and Practices,* Manchester: Manchester University Press, 1990, pp. 1–3). Moreover, I would not echo Luz's assertion that all exegesis after the Enlightenment is somehow more objective and thus call into question all early Christian exegesis (so his *The Theology of the Gospel of Matthew,* translated by J. B. Robinson, New Testament Theology, Cambridge: Cambridge University Press, 1995, pp. 40–1).

hermeneutic'.[3] Early Christianity developed and grew in an environment that strongly emphasized the importance of text, and one is not surprised to discover considerable continuity between Jewish and early Christian usage of the Scriptures.

Research has confirmed that a high level of continuity existed between Jewish and early Christian exegesis.[4] Because the Scriptures were deemed authoritative, they formed the basis for thought and practice, for answers to the problems of change, for the defence of the faith and, ultimately, for the construction of worldviews. Vermes observes,

> Religious teachers . . . confronted with new situations unforeseen by the legislators, found themselves faced with the task of associating them with that message and of giving them scriptural relevance. In addition, Palestinian Jewry was divided, from the second century B.C. to the end of the Second Temple, into separate and rival groups (Pharisees, Sadducees, Essenes, Judeo-Christians), each of which slanted its interpretative system to justify the biblical authenticity of its beliefs and way of life. Here then were two other demands: exegesis was required to adapt and complete scripture so that it might on the one hand

---

[3] 'The Theological Appropriation of the Old Testament by the New Testament', *SJT* 39 (1986): 2. See especially C. Rabin, 'The Translation Process and the Character of the Septuagint', *Textus* 6 (1968): 1–26.

[4] The interaction between Jews and Christians on the interpretation of Scripture has an intriguing history. One need only consult Jerome's *Dialogues* to see the extent to which the debate ultimately devolved to the level of interpretation. The literature on ancient approaches to Scripture is vast, with specialist and general studies accumulating. For general introductions see the diverse essays in the two massive volumes of M. J. Mulder, ed., *Mikra: Text, Translation, and Reading and Interpretation of the Hebrew Bible in Ancient Judaism and Early Christianity*, CRINT 2.1, Assen and Maastricht: Van Gorcum; Philadelphia: Fortress, 1988, and M. Saebo, ed., *Hebrew Bible/Old Testament: The History of Its Interpretation*, vol. I: *From the Beginnings to the Middle Ages (until 1300). Part 1: Antiquity*, Göttingen: Vandenhoeck & Ruprecht, 1996. See also the helpful collection of essays in G. K. Beale, ed., *The Right Doctrine from the Wrong Texts? Essays on the Use of the Old Testament in the New*, Grand Rapids: Baker, 1994. The studies of C. H. Dodd, *According to the Scriptures: The Substructure of New Testament Theology*, London: Nisbet & Co., 1952; F. F. Bruce, *Biblical Exegesis in the Qumran Texts*, London: Tyndale Press, 1960; R. N. Longenecker, *Biblical Exegesis in the Apostolic Period*, Grand Rapids: Eerdmans, 1975; D. Patte, *Early Jewish Hermeneutic in Palestine*, SBLDS 22, Missoula: Scholars, 1975; and D. J. Moo, *The Old Testament in the Gospel Passion Narratives*, Sheffield: Almond, 1983, pp. 1–78, remain valuable. See also D. Instone-Brewer, *Techniques and Assumptions in Jewish Exegesis before 70 CE*, TSAJ 30, Tübingen: Mohr (Paul Siebeck), 1992, *passim*, and C. M. Tuckett's comments in *The Scriptures in the Gospels*, BETL 131, Leuven: Leuven University Press, 1997, pp. xxiii-xxiv. For a useful introduction to Talmud and Midrash, see H. L. Strack and G. Stemberger, *Introduction to the Talmud and Midrash*, translated and edited by M. Bockmuehl, Edinburgh: T. & T. Clark, 1992.

apply to the present time, and on the other, satisfy the requirements of polemics.[5]

Thus, it is not surprising to discover that the Scriptures and their interpretation played a profound role in the formation of communal self-definition
vis-à-vis the parent body in the communities of the Dead Sea and early
Christianity.[6] Evidence for this may be found, for example, in the import
afforded the interpretation of the Teacher of Righteousness in the Dead
Sea community[7] and the teachings of Jesus in Matthew.

The appeal to the Scriptures in the early Christian movement seems to
have originated in attempts to explain the Christ event within the broader
scope of God's plan and salvation history. Whether it began as part of
a defensive apologetic,[8] an aggressive evangelistic/missions campaign,[9]
or out of a need to shore up inner support[10] has long been disputed.[11]
Part of the difficulty in determining the motivating factors behind the
earliest usage of the Old Testament by Christians lies in the lacunae in
the sources from this period. If Matthew is dated after AD 70, then the
four decades that followed the Christ event may have witnessed substantial development. Thus, the urgencies behind Matthew's use of Scripture
may be somewhat different from those in the days which shortly followed
the death and resurrection of Jesus. Overman, for example, suggests that
the use of the Old Testament in Matthew was part of the process of legitimation as the Matthean community struggled to gain the upper hand with

---

[5] 'Bible and Midrash', p. 202.

[6] A perusal of CD, 1QS, 4QMMT, 1QH^a and the various *pesherim* reveals a broad usage
of the Old Testament which serves to distinguish the Qumran community. See Stanton,
Gospel for a New People, pp. 90–3, on sectarianism in the Damascus Document. On Qumran
sectarianism see L. H. Schiffman, *Sectarian Law in the Dead Sea Scrolls: Courts, Testimony,
and the Penal Code*, Chico: Scholars, 1983, pp. 211–20, and B. Z. Wacholder, *The Dawn
of Qumran: The Sectarian Torah and the Teacher of Righteousness*, Monographs of the
Hebrew Union College no. 8, Cincinnati: Hebrew Union College Press, 1983, pp. 33–98.

[7] J. C. VanderKam, *The Dead Sea Scrolls Today*, Grand Rapids: Eerdmans, 1994, pp.
100–4; H. Ringgren, *The Faith of Qumran: Theology of the Dead Sea Scrolls,* expanded
edn, edited with a new introduction by James H. Charlesworth, New York: Crossroad, 1995,
pp. 31–43.

[8] So E. Massebieau, *Examen des citations de l'Ancien Testament dans l'évangile selon
Saint Matthieu*, Paris, 1885, and Lindars, *New Testament Apologetic*, p. 19.

[9] B. Gärtner, 'The Habakkuk Commentary (DSH) and the Gospel of Matthew', *ST* 8
(1954): 23; McConnell, *Law and Prophecy*, p. 138; G. Schille, 'Bemerkungen zur Formgeschichte des Evangeliums II. Das Evangelium des Matthäus als Katechismus', *NTS* 4
(1957): 113.

[10] Brown, *Birth*, p. 98, argues that the Matthean formula citations 'had a didactic purpose,
informing the Christian readers and giving support to their faith'.

[11] The original purpose of the formula quotations is likewise debated. See, for example,
in response to Stendahl, Gärtner's arguments in 'Habakkuk Commentary', 23, which favour
a missionary preaching milieu.

the increasingly dominant post-70 formative Judaism.[12] Almost certainly the struggle for self-identity and legitimation were contributing factors to OT usage, as is evidenced in both Matthew and the sectarian texts from the Dead Sea Scrolls. This process took on greater significance as Christianity parted ways with Judaism, and early believers sought to reformulate numerous issues pertinent to their communities. Regardless of the precise milieu in which early Christian exegesis occurred, it is sufficient to note that the resulting perspective on the life, ministry, death and resurrection of Jesus of Nazareth and its repercussions upon issues such as the role of the Law, identity of the people of God, means of salvation, christology, *theo*logy, eschatology, and so on, were ultimately validated by OT texts.[13]

In what remains of this chapter, I shall present something of a history of scholarship of Matthew's use of the Old Testament and, more specifically, the formula quotations. This will, it is hoped, provide a base upon which to build in the following chapters. And given that Isa. 42.1–4 has been traditionally considered one of the four *Ebed Yahweh* passages, it seems that what is meant by the construct 'S/servant of the Lord' should be addressed. In order to get at this issue, the final section of the chapter will offer a semantic analysis of this important and much discussed phrase.

Matthew's use of the Old Testament

Characterized by M. D. Goulder as 'highly complex', Matthew's use of the Old Testament is more thoroughgoing than that of the other Synoptic Gospels.[14] The frequent explicit citations, forty in all, implicit quotations, of which there are twenty-one, and numerous allusory references to the Old Testament are central to his narrative development.[15] The fact that

---

[12] Overman's study *Matthew's Gospel and Formative Judaism* is beneficial in many respects. On this topic see also P. Sigal, *The Halakah of Jesus of Nazareth according to the Gospel of Matthew*, Lanham, MD: University Press of America, 1986, and Saldarini, *Matthew's Christian-Jewish Community*. Overman's description, p. 72, of a 'fluid and fragmented' post-70 Judaism also aptly depicts pre-70 Judaism, at least what we know of it through the Dead Sea Scrolls.

[13] In this sense Dodd's suggestion, *According to the Scriptures*, pp. 132–8, that the Old Testament forms the substructure of NT theology may be cautiously affirmed (so also J. Marcus, *The Way of the Lord: Christological Exegesis of the Old Testament in the Gospel of Mark*, Louisville: Westminster/John Knox Press, 1992, pp. 202–3).

[14] *Midrash and Lection in Matthew*, London: SPCK, 1974, p. 124.

[15] So Senior, 'Lure of the Formula Quotations', p. 89 n. 1. B. W. Bacon, *Studies in Matthew*, London: Constable, 1930, p. 470, is more optimistic and less precise in suggesting that Matthew cites the Old Testament over one hundred times. One must further classify the citations into explicit (those which include a formula and a section of an OT

Matthew also includes all citations from parallel passages in both Mark and Q and further expands upon Marcan allusions is duly illustrative of the import of the Old Testament in the Gospel.[16] As a result, there is a sound basis for the argument that the theme of fulfilment undergirds the Gospel from beginning to end. Jesus' statement in 26.54 perhaps captures this best: 'But how then would the scriptures be fulfilled, which say it must happen in this way?'[17]

Thus fulfilment is one of the great assumptions of the Matthean narrative. While the recurrence of πληροῦν demonstrates Matthew's interest in the theme,[18] it seems that this verb is but one component in a much more comprehensive development of fulfilment in Matthew.[19] Similarly, the OT usage, although significant, primarily contributes to Matthew's overall narrative strategy of demonstrating the continuity of God's purposes in the life and ministry of Jesus of Nazareth with the history of the Jewish people. The opening section of the Gospel, for example, intimates as much when it commences, 'A book of the beginnings of Jesus

passage), implicit (a lengthy citation without explicit reference to its origin; so Moo, *Passion Narratives*, p. 19), and allusory categories.

[16] Davies and Allison, *Matthew*, I.44. The difficulty in determining the allusory material is due to the subjectivity of the exercise. See Moo, *Passion Narratives*, pp. 20–1, who argues that the inclusion of 'Scriptural words and phrases' is the determinant for an allusion. R. B. Hays, *Echoes of Scripture in the Letters of Paul*, New Haven: Yale University Press, 1989, pp. 18–21, offers a more careful description of how allusion is defined in literary critical approaches. Studies of Matthew's use of the Old Testament ought to take such usages into account; the difficulty, of course, arises in attempting to establish boundaries to contain the inherent self-indulgence.

[17] Cf. 26.56. D. B. Howell, *Matthew's Inclusive Story: A Study in the Narrative Rhetoric of the First Gospel*, JSNTSup 42, Sheffield: JSOT Press, 1990, p. 189, comments regarding Jesus' statement at his arrest in 26.56 ('all this has taken place so that the scriptures of the prophets may be fulfilled'): 'Only here in the entire narrative does Jesus express on the phraseological plane with the same words what the narrator has been stating throughout the Gospel in the fulfillment quotations: the events in Jesus' life fulfil the Old Testament Scriptures'.

[18] πληροῦν occurs in Matthew twelve times, eight times in John, twice in Luke and once in Mark. H. Frankemölle, *Jahwebund und Kirche Christi*, NTAbh, n.F. 10, 2nd edn, Münster: Aschendorf, 1984, pp. 388–9, emphasizes the centrality of πληροῦν to Matthew's understanding of fulfilment. France, *Evangelist and Teacher*, pp. 166–205, demonstrates the broader significance of fulfilment in the Gospel. G. Delling, 'πληρόω', *TDNT* VI.297, observes that the πληρόω formulae are limited exclusively to the Gospels and Acts (except for Jas. 2.23) on those occasions when accompanying proofs from Scripture refer only to the Christ event. The expression never occurs in Paul. On fulfilment citations in John, see Rothfuchs, *Erfüllungszitate*, pp. 151–4.

[19] Moule's restriction, 'Fulfilment-Words', 297–8, of Matthew's usage of πληροῦν to simplistic prediction-fulfilment may need revision. Similarly, R. A. Greer, 'The Christian Bible and Its Interpretation', in *Early Biblical Interpretation*, edited by J. Kugel and R. A. Greer, Philadelphia: Westminster, 1986, p. 135, also affirms a Matthean emphasis upon the 'predictive aspect of Scripture'. *Pace* Brown, *Birth*, p. 97 n. 3, who opines that Moule's categorization of Matthew is too restrained.

the Messiah, son of David, son of Abraham'. Likewise, in the curious genealogy which follows (1.2–16) and the unusual circumstances surrounding his conception (1.18–25), Jesus is presented as the fulfilment of the promises of God to his people. From Matthew's perspective at least, Jesus is the long-awaited one, who is not only the presence of God among his people (1.23) but also their saviour from sin (1.21). He is the fulfilment of the Scriptures and Israel's hopes, the anticipated king/messiah who marks the beginning of the end (2.6).[20] Thus his relationship to the Law (5.17–20), Israel and the nations is of ultimate importance. Furthermore, that Matthew's usage and development of OT themes exceeds that of the other Synoptic Gospels would seem to demonstrate that he was a Jewish author thoroughly *au fait* with the Scriptures and knowledgeable about eschatological expectations within Judaism;[21] this is perhaps most clearly articulated in his employment of the ten so-called formula citations.[22]

Matthew's use of the Old Testament is commonly divided into two categories, those references already present in his sources (i.e. Mark, Q and possibly M) and those peculiar to Matthew himself.[23] Among the latter group, the formula quotations are perhaps the most distinctive. Such distinctiveness has led to the supposition that due to their redactional nature they comprise a sure guide to understanding Matthew's usage of the Old Testament, which in turn has created a tendency to focus too quickly upon the formula citations alone. In response, some scholars have increasingly lamented that such overemphasis has led to an impoverished view of Matthew's OT usage in general.[24] Giving greater weight to the

[20] D. C. Sim, *Apocalyptic Eschatology in the Gospel of Matthew*, SNTSMS 88, Cambridge: Cambridge University Press, 1996, pp. 87–91, locates Matthew's fulfilment in an apocalyptic worldview which is framed in terms of a mechanistic determinism.

[21] *Pace* Clark, 'Gentile Bias', 165–8; Nepper-Christensen, *Matthäusevangelium*, pp. 202–7; Trilling, *Das wahre Israel*, pp. 219–24; and Strecker, *Weg*, pp. 15–35, who all argue for gentile authorship. For a critique of Clark on this point, see Davies and Allison, *Matthew*, I.29–32, and Stanton, 'Origin and Purpose', pp. 1916–21.

[22] *Pace* Luz, *Matthew*, p. 162. The commonly agreed-upon ten quotations include 1.23; 2.15, 18, 23; 4.15–16; 8.17; 12.18–21; 13.35; 21.5; 27.9–10. Beyond these ten, which all contain the standard formula and are asides by the author, some scholars have cautiously nominated additions. Stendahl, *School*, pp. 99–101, and Soares Prabhu, *Formula Quotations*, p. 41, tentatively include 2.6 in this group, as does I. H. Jones, *A Commentary on the Gospel of St Matthew*, Epworth Commentaries, London: Epworth, 1994, p. 6, who further includes Matt. 13.14 for a total of twelve. Soares Prabhu, *Formula Quotations*, pp. 18–62, and Rothfuchs, *Erfüllungszitate*, pp. 27–56, both offer excellent summaries of the formula quotations.

[23] Already in Massebieau, *Examen des citations*, and B. F. Westcott, *An Introduction to the Study of the Gospels,* 8th edn, London: Macmillan and Co., 1895, p. 229. See also the later studies of Stendahl, *School*, and Gundry, *Use of the Old Testament*.

[24] Most recently Senior, 'Lure of the Formula Quotations', p. 95. A more general critique is found in Stanton, *Gospel for a New People*, p. 346, and Luz, *Matthew*, p. 157.

other explicit, implicit and allusory references to the Old Testament in the Gospel, including those adopted from the major sources, can only offer a more balanced view and provide a substantial base from which to contemplate the role of the formula quotations themselves. A brief review of recent findings regarding Matthew's use of the Old Testament in general may serve to place the analysis of the text under investigation here in broader perspective.

The observation that Matthew includes all OT passages cited in the sources he draws upon, while of some interest, offers little assistance in understanding the background for his usage of the Old Testament except perhaps as a general comment upon his preoccupation with the theme of fulfilment. Any redactional adjustments Matthew made to these quotations may be significant, however, due to the potential insight they might afford into Matthew's concerns, theological or otherwise.[25] Senior, taking up Stanton's suggestion that the non-formula quotations be considered more seriously,[26] has recently commented upon Matthew's use of the Old Testament in the Passion narrative. He argues that the Passion narrative, in which there are few formula citations,[27] reveals 'a depth and variety' in Matthew's use of the Old Testament that places the usage of the formula quotations on a broader canvas. He concludes that they are but part of a 'full repertoire of the ways Matthew uses the Old Testament to underwrite the story of Jesus for his community and, at the same time, to provide his community with a new reading of their scriptures in the light of the faith in Jesus' identity as Messiah and Son of God'.[28] They are distinct not because of their theology or their placement, 'but mainly because in these instances it is the narrator rather than other characters in the narrative world of Matthew who makes this recurring and fundamental affirmation'.[29] Thus the formula quotations, the explicit and implicit non-formula quotations, and numerous allusions all may potentially contribute to an understanding of Matthew's use of the Old Testament. Of significance in this regard has been the recent interest

[25] This is, of course, dependent upon whether the sources Matthew drew upon were the same as our text of Mark and Q.

[26] Stanton, *Gospel for a New People*, p. 346, in particular observes that 'the evangelist's modifications of the quotations found in his sources and the additional references he includes without using his "introductory formula" ' have been neglected (also cited in Senior, 'Lure of the Formula Quotations', p. 95).

[27] There is some debate concerning whether or not Matt. 26.54, 56 qualify as formula quotations. The fact that no OT text is explicitly cited is problematic, as is the fact that both references to the fulfilment of Scripture are placed on the lips of Jesus; these stand in contrast to all other formula quotations which are asides provided by the author.

[28] 'Lure of the Formula Quotations', p. 115.   [29] *Ibid.*

in the quotations incorporated from Mark and Q, and whether they have indeed been adjusted towards the LXX by Matthew.

Although the data do not prove as incontrovertible as some would like, Matthean adjustments to the quotations adopted from Mark and Q appear to have been made in order not to achieve greater conformity to the LXX[30] but to incorporate Matthew's own contextual and theological interests. Both Soares Prabhu and Stanton have demonstrated that the citations taken over from Mark and Q betray the redactional tendencies found in Matthew's handling of the major sources in general.[31] Stanton's conclusions are clear; the OT citations from Mark and Q are generally septuagintal, and Matthew retains them in that form: '*Matthew's primary allegiance is to the textual form of the quotations in his sources rather than to the LXX as such*'.[32] The importance of the Marcan and Q (Lucan) parallels is that they provide reasonably established sources with which to make comparisons; in other words, they stand in contrast to those citations peculiar to Matthew. The fact that Matthew adjusts Mark, Q and M and also the quotations taken over from them would suggest that one should not be surprised to discover that he also modified the OT quotations he derived from other sources.

Much of this argument, however, is reliant upon extant text-forms and the ability of a modern investigation to determine intended meaning through a comparison of those text-forms. Redaction criticism remains one of the few methods that can be used to ascertain Matthew's agenda in his use of the Old Testament; however, its application, while a provocative exercise, has not won unanimous support among the scholarly community. The hesitancy which exists with respect to studies claiming to

[30] *Pace* W. C. Allen, *A Critical and Exegetical Commentary on the Gospel according to St Matthew*, 3rd edn, ICC, Edinburgh: T. & T. Clark, 1912, p. lxii; Kilpatrick, *Origins*, p. 56; Stendahl, *School*, p. 148; and Goulder, *Midrash and Lection*, p. 125, who, for example, argues that Matt. 15.8 (Mark 7.6) and 19.18 (Mark 10.19) are brought closer to the LXX. At the heart of this issue is the contention that Matthew's Bible was the LXX (so Bacon, *Studies in Matthew*, p. 477; Strecker, *Weg*, pp. 24–85; and most recently supported by New, *Old Testament Quotations*, p. 122).

[31] Stanton, *Gospel for a New People*, pp. 354–5; Soares Prabhu, *Formula Quotations*, pp. 77–84; and Davies and Allison, *Matthew*, I.35. Stanton observes that Matt. 16.9 (Jer. 5.21) omits the harsh elements of Mark 8.18; the alterations in Matt. 19.18 (Mark 10.19) may be stylistic in nature, although the text is too difficult to be certain; Matt. 21.9 includes a Son of David reference not in the LXX. Similarly, Matt. 22.32 (Mark 12.26) and 24.30 (Mark 13.26) may also evince stylistic embellishments nonexistent in the LXX (cf. also Matt. 21.13 (Mark 11.17); Matt. 24.15 (Mark 13.14); Matt. 26.47–56 (Mark 14.43–52); Matt. 9.13 and 12.7 (Hos. 6.6); Matt. 3.3 (Mark 1.3); Matt. 11.10 (Mark 1.2)). It seems evident, then, that Matthean redactional concerns are the likely impetus behind the textual adjustments rather than an overriding concern to bring the text into alignment with the LXX. In fact, the author introduces key interpretative elements not found in the LXX.

[32] *Gospel for a New People*, p. 358.

discern Matthew's theological interests based upon comparative analyses of the text-form of the shared quotations from Mark and Luke becomes even more pronounced with respect to the textually complex formula quotations.[33]

The formula quotations

The quandary which Matthew's formula citations have presented to interpreters is legendary. The issues that these texts raise are in reality quite straightforward, but their resolution is rendered difficult due to lacunae in our knowledge of text-forms, translation techniques and hermeneutics during the period prior to AD 70. Thus, questioning the function of a quotation in its context, while initially appearing to be an elementary exercise, can in fact be exceedingly complicated. And while the formula quotations should probably not be considered a 'special' group of Matthean citations, the fact that they are unique in Jewish literature warrants comment.[34] Scholarship has arrived at several conclusions concerning this group of citations that may provide a starting point from which to proceed.[35]

Perhaps the most conspicuous element of the formula quotations is their distinctive Hebraic text-form, and it is this 'Hebrew character' that first set the quotations apart as a group.[36] Another notable characteristic involves the obvious way in which the citations have been inserted into the narrative, possibly in the final edition, rendering them easily recognizable as interjections by Matthew.[37] This is evident on several levels. First, the formulae that introduce the citations bear all the hallmarks of Matthew's vocabulary and theology.[38] Second, four of the quotations have been

---

[33] Luz, *Matthew*, p. 161, for example, concludes that the import of 'the wording of the quotations for the understanding of the theology of Matthew is minimal'.

[34] The eight Johannine formula quotations (12.38; 13.18; 15.25; 17.12; 18.9, 32; 19.24, 36), while sharing a similar motif, are distinct from those of Matthew. See further Rothfuchs, *Erfüllungszitate*, pp. 151–77.

[35] One may consult the numerous summaries for detailed treatments, e.g. Brown, *Birth*, pp. 96–104; van Segbroeck, 'Les citations d'accomplissement', pp. 107–30; Soares Prabhu, *Formula Quotations*, pp. 18–40; Jones, *Matthew*, pp. 5–7; Davies and Allison, *Matthew*, III.573–7; Luz, *Matthew*, pp. 156–64.

[36] While this traditional characterization is true for some of the formula quotations, it does need to be qualified somewhat. A better characterization of the quotations might describe them as possessing a 'mixed text-form', meaning that they are both the same and yet different from the LXX and MT. See below for a fuller discussion.

[37] J. Hawkins, *Horae Synopticae: Contributions to the Study of the Synoptic Problem*, Oxford: Clarendon, 1909, p. 154, asserts that they were 'avowedly introduced by the author'.

[38] See the full treatment of this issue in Rothfuchs, *Erfüllungszitate*, pp. 33–43, and Soares Prabhu, *Formula Quotations*, pp. 46–62. The vocabulary involved is Matthean

inserted into Marcan and Q material (4.15–16; 8.17; 12.18–21; 13.35). Third, the citations clutter the narrative, creating a disjointed, uneven reading, while their removal produces a flowing text (1.23; 2.15; 2.23; 4.15–16; 8.17; 12.18–21).[39] Fourth, several of the citations seemingly can only function within their setting in the Matthean narrative (e.g. Hos. 11.1 in Matt. 2.15). Fifth, the contexts surrounding several of the citations contain similar terminology and themes found in the citations themselves, suggesting a cross-pollination during the composition of the Gospel.[40] When taken together, these factors contribute to a strong case in favour of the position that the citations have been added by Matthew to the narrative.

Scholarly agreement is substantial regarding the general function and purpose of the formula quotations. They are understood as authorial comments that serve Matthew's programmatic development of the theme of Jesus' fulfilment of the will of God.[41] This is perhaps most clearly witnessed in the language and use of the formula that precedes this group of citations. The frequent usage of fulfilment language (πληροῦν) in Matthew and John is distinct when compared to the contemporary Jewish sources. For example, its translational equivalent never occurs in the Mishnah and J. Fitzmyer observes that no real parallel to the NT fulfilment formulae is found in the Qumran literature either.[42] B. Metzger's oft-cited study concludes that the reason for the difference transcends the issue of genre and may ultimately 'be traced to two differing interpretations of history'.[43]

(Strecker, *Weg*, p. 50). That the basic formula is dependent upon Mark 14.49 is probable; nevertheless, the language and form are distinctly Matthean. The one formula that occurs in 13.14 may complicate the discussion because it contains little, if any, Matthean vocabulary (Jones, *Matthew*, p. 6).

[39] This is particularly the case in the Infancy narrative. This point does not in and of itself prove Matthean interests are behind the text because the unevenness could have preceded Matthew's handling of it.

[40] See especially Cope, *Matthew*, pp. 6–10.

[41] Jones, *Matthew*, p. 6; Howell, *Matthew's Inclusive Story*, pp. 251–4.

[42] 'The Use of Explicit Old Testament Quotations in Qumran Literature and in the New Testament', *NTS* 7 (1960–1): 303. For a detailed study on the formulae in the Dead Sea Scrolls, see also F. L. Horton, 'Formulas of Introduction in the Qumran Literature', *RevQ* 7 (1971): 505–14. In an attempt to explain the disparity, Fitzmyer suggests that the fulfilment formulae 'are fundamentally a New Testament type. More fundamental still is probably the difference in outlook which characterizes the two groups.' He further urges a theological distinction, suggesting that the Qumran community is still 'forward looking' in its anticipation of the eschaton whereas Christian theology is 'characterized by a backward glance'.

[43] 'The Formulas Introducing Quotations of Scripture in the NT and the Mishnah', *JBL* 70 (1951): 306–7. On the rabbinic formulas, see J. Bonsirven, *Exégèse rabbinique et exégèse paulinienne*, Paris: Beauchesne et ses fils, 1938, pp. 29–32.

Beyond these acknowledged points, however, common ground is less easy to locate concerning the formula quotations. In fact, since Massebieau first popularized the concept that they form a distinctive group,[44] agreement on their particular characteristics has not been uniform. Two interrelated issues have dominated scholarly discussion on the formula quotations in the past. First, the question of the source of Matthew's text-form has perplexed scholars and shows no sign of resolution. Doubt continues to exist regarding whether Matthew is himself responsible for the anomalous text-form of the citations and also whether one may plot Matthean theological interests based upon the discrepancies in his text-form.[45] The assertion that the citations consist of the author's own work and are 'closely related to Matthew's thought' risks the danger of diagnosing 'the theological point of the citation precisely against the background of what are recognized as Matthean interests', thereby opening itself up to the charge of circular reasoning.[46] Second, the specific role of the quotations within their given contexts remains somewhat obfuscated, and questions linger concerning whether there is any direct relationship between the content and the surrounding context. Are they, for example, mere proof-texts cited to validate historical elements within Matthew's presentation of the life of Jesus, or do they make a more significant contribution to his christology? However one resolves such issues, directly at the centre of this debate resides the question of Matthew's text-form.

Source and text-form of the formula quotations

As observed above, one of the defining characteristics of the formula quotations is their distinctive text-form. They both resemble and yet

---

[44] In Massebieau's short study of 1885, *Examen des citations*, he groups twenty-three quotations as Matthean, eleven of which he designates 'apologetic citations'. H. J. Holtzmann, *Hand-Commentar zum Neuen Testament: Die Synoptiker*, Freiburg, 1889–91, p. 41, distinguishes between *Reflexionszitate* and *Contextcitate*. This is perhaps the earliest use of these terms with reference to Matthean citations in German. Westcott, *Introduction*, p. 229, notes two groups of Matthean citations that resemble Holtzmann and Massebieau's categories.

[45] Note that the recent studies by Weren, 'Quotations from Isaiah', pp. 447–65, and 'Jesus' Entry into Jerusalem', 117–41, are more optimistic about this method.

[46] Brown, *Birth*, p. 104. Brown's point that only the citations that Matthew introduced into Christian tradition may be thought to provide a clear analysis of Matthean theology is a reasonable caution. The adjustment of Marcan and Q citations, however, also demonstrates Matthew's theological interests. As noted earlier, if Matthew has redactionally modified the narratives and the citations of Mark and Q to suit his theological interests, then one may legitimately ask whether he has not also adjusted other texts taken from Jewish or Christian tradition.

differ from the MT and LXX, and, to complicate matters further, at various points the quotations contain readings completely at variance with all known textual traditions. Their uniqueness has in turn led to innumerable theories concerning their source, many of which are inextricably bound to the broader issues of Matthean composition and the author's linguistic abilities.[47] In fact, there has been a proclivity among scholars to subordinate ideas concerning the significance and function of the citations to assumptions about the possible origins of the Gospel. As I shall argue, however, this subordination is not necessarily a logical one. Similarly, scholarship has tended to view the quotations as a monolithic group, relegating them all to one particular source.[48] Such an extreme representation is probably not historically credible, and the source(s) from which they were obtained are in reality much more diverse.

Already by the time of Jerome the conundrum of the distinctive text-form was confounding biblical scholars.[49] Attempts to respond to the issues involved are as diverse as they are creative. A minimalist approach argues that the text-form existed prior to Matthew either in an oral tradition, a Testimony collection, or an as yet unknown version, rendering any proposed links between the citation and its surrounding context unlikely. The Testimony hypothesis[50] was most clearly articulated by J. R. Harris in his two-part work, *Testimonies*, in which he postulated the existence of early Christian collections of significant OT passages.[51] Proponents of the Testimony hypothesis suggest that adherents of the early church, like their Jewish counterparts, collected OT passages for encouragement,

---

[47] Bacon, *Studies in Matthew*, pp. 470–7, for example, argues that the citations were derived from 'Aramaic Targumic' material. Similarly, Torrey, *Documents of the Primitive Church*, pp. 65–6, suggests that Matthew was composed in Aramaic using an Aramaic Mark as his primary source; however, the quotations point to a Hebrew original which was rendered quite freely.

[48] See Davies and Allison, *Matthew*, III.575.

[49] Jerome of Bethlehem, *Apologia contra Rufinum*, 2.34, notes that 'Wherever the Seventy agree with the Hebrew, the Apostles took their quotations from that translation. But where [the two] disagree, they set down in Greek what they had found in the Hebrew.'

[50] For a recent treatment see Martin C. Albl,'*And Scripture Cannot Be Broken*'. *The Form and Function of the Early Christian Testimonia Collections,* NovTSup 96, Leiden: Brill, 1999.

[51] J. R. Harris, *Testimonies,* with the assistance of Vacher Burch, 2 vols., Cambridge: Cambridge University Press, 1916-20. Others who have subscribed to this position include F. C. Burkitt, *The Gospel History and Its Transmission,* 3rd edn, Edinburgh: T. & T. Clark, 1911, p. 126; Allen, *Matthew,* p. lxii; E. Lohmeyer, *Das Evangelium des Matthäus,* revised by W. Schmauch, 4th edn, MeyerK, Göttingen: Vandenhoeck & Ruprecht, 1967, p. 23; and L. Vaganay, *Le problème synoptique: une hypothèse de travail,* Paris: Desclée et Co., 1954, pp. 237ff. For an incisive critique by a scholar who worked with the idea for some time, see Dodd, *According to the Scriptures*, p. 26, who ultimately rejected the position after having been nearly convinced.

edification and apologetical purposes.[52] Strecker posits that the formula quotations derive from a written source (Testimony collection)[53] and further argues that the citations only evince minor Matthean redaction and thus are loosely related to the context in their employment in Matthew's historicization of Jesus' life.[54] One might also include among this group Moule's thesis that Matthew's quotations are examples of primitive proof-texting, which assumes access to a text-form already in existence.[55] Kahle has postulated that the formula quotations originated in written Greek Targums, for which no records exist.[56] On a slightly different tack, Kilpatrick[57] and, most recently, Luz have suggested that the quotations were passed down as part of an oral tradition. Luz extends the argument to suggest that the formula quotations accompanied the narratives to which they are attached.[58]

All these positions are characterized by their propensity to minimize possible links to the surrounding Matthean context and potential

[52] Although a reasonable theory, this supposition appeared to be little more than speculation until the discovery of 4QTest and 4QFlor in the Dead Sea Scrolls, Jewish examples of messianic texts compiled in one document that provides the best evidence to date in support of the existence of collected testimonies. J. M. Allegro, 'Further Messianic References in Qumran Literature', *JBL* 75 (1956): 186, writes concerning the implications of the Dead Sea Scrolls upon the theory of Christian testimonia, 'There can be little doubt that we have in this document a group of *testimonia* of the type long ago proposed by Burkitt, Rendel Harris, and others to have existed in the early Church. Our collection has the added interest of including two testimonies used by the early Christians of Jesus.' Possible Christian examples of Testimony collections might include texts such as PapRyl 460; however, whether this text comprised a memory aid, list of liturgical texts or Testimony is uncertain. C. H. Roberts, *Two Biblical Papyri in the John Rylands Library Manchester,* Manchester: University of Manchester Press, 1936, pp. 49ff., asserts that it is indeed an example of a Testimony collection. Most recently, see G. N. Stanton's, 'The Fourfold Gospel', *NTS* 43 (1997): 336–41, promising investigations into the codex and its role and importance in early Christianity.

[53] *Weg*, pp. 49ff., pp. 183ff. McConnell, *Law and Prophecy*, p. 135, finds Strecker's arguments partially convincing and surmises that it is 'probable that Matthew drew at least some of these quotations from a collection of quotations'.

[54] Strecker, *Weg*, p. 69 (see also his 'The Concept of History in Matthew', in *The Interpretation of Matthew,* edited by G. N. Stanton, Studies in New Testament Interpretation 3, Edinburgh: T. & T. Clark, 1995, p. 86).

[55] 'Fulfilment-Words', 293–320.

[56] *Cairo Geniza*, pp. 209–64. This view, based upon his ideas concerning the origin of the LXX, has largely been discounted in light of the presence of LXX texts in the Dead Sea Scrolls and Greek texts from Naḥal Ḥever.

[57] *Origins*, pp. 96–7.

[58] *Matthew*, pp. 160–1. Practically, this theory is very cumbersome and inconsistent. Given that the formula which precedes the quotations is Matthean and has been inserted into Marcan material, one would assume that the other citations have been inserted into their narrative contexts; one must be cautious, however, about demanding uniformity on this issue. Nonetheless, Luz has not explained the aberrant text-form, although he is correct that other explanations such as a lapse in memory may be possible.

theological usage. Such a stance is arguable, for if Matthew is not directly responsible for the text-form, then the contention that textual idiosyncrasies betray Matthew's interests fails. For example, writing concerning the text under analysis in this thesis, Isa. 42.1–4 in Matt. 12.18–21, Lindars opines that the quotation was modified in a pre-Matthean apologetical context within the church and 'owes nothing to its present context'.[59] He avers that the text enjoyed a long history that was shaped by the apologetical concerns of early Christianity.[60] As a result of the use of the Old Testament in various contexts, he postulates that developmental stages are distinguishable in the text-form. For example, Matt. 12.18–21 contains four such redactional periods linked to apologetic interests regarding Jesus' resurrection, baptism, and gentile mission.[61] He surmises that the final redactor of Matthew, apparently unaware of the prior history of the adjustments, merely employed the text in ignorance. While Lindars' position has largely been discounted, he does raise an important question. If the quotations have been employed, even adjusted, in early Christian usage prior to Matthew, may one argue that Matthew intends the entire quotation to be of significance within his narrative? The point is similar in many respects to those of Luz, Kilpatrick and, ultimately, Moule. When one bases the work upon redaction criticism and its assumption that Matthew's interests are discernible in the adjustments to the text, one must ascertain that such adjustments were actually undertaken by the author in question.

The most dominant position on the text-form of the formula quotations maintains that Matthew, by drawing upon Hebrew, Aramaic and Greek sources, modified the text, and that these distinctive characteristics instituted by Matthew point to possible authorial concerns.[62] As noted earlier, the assumption which underlies this conception is essentially that of redaction criticism, namely that, through cautious investigation of the adjustments, one may determine the emphases of the author. This, of course, assumes a stable text-form by which a comparison may be made. Stendahl, whose classic study continues to endure due to its comprehensive

---

[59] *New Testament Apologetic*, p. 145 n. 1. Lindars, p. 150, further notes that Isa. 42.1–4 (Matt. 12.18–21) is employed in its present form to validate the version of Mark's 'messianic secret', which the author imported from 3.7–12.

[60] Lindars, *ibid.*, pp. 147–52. He contests, p. 148, that the 'process of adaptation is complete before they are incorporated into the Gospel' (see further pp. 117–22) and thus that 'Following the normal procedure of Form Criticism, we must interpret the passage out of itself without regard to its present context.'

[61] *Ibid.*, pp. 148ff.

[62] See Gundry, *Use of the Old Testament*, p. 172 n. 2, for a short bibliography supporting this claim. He argues that 'this must be the supposition, unless pre-Christian MSS are discovered which agree with the aberrant text of the quotations'.

examination of the text-form of the citations, ventured to argue that the text provides evidence that Matthew was written by a 'school' that utilized a midrashic *pesher* technique.[63] Most provocative perhaps is his assertion that this school made conscious use of a great variety of readings, intentionally selecting one reading over another in support of its message.[64] Importantly, he reaffirmed the existence of a 'strong LXX element in the formula quotations', which, he argued, indicated that 'they originated in Greek form' and, accordingly, that Matthew's church was Greek-speaking.[65] The modifications made to the text relate to the context into which the quotations have been inserted. He concluded that 'all of Matthew's formula quotations give evidence of features of text interpretation of an actualizing nature, often closely associated with the context in the gospel'.[66]

Barth concurs with this assessment, arguing that adjustments to the quotation must have been 'a matter of conscious alteration' by the author himself to suit his theological interpretation.[67] Barth's position, while not directly followed, is similar to those of Gundry, who describes Matthew as a Targumist,[68] Soares Prabhu,[69] Rothfuchs,[70] McConnell,[71] van Segbroeck[72] and many recent commentators.[73] Theirs is a stance that relies heavily upon assumptions concerning the author/redactor of Matthew and the postulate that a linkage exists between the distinctive text-form of the quotations and Matthew's concerns in the narrative. Soares Prabhu, after a thorough treatment, concludes that 'text or formula showed a conscious and deliberate adaptation to the particular context in which it occurred [*sic*] a fact suggesting that the editor who put the quotations into the Gospel was responsible for their closely adapted form'.[74]

[63] Stendahl, *School*, pp. 109–15.

[64] In support of this procedure Stendahl, *ibid.*, pp. 183–202, cites 1QpHab (his DSH). Gärtner, 'Habakkuk Commentary', 2–6, rejects this comparison by noting the presence of wordplay.

[65] Stendahl, *School*, p. 203.   [66] *Ibid.*, pp. 200–1.

[67] Barth, 'Matthew's Understanding of the Law', pp. 125–8.

[68] *Use of the Old Testament*, pp. 172–4. He is consistent at least in urging that the formula quotations are not unique in their text-form but are similar to other non-Marcan quotations in Matthew.

[69] *Formula Quotations*, pp. 104–5.   [70] *Erfüllungszitate*, p. 89.

[71] *Law and Prophecy*, pp. 134ff.   [72] 'Les citations d'accomplissement', pp. 128–30.

[73] E.g., A. Sand, *Das Matthäus-Evangelium*, ErFor 275, Darmstadt: Wissenschaftliche Buchgesellschaft, 1991, pp. 151ff.; D. E. Garland, *Reading Matthew: A Literary and Theological Commentary on the First Gospel*, New York: Crossroad, 1993, pp. 138–9; Davies and Allison, *Matthew*, II.323–4; D. A. Hagner, *Matthew 1–13*, WBC 33a, Dallas: Word Books, 1993, pp. 337–9.

[74] *Formula Quotations*, p. 107.

However appealing the position describing Matthew as Targumist is, in its present form it lacks the nuance and precision necessary to be wholly convincing. And despite their exhaustive and meticulous examinations and listings of the OT citations in Matthew, the early studies of Gundry, Stendahl and, most recently, New are based upon certain assumptions concerning the state of the text prior to AD 100 that are in need of modification in light of the more recent textual discoveries of the last century. Stendahl's frequently cited preface to his second edition of *The School of St Matthew*, published in 1968, allows as much. He observes that

> the present state of O.T. textual criticism is one of greater flux than I surmised ... Such a promising yet unfinished state of affairs both hinders and helps further progress in the study of the Matthean quotations. It makes it more probable that readings found in Matthew could witness to text forms actually available in Greek, prior to Matthew [emphasis mine].[75]

Given what we know of the state of the text in the first century, it comes as no surprise that investigations into the *Textgestalt* of Matthew's OT citations have not yielded a consensus. In fact, New's recent, and somewhat unexpected, re-articulation of the theory that the LXX was Matthew's Bible indicates that the issue is far from settled.[76] Most scholars are willing to concede varying degrees of Matthean editorial activity with regard to the quotations, particularly the formula citations. The primary question, of course, concerns the extent of the modifications and the relationship, if any, between the quotation and its context. Given the import of these issues and the potential contribution to understanding Matthew's Gospel, this seems one step in the process that cannot be overlooked. Thus, I shall explore the text-form of Matthew's quotations in more detail in chapters 4 and 5. Fortunately, scholars have moved beyond

[75] Stendahl, *School*, p. iv. As Stanton, 'Origin and Purpose', p. 1933, observes, the potential impact of recent textual discoveries upon Matthew's use of the Old Testament has yet to be fully extrapolated. New, *Old Testament Quotations*, p. 9, following many others cites Stanton and promises much in his introduction; however, the text itself does not greatly advance the discussion. See also the unpublished paper by G. I. Davies, 'Did Matthew Know Hebrew?', and more recently Menken, 'Isaiah 42,1–4 in Matthew 12,18–21', who argue that Matthew exhibits little evidence of a knowledge of Hebrew and postulate that he was dependent upon Greek versions which were corrected towards the MT.

[76] New's work, *Old Testament Quotations*, has updated the LXX evidence. M. Davies, *Matthew. Readings: A New Biblical Commentary,* Sheffield: JSOT Press, 1992, p. 210, is another proponent of a position perhaps too focused upon the LXX as a standard translation from which the early church worked. She urges that 'Where the quotations differ markedly from our Septuagint . . . the variations may be explained in one of two ways: the Matthean text is an allusion to scriptural passages rather than a quotation, or the author's text of the Septuagint was different from ours.'

the well-worn issue of text-form and have begun to enquire further regarding the rhetorical function the quotations play in Matthew's narrative and his presentation of Jesus.

Rhetorical function

Beyond the question of text-form, more pressing issues confront an investigation into the formula citations. If one considers the citations as simple proof-texts, then explicating their relationship to the surrounding context should be straightforward. One of the shortcomings of this position, however, is that it cannot adequately account for extended, seemingly superfluous segments of material in numerous citations (e.g. 4.15–16; 12.18–21). It may well be that Matthew personally enjoyed or found this extraneous material meaningful on some level, or accepted it as part of the wider tradition; given his editorial economy elsewhere, however, this seems rather unlikely. Justifying the inclusion of these superfluous lines of OT text is only one element in the equation. As noted in chapter 1, the modified text-form contains within it a new set of linguistic relationships, which subtly adjusts the message that the text communicates. Concomitant with the distinct message is the rhetorical force the final form of the quotation exerts within the narrative into which it has been introduced.

To enquire about the function of a quotation and to argue for a more complex usage raises legitimate questions concerning the genre of Matthew's Gospel as a whole. In the past, the consensus amongst critical scholars has maintained that the work of the Gospels is best considered *Kleinliteratur*, that is, low literature marked by a lack of literary sophistication.[77] There are signs that this edifice is beginning to crumble, especially in light of the use of literary criticism. Numerous studies have explored the complexity and thoughtfulness of the Matthean narrative, implying that the narrative be considered if not *Hochliteratur*, then at least somewhere in between.[78] In a recent contribution to the discussion, Jones, proposing that Matthew developed a new genre, argues,

> a Gospel which has redrawn the function and significance of
> narrative as effectively as the Gospel of Matthew, which emerged

[77] See R. Bultmann, *History of the Synoptic Tradition,* translated by J. Marsh, New York: Harper and Row, 1963, pp. 368–74.

[78] See, for example, J. C. Anderson, *Matthew's Narrative Web: Over, and Over, and Over Again,* JSNTSup 91, Sheffield: JSOT, 1994; J. D. Kingsbury, *Matthew as Story,* 2nd edn, Philadelphia: Fortress, 1988; and Howell, *Matthew's Inclusive Story.* The suggestion that one must employ a virginal reading (so R. A. Edwards, *Matthew's Story of Jesus,* Philadelphia: Fortress, 1985, pp. 9–10) seems to ignore the fact that there are legitimate elements of complexity which may only be noticed upon several readings (e.g., see Matt. 13.52).

from a unique contract between writer and audience, which was based on lengthy preparatory work and provided in imagery, metaphors and parables a focus for distinctive expressions of Christian spirituality, has surely moved into a genre without parallel in the history of literature.[79]

Jones' evaluation of genre, although controversial, underscores the value of examining the evocative imagery and metaphors found within the quotations and their role in the narrative. Likewise, recent works on the formula quotations are generally agreed that while they superficially supply a simple this-for-that reference, upon closer inspection the richness of their contribution to Matthew's christology emerges. Numerous approaches have been adopted in an attempt to plumb the depths of Matthew's idiosyncratic usage in order to distinguish the function of the citations within his theology and narrative.

Assuming that the text-form is a Matthean phenomenon and that the author's theological emphases may be identified in it, scholars have conducted brief explorations into select formula citations in order to determine whether they make a theological contribution to the Gospel.[80] The works of Rothfuchs[81] and McConnell[82] represent increasingly sophisticated and focused efforts in demonstrating more precisely the theological function of the citations.[83] Their method is straightforward. Noting distinct textual characteristics and prominent vocabulary and themes, they plot the broader theological significance of the quotations within Matthew's thought. While this exercise has opened up new vistas for understanding Matthew,[84] this approach, like those of intertextual studies in general, is prone to a degree of circularity and Eco's 'smart reader'

[79] *Matthean Parables*, p. 169. See the review by Stanton in *Epworth Review* 25 (1998): 100–1, in which he challenges Jones' assertion concerning a new genre.

[80] This approach is evidenced in the earlier works of Stendahl, *School*, and Gundry, *Use of the Old Testament*.

[81] *Erfüllungszitate*. [82] *Law and Prophecy*.

[83] Cope's argument in *Matthew* is similar to and yet distinct from this group. He claims that beyond providing an initial direct link to the surrounding context, the formula citations function as generative 'mid-point' texts around whose themes and key words the material has been composed and structured. In the case of Matt. 12.18–21, for instance, the retiring, compassionate nature of Jesus presented in vv. 15–16 is what initially prompted the citation and it finds validation in v. 19. But Cope maintains that a realm of reference exists outside this obvious fulfilment. (Soares Prabhu, *Formula Quotations*, p. 107, argues in a similar vein. In contrast to Cope's and Soares Prabhu's suggestion of a more complicated interrelationship, Strecker, *Weg*, pp. 82-3, argues that Matthew reworked the contexts following 4.15–16, 21.5–6, and 27.9–10.) As insightful as Cope's work is, it supplies few answers to the problems of the superfluous content and the rhetorical function of the citations.

[84] See the fine summary by van Segbroeck, 'Les citations d'accomplissement', pp. 107–30.

syndrome. Additionally, these studies, although stimulating, do not fully probe the rhetorical force of Matthew's usage.

An early exploration endeavouring to address the question of rhetorical force is that of L. Hartman.[85] Hartman argues that an analysis of the citations must consider their communicative function. Citations are added to reinforce opinion, to colour with a more illustrative or accurate formulation, and 'to create a certain set of associations in his reader'.[86] This last point leads him to the conclusion that a quotation elicits 'a bundle of ideas connected with its context and/or its interpretation and usage'.[87] Hartman's work underscores the fact that interpretations derive from communities and that for communication to be effective it must draw upon or interact with known interpretative traditions. Thus, his hunch that something more lies behind the usage of many formula citations may prove accurate. The challenge lies in establishing a reasonable method to move from instinct to a demonstrable thesis. And while determining the interpretation behind Matthew's usage is challenging, it is, nevertheless, a useful exercise because it locates the interpretation presented in Matthew within a historical and cultural milieu, adding a valuable element to the investigation.

The discussion concerning the quotations has been redirected by J. D. Kingsbury, who argues that the rhetorical force of the formula citations in Matthew is focused on providing God's evaluative point of view in the narrative.[88] 'By cloaking the life of Jesus and many of his words in the aura of the Old Testament scripture, Matthew establishes Jesus as the thoroughly reliable exponent of God's evaluative point of view.'[89] Although Kingsbury has no doubt captured an element of what Matthew is about, D. Hill accurately observes that the narrator's and God's points of view 'are aligned to affirm who Jesus is'.[90] In another attempt to answer this question of rhetorical force, D. B. Howell pursues ideas first detailed in Chatman's *Story and Discourse*.[91] Howell proposes that the formula

---

[85] 'Problem of Communication', pp. 131–52. See also R. T. France, 'The Formula-Quotations of Matthew 2 and the Problem of Communication', *NTS* 27 (1980): 233–51, who engages with Hartman on numerous issues. An article rarely mentioned, P. Grech's 'The "Testimonia" and Modern Hermeneutics', *NTS* 19 (1972): 318–24, examines OT citations in light of the issues raised by the recent hermeneutical discussion.

[86] Hartman, 'Problem of Communication', p. 134.   [87] *Ibid.*

[88] Kingsbury, *Matthew as Story*, p. 33; 'The Figure of Jesus in Matthew's Story: A Literary-Critical Probe', *JSNT* 21 (1984): 5ff.

[89] Kingsbury, 'Figure of Jesus', 6.

[90] 'The Figure of Jesus in Matthew's Story: A Response to Professor Kingsbury's Literary-Critical Probe', *JSNT* 21 (1984): 40.

[91] *Story and Discourse: Narrative Structure in Fiction and Film*, Ithaca and London: Cornell University Press, 1978.

citations are examples of the use of generalized commentary in Matthew, a function which 'fulfils the need for verisimilitude'.[92] Rightly challenging the ingrained supposition that the citations are merely 'asides' of the author and thus, for all intents and purposes, not part of the story, he proposes that the citations possess a crucial rhetorical function in the narrative.[93] The formula quotations do not exclusively provide the evaluative viewpoint of God as Kingsbury upheld; instead, they 'establish the reliability and authority both of the narrator and of Jesus'.[94] Given that the Old Testament and its authority 'exist independently of the Gospel narrative world', an appeal to sacred text gives Matthew's story 'plausibility' and 'reinforces truth claims about Jesus'.[95] As McConnell observes, the formula citations 'present an outline of Jesus' whole life and ministry'.[96] From this perspective, the citations are viewed as fundamentally christological and serve to highlight that Jesus is the messiah of Israel, who completely fulfils the will of God.

Kupp's thoughtful study incorporates and builds upon these ideas, specifically in relationship to the christological import of the presence motif in Matthew. He suggests that the text of Isa. 7.14 cited in Matt. 1.23 functions on two levels. On the narrative level, the text serves to provide 'basic surface congruity' and validate the unusual conception (Isa. 7.14a). On a second, 'deeper level', the christological theme of presence is given expression, a significant motif in the Gospel which reappears at various points in the narrative.[97]

Although it is perhaps assumed, the importance of the final form of the citation for Matthew's rhetoric is seldom explicitly addressed by those who argue in favour of a theological usage. The final form becomes particularly significant in Matthew's formula citations, whose text is distinct from other known versions. It is doubtful whether the participants in an actual reading event, those either hearing the text spoken aloud in a corporate gathering or reading their texts privately, possessed the linguistic skill to recall or differentiate between the variant readings found in the LXX, MT or Aramaic texts. Yet one must acknowledge, as Hartman

---

[92] *Matthew's Inclusive Story*, pp. 185–6. A similar usage of generalized commentary is found in the study by J. C. Anderson, *Matthew's Narrative Web*, pp. 52–3, 59–61.

[93] Howell, *Matthew's Inclusive Story*, p. 185.   [94] *Ibid.*, p. 186.   [95] *Ibid.*

[96] *Law and Prophecy*, p. 134. So also Howell, *Matthew's Inclusive Story*, p. 186, who does not make reference to McConnell. McConnell, p. 124, further outlines Jesus' life and ministry using four categories: '1. Jesus kept his messiahship hidden from the public as a whole; 2. Jesus went primarily to the oppressed and socially outcast; 3. this hidden ministry ended in victory; 4. this ministry was ultimately valid for all nations.'

[97] See above, p. 19 n. 20. Kupp, *Matthew's Emmanuel*, pp. 157–219. See also Luz, *Theology*, p. 31.

indicates, that OT quotations carry with them a web of associations that are evoked when read, particularly if they are well known, as for example Isa. 11.1ff. would have been. That much has been established in the recent discussion concerning intertextuality. A discussion concerning the web of associations a passage may evoke must, it seems, also consider the question of text-form. The fact that the Targums and, more recently, the LXX are recognized as having within their text-forms the interpretative commitments of the scribe or community is evidence that a change in the text-form creates a new set of associations and meaning.[98] Similarly, the peculiarities in Matthew's version of the quotations may point to interpretative concerns within the early Christian movement. What recent research has demonstrated is that it is a mistake to separate the discussion of text-form, as significant as it is, from that of the rhetorical force of the final form. The grammatical and syntactical relationships in the redacted text-form create a distinct meaning and rhetorical force that ought to be considered within the thrust of the narrative. As Howell observes, the rhetorical effect of the citations urges that they be considered much more than mere asides by the author; rather, their content, whether intended or not, contributes to the narrative and, in the case of the formula quotations, to the portrait of Jesus presented in Matthew.

A way forward, then, ought to include an exploration into the text-form and Jewish milieu in order to provide a context and basis for the investigation of Matthew's usage. But this does not proceed far enough. In addition to the verbal and thematic emphases of the citation, one must also consider the rhetorical force of the quotation's final form within its immediate and remote contexts and the overall impact of the citation upon Matthew's presentation of Jesus. When such a comprehensive investigation is conducted, the full extent of Matthew's usage of Isa. 42.1–4 may be revealed. Before proceeding further, however, it might be prudent to address the veracity of one of the persistent assertions about Matthew's usage of Isa. 42.1–4, namely, that the passage constitutes what is traditionally thought of as a 'Servant of the Lord' text.

The Servant of the Lord

The concept that the four 'Servant Songs' (Isa. 42.1–4; 49.1–6; 50.10–11; and 52.13–53.12) comprise a composite portrait of an eschatological

---

[98] For recent treatments of this issue as it pertains to the LXX, see A. van der Kooij, *The Oracle of Tyre: The Septuagint of Isaiah XXIII as Version and Vision*, Leiden: Brill, 1998, pp. 1–19, and D. A. Baer, *When We All Go Home: Translation and Theology in LXX Isaiah 56–66*, The Hebrew Bible and Its Versions, vol. I, JSOTSup 318, Sheffield: Sheffield Academic Press, 2001, pp. 23–159.

individual was first expounded in B. Duhm's *Das Buch Jesaia* of 1892.[99] Duhm's position inevitably raises concerns about whether one may actually speak of 'the Servant', suffering or otherwise, as a figure or concept.[100] Numerous older studies uncritical of Duhm's work perpetuated an assumed ontological status for 'the Servant' and continued working with the conjecture that Jesus fulfilled the Jewish expectations of this figure. Several studies, the most prominent being that of M. D. Hooker, have challenged this stance by arguing that no evidence from the period exists to justify such claims.[101] D. H. Juel concurs, 'The Isaiah material... was not used to prove that Jesus was the Servant, since there existed no such figure in the interpretive tradition.'[102] J. Jeremias moderated Duhm's portrait somewhat by employing language that designates 'servant of the Lord' as an honorary title.[103] Similarly, numerous scholars have presented Jesus not as 'the Servant' but as a servant *par excellence*.[104] The topic has not received much attention of late; perhaps Mettinger's aptly titled *A Farewell to the Servant Songs* accurately portrayed scholars' waning interest. However, there are signs of a resurgence.[105]

[99] E. Ruprecht, 'Die Auslegungsgeschichte zu den sogenannten Gottesknecht liedern im Buch Deuterojesaja unter methodischen Gesichtspunkten bis zu Bernard Duhm', unpublished dissertation, Heidelberg, 1972, traces the history of these ideas back to Duhm. Unfortunately, I was unable to obtain access to Ruprecht's dissertation; see Mettinger, *Farewell to the Servant Songs*, p. 9.

[100] This position assumes an ontological status for an expected eschatological redeemer figure. The question of the existence of a suffering or weak messianic figure in Judaism is, to a certain extent, a separate issue from the question regarding the existence of a suffering servant figure based upon Isa. 53. Unfortunately, studies have tended to collapse the two questions into one and ignore the distinction.

[101] *Jesus and the Servant*, pp. 58–61. Such a contention, however, has created problems of its own because it cannot account for the traditional connection of Jesus with the servant. This is a general weakness in Hooker's approach, which may be attributed not so much to her own work as to the deeply embedded assumptions which already existed in and permeated the debate. For example, her third chapter, 'Jewish Interpretation of the Servant', presents a brief search for a 'Servant concept' or theme which, Hooker contends, cannot be found. Probable links between servant and messiah are not explored, nor is the ascriptive element of the servant pursued. (See J. E. Ménard, 'Pais Theou as Messianic Title in the Book of Acts', *CBQ* 19 (1957): 83–92, for the inventive position that the background for παῖς θεοῦ is located in the prophets of the past, who were 'prototypes' of Jesus the Prophet and Suffering Messiah.)

[102] *Messianic Exegesis: Christological Interpretations of the Old Testament in Early Christianity*, Philadelphia: Fortress, 1988, p. 131.

[103] J. Jeremias, 'παῖς θεοῦ', *TDNT* V.677–717; see also E. Lohmeyer, *Gottesknecht und Davidssohn,* 2nd edn, FRLANT, Göttingen: Vandenhoeck & Ruprecht, 1953, pp. 2–8.

[104] See R. N. Longenecker, *The Christology of Early Jewish Christianity,* SBT Second Series 17, London: SCM Press, 1970, p. 105.

[105] See the several essays in B. Janowski and P. Stuhlmacher, *Der Leidende Gottesknecht: Jesaja 53 und seine Wirkungsgeschichte mit einer Bibliographie zu Jes 53,* Forschungen

Since Duhm, Isa. 42.1–4 has been traditionally grouped within the four 'Servant Songs' and naturally assumed to refer to the 'suffering' Servant of Deutero-Isaiah. One might legitimately inquire, however, whether there is any evidence that Isa. 42.1–4 was employed in connection with the other servant songs or used to allude to a figure known as the 'Servant of the Lord' within Second Temple Judaism. The difficulty is that there is little documentation to confirm the existence of a figure designated 'Servant of the Lord'.[106] The primary evidence has derived from Duhm's assertion that the four songs of Isaiah were originally one source and were later spliced into the Isaianic text. In addition to the lack of evidence from the period, it seems that there is a degree of semantic confusion surrounding the use of 'servant'. A closer inspection of the grammatical and semantic function of the nominal servant may permit greater precision in the categorization of this theoretical construct.

A semantic description of usage

Jeremias' descriptive labels effectively serve the practical function of categorizing the various usages of 'servant'; however, it is not immediately obvious whether the meaning[107] of 'servant' changes with certain referents. An analysis of a few representative uses may help to provide a more nuanced description of the term's usage and test whether proposed distinctions reflect shifts in meaning. Particularly important in this regard is a semantic description of the uses of the nominal.

The noun-phrases which include עֶבֶד appear to be established within religious usages. עֶבֶד rarely occurs in the absolute[108] and is generally modified by a possessive pronoun, usually in the first-person and usually with reference to God.[109] The term most frequently occurs in either of two

---

zum Alten Testament 14, Tübingen: Mohr (Paul Siebeck), 1996, and P. Satterthwaite, R. Hess and G. Wenham, *The Lord's Anointed: Interpretation of Old Testament Messianic Texts,* Carlisle: Paternoster, 1995. Studies concerning the servant in Matthew include B. Gerhardsson, 'Gottes Sohn als Diener Gottes: Messias, Agape und Himmelsherrschaft nach dem Matthäusevangelium', *ST* (1973): 73–106; Lohmeyer, *Gottesknecht und Davidssohn*; J. D. Kingsbury, *Matthew: Structure, Christology, Kingdom,* Philadelphia: Fortress, 1975, pp. 93–5; 'Figure of Jesus', 3–36; and D. Hill, 'Son and Servant: An Essay on Matthean Christology', *JSNT* 6 (1980): 2–16, and his reply to Kingsbury in 'A Response', 37–52.

[106] S. H. T. Page, 'The Suffering Servant between the Testaments', *NTS* 31 (1985): 481–97.

[107] The term 'meaning' is appropriate in this context due to the assumption that a shift in meaning occurs in the transition from a lively usage to a hardened one.

[108] The absolute העבד in fact only occurs a total of thirteen times in the Old Testament, eight of which appear in Gen. 24.

[109] As is frequently noted, the occurrence of a possessive pronoun suggests a special status of election.

grammatical forms, in construct (3) or in apposition with a designated referent (1, 2), which serves to name the particular servant or servants being mentioned. These forms are:

(1)   דָּוִד עַבְדִּי   apposition
(2)   עַבְדִּי מֹשֶׁה   apposition
(3)   הַלְלוּ עַבְדֵי יְהוָה הַלְלוּ אֶת־שֵׁם יְהוָה   (Ps. 113.1) construct plural

The plural construct form (3) with a genitive of possession often occurs to create the phrase 'servants of the Lord', while both noun-phrases in (1) and (2) are examples of predication and apposition.[110] It seems that most examples of the OT religious use of עֶבֶד in the singular are found in apposition with a designated referent.[111] The classification of the appositional noun-phrase is the point at which most studies become obfuscated. Surveys such as that of Jeremias too quickly jump to the conclusion that the appositive functions as a title, given the direct correspondence between it and the referent. One must question, however, whether the appositive element 'my servant' is merely a title bestowed upon honourable individuals. Unfortunately, the ambiguity that surrounds the exact function and definition of apposition or predication complicates matters. Thus, a discussion of predication and apposition may help in determining the use and meaning of 'servant' in these texts.

In his comprehensive two-volume series *Semantics*, J. Lyons[112] offers an illuminating discussion on apposition and predication. Lyons defines a predicate as 'a term which is used in combination with a name in order to give some information about the individual that the name refers to: i.e. in order to ascribe to him some property'. This much is straightforward and perhaps too general to be useful for present purposes. He further argues, however, that greater specificity can be attained by ascertaining whether the predicate is equative or ascriptive, a distinction which also holds true for apposition.

Equative sentences 'have as their most characteristic function that of identifying an entity referred to by means of one expression with an

---

[110] Technically, the distinction between apposition and predication is not sharp. In fact, both function in what is virtually a synonymous fashion. The only difference is that the appositive is attached directly to the noun-phrase whereas the predicate is a noun-phrase separated by a copula.

[111] Except, of course, Isa. 42.1–4; 49.1–6; 50.10; 52.13; 53.11; the great difficulty is the fact that there is no designated referent for the servant in the Isaianic servant songs. Note that in the uses of the plural in texts such as Pss. 113.1, 134.1, 135.1 and Isa. 54–66 (54.17; 65.8, 9, 13, 14, 15) the referent is obviously the people of God. Such a referent does not need to be identified any more than 'my chosen ones' of Isa. 65.15.

[112] *Semantics*, 2 vols., Cambridge: Cambridge University Press, 1977, vol. I, p. 148.

entity referred to by another expression'.[113]   On the other hand, an ascriptive sentence assigns 'the referent of the subject-expression a certain property'.[114] The equative must be a nominal while the ascriptive may be either a nominal or an adjective. A further distinction noted by Lyons is that unlike the ascriptive sentence, the equative is permutable.[115] Based upon these criteria, he concludes that a point of confusion occurs in English when one classifies 'both kinds of complements as nominal (in what is arguably an equivocal use of the term "nominal")';[116] this is a complication that seems to have also occurred in discussions concerning the servant in Jewish literature. Additionally, some terms remain difficult to classify, which Lyons deems ultimately as 'ambiguous'.

Unlike other nominals (e.g., king, priest or prophet), the determination of whether servant should be deemed equative, ascriptive or ambiguous is a complex affair. It is at this point that Lyons' distinction may provide assistance. He contests that for the appositive to be considered equative, one entity must refer to another by means of differing expressions. In Lyons' own example, 'The Chairman, John Smith, proposed a vote of thanks', 'the Chairman', one entity, is permutable with another entity, 'John Smith'. In the case of servant, one must decide whether it is permutable with the named element, Moses, David, or whomever. Several factors impinge upon how servant is conceived of. First, the presence of the personal pronoun renders the nominal servant definite. Thus, the articular servant designates one particular servant, in which case the two entities are permutable. For example, God's query to the Adversary in Job 1.8 'Have you considered *my servant Job?*' places a particular servant of God, one named Job, under scrutiny. Secondly, in addition to definiteness is the fact that servants possessed a specific position and status within society in the ancient world and thus may be considered an 'entity'. Thirdly, servant often appears in the first position, which is usually the location of the subject, as in the noun-phrase 'my servant Job'. In this noun-phrase, 'Job' is placed in apposition to 'my servant'. Thus, there seems good evidence to contend that 'my servant' be classified as equative. Yet there are other usages which bear within them hints of an attributive dimension and cast doubt upon this assertion.

If the equative links two entities, the ascriptive use ascribes a certain property or attribute to an individual or class. Lyons' example, 'The Chairman, a prominent local author, proposed a vote of thanks', provides room for exploration. The phrase 'a prominent local author' is anarthrous and thus descriptive of 'the Chairman'. 'The Chairman' is one of the

---

[113] *Ibid.*, II.473.   [114] *Ibid.*, II.472.   [115] *Ibid.*, II.471.   [116] *Ibid.*, II.472.

group of prominent local authors. Based upon this analysis, the fact that 'my servant' is definite, and thus designatory, seems to rule out any as-criptive classification; however, the term may also contain an ascriptive element,[117] as is demonstrated in the uses in Isa. 44.21 and 49.6. The passages read as follows:

זְכָר־אֵלֶּה יַעֲקֹב וְיִשְׂרָאֵל כִּי עַבְדִּי־אָתָּה
יְצַרְתִּיךָ עֶבֶד־לִי אַתָּה יִשְׂרָאֵל לֹא תִנָּשֵׁנִי׃

(Isa. 44.21)

Remember these things, O Jacob, and Israel, for you are my
  servant;
I formed you, you are my servant; O Israel, you will not be
  forgotten by me.

וַיֹּאמֶר נָקֵל מִהְיוֹתְךָ לִי עֶבֶד לְהָקִים אֶת־שִׁבְטֵי יַעֲקֹב
וּנְצִירֵי יִשְׂרָאֵל לְהָשִׁיב וּנְתַתִּיךָ לְאוֹר גּוֹיִם
לִהְיוֹת יְשׁוּעָתִי עַד־קְצֵה הָאָרֶץ׃

(Isa. 49.6)

And he says, 'It is too light a thing that you should be my servant
  to raise up the tribes of Jacob and to restore the survivors of
  Israel;
I will give you as a light to the nations, that my salvation may
  reach to the end of the earth.'

The presence of the infrequent עֶבֶד־לִי (44.21) and לִי עֶבֶד (49.6) attracts interest. Grammatically, the point at issue concerns the translation of this noun-phrase, paying particular attention to the לְ. The common practice in English translation is to classify the לְ as a genitive of possession,[118] thereby stressing the elect status of the individual. This solution effec-tively advances the movement towards perceiving 'servant' as an honorary

[117] This may simply be due to the fact that the noun 'servant' is closely related to the verb 'to serve'. Other examples of terms in which the nominal and verbal forms are similar are 'ruler' = to rule; 'founder' = to found; 'leader' = to lead. With terms such as these the verbal element within the nominal is almost inseparable.

[118] Interestingly, most commentators from the English-speaking world translate the phrase as 'my servant' (so J. L. McKenzie, *Second Isaiah,* AB, Garden City, New York: Doubleday, 1968, p. 70; cf. J. D. Watts, *Isaiah 34–66,* WBC, Dallas: Word, 1987, p. 139, who inconsistently translates 44.21 as 'servant for me' and 49.6 with 'my servant'), whereas most German-speakers translate the phrase in a manner similar to W. Grimm: 44.21, 'Knecht bist du mir' and 49.6, 'du mir Knecht bist', suggesting the dative (see W. Grimm, *Das Trostbuch Gottes: Jesaja 40–55,* Stuttgart: Calwer Verlag, 1990, pp. 39, 62). That the LXX translates the לְ with μοῦ is not surprising given the translator's tendency elsewhere to harmonize readings.

title.[119] That one may consider the לְ as denoting specification rather than possession is possible, if not probable, given the contexts. If this is the case, the translation would read 'a servant for/to me',[120] highlighting the role of the individual before God. Several reasons can be adduced in support of the contention that the לְ might be better taken as specification. First, the form עֶבֶד־לִי is unusual, occurring only four times in the Old Testament.[121] This infrequency, when combined with the fact that עַבְדִּי appears to have been a standardized form to express 'my servant', may denote more than mere poetic variation.[122] Secondly, although the context of 44.21 is ambiguous, the context of 49.6 delineates the mission of the servant, implying that the translation 'servant to/for me' is more appropriate than 'my servant'. The mission of the servant in 49.6, 'to restore the tribes of Jacob' and 'to bring back those of Israel I have kept' in addition to his role of functioning as a 'light to the gentiles' and as an agent to bring 'salvation to the ends of the earth', confirms a reading which focuses not upon whose servant he is but on the fact that he is a servant who serves Yahweh's purposes in the world.

Furthermore, the parallelism in 44.21 does not necessarily endorse the position that עַבְדִּי is the direct equivalent of עֶבֶד־לִי. If the לְ is taken as denoting specification, then the translation would read 'Remember these things, O Jacob, and Israel, for you are my servant; I have formed you, you are a servant for me.' If this is the case, then the translation 'I have formed you, you are a servant for me' suggests a functional element, that somehow God's election and formation of the servant have a concomitant practical side, namely, service to Yahweh.

These texts appear to support the case that the nominal 'servant' possesses both an equative and an ascriptive element, which should caution against overstatements concerning the hardening of the term into an honorary title, concept or name. The implication is that when God labels an individual his servant, an ascriptive element may be present as well, as is evidenced in the more complex examples of Moses and Job. In describing Moses, the frequently cited Num. 12.7 reads,

לֹא־כֵן עַבְדִּי מֹשֶׁה בְּכָל־בֵּיתִי נֶאֱמָן הוּא׃

Not so with my servant Moses; he is trustworthy in all my house.

---

[119] Or, one may argue that the translation reflects translators' *a priori* assumptions that 'my servant' was a title in this period.

[120] So B. K. Waltke and M. O'Connor, *An Introduction to Biblical Hebrew Syntax*, Winona Lake: Eisenbrauns, 1990, 11.2.10d.

[121] In addition to Isa. 44.21 and 49.6, it occurs in Gen. 44.10 and 17.

[122] One might argue that the difference in expression is merely for the sake of variety; however, other occurrences exist which display no variety, containing repetitions of עַבְדִּי or עֶבֶד־י in the same context (e.g. Isa. 65.13).

In this text, the second clause, 'he is trustworthy in all my house',[123] further elaborates upon the initial line, 'Not so with my servant Moses.' Thus, because the phrase 'my servant Moses' is qualified by the descriptive element of faithfulness, one suspects that the expression 'my servant' in some way contains a contingent element of faithfulness.[124] The implication is that rather than merely an honorary title used for important figures, the noun-phrase 'my servant' possesses an ascriptive force. Similarly, the opening line in Job 1.8, 'Have you considered my servant Job?', is further amplified in the following lines: 'There is no one like him on earth, a blameless and upright man who fears God and turns away from evil.' While it is true that in both of these examples the description is directed towards the named individual, the fact that the phrase 'my servant' is the subject and the name is appositional strongly suggests a descriptive element be attributed to the phrase 'my servant'.

Having emphasized the ascriptive aspect of the term, however, an account must be rendered for the actuality that the noun-phrase 'servant of the Lord' or 'my servant' appears to have undergone a degree of hardening to the extent that it seems to function as an honorary title. Although the text originates from a much later era,[125] the following verse of *2 Baruch* 70.9 provides evidence of such a usage: 'And it will happen that everyone who will save himself and escape from all things which have been said before – both those who have won and those who have been overcome – that all will be delivered into the hands of *my Servant*, the Anointed One.'[126]

Yet even in what would seem to be as clear an example as one could find of its usage as an honorary title, one cannot completely extricate 'servant' from the practical implications of a master–servant relationship.[127] Perhaps it is the employment of the possessive pronoun that shifts the focus. The emphasis rests upon the fact that the person is a servant of Yahweh, who, as an ethical God, requires qualities that reflect his own nature and character in his servants. The noun-phrase 'the Anointed One' is clearly

---

[123] Note the NRSV translates with the gloss 'he is entrusted with all my house'.

[124] This is a difficult example due to the fact that 'my servant' is an articular phrase, 'the servant of mine'. The definiteness itself strongly implies that the phrase be taken as equative; however, the second line of v. 7 hints at the presence of an attribute of faithfulness. Thus, as a servant in the household of God, Moses is deemed the most faithful. If such is the case, then in addition to the equative, an ascriptive element is also present.

[125] A. Klijn, '2 Baruch', in *The Old Testament Pseudepigrapha*, edited by J. H. Charlesworth, vol. I, Garden City, NY: Doubleday, 1983, p. 617, dates *2 Baruch* to the first two decades of the second century AD, based upon its relationship to *4 Ezra*.

[126] The translation is that of Klijn, '2 Baruch', 645.

[127] Note the language 'delivered into the hands of *my Servant*', which emphasizes the function or servanthood of the servant.

a title; however, the usage of 'servant' ultimately remains equivocal.[128] If such is the case, then one must enquire further regarding the relationship between the servant and messiah.

Servant and messiah

Juel has argued that since no servant figure existed during the Second Temple period, one must explain why Jesus was equated with a servant at all.[129] The answer, he suggests, is to be found in the exegetical links between servant and messiah. There seems little doubt that the messiah was also designated 'servant',[130] but efforts to construct a 'servant' from these passages are perhaps misguided.[131]

If the ascriptive element is prominent in forms in which 'my servant' stands in apposition to important figures in Israel, there is seemingly no logical reason why a messianic figure could not also be considered 'my servant', potentially with an ascriptive sense. One might even argue that the messiah could be considered servant *par excellence*.[132] Such a formulation may lie behind the designation of Jesus as τὸν ἅγιον παῖδά σου Ἰησοῦν ὃν ἔχρισας in Acts 4.27 and τοῦ ὀνόματος τοῦ ἁγίου παιδός σου Ἰησοῦ in 4.30.[133] In a manner similar to the forms found in the Old Testament, the nominal, Jesus, is in apposition to 'servant' in both of these texts. Once again it is ambiguous and difficult to determine whether the stress is upon the ascriptive qualities of a servant or on equating Jesus with a servant, perhaps even 'the servant' from Isa. 40–55.[134] Also of interest

---

[128] See Lyons, *Semantics*, 10.4, regarding grammatical ambiguity.

[129] *Messianic Exegesis*, p. 131.

[130] Passages such as Zech. 3.8, 'my servant, the Branch', in addition to later texts, indicate that this may be the case. See the much fuller treatment in R. Beaton, 'Justice and Messiah: A Key to Matthew's Use of Isa 42:1–4?', *JSNT* 75 (1999): 5–23.

[131] See the Qumran Hymns, *Hodayoth*, in which the composer presents himself to Yahweh as 'your servant'. Consider several of the uses in 1QH[a]: 4.26 reads, 'you have spread your holy spirit upon your servant . . .'; 5.24–5, 'And I, your servant, have known thanks to the spirit you have placed in me'; 6.8, 'for putting wisdom in the heart of your servant to know these matters'. The reference here to servant is not titular; rather, it reflects the posture and status of one before Yahweh. While it may be argued that these usages are significantly removed from messianic associations of the servant, they do intimate that the term has retained an ascriptive element during this period.

[132] T. W. Manson, *The Servant-Messiah: A Study of the Public Ministry of Jesus*, Cambridge: Cambridge University Press, 1953, p. 73.

[133] A correlation between the servant of Isa. 42.1–4 and these two texts may be present in the anointing and the use of ὄνομα (LXX Isa. 42.4/Matt. 12.21).

[134] An equative designation has on its side the liturgical usage evident in the references to Jesus as servant in *Did.* 9.2, 3. On the other hand, there are grounds for discerning an ascriptive element. The reference to David in Acts 4.25 as Δαυὶδ παιδός σου may have created the need to further enhance the reference to Jesus as ἅγιον παῖδά σου to distinguish between them (so Jeremias, 'παῖς θεοῦ', p. 704 n. 378).

in this regard is Matthew's use of the servant motif in Isa. 42.1–4, which has long been considered indecipherable. Hooker insightfully observes that 'Matthew's partiality for Old Testament prophecies suggests that the significance of these quotations *lies in his desire to find passages which foreshadow particular events, and not in any intention to identify Jesus with the Servant of the Songs*' (emphasis mine).[135] However, Matthew may not be concerned so much with validating the events of Jesus' life and ministry foreshadowed in Scripture as he is in employing an accepted messianic text to describe them. Support for this may be located in the description of the mission in Isa. 42.1–4, that is, in the attributes of Spirit endowment, announcement of justice, compassion for the tired and weak, and the universal mission found therein.[136]

Evidence is scant in support of a Servant of the Lord figure during this period; however, there may be another way of describing the use of 'servant'. It is conceivable that it was employed in a titular sense, but accompanied with an ascriptive force. If so, then its use with 'messiah' could have taken on a quintessential or idealized sense in which it ascribed qualities or characteristics to the messiah. Attributes such as faithfulness, trustworthiness, loyalty, and willingness to put completion of God's will ahead of one's own, which marked servants of God in the Old Testament, may have been transferred to the messiah. Furthermore, Isa. 42.1–4; 49.1–6; 50.10–11; and 52.13–53.12 serve to expand upon the status, character and mission of one or more of God's servants in a way which, due to the ambiguous referent, opened the way for an eschatological interpretation, probably shortly after composition.

Even a brief survey such as this reveals that the two fundamental questions which confront this investigation concern the state of the text-form prior to AD 100 and the early Jewish usage of Isa. 42.1–4. A more enlightened perspective on these topics may assist in ascertaining the background to Matthew's usage.

---

[135] *Jesus and the Servant*, p. 150.

[136] On the importance of these ideas in messianic thought, see Beaton, 'Justice and Messiah'.

3

TEXTS AND EARLY JEWISH EXEGESIS

A common assumption when examining the usage of an OT passage in later literature is that such an exercise ought to be accompanied by an investigation into possible historical antecedents. This in turn helps to determine whether the passage under scrutiny is in continuity or discontinuity with other uses from the period. What is perhaps unfortunate in a task of this nature is its relative complexity, for an investigation quickly encounters various and frequent lacunae, prohibiting a complete description and yielding only tentative results. This is especially true for studies on Matthew's formula citations which, as observed earlier, are complicated by the anomalous text-forms,[1] unusual usage[2] and unattested introductory formulae.[3] The situation has been eased somewhat with the publication of the texts from Masada, Naḥal Ḥever, Wadi Murabbaʿat and Khirbet Qumran and the insights these texts have afforded into the text-form, exegesis and hermeneutics in the period immediately prior to and contemporaneous with the composition of the New Testament. Given

---

[1] Most recently see New, *Old Testament Quotations*, pp. 122–3, for whom the text-forms of 12.18–21 (Isa. 42.1–4), 21.5 (Isa. 62.11/Zech. 9.9) and 26.31 (Zech. 13.7) pose some difficulty in his argument that the LXX was Matthew's Bible. Beyond these three citations, New argues that Matt. 4.14–16 (Isa. 8.23–9.1) is an extensively 'edited' LXX text; however, the editorial work suggested, although possible, raises the question whether the text is septuagintal at all and not another Greek version or rendering of the Hebrew.

[2] As maintained earlier, *pesher* does not occur in Matthew; the formula quotations do not parallel rabbinic usages; nor does Matthew initially appear to utilize the techniques of rabbinic exegesis. Furthermore, Matthew proffers no comment on the passages adduced. The citations either fit within their context (*Kontextualszitate*) or serve as commentary upon the narrative (*Reflexionszitate/Erfüllungszitate*).

[3] Metzger, 'Formulas Introducing Quotations of Scripture', 297–307. After a thorough analysis of the various formulae used in the Mishnah and New Testament, Metzger concludes that 'the characteristically Christian view of the continuing activity of God in the historical events comprising the life, death and resurrection of Jesus of Nazareth, fulfilling and completing the divine revelation recorded in the OT, is reflected even in the choice of formulas introducing quotations of Scripture in the NT'. See also Bonsirven, *Exégèse rabbinique*, pp. 27–33; Fitzmyer, 'Explicit Old Testament Quotations', 297–333; and Horton, 'Formulas of Introduction', 505–14.

this state of affairs, it seems prudent to scrutinize recent investigations into the biblical text-form for any possible clues concerning Matthew's distinctive text-form and usage of biblical quotations.[4] This method of examination, it is hoped, will set the stage for an analysis of the distinctive text of Isa. 42.1–4 in Matt. 12.18–21 and aid in determining whether the textual peculiarities were drawn from Judaism and used in support of its ideology, or whether they represent early Christian historical and/or theological reflection upon the life and times of Jesus of Nazareth.

This chapter seeks to examine the transmission, translation and usage of Jewish sacred texts in general and, more specifically, Isa. 42.1–4, in the hope of placing Matthew's usage of Isaiah within a historical context. In order to accomplish this task, the chapter will begin with an overview of Jewish exegesis, followed by a discussion of the OT textual status during the Second Temple period and the proposed links between exegesis and text-form. The text-form, it is contended here, potentially offers a window into the turbulent world of the early Christian movement as it sought to define itself against the various expressions of Judaism during this period.[5] The second part of the chapter will explore, in greater depth than has otherwise been done, the Jewish usage of Isa. 42.1–4, in an attempt to establish the Jewish interpretation of the passage and the ideas associated with it which served to form the world of ideas upon which Matthew and the early Christians may have drawn.

Jewish exegesis

The asseveration that the Hebrew Bible was a '*document extraordinaire*' which was 'not limited by time and space' and in which 'all worthwhile knowledge relating to human conduct as well as a proper understanding and interpretation of events past, present and future, is to be found'[6]

---

[4] See the essays in Mulder, ed., *Mikra*, and Moo, *Passion Narratives*, pp. 1–78. See also the recent study of T. H. Lim, *Holy Scripture in the Qumran Commentaries and Pauline Letters*, Oxford: Clarendon, 1997, for an examination of Pauline OT texts in light of the DSS evidence.

[5] Both unity and diversity within Judaism are assumed throughout the thesis. Although much recent discussion concerning the Law has focused upon Paul and the Law, several studies on Matthew are worth noting. See Overman, *Matthew's Gospel and Formative Judaism*, pp. 73–90; Saldarini, *Matthew's Christian-Jewish Community*, pp. 124–64; and K. Snodgrass, 'Matthew and the Law', in *Treasures Old And New: Recent Contributions to Matthean Studies*, edited by D. R. Bauer and M. A. Powell, SBL Symposium Series, Atlanta: Scholars, 1996, 99–127.

[6] E. Slomovic, 'Toward an Understanding of the Exegesis in the Dead Sea Scrolls', *RevQ* 7 (1969–71): 3, citing *m. Abot* 5.22. Regarding the importance or role of Torah, see also *m. Abot* 1.1.

reveals the reason for the central locatedness of the Jewish Scriptures in both the early Jewish and Christian communities.[7] Because the text was neither temporally nor spatially bound, an awareness by each subsequent generation of the cultural and temporal gulfs between the past and the present necessitated the exegetical enterprise. As Fishbane observes, 'the central task of the exegetical tradition is to demonstrate the capacity of Scripture to regulate *all* areas of life and thought'.[8]

Given the centrality of the Jewish Scriptures, the interpretation of the Hebrew Bible by the communities of Jews and Christians was of paramount importance, and their distinctive interpretations provided structure and definition to their worlds, serving to shape the various communities' understandings of 'faith and practice, affecting such items as cult, theology, and worldview, halakhah, calendar, prophetic fulfilment, and eschatology'.[9] The result was such that both internal and external dialogues and conflicts necessarily invoked a community's distinctive interpretation of the sacred text. A noteworthy example is offered by the Dead Sea community, which seems to have employed texts to marshal 'scriptural authority in service of [their] ideology',[10] a propensity that J. A. Sanders has labelled the constitutive element in their hermeneutic.[11] And while a 'prophetic critique' towards those outside the sect was voiced, the lack of such a critical gaze directed towards its members depicts a group keen to demonstrate that they were the true way, so much so that texts were apparently altered to keep such a focus intact.[12]

---

[7] The bibliography on this topic is immense. For a more general treatment of biblical exegesis, see Vermes, 'Bible and Midrash', pp. 199–231, and Patte, *Early Jewish Hermeneutic*, *passim*, who stresses the hermeneutical issues involved. The recent collection of essays in L. V. Rutgers, et al., eds., *The Use of Sacred Books in the Ancient World*, Biblical Exegesis and Theology 22, Leuven: Peters, 1998, offers discussions on broader issues related to this theme.

[8] *Biblical Interpretation*, p. 3.

[9] W. Brownlee, 'The Background of Biblical Interpretation at Qumran', in *Qumran: sa piété, sa théologie et son milieu*, edited by M. Delcor, BETL XLVI, Paris: Gembloux, 1978, p. 183.

[10] So J. A. Sanders, 'From Isaiah 61 to Luke 4', in *Christianity, Judaism and Other Greco-Roman Cults: Studies for Morton Smith at Sixty. Part One: New Testament*, edited by J. Neusner, SJLA 12, Leiden: Brill, 1975, p. 95.

[11] Sanders, *ibid.*, here cites K. Elliger, *Studien zum Habakuk-Kommentar vom Toten Meer*, BHT 15, Tübingen: Mohr (Paul Siebeck), 1953, who argues, 'Der Ausleger hat ein ganz bestimmtes hermeneutisches Prinzip als Richtschnur. Und dieses lässt sich in zwei Sätzen zusammenfassen: 1. Prophetische Verkündigung hat zum Inhalt das Ende, und 2. die Gegenwart ist die Endzeit.' ('The interpreter has a very definite hermeneutical principle as a guide. And this allows him to bring together the two sentences: 1. The prophetic proclamation has the end as its subject matter and 2. the present time is the end.')

[12] C. Evans, '1 Q Isaiah[a] and the Absence of Prophetic Critique at Qumran', *RevQ* 11 (1984): 537–44.

The manner in which a citation from sacred writ was employed to substantiate various positions is perhaps the most interesting element in a study of this nature, for in it one encounters firsthand a community's interpretations that were thought to validate its perception of reality.[13] Individual studies have been undertaken on the uses in the Dead Sea Scrolls, pseudepigrapha, New Testament, Josephus, Philo, and the Rabbis, which demonstrate that the usage of the Old Testament by the various authors contains elements of continuity as well as discontinuity with one another.[14] In an article exploring only explicit quotations from Qumran, Fishbane offers two general categories of biblical quotation: (1) citations preceding comments made concerning the citation,[15] and (2) citations used to 'justify' a 'point previously made in the text'.[16] The Jewish exegetical techniques to which scholarship typically appeals in order to explain the use of the Scriptures in the New Testament most obviously fit into his first category. An examination of the use of the Old Testament in these contexts does not evince unbounded, subjective interplay with the text; instead, early biblical interpretation appears to have been limited by the use of exegetical devices as, for example, in the seven *middot*, initially attributed to Hillel.[17] The second category of texts Fishbane designates as 'prooftexts', which, he argues, 'can *almost never*

---

[13] For the Dead Sea community and early Christianity, it is perhaps their eschatological self-understanding that most distinguished their interpretation of Scripture. (For specific discussions on eschatology in Qumran, see J. J. Collins, 'Patterns of Eschatology at Qumran', in *Traditions in Transformation: Turning Points in Biblical Faith*, edited by B. Halpern and J. Levenson, Winona Lake: Eisenbrauns, 1981, pp. 351–75; P. R. Davies, 'Eschatology at Qumran', *JBL* 104 (1985): 39–55). Such a worldview contributed to their identification as the people of God, the establishment of boundaries within which they should live, and the affirmation that they lived in the end of times and were expecting, or had already experienced, the arrival of the messiah of Israel.

[14] When one compares the eschatological framework of Qumran with Philo's somewhat allegorical exegesis, the contrast becomes obvious. On exegesis in the pseudepigrapha, see J. H. Charlesworth, 'The Pseudepigrapha as Biblical Exegesis', in *Early Jewish and Christian Exegesis: Studies in Memory of William Hugh Brownlee*, edited by C. A. Evans and W. F. Stinespring, Atlanta: Scholars, 1987, pp. 139–52.

[15] 'Use, Authority and Interpretation', p. 350. Fishbane further qualifies this category with 'the pseudepigraphic, the pesherite, the anthological, and the explicatory form'.

[16] *Ibid.*, p. 348.

[17] While the attribution to Hillel is questionable, an early date for these rules seems reasonable. See *p. Pesaḥ*. 6.1, 33a; *t. Pesaḥ*. 4.13; *t. Sanh*. 7.11. The seven *middot* include *qal wa-ḥomer, gezerah shawah, binyan ab mi-katub eḥad, binyan ab mi-shnê ketubim, kelal u-ferat u-kelal, ke-yoṣe bô be-maqom aḥer, dabar ha-lamed me-'inyanô*. As is well documented, these seven guidelines were expanded upon to include the thirteen *middot* of R. Ishmael and, subsequently, the thirty-two *middot*. See Strack and Stemberger, *Introduction*, pp. 17–30. The *middot* are important for the implication that limitations to interpretation had already been established by the NT period.

be read according to their plain-sense' (emphasis mine). Instead, he proposes that they must be 'construed relative to the point which precedes
them'; the 'original sense of the prooftext must be disregarded in order
to understand how the writer has exegetically appropriated it'; and he
concludes that whether the 'citation sponsors or supports the new issue'
must be determined on an individual basis.[18] While it is open to debate
how much of the original context the author had in mind,[19] Fishbane
seeks to free the investigator to think in categories which stretch beyond
grammatical/historical exegesis.

The difficulty which confronts an investigation into Matthew's use of
explicit citations from the Old Testament is that commentary concerning
the citation never occurs, denying identification of authorial intent and
understood meaning. In this respect Matthew's usage is unlike Fishbane's
first category but similar to the second. His ambiguous usage of the Old
Testament and lack of explicit commentary force one to the text of the citation itself and its surrounding context.[20] Furthermore, while Matthew's
quotations may be categorized as proof-texts, they also appear to be distinguished by theological complexity.[21] Whether he has been faithful to the
prior context and employed the text in a manner congruent with its historical usage is debatable. The mixed text-form, however, which characterizes
several of the formula quotations, especially 12.18–21, may suggest that
clues as to how it was interpreted reside within the text-form itself. Such a
postulate infers a relationship between text-form and exegesis or text and
hermeneutics. While this idea may at first sound far-fetched, numerous
careful and detailed studies have recently been published which indicate
that such may be the case.[22] Until the ascendancy of the MT and reforms
evidenced in the Greek texts of Aquila, Symmachus and Theodotion occurred in the late first and second centuries, the OT text was characterized

---

[18] Fishbane, 'Use, Authority and Interpretation', p. 348.

[19] See Dodd, *According to the Scriptures*, pp. 61–110, for arguments in favour of the
view that the NT authors cited passages in light of the context. S. L. Edgar, 'Respect for
Context in Quotations from the Old Testament', *NTS* 9 (1962): 55–62, holds the curious
viewpoint that while the Gospel authors disregarded context, Jesus cited the Old Testament
in context.

[20] Even in texts such as Matt. 27.3–10, one only glimpses the remnants of a midrashic
approach, the completed results rather than the process.

[21] See especially Rothfuchs, *Erfüllungszitate*, pp. 89, 181, and McConnell, *Law and
Prophecy*, pp. 134–8.

[22] As E. E. Ellis, *The Old Testament in Early Christianity: Canon and Interpretation in
the Light of Modern Research*, WUNT 54, Tübingen: Mohr (Paul Siebeck), 1991, p. 74,
observes, 'in recent decades the research has shown that, in part, the textual question is itself
a hermeneutical question and that textual variations are sometimes deliberate alterations, a
kind of implicit midrash adapting the text more clearly to its present application'.

by fluidity and variety.[23] Thus, an examination of the state of the OT text may yield insights which will aid in untying the knot of Matthew's usage.

Exegesis and the biblical text in Second Temple Judaism

Current OT text critics generally agree that the biblical texts found among the Dead Sea Scrolls in 1947 have had a phenomenal impact upon the discipline,[24] so much so that this date has come to mark something of a watershed, leading one scholar to opine, 'We are now in a totally new era in the study of biblical exegesis.'[25] This is primarily due to the fact that prior to the discovery of the Dead Sea Scrolls, the earliest manuscript of the entire Old Testament was the medieval eleventh-century manuscript Leningrad B 19^A.[26] In the Dead Sea Scrolls, scholars have in their possession for the first time manuscripts from an early date with which to compare other traditions. In addition to the more publicized Dead Sea Scrolls, there are also important manuscripts that were unearthed in Masada, Naḥal Ḥever and Wadi Murabbaʿat.

With an ever burgeoning abundance of textual data to process as a result of the final publication in recent years of the remaining Dead Sea Scrolls, some tentative conclusions concerning textual history and transmission are being proffered. Before one may draw specific correlations between these texts and Matthew's OT text-form, however, a more precise description of the state of the OT text is required. The value of these texts for NT

---

[23] See Lim, *Qumran Commentaries and Pauline Letters*, pp. 69–94. Vermes, 'Bible and Midrash', p. 203, notes that 'it should be remembered that the ancient versions of the Bible are themselves also part of exegetical literature. A considerable amount of interpretative material found its way into the Septuagint, the Palestinian Targums, and occasionally the peshiṭta, only to be more or less thoroughly eliminated in the subsequent revisions or translations of Aquila, Symmachus, Theodotion and Onkelos.'

[24] Books, articles and essays on this topic have proliferated. For a sampling see F. M. Cross and S. Talmon, eds., *Qumran and the History of the Biblical Text*, Cambridge, MA: Harvard University Press, 1975; S. Talmon, 'The Old Testament Text', in *The Cambridge History of the Bible*, vol. I: *From the Beginnings to Jerome*, edited by P. R. Ackroyd and C. F. Evans, Cambridge: Cambridge University Press, 1970, p. 184; E. Tov, 'Hebrew Biblical Manuscripts from the Judaean Desert: Their Contribution to Textual Criticism', *JJS* 39 (1988): 19–37; and E. Ulrich, 'Multiple Literary Editions: Reflections toward a Theory of the History of the Biblical Text', in *Current Research and Technological Developments on the Dead Sea Scrolls: Conference on the Texts from the Judean Desert, Jerusalem, 30 April 1995*, edited by D. W. Parrey and S. D. Ricks, Leiden: Brill, 1996, pp. 80–1.

[25] Charlesworth, 'The Pseudepigrapha as Biblical Exegesis', p. 140.

[26] This manuscript dates to AD 1008 or 1009. See Kahle, *Cairo Geniza*, p. 60; G. Vermes, *The Dead Sea Scrolls: Qumran in Perspective*, London: SCM Press, 1973, p. 35; and E. Y. Kutscher, *The Language and Linguistic Background of the Isaiah Scroll (1QIsaᵃ)*, STDJ 6, Leiden: Brill, 1974, p. 3.

studies depends, of course, upon their dating, geographical distribution and the degree to which they represent the ideological framework of the general populace. Thus, these issues ought to be addressed.

The dating of the manuscripts has proved to be a long and arduous task, at times appearing to be more 'art' than 'science'.[27] The historical events of revolutions and political upheavals at Naḥal Ḥever, Wadi Murabbaʿat and Masada may provide solid boundaries for dating, rendering the establishment of a *terminus ad quem* a relatively straightforward task.[28] Texts found at Naḥal Ḥever and Wadi Murabbaʿat, which date no later than the Bar Kochba revolt (AD 132–35), are the latest in this group, preceded by those found in Masada, which was conquered in AD 73. The Khirbet Qumran site appears to have been active from 150 BC, only to be abandoned c. AD 68.[29] This, however, does not establish a *terminus a quo* as it appears that many manuscripts were brought to the community with the settlers;[30] thus, each text must be dated individually. For present purposes, however, it is sufficient to note a dating prior to the composition of the Gospel of Matthew.[31]

A second important question concerns whether the texts are representative of Palestine as a whole or merely of an isolated sect. Tov purports that it is 'superfluous' to assert that the texts may *only* 'typify' the various groups who possessed the scrolls.[32] In support of this contention, he

---

[27] On the palaeographic dating, see F. M. Cross, 'The Oldest Manuscripts from Qumran', *JBL* 74 (1955): 147–72, and A. Birnbaum, 'The Qumrân (Dead Sea) Scrolls and Paleography', *BASOR* Supplementary Studies, 13–14, New Haven, 1952, pp. 9–14. See the helpful chart that compares the dates achieved by palaeography and AMS tests in VanderKam, *The Dead Sea Scrolls Today*, p. 18.

[28] This, of course, assumes that the texts were not placed in these caves at a later date. See the discussion in Tov, 'Hebrew Biblical Manuscripts', 8.

[29] The early dates first postulated by Cross and other palaeographers have generally been confirmed by the 'more scientific' means of radiocarbon dating.

[30] Assigning a *terminus ad quo* is a much more difficult task. While no secure date may be suggested for Naḥal Ḥever and Masada, R. de Vaux, *Archaeology and the Dead Sea Scrolls*, The Schweich Lectures of the British Academy, London: Oxford University Press, 1973, pp. 53–7, opts for a date of AD 42–43 for Wadi Murabbaʿat. See also Cross, 'Oldest Manuscripts', 167–9. The oldest manuscripts are 4QExod[f]* (250 BC), 4QSam[b] (second half of the third century BC), and 4QJer[a]* (200 BC) (D. N. Freedman, 'The Masoretic Text and the Qumran Scrolls: A Study in Orthography', in *Qumran and the History of the Biblical Text*, edited by Cross and Talmon, p. 93; Cross, 'Oldest Manuscripts', 167–9).

[31] I am not necessarily arguing for direct dependence upon any of these manuscripts. Instead, the importance of determining a date prior to the composition of Matthew, however one views this issue, is due to the fact that accompanying the writing of the texts was the codification of the ideas, theological or otherwise, which were 'in the air' at the time. It is thus assumed that while Matthew may not have been reliant upon these traditions, he or members of his community may have come into contact with them or at least the ideas contained therein.

[32] Tov, 'Hebrew Biblical Manuscripts', 7.

observes that it seems that the texts discovered at Murabbaʿat and Naḥal Ḥever, as well as some of those found at Masada, were all copied else-where.[33] Qumran, however, represents a somewhat different situation. Although there was a strong sectarian element, not all the texts from the Dead Sea community are sectarian. The discussion concerning the 'scriptorium' aside, studies on orthography and palaeography at Qumran indicate that some of the scrolls were copied on site while others orig-inated from outside the community and presumably accompanied the converts to Qumran, where they were placed in the library.[34]

Finally, given that there continues to be considerable doubt concerning Matthew's linguistic abilities, a brief description of the language situation in Palestine may also be appropriate at this point. The manuscripts have served to confirm previous studies that asserted a bi- or even trilingual language environment in Palestine.[35] In most respects this is a dated issue, a subject upon which most scholars are now in general agreement; thus the point is only worth summarizing. At the time of Matthew's composition, the texts in circulation were written in Hebrew, palaeo-Hebrew, Aramaic and Greek. Perhaps the greatest surprise has been the quantity of Greek texts, some of which, it seems, are distinct from the LXX tradition,[36] suggesting a greater diversity of language usage in Palestine than is sometimes acknowledged.

Thus, given the manuscripts' dating, their broad geographical distri-bution and the linguistic diversity, one cannot but conclude with Tov that 'most scrolls found in the Judaean Desert are relevant to our understand-ing of the state of the text of the Bible in *Palestine as a whole* from the third century B.C.E. until the second century C.E.' (emphasis mine).[37]

[33] *Ibid.*, 10.

[34] On this see Tov's helpful article, 'The Orthography and Language of the Hebrew Scrolls Found at Qumran and the Origins of these Scrolls', *Textus* 13 (1986): 31–57; see also the articles by Cross, 'Oldest Manuscripts', 147–72, and Freedman, 'Study in Orthography', pp. 196–211. A further point requiring mention is the fact that because not all the DSS texts are sectarian, some of the manuscripts may have been broadly disseminated throughout Palestine.

[35] For a comprehensive survey of Aramaic and Greek in Palestine, see M. McNamara, 'The Language Situation in First Century Palestine: Aramaic and Greek', *Proceedings of the Irish Biblical Association* 15 (1992): 7–36, and M. Hengel, *Judaism and Hellenism: Studies in Their Encounter in Palestine during the Early Hellenistic Period*, translated by J. Bowden, London: SCM Press, 1974, pp. 103ff. For a discussion concerning how this relates to the Matthean citations, see Gundry, *Use of the Old Testament*, pp. 174–8.

[36] Kahle's theory, *Cairo Geniza*, pp. 246–7, that the LXX derives from earlier Greek Targums has come under increasing attack in light of Hebrew texts in the Dead Sea Scrolls which appear to offer support for distinct LXX readings.

[37] Tov, 'Hebrew Biblical Manuscripts', 7.

Current state of research

Study of the manuscripts has occasioned a paradigm shift in the under-standing of the status of the texts prior to the second century AD. In light of the new evidence provided by the Dead Sea Scrolls, recent authors have challenged the longstanding assumption, held since the seventeenth century, that the MT, LXX, and SP together represent three stable 're-censions' or 'text-families'.[38] Increasing recognition is now being given to the idea that the biblical texts in early Judaism were characterized by greater fluidity and variety than previously thought. Nevertheless, old positions die hard. As recently as 1988 Tov wrote,

> According to the old-fashioned concepts with which most schol-
> ars still work, all the Qumran texts can somehow be fitted into
> that tripartite picture of the MT, LXX and Samaritan Pentateuch
> in the case of the Pentateuch and under a different name in
> the other books of the Bible. However, it has now been recog-
> nised that several texts do not fit within any such framework,
> and must consequently be taken as sources *additional* to those
> known before.[39]

Unfortunately, not only have many OT textual critics failed to account fully for this situation, studies of Matthew's use of the Old Testament also have to a large degree overlooked it, even though these ideas have been extant since Stendahl's preface to his second edition.[40] Currently, the contentious issue among scholars concerns the classification of 'variant readings'. Are they in fact textual 'variants', or do they reflect exegetical alterations? The obvious question that arises for many scholars concerns whether the MT (based upon late manuscripts) ought to remain the 'yard-stick to measure the textual tradition'.[41]

---

[38] E. Tov, 'A Modern Textual Outlook Based on the Qumran Scrolls', *HUCA* 53 (1982): 11–19, and Ulrich, 'Multiple Literary Editions', *passim*. Cf. F. M. Cross's theory of local texts in 'The Evolution of a Theory of Local Texts', in *Qumran and the History of the Biblical Text*, edited by Cross and Talmon, pp. 306–21. This development is likewise evident when one compares the work of P. W. Skehan, 'The Qumran Manuscripts and Textual Criticism', in *Volume du Congrès Strasbourg, 1956*, Society for Old Testament Study, VTSup 4, Leiden: Brill, 1957, pp. 148–58, with that of S. Talmon, 'DSIa as a Witness to Ancient Exegesis of the Book of Isaiah', in *Qumran and the History of the Biblical Text*, edited by Cross and Talmon, pp. 116–26.

[39] 'Hebrew Biblical Manuscripts', 31–2.   [40] *School*, pp. i–xiv.

[41] Talmon, 'DSIa as a Witness to Ancient Exegesis', p. 117. While this second issue is perhaps the more interesting point to pursue, this OT critical concern is beyond the parameters of this study.

The simple terms 'fluidity' and 'variety' have become standard technical expressions used to mark the state of the text prior to AD 200.[42] A fluid state merely points to the numerous readings present in the texts, suggesting non-standardized manuscript traditions. It appears that the MT did not attain pre-eminence as the accepted text until much later; prior to its ascendancy, texts tended to be more free in their renderings. Likewise, the term 'variety' refers to the great number of distinct texts which have been discovered from this period. For example, the fact that Qumran could have three versions of Isaiah in its library is indicative of the textual state and attitudes towards the text.

One must be cautious, however, in making sweeping assertions regarding the diversity in the Qumran manuscripts.[43] The proto-Masoretic manuscripts include texts such as 4QExod[f*] (which dates to around 250 BC and is very close to the MT), numerous palaeo-Hebrew texts such as 4QJer[a*] (which appears to be corrected towards the MT)[44] and 1QIsa[b] (whose conservative text is almost identical to the MT).[45] Careful analysis has determined that the texts found in Masada, Naḥal Ḥever, Wadi Murabbaʿat, and most of those at Qumran ought to be classified as proto-Masoretic. In addition to these, several other texts exist which may be considered proto-Samaritan[46] or septuagintal.[47] Perhaps D. Barthélemy's

---

[42] So S. Talmon, 'Aspects of the Textual Transmission of the Bible in Light of Qumran Manuscripts', in *Qumran and the History of the Biblical Text*, edited by Cross and Talmon, pp. 226–63, and 'DSIa as a Witness to Ancient Exegesis', pp. 116–26; J. Ziegler, 'Die Vorlage der Isaias-Septuaginta (LXX) und die erste Isaias-Rolle von Qumran (1QIsa[a])', in *Qumran and the History of the Biblical Text*, edited by Cross, and Talmon, pp. 90–115. Charlesworth, 'The Pseudepigrapha as Biblical Exegesis', 139–52, suggests that select 'variants' in the pseudepigrapha likewise represent exegetical traditions.

[43] Reasons for caution against overgeneralization concerning the apparent fluidity and variety among the manuscripts include the following. First, if one works from the assumption that the MT represents the standard received text, then each variant must be considered on its own in relation to the MT. Such analyses usually result in an affirmation or a rejection based upon their closeness to the MT. Second, the divergences of a more 'free' rendering, such as that of 1QIsa[a] or the LXX, could be accounted for by the 'sloppy, stupid scribe' theory; however, when this position is forsaken, one is left with the assertion that select adjustments to the text are not necessarily errors but exegetical/interpretative judgments reflected in the language, grammar or syntax. Such a position has become increasingly popular, and with good reason, for the evidence in its favour is now extensive.

[44] Tov, 'Hebrew Biblical Manuscripts', 29.   [45] See n. 60 below.

[46] Tov, 'Hebrew Biblical Manuscripts', 30–1, lists under this rubric 4QpaleoEx[m*], 4Q158, 4Q364, 4QNum[b*], 4QTest (175), 4Qdeut[n].

[47] These are 4QLXXLev[a], pap4QLXXLev[b*], 4QLXXNum, 4QLXXDeut, pap7QLXXEx; some also include 7Q3–19 (Tov, 'Hebrew Biblical Manuscripts', 18). See also 8 ḤevgrXII*. There is some disagreement as to whether the following texts may be considered close to the LXX: 4QJer[b], 2QDeut[c], 4QEx[a*], 4QDeut[q]. Tov, *ibid.*, 29 n. 91, argues that of these the only obviously LXX text is 4QJer[b].

seminal and frequently cited work *Les devanciers d'Aquila* should also be mentioned at this point.[48] In it Barthélemy describes a LXX text corrected towards the MT, which he designates the καιγε recension. This text provides further support for the consolidation and standardization of the MT in the late first century, most probably as a result of the fact that it was the text of the Pharisees, who became dominant after AD 70.[49] In fact, Greek texts found at Naḥal Ḥever which have been dated to the mid first century BC represent a text-form which has been corrected towards the MT.[50]

Even when this latter conformist trend towards the MT is taken into consideration, however, numerous texts resist classification within the tripartite division and effectively challenge this model. As I explore the textual variations of the period in the hope of determining a model for Matthew's mixed-text citations, I shall survey the DSS texts which are not proto-Masoretic. It is this grouping of texts that may hold the greatest promise for attempts to categorize the 'mixed-text' formula quotations in Matthew.

The texts which fall outside the tripartite division are frequently referred to as either 'independent' or 'non-aligned'. Tov offers a description of these non-aligned texts, which might prove helpful in describing Matthew's own mixed-text forms:[51]

1. Non-aligned texts are not 'exclusively close' to the MT, LXX, or SP.
2. Non-aligned texts may agree, sometimes significantly, with the MT, LXX or SP against other texts (i.e. the MT, LXX, SP), but, importantly, they *'also disagree with the other texts to the same extent'* (emphasis mine).
3. Non-aligned texts 'contain readings not known from one of the other texts, so that they are not exclusively close to one of the other texts or groups'.
4. 'Usually the employment of the term *non-aligned* merely implies that the texts under consideration follow an inconsistent

---

[48] *Les devanciers d'Aquila: première publication intégrale du texte des fragments du dodécaprophéton*, VTSup X, Leiden: Brill, 1963.

[49] Note, however, that A. Cadwallader, 'The Correction of the Text of Hebrews towards the LXX', *NovT* 34 (1992): 257–92, argues that the citations in Hebrews are generally corrected towards the LXX, not the MT.

[50] See E. Tov, ed., *The Greek Minor Prophets Scroll from Nahal Hever (8HevXIIgr)*, DJD VIII, Oxford: Clarendon, 1990, pp. 24–6; he now dates these texts as early as 50 BC and as late as AD 50.

[51] E. Tov, *Textual Criticism of the Hebrew Bible*, Minneapolis: Fortress, 1998, pp. 116–17.

pattern of agreements and disagreements with the MT, SP and LXX, as in the case of 4QDeut[b,c,h,k], 4QIsa[c]*, 4QXII[c,e], 4QDan[a], and 11QpaleoLev[a].'

5. Texts which are most manifestly non-aligned, and actually independent, are texts which contain readings that diverge significantly from the other texts, such as 4QDeut[j,n], 4QJosh[a]*, 4QJudg[a], and 5QDeut.

6. 4QSam[a] holds a special position in this regard since it is closely related to the *Vorlage* of the LXX while also reflecting independent features.[52]

These observations have served to challenge the tripartite view, offering a fresh perspective of the development of the OT text. Especially pertinent to this study are Tov's observations that non-aligned texts exhibit 'inconsistent agreements and disagreements' with the three versions, significant agreement with and divergence from other texts and the possession of unique readings.[53] This in turn raises the question of how one should determine whether a text is septuagintal, proto-Masoretic, and so forth. Identifying criteria have proved elusive. Traditionally, calculating the percentage of verbal similarity to one of the three established traditional manuscripts has been the method employed. Critical of this approach, Tov proposes that account should also be taken of 'disagreements', and, more importantly, 'unique readings',[54] 'with an open mind for the possibility that some scrolls are not to be linked with any of the known textual documents'.[55] Initial conclusions drawn from the study of the scrolls have engendered caution in ascertaining whether a text is septuagintal, proto-Masoretic, or proto-Samaritan. The DSS texts of Isaiah are of special interest in this regard not only because of Isaiah's prominence in Matthew's usage, but also because of the significant role Isaiah plays in the Dead Sea Scrolls and the early Christian community.[56] Given the above discussion, one might expect

---

[52] Although cf. F. M. Cross, *The Ancient Library of Qumran*, 3rd edn, Sheffield: Sheffield Academic Press, 1995, p. 42, who asserts that 4QSam[a] provides the Hebrew *Vorlage* for the LXX.

[53] As an example, Tov, 'Modern Textual Outlook', 9, cites his own early work in 11QpaleoLev, which 'often agrees with the MT against the others, with the Sam. Pent. against the others, and also with the LXX against the others'.

[54] *Ibid.*, 10–11.   [55] *Ibid.*, 12.

[56] The most frequently cited biblical books in Qumran include Deuteronomy, Psalms, Isaiah, and Exodus; of these, Skehan, 'Qumran Manuscripts', p. 152, observes that 'Isaias was quite evidently the most studied book outside the Pentateuch'. On the importance and use of Isaiah in Christianity throughout its history, see Sawyer, *The Fifth Gospel*.

to discover that variety and diversity exist even amongst the Isaiah manuscripts.

Manuscripts of Isaiah

The textual history of the Isaiah manuscripts is as complex as the book was popular. Regarding 1QIsa[b], P. W. Skehan observes that 'the text of DSIb [= 1QIsa[b]] is an excellent ancient witness to the integrity of transmission, within extremely narrow limits, of the consonantal text of Isaias as we now know it'.[57] The texts of 1QIsa[a], the 4QIsa[a-r] fragments, 5QIsa (5Q3) and the LXX, however, are a different matter altogether. In a recent article, van der Kooij,[58] following the dissertation of F. J. Morrow,[59] reassesses the Isaianic texts found in Qumran and their relation to the LXX. He proposes that the Isaiah manuscripts found among the Dead Sea Scrolls represent three unique textual traditions and that LXX Isaiah remains unattested in the Dead Sea Scrolls.[60] Furthermore, the MT is unique in many respects when compared with 1QIsa[a], 1QIsa[b], and the 4QIsa fragments. Summarizing scholarship's assessment, he notes that the nature of each text is as follows:

1. 1QIsa[b] bears great similarity to the MT. It is a conservative text with few significant variants, suggesting that it be considered pre-Masoretic or proto-Masoretic.[61]

---

[57] 'The Text of Isaias at Qumran', *CBQ* 17 (1955): 38–43. Given the fragmentary nature of 1QIsa[b], however, one must be cautious of too quickly labelling it proto-Masoretic; perhaps pre-Masoretic is adequate (A. van der Kooij, 'The Old Greek of Isaiah in Relation to the Qumran Texts of Isaiah: Some General Comments', in *Septuagint, Scrolls and Cognate Writings*, edited by G. J. Brooke and B. Lindars, SBLSCS 33, Atlanta: Scholars, 1992, p. 199).

[58] 'Old Greek of Isaiah', pp. 195–213.

[59] 'The Text of Isaiah at Qumran', unpublished PhD dissertation, The Catholic University of America, 1973, Ann Arbor, Michigan: University Microfilms, 1977.

[60] Van der Kooij, 'Old Greek of Isaiah', p. 198, observes that (1) the LXX 'is not a text written in the language of the Hebrew Bible itself' and (2) the 'Old Greek is not attested by any manuscript dating from the time when the original translation was presumably made...LXX Isa is in fact only an indirect witness to the early history of the text of Isaiah.' Thus, scholars continue to put forth the supposition that the LXX is an interpretative translation and may even be based upon any of the texts that were in existence. Space does not allow a thorough discussion of the LXX here. The question of the source for the LXX is disputed, as is the question regarding how free a rendering the LXX really is. See J. Koenig, *L'herméneutique analogique du Judaïsme antique d'après les témoins textuels d'Isaïe*, VTSup 33, Leiden: Brill, 1982, pp. 3–30; I. L. Seeligmann, *The Septuagint Version of Isaiah*, MVEOL 9, Leiden: Brill, 1948, pp. 95–121; and most recently, D. Baer, *When We All Go Home*, pp. 11–22.

[61] Already Skehan, 'Text of Isaias', 40–1.

2. 1QIsa[a], the oldest of the Isaiah texts,[62] represents a different tradition or a 'freer' translation.[63] It is common now to acknowledge a 'freer approach' to the *Vorlage*, evidenced in the 'deviations and variant readings of a linguistic nature', and 'contextual changes such as harmonisations'.[64]

3. The fragments of 4QIsa stand somewhere between 1QIsa[a] and 1QIsa[b].[65]

Morrow concludes regarding the diversity of Isaiah manuscripts that 'One may speak of three kinds of texts: the Massora, representing a fixed tradition; the great scroll from Cave 1, aberrant even by Qumran standards ... and lastly, the whole Qumran tradition aside from 1QIs[b], which can be regarded as fluid and which is, on the whole, closer to the MT than to 1QIs[a].'[66] Thus, one may postulate three distinct traditions of Isaiah in the Qumran community. If, however, one includes the unattested LXX Isaiah and early strata in the Targums, the number of Isaiah traditions in existence in Palestine prior to the period of the penning of the New Testament is augmented, rendering Matthew's unique text of Isaiah less conspicuous than is often otherwise understood.

Exegesis and the manuscripts

As noted above, affirmation of the argument that the text-form was characterized by fluidity and variety until the second century AD carries with it important implications regarding how one approaches variants found in the texts. It is a difficult matter to determine the provenance of

---

[62] Kutscher, *Linguistic Background*, p. 3, dates the manuscript as second century BC, citing Birnbaum, 'The Qumrân Scrolls and Paleography', p. 43. See also Skehan, 'Text of Isaias', 42.

[63] Cf. W. F. Albright, 'New Light on Early Recensions of the Hebrew Bible', *BASOR* 140 (1955): 30, who maintains that 'the prototype of the first Isaiah Scroll came from Babylonia', and is thus an 'offshoot of the proto-Masoretic text-tradition in Babylonia'. According to Albright's scheme, the fact that 1QIsa[a] developed apart from Babylonia accounts for the numerous variants and generally inferior character when compared with 1QIsa[b].

[64] Van der Kooij, 'Old Greek of Isaiah', p. 197.

[65] Morrow, 'The Text of Isaiah at Qumran', p. 171 (also cited in van der Kooij, 'Old Greek of Isaiah', p. 197), notes five characteristics of the variants of the 4QIsa fragments: (1) 'breakdown of grammar and usage', (2) 'breakdown of Hebrew pronunciation', (3) 'substitution of more normal or current diction, including the interpretation of unusual words in terms of what is known', (4) 'harmonising tendency with regard to person', and (5) 'the influence of similar Biblical passages on each other'. These tendencies suggest that the 4QIsa[a-r] fragments are closer to 1QIsa[b] and the proto-Masoretic text. See also Skehan, 'Text of Isaias', 42, who argues that 4QIsa[c] 'has no special connection textually with DSIa'.

[66] Morrow, 'The Text of Isaiah at Qumran', p. 171.

a 'variant' reading. It may have derived from a previously extant text-form, or resulted from exegetical alterations made to the text in light of the theological, practical or apologetical issues confronting the scribe or community. Or its origins may in fact have derived from scribal sloppiness. There seems to be little doubt that it was not only the meturgeman who altered and shaped the biblical text to reflect interpretations popular in the synagogue. Such a 'free' approach to the texts is worth noting. Tov outlines several characteristics indicative of such an approach: (1) a displayed 'tendency to modernise the spelling and language of the Bible'; (2) numerous mistakes; (3) 'untidy corrections'; and (4) 'frequent contextual changes'.[67] The first three observations, interesting for what they say concerning scribal habits and attitudes of the period, are worth bearing in mind as Matthew's texts are examined, but it is the fourth point which will command greater attention in this investigation. LXX Isaiah, 1QIsa[a] and the 4QIsa fragments all exhibit examples of these four characteristics, and there are numerous illustrations of exegetical alterations. One could list numbers of relevant texts in this regard which would serve present purposes well; however, given that the study concerns Matthew's use of Isaiah, it seems appropriate to employ examples from the Isaianic tradition which will resurface later in the thesis.

As is well known, LXX Isa. 42.1a contains two additions that serve to clarify the ambiguous subject of the MT's anonymous servant passage. The inclusion of Ιακωβ and Ισραηλ in the LXX seems to reflect the redactor's attempt to identify unequivocally what had been an uncertain subject. The fact that the revisions of Aquila, Symmachus and Theodotion bring the text into line with the MT is expected given Barthélemy's work and the texts found at Naḥal Ḥever. A more difficult variant in LXX Isa. 42.4 contains the peculiar ἐπὶ τῷ ὀνόματι in place of the MT's וּלְתוֹרָתוֹ. This variant occurs only in the LXX. Perhaps not surprisingly, J. Ziegler concludes that the LXX text is a Greek corruption.[68] Acting upon this dubious assumption without supporting textual evidence, Ziegler emends the text to read νόμῳ rather than ὀνόματι. Koenig, perhaps more wisely, observes that 'La var. de Qa en 42,4 compte, du point de vue qualitatif et historique parmi les plus importantes. C'est peut-être la plus importante. Mais elle est aussi l'une des plus embarrassantes.' ('The variant of Qa in 42, 4 counts as among the most important from a qualitative and historic

---

[67] Tov, 'Hebrew Biblical Manuscripts', 15. The contrast between Tov's postulated 'Qumran system' and the other scrolls is particularly acute with regard to the handling of the text. The other scrolls are much more conservative in both spelling and content.

[68] *Untersuchungen zur Septuaginta des Buches Isaias,* Alttestamentliche Abhandlungen, XII, Münster: Verlag der Aschendorffschen Verlagsbuchhandlung, 1934, p. 277.

point of view. It is perhaps the most important, but it is also one of the most embarrassing.')[69] To argue this case, however, Koenig must postulate an interpretative strategy outside Isa. 42.4 which includes a 'name' theme. The fact that Matthew abandons the MT and follows the LXX assiduously may reflect an exegetical tradition known in the Jewish community that would be easily overlooked if the variant was too quickly tossed aside as insignificant.

A second and perhaps more controversial text is 1QIsa[a] 51.4–6. While the MT, LXX, and Targum are all in general agreement, 1QIsa[a] contains variants in the subject of the clauses in verse 5. Whether the text ought to be read messianically is questionable and irrelevant to the discussion at this point.[70] The MT translated reads, 'for a teaching will go out from me, and my justice for a light to the peoples. I will bring near my deliverance swiftly, my salvation has gone out and *my* arms will rule the peoples; the coastlands wait for *me*, and for *my* arm they hope.' In contrast, 1QIsa[a] reads, 'My salvation has gone forth, and *his* arms will rule the peoples; the coastlands wait for *him* and for *his* arm they hope.' It is acknowledged that the only distinction between two of these three variants involves a *waw* and a *yod*, which in the Dead Sea Scrolls are poorly written and thus frequently confused; however, in these particular verses the *waw* seems the better choice. Further supporting a *waw* is the fact that 1QIsa[a] includes אלױ in verse 5 for the MT's אלי, which is more difficult to explain as a scribal slip.[71] Finally, that the three variants occur together in this one verse is rather extraordinary.[72] It is perhaps easier to argue that the verse has been shaped by a scribe in light of theological concerns. Whether the variants represent the original text or a later alteration by the sect remains unclear.

[69] *L'herméneutique analogique*, p. 355. The fact that Matthew opts for the LXX rather than the MT reading at this point is perhaps equally *important et embarrassant*.
[70] See W. H. Brownlee, *Meaning of the Qumran Scrolls for the Bible*, New York: Oxford University Press, 1964, p. 197, and D. Barthélemy, 'Le grand rouleau d'Isaïe trouvé près de la mer morte', *RB* 57 (1950): 548, who both consider the variants as legitimate readings which reflect a messianic reading. Barthélemy in particular considers the variants as the original readings.
[71] So Brownlee, *Meaning of the Qumran Scrolls*, p. 197. Upon closer inspection, the manuscript does appear to contain two *waws*, which would suggest a third-person singular form. *Pace* R. E. Brown, 'The Qumran Scrolls and the Johannine Gospel and Epistles', in *The Scrolls and the New Testament*, edited by K. Stendahl, London: SCM Press, 1958, p. 204, whose critique of Brownlee rightly notes the frequent confusion between *waw* and *yod* in the Dead Sea Scrolls but fails to comment on אלױ.
[72] Barthélemy, 'Le grand rouleau d'Isaïe', 548, observes, 'Voilà trois suffixes de la troisième personne qui correspondent à trois suffixes de la première personne dans le texte massorétique.' ('Here are three suffixes of the third person that correspond to three suffixes of the first person in the Masoretic Text.')

The question arises whether these three readings in 1QIsa[a] 51.5 should be considered in isolation or, as Barthélemy asserts, alongside the variants in 52.14, 53.11, 41.2 and 42.1. When such an exercise is performed, the conclusion that the manuscript has undergone scribal modification seems reasonable.[73] This is also evident in LXX Isaiah, which appears to have been shaped by an author with a theological agenda. Thus, rather than a free translation by an inept or haphazard scribe, it reflects the theological emphases of the translator. Concerning 1QIsa[a] Barthélemy writes,

> Voilà donc un ensemble convergent de variantes, toutes can-
> tonnées dans l'ensemble *Is.* XLI-LIII. On peut les envisager sous
> deux jours différents: Ou bien les Sophérim ont voulu réduire
> la portée messianique de certains textes prophétiques, probable-
> ment pour des raisons de controverse avec telle ou telle secte.
> Ou bien l'espérance messianique des milieux sectariens a déteint
> sur le texte des manuscrits qu'ils utilisaient. La déformation a
> d'ailleurs bien pu avoir lieu dans les deux sens à la fois, certaines
> 'variantes messianiques' constituant un bien primitif, d'autres
> des interpolations sectariennes. Pourra-t-on jamais se prononcer
> avec certitude sur chacun de ces cas?[74]

> Here, therefore, is a convergent body of variants, all located
> in the section of Isaiah 41–53. One can envisage them in two
> different ways: the Sophérim may well have wanted to reduce the
> messianic reach of certain prophetic texts, probably for reasons
> of controversy with this or that sect. Or, the messianic hope of
> the sectarian environments may have faded in the text of the
> manuscripts that they used. Moreover, the distortion may well
> have taken place in both directions at the same time, certain
> 'messianic variants' constituent of a good original, the others
> of sectarian interpolations. Will one ever be able to pronounce
> with certainty on each of these cases?

Conclusion

Several conclusions germane to the study of Matthew's use of the Old Testament arise from these data. First, the overview of text-forms se-curely places the penning of Matthew during a period of textual fluidity

---

[73] For similar arguments concerning the LXX and Targum, see P. Churgin, 'The Targum and the Septuagint', *AJSL* 50 (1933–4): 41–65, and L. H. Brockington, 'Septuagint and Targum', *ZAW* 66 (1954): 80–6.

[74] 'Le grand rouleau d'Isaïe', 549.

and variety. Second, the contention that exegetical decisions were incorporated into texts, even into those that were considered sacred, seems well founded. Although Fishbane's description of the results as 'the divinization of the content of exegetical traditions' is perhaps too lofty, a certain 'authoritative status' is inherent within the exegetical traditions which are evident in the mixed quotations in Matthew.[75] Closely linked to the exegesis of the text were two components, the interpretation of the surroundings through an eschatological grid and the constitution of the group's self-identity. I shall turn next to how this worked itself out in early Christianity.

Early Christian use of the Old Testament: text and exegesis

Given that Christianity originated as a movement within Judaism, the supposition that early Christian OT usage would bear the hallmarks of Jewish exegesis is not far-fetched, especially if Jewish scribes participated in the new movement (Matt. 13.52).[76] Continuity has indeed been found to exist between early Christian usage and that of several of the strands of Judaism on ideological and practical levels. This includes awareness and use by NT authors of the various Jewish *middot*,[77] midrash, explicit and implicit citations and allusions. As in Jewish apocalyptic literature, there is within early Christian writings a clear eschatological emphasis that permeates the compositions. Diversity in usage is also apparent and is manifest particularly in the assumptions behind the uses. This renders generalizations tenuous and almost demands the intensive investigation of a specialist study, many of which have been conducted on authors such as Paul, Philo, Josephus, Luke and Matthew.

Accounting for the discontinuity between early Christianity and Judaism is not necessarily as straightforward as it seems, especially in view of the recent emphasis upon the Jewishness of early Christianity. Commonplace now is the assertion that the key distinction between the

---

[75] Fishbane, *Biblical Interpretation*, p. 4, describes this process as 'the remarkable attribution in certain groups of a revealed status to the human exegesis of implicit Scriptural meanings'. See, for example, 1QpHab 7.1, 'And God told Habakkuk to write what was going to happen ²to the last generation, but he did not let him know the end of the age. ³[blank] And as for what he says: [*Hab 2.2*] "So that the one who reads it /may run/". ⁴*Its interpretation concerns the Teacher of Righteousness, to whom God has disclosed ⁵all the mysteries of the words of his servants, the prophets*' (emphasis mine).

[76] D. E. Orton, *The Understanding Scribe: Matthew and the Apocalyptic Ideal*, JSNTSup 25, Sheffield: JSOT Press, 1989, pp. 137–63.

[77] For a listing and history of the various *middot*, see Strack and Stemberger, *Introduction*, pp. 15–30, and Instone-Brewer, *Techniques and Assumptions*, *passim*.

two is the christocentric element within NT usage. As Ellis observes, 'Jesus and his apostles and prophets ... make their unique contribution to first-century Jewish exposition by their thoroughgoing *reinterpretation of the biblical writings to the person, ministry, death and resurrection of Jesus the Messiah.*'[78] This reinterpretation affects a host of topics, such as the view of salvation history, the future, the basis for ethics, the identity of the people of God, and so on. Of all the emphases and uses, however, it is the use of the Old Testament in support of christology which is of concern here, a practice known in modern parlance as 'christological exegesis'.

Juel, whose *Messianic Exegesis* examines NT christology from the vantage point of early Christianity's exegesis of the Old Testament, places the development of pre-literary christology within the comparative framework of Christian and Jewish exegesis in the hope of 'noting what is distinctive about Christian interpretation'.[79] By delineating elements of the particular exegetical developments in early Christianity, he succeeds in demonstrating the importance of historical background studies to christological inquiry. Marcus, in a more thorough and detailed manner than Juel, also investigates the phenomenon of 'messianic exegesis' in his analysis of christological exegesis in Mark. Marcus postulates that in support of its christology, early Christianity employed many of the same exegetical techniques found in contemporaneous Judaism. These similarities include (1) a tendency towards an eschatological interpretation; (2) the 'conjuring up' of the broader context along with the verse(s) cited; (3) the awareness and use of multiple versions; (4) adjustment of the OT text to support a point; (5) conflation of OT texts (e.g., Mark 1.2, 3); (6) 'reconciliation of scriptural contradictions'; and (7) the blurring of the lines between Scripture and interpretation.[80] Marcus concludes that 'Old Testament patterns and themes used by Mark have thus suffered an

---

[78] E. E. Ellis, 'Biblical Exegesis in the New Testament Church', in *Mikra*, edited by Mulder, p. 691.

[79] *Messianic Exegesis*, p. 23. Juel's work progresses on the level of parallels and themes, and does not address text-form, versions, and so on, in depth. While Juel's overall hypothesis is welcomed, he downplays, perhaps too much, ideas which may have originated with Jesus himself; he is also overly committed to a developmental approach, leaving little room for ingenuity or creative postulates on the part of Jesus or early Christians.

[80] *Way of the Lord*, p. 200. See also his 'Mark and Isaiah', in *Fortunate the Eyes that See: Essays in Honor of David Noel Freedman in Celebration of his Seventieth Birthday*, edited by A. Beck, et al., Grand Rapids: Eerdmans, 1995, pp. 449–66, and other works such as R. E. Watts, *Isaiah's New Exodus and Mark*, WUNT 88, Tübingen: Mohr (Paul Siebeck), 1997, pp. 85–6.

alchemical transformation based upon a logically prior belief, the good news of the arrival of the eschaton in the event of Jesus Christ.'[81]

The work by Marcus complements numerous other NT studies which evince a similar conclusion that quotation of the Old Testament often included interpretative modifications to the text in support of theological concerns and that this reinterpreted text was considered authoritative. The early treatise by J. de Waard is interesting in this regard as he points to possible textual similarities between NT citations of the Old Testament and quotations in the new texts discovered in Qumran.[82] De Waard also notes citations common to both the Dead Sea Scrolls and the New Testament, which he suggests are quoted out of context by both groups of authors yet are employed with the same meaning in the two traditions. This appears to establish that a common understanding of the text existed within Judaism, upon which the NT writers drew. More recent studies continue to confirm that this observation is indeed correct. Lim's study on the textual nature of Paul's OT quotations, for example, contests that variants in his text resemble the Dead Sea Scrolls at points.[83] A comparison of other quotations in the New Testament reveals evidence of similarities with the rabbis.[84] A survey of the use of Scripture in Q[85] further confirms that the tack is a good one.[86] Initially, therefore, it appears that the fluid textual state that was identified in Judaism during this period is also evident within early Christian documents.

This raises several issues relevant to the discussion of Isa. 42.1–4. In order to locate a quotation from the Old Testament in the New Testament within a history of ideas or interpretation, an analysis of the text and usage ought to begin with the Jewish literature. This becomes even more critical for Matthew's quotation of Isa. 42.1–4 because its use in Matthew

---

[81] Marcus, *Way of the Lord*, p. 203. He thus arrives at the conclusion that Mark's exegesis is in both continuity and discontinuity with Judaism (pp. 201–2), leading him to cautiously affirm Dodd's contention that the Old Testament indeed forms the 'substructure of New Testament theology'.

[82] *A Comparative Study of the Old Testament Text in the Dead Sea Scrolls and in the New Testament*, STDJ 4, Leiden: Brill, 1965. For example, de Waard, p. 9, suggests the possible variant of 1QIsa[a] 7.14 וקרא for Matthew's distinctive καλέσουσιν in 1.23.

[83] *Qumran Commentaries and Pauline Letters*, pp. 142–9. Cf. C. D. Stanley, *Paul and the Language of Scripture: Citation Technique in the Pauline Epistles and Contemporary Literature*, SNTSMS 74, Cambridge: Cambridge University Press, 1992, and D. A. Koch, *Die Schrift als Zeuge des Evangeliums*, Tübingen: Mohr (Paul Siebeck), 1984.

[84] Bonsirven, *Exégèse rabbinique, passim*.

[85] C. M. Tuckett, 'The Use of the Scriptures in Q', in *The Scriptures in the Gospels*, edited by Tuckett, pp. 7–26. See in particular his discussion concerning intertextuality in the section entitled 'Isaiah 53 and related texts', pp. 15–20.

[86] *Pace*, Cadwallader, 'Correction of the Text of Hebrews', 257–92.

is the sole explicit citation in the New Testament and thus finds no basis for comparison within the New Testament itself.[87] Such a study might resolve whether Matthew drew upon a translation or tradition known within Judaism, or whether the modifications to the text were made in light of his own theological or contextual concerns. The resolution of this issue would remove one of the primary obstacles in determining Matthew's usage. Furthermore, speculation regarding Matthew's 'christological' exegesis and usage would thus be greatly enhanced by an analysis of usage during the period prior to Matthew's composition.[88] This may also assist in the determination of whether Isa. 42.1–4 was considered of a piece with 52.13–53.12 and, similarly, whether it was associated with the theme of suffering and death. It would also serve to establish a basis on which one might distinguish continuity and discontinuity with Judaism, or plot 'trajectories', to use Marcus' expression.[89]

Historical antecedents and early Jewish usage of Isaiah 42.1–4

Before embarking on an examination of early Jewish literature, a few words of caution are in order. The relative dearth of literature from this period recommends tentative conclusions. Similarly, because the dating of many of the documents is disputed, one must take care in order to avoid the too frequently anachronistic[90] and loose usage of Jewish citations[91] to validate spurious interpretations. It is the aim of this section to collect and investigate Jewish texts that include reference to Isa. 42.1–4 in order to determine the function and interpretation of the passage, with the hope of establishing a framework within which Matthew's use of Isa. 42.1–4 may be analysed. The diversity in Judaism during this era opens the door to the possibility of competing usages and interpretations. The LXX and Targums will also be included here in acknowledgment of the notion

---

[87] The influence of the text upon the Baptism and Transfiguration narratives and 2 Peter 1.17 are hereby acknowledged; however, the usages do not offer extended explicit citation of the text with which to compare Matthew's usage here. In *Dial.* 123 and 135, Justin cites the LXX version.

[88] If it stands in discontinuity, then one must come to terms with where, when and how Matthew's understanding of the passage developed historically. Did it evolve in the church or represent a tradition from Jesus' own self-understanding? Or, was Matthew himself the source of this insight?

[89] *Way of the Lord*, p. 10.

[90] P. S. Alexander, 'Rabbinic Judaism and the New Testament', *ZNW* 74 (1983): 237–45.

[91] See the extensively cited S. Sandmel, 'Parallelomania', *JBL* 81 (1962): 1–13.

that translation is not conducted in a vacuum but instead reflects the theological and cultural emphases of the time.[92]

Non-messianic usages

The Septuagint and corporate Israel

In the quest for the source of Matthew's text-form, the first stop is usually the LXX, where a textual comparison is undertaken.[93] Recent investigation into LXX Isaiah has been moving towards the assertion that many of the 'variants', when compared with the MT, reflect exegetical alterations made to the text.[94] Koenig observes,

> Il est vrai que si l'on considère l'évolution des questions depuis la fin du XIXe siècle, une part grandissante a été faite à la réflexion et aux initiatives des anciens interprètes. De plus en plus fréquemment les critiques modernes ont parlé d'une Exégèse à l'oeuvre. Le crédit de mieux en mieux affermi de cette conception marque un contraste avec la prédominance des explications par les accidents.[95]

> It is true that if one considers the evolution of the question since the end of the 19th century, an increasing portion has been done based on the reflection and initiatives of the ancient interpreters. More frequently, modern critics have spoken of an exegesis within the work. The benefit of this conception, which is increasing in support, stands in contrast to the prevalence of explanations by the variants.

Whether one may, with Koenig, argue that the scriptural borrowings (*emprunts Scripturaires*) and verbal analogies (*analogies verbales*) are

---

[92] Although some passages and translations are more affected than others in this regard, one should not assume that the major translations provide purely objective renderings. Koenig's work, *L'herméneutique analogique*, is helpful at this point.

[93] Most recently, New, *Old Testament Quotations*.

[94] A. Sperber, 'The New Testament and the Septuagint', *Tarbis* 6 (1934): 1–29 and 'New Testament and Septuagint', *JBL* 59 (1940): 193–293.

[95] Koenig, *L'herméneutique analogique*, p. 195. See also van der Kooij, *The Oracle of Tyre*, and D. A. Baer, 'Stumbling towards Eloquence: The Translator of Septuagint Isaiah', unpublished paper, Cambridge, 1995, who describe a translation consciously shaped in view of oral presentation; similarly, but in a less thoroughgoing manner, Seeligmann, *Septuagint Version*, pp. 95–121. Cf. Ziegler, *Untersuchungen*, *passim*, who lists the variants but draws no systematic conclusions from them.

techniques consistently applied is debatable; however, there does appear to be an overarching theological motive on the part of the translator, resulting in what appears to be a Targumic type of translation of the Hebrew *Vorlage*.[96] This, of course, assumes that the Hebrew *Vorlage* which the translator worked from is identical or similar to the MT. If the LXX is indeed such a translation, as now seems likely, its variant readings, whether exegetically or theologically motivated, present a window into the thought-world of this early Jewish translator and, by implication, the community for which it served as Scripture. Furthermore, it may provide the clearest and fullest example of a sustained interpretation of the passage evidenced by its textual 'variants' when compared to the MT, 1QIsa, and so on. By virtue of its early and fairly secure dating, LXX Isaiah offers a fixed point from which to begin the study. Therefore, rather than merely appealing to it for textual variants with which to compare Matthew's text-form, the passage will be examined to determine the emphases of the translator.

The most obvious modification is the septuagintal identification of the servant in 42.1. It offers a clearly articulated corporate interpretation;[97] furthermore, it appears to substitute an entrenched particularism in place of the universalism of the MT. Such an interpretation is evidenced by the inclusion of Ιακωβ and Ισραηλ, interpretative additions which serve to clarify the ambiguous subject and to harmonize 42.1 with the explicitly designated 'servant' in Isa. 41.8,9 and 44.1, in which Israel is openly identified as the servant in both the LXX and MT.[98] This initial clarification

---

[96] It is interesting that LXX Isaiah betrays similar interpretative emphases as does the Targum to Isaiah. See Brockington, 'Septuagint and Targum', 80–6; Churgin, 'The Targum and the Septuagint', 41–65; Rabin, 'Translation Process', 1–26; and, most recently, van der Kooij, *The Oracle of Tyre*. Brockington, 80, for example, points out that the term σώζειν and its derivatives occur more frequently in the LXX than ישׁע in the MT (the former is inserted at 10.22; 12.2; 14.32; 33.20; 38.11; 40.5; 51.14; 60.6). This trend is also apparent in the Aramaic Targum, here with the verb פרק (18.3; 44.23; 50.10; 60.1; 61.10; 62.1). That the LXX is independent of the Targum is evidenced in the fact that each inserts the terms in different locations, leading Brockington to argue that both evince a primarily oral 'common tradition'.

[97] The use of the term 'corporate' is not meant in the manner described by H. W. Robinson's now questioned conception of 'corporate personality', so popular amongst OT scholars some years ago. For an explication of the concept, see H. W. Robinson's *The Christian Doctrine of Man*, Edinburgh: T. & T. Clark, 1911, pp. 27–41. See the perceptive critique by J. W. Rogerson, 'The Hebrew Conception of Corporate Personality: A Re-Examination', *JTS* 21 (1970): 1–16, and the investigation of relevant OT passages by J. R. Porter, 'The Legal Aspects of the Concept of "Corporate Personality" in the Old Testament', *VT* 15 (1965): 361–80.

[98] This is such an obvious exegetically motivated change that there seems little reason to argue for it. Given that the servant is specifically identified as Israel in 41.8, 9; 44.1, 2, 21 and 45.4, it no doubt seemed a reasonable exegetical solution. Such an identification also

is supported throughout the passage. A second notable modification occurs in 42.4a, in which ἀναλάμψει καὶ οὐ θραυσθήσεται (he will shine
forth and not be shattered) translates לֹא יִכְהֶה וְלֹא יָרוּץ (he will not grow
faint or be crushed). Although similar to the MT, the LXX makes explicit
the sustaining power of God on Israel's behalf by omitting the negative
particle and translating לֹא יִכְהֶה with ἀναλάμψει.[99]

Finally, the text of LXX Isa. 42.4b, which reads ἐπὶ τῷ ὀνόματι αὐτοῦ
ἔθνη ἐλπιοῦσιν and to which Matthew subscribes over against the MT's
וּלְתוֹרָתוֹ אִיִּים יְיַחֵילוּ, complicates the discussion. Ziegler's assertion that
ὀνόματι is a Greek corruption is certainly plausible, but good evidence
exists which adjudges his textual emendation as overly hasty.[100] First,
Ziegler provides no textual evidence to substantiate such an alteration,
apart from the obvious morphological affinity between ὀνόματι and
νόμῳ.[101] Second, given the importance of Torah in Jewish thought, one
wonders whether such a mistake would have gone unnoticed.[102] Third,
the difficulty of the reading ὀνόματι renders it the *lectio difficilior* in this
situation. Fourth, one could imagine a scribe inserting Torah,[103] but not
'name'.[104]

If one accepts ὀνόματι as the original reading, the motivation driving
the LXX translator and his intended meaning become problematic. The
apparent referent of 'name' is the servant, namely, Israel; thus, it is in
the name of Israel that the ἔθνη will find hope – an unusual meaning
indeed. One possible reason for the adjustment is a theological linkage
between law and the divine name. Koenig observes that 1QIsa[a] 26.8
includes a variant which reads 'your name and your Law' instead of

fits well with the LXX author's tendency towards harmonization. Note also that in *Ps. Sol.*
17.21 Israel is identified as a servant in contrast to the messiah, Son of David.

[99] LSJ, p. 110, suggests the definitions 'flame up' or 'shine out' for ἀναλάμπω. It is also
used metaphorically to mean 'break out' or 'to revive/come to oneself'. Cf. LXX Isa. 42.6,
in which again a more positive emphasis is apparent.

[100] J. Ziegler, ed., *Isaias: Septuaginta Vetus Testamentum Graecum*, vol. XIV, Göttingen,
1939, p. 277, suggests that τῷ νόμῳ is the original reading (so also Jeremias, 'παῖς θεοῦ',
p. 698).

[101] This substitution, however, is not without parallel. Ziegler, *Untersuchungen*, p. 141,
observes that ὄνομα occurs in the place of νόμος (= MT) in LXX[A] Exod. 16.4 and Ps.
118(119).165.

[102] For the same reason, however, it is doubtful whether a scribe would substitute 'name'
for 'Torah' to suit his interpretative bias. This is most evident in the later Jewish versions
of the Old Testament in Greek (Aquila, Symmachus, Theodotion), which all contain the
correction towards the MT.

[103] Gundry, *Use of the Old Testament*, p. 115, suggests that a scribe might conform the
text to agree with the Jewish concept of the 'Messiah expounding Torah in his kingdom'.

[104] Previous speculation that the LXX may reflect an earlier text than the MT, and may
even point back to a vulgar Hebrew text, seems a less likely option given recent finds in
Qumran and study of the LXX itself.

the MT's 'your name and your renown'.[105] Such a nexus between the
divine name and Law is further evidenced by Ps. 119.55, which reads,
'I remember your name O Lord in the night, and keep your Law.'[106]
Koenig proposes that responsibility for the adjustment lay with the Jewish
pietists, whose thoughts were tuned to divine judgment and justice and the
tensions between the legalist and the mystic.[107] As usual, Koenig's idea
is inventive and worth exploring; however, his position is complicated
by the fact that the referent of 'name' appears to be the servant, not the
Divine.

To summarize, the LXX's adjustments to the MT present the reader
with a heightened particularism that extols YHWH's support for Israel
and its mission to the nations.[108]

Non-messianic individual readings

In contrast to the corporate identification found in the LXX, the designation of 'servant' in several passages in 1QH[a] (*Hodayot*) with regard to an
individual subject of the hymns (perhaps the Teacher of Righteousness)

---

[105] The LXX follows the MT in this text.

[106] Koenig, *L'herméneutique analogique*, p. 236, observes, 'La valeur édifiante de
l'introduction de la Loi dans la recension Qa du passage est manifeste. Au lieu du Nom +
l'invocation (du Nom), l'association du Nom et de la Loi reflète la succession de deux
moments constitutifs du culte. Le souci d'instruire la communauté religieuse est patent,
et il trahit une inspiration légaliste qui est bien conforme à l'orientation prédominante du
Judaïsme, à partir de la fin de l'exil. Il est probable que le souci légaliste s'est combiné avec
une réaction contre une interprétation trop mystique, qui aurait tiré de l'espérance ... en
"ton Nom et ton invocation" l'idée d'une relation avec Dieu, plus ou moins dégagée de
l'assujétissement à la Loi et aspirant à devenir directe.' ('The edifying value of the introduction of the Law in the passage in the recension of Qa is evident. Instead of the Name + the
invocation (of the Name), the association of the Name and the Law reflects the succession
of two constituent moments of the cult. The concern to instruct the religious community is
obvious, and it betrays a legalistic inspiration that is well in accordance with the predominant orientation of Judaism at the end of the exile. It is probable that the legalistic concern
is itself combined with a reaction against an overly mystical interpretation, which would
have drawn on hope ... in "your Name and your invocation" the idea of a relation with God,
which is more or less released from the subjugation to the Law and tends towards direct
access'.)

[107] *Ibid.*

[108] A corporate conception which views Israel as servant of the Lord is not unique to
the LXX, however, as texts such as *Ps. Sol.* 17.21 and *Pesiq. Rab.* 36 also attest to a similar
conception. (As noted below, the corporate reference in *Pesiq. Rab.* refers to the generation
of the messiah. The referent of *Midr. Ps.* 2.7 is difficult to determine; see discussion below.)
Pace Jeremias, 'παῖς θεοῦ', pp. 684, 699, who suggests that the corporate identification of
the servant of the Lord in Isaiah is limited to the Diaspora, while Palestine supported the
individualistic messianic reading.

who receives the bestowal of spirit provides another vantage point.[109] It is this association of the 'holy spirit' with an individual 'servant', a nexus rarely found outside Isa. 42.1–4, which has led scholars to suggest that Isa. 42.1 may have influenced the composition (cf. Isa. 61.1, 2).[110] A few representative examples in 1QH^a include 5.24, 25 (= 13.24, 25); 6.25 (= 14.25); 4.26 (= 17.26 + frag. 14); 15.6–7 (= 7.6–7); and 17.32 (= 9.32).[111] In these texts the reader is introduced to an individual who is presented as a servant who enjoys a relation to the spirit. Although he is not considered messianic, the frequently mentioned bestowal of spirit is an intriguing development.[112] The servant 'knows' by the spirit (6.25), has the 'holy' spirit 'stretched out' over him (4.26; 15.7), is strengthened by the holy spirit (15.5f.), and is favoured by the 'spirit of knowledge' (6.25). One must be cautious, however, in postulating the direct influence of Isa. 42.1 due to the fact that the ideas found in 1QH^a are also present in the important and frequently cited texts of Isa. 11.1–5 and 61.1–2. But if Delcor is correct that Isa. 42.1 lies behind 15.6–7 and possibly 17.32, perhaps the passage contributed to the concept of the spirit and the servant in other texts as well. Of equal importance is the fact that the psalms appear to have been widely distributed and employed in a liturgical setting,

[109] The difficulty presented by the genre and function of the hymns within the community renders deciphering whether the 'I' statements refer to the corporate community or the individual composer a complex undertaking.

[110] Brownlee, *Meaning of the Qumran Scrolls*, pp. 140–3; Bruce, *Biblical Exegesis*, pp. 60–1. Bruce is more careful in his designation of the identity of the 'spokesman', observing only that he claims to be the servant of the Lord and to be endowed by the spirit. One might also point to Isa. 11.1–5, in which 'Branch' is linked with the spirit, although the language of servant does not occur here.

[111] M. Delcor, *Les hymnes de Qumran (Hodayot)*, Paris: Letouzey et Ané, 1962, notes the possible influence of Isa. 42.1 in 15.6–7 (pp. 186–7) and 17.32 (p. 221) in the use of the themes of spirit and truth.

[112] For more detailed studies on the spirit in Qumran, see A. E. Sekki, *The Meaning of* Ruaḥ *at Qumran*, SBLDS 110, Atlanta: Scholars, 1987; A. A. Anderson, 'The Use of "Ruah" in IQS, IQH, and IQM', *JSS* 7 (1962): 293–303; and the section in R. Beaton, 'Messianism, Spirit, and Conflict' (unpublished conference paper, Aberdeen, 1996), entitled 'An Eschatological Spirit in Judaism?'. A. Hultgard, *L'eschatologie des Testaments des douze Patriarches*, vol. I: *Interprétation des textes*, Acta Universitatis Upsaliensis Historia Religionum 6, Uppsala: Almqvist & Wiksell, 1977, pp. 281, 323–4, observes the import of the bestowal of the spirit on the messiah in the Greek and Roman periods evidenced in *1 Enoch* 49.1–3, *Ps. Sol.* 17.42 [37], 11QMelch 18. He argues that all these texts are influenced by Isa. 11.1 and 61.1–2. So also W. Horbury, 'Messianism in the Old Testament Apocrypha and Pseudepigrapha', in *King and Messiah in Israel and the Ancient Near East: Proceedings of the Oxford Old Testament Seminar*, edited by J. Day, JSOTSup 270, Sheffield: Sheffield Academic Press, 1998, p. 429 (who cites Hultgard). On the spirit in rabbinic literature see P. Schäfer, *Die Vorstellung vom heiligen Geist in der rabbinischen Literatur*, SANT 28, Munich: Kösel, 1972.

which may indicate that the ideas contained therein were disseminated throughout the popular culture.

Possible employment with messianic readings

Due to a dearth of evidence, scholars have essentially abandoned the idea of an eschatological 'Servant' figure in early Judaism.[113] As noted in chapter 2, however, this conclusion may be a too hasty and simplistic overreaction to the excesses of previous generations. A helpful caution against this response resides in the association of 'servant' with 'Branch' in Zech. 3.8, a combination which colours both terms with messianic connotations.[114] This would suggest that it is at least conceivable that the mention of the servant of the Lord might conjure up images of a messianic figure of some sort. This section seeks to explore uses of Isa. 42.1–4 in Jewish literature which directly or indirectly influenced the confluence of diverse conceptualizations of messianism and upon which Matthew may have drawn. It must be acknowledged at the outset that this may or may not include ideas concerning a quintessential servant.[115] Earlier scholars, such as J. Brierre-Narbonne, contended that Isa. 42.1–4 contributed to the background of messianic figures found in works[116] like *Ps. Sol.* 17, *1 Enoch* 37–71 and the Targums (cf. Isa. 43.10; 52.12). Jeremias goes so far as to argue that in Palestine a messianic interpretation of Isa. 42.1–4 'was constant from pre-Christian times'.[117]

An investigation of this nature, however, is encumbered by several weighty matters. Perhaps most controversial is the debate concerning how widespread and coherent messianic expectation was in early Judaism. In

---

[113] See as early as Jeremias, 'παῖς θεοῦ', p. 682; Hooker's challenge, *Jesus and the Servant*, is perhaps the most notable. For an examination of textual evidence, see Page, 'Suffering Servant', 481–97. Concerning the OT discussion, see Mettinger, *Farewell to the Servant Songs*, pp. 44–5. For more sophisticated discussions on the servant of Isa. 53, see the most recent contributions to the debate in the two collections of essays by W. Bellinger and W. Farmer, eds. *Jesus and the Suffering Servant: Isaiah 53 and Christian Origins*, Harrisburg: Trinity Press International, 1998, and Janowski and Stuhlmacher, *Leidende Gottesknecht*.

[114] Juel, *Messianic Exegesis*, p. 126; so also B. D. Chilton, *The Glory of Israel: The Theology and Provenience of the Isaiah Targum*, JSOTSup 23, Sheffield: JSOT Press, 1982, p. 115.

[115] See especially Hooker, *Jesus and the Servant*, pp. 53–61. On this issue see Mettinger, *Farewell to the Servant Songs*, p. 46 n. 83, who suggests that although he does not think that the four servant songs as we know them today existed at the time of the book's writing, he has no comment about how the text was read during the period of the New Testament.

[116] *Exégèse apocryphe des prophéties messianiques*, Paris: Librairie Orientaliste Paul Geuthner, 1937, p. 41. These include *Ps. Sol.* 17.28, 31, 35 and *1 Enoch* 39.6; 40.5; 48.4.

[117] 'παῖς θεοῦ', p. 697.

view of this, a brief discussion of messianism will be addressed first. A further issue derives from the realization that the argument in favour of a messianic interpretation and usage of Isa. 42.1–4 assumes the existence of exegetical interconnections between messianically interpreted texts. The present study ought also to explore texts which may include direct and indirect use of Isa. 42.1–4 and to investigate the extent to which this passage contributed, if at all, to the range of messianic ideas in the period.[118] In connection with this, one must remain aware of the possibility that verbal, thematic and phraseological allusions may also be present. Finally, attentiveness to the thorny issue of the dating of the various texts must be maintained.

Messianism

The topic of messianism, one aspect of Jewish corporate eschatology, has proved to be a storm centre of controversy. Recent investigations have challenged the former consensus which opined a widespread, unified messianic hope during the first century in a deliverer known as 'The Messiah'.[119] An early note of dissent was sounded in an article by M. de Jonge, who urged that any discussion concerning a messianic personage be limited to texts which included the infrequently occurring term מָשִׁיחַ, thereby reducing the 'confusion' and the impact of ahistorical assumptions.[120] Regarding these usages de Jonge observes, 'One should realize that in the OT the term "anointed" is never used of a future savior/redeemer, and that in later Jewish writings of the period between 200 B.C. and A.D. 100 the term is used only infrequently in connection with agents of divine deliverance expected in the future.'[121] More

---

[118] Horbury, 'The Messianic Associations of the "Son of Man"', *JTS* 36 (1985): 34–55.

[119] The two representative examples of this perception are E. Schürer, *The History of the Jewish People in the Age of Jesus Christ*, revised and edited by G. Vermes, F. Millar and M. Black, 3 vols., Edinburgh: T. & T. Clark, 1973–87, and G. F. Moore, *Judaism in the First Centuries of the Christian Era*, 2 vols, New York: Schocken, 1971 (originally published 1927).

[120] 'The Use of the Word "Anointed" in the Time of Jesus', *NovT* 8 (1966): 132–48. De Jonge notes thirty-eight occurrences of מָשִׁיחַ in the entire Old Testament. Of these, seven refer to priests, two to the patriarchs, twenty-nine to kings; none refers to an eschatological saviour figure. Surprising to many is the fact that prior to the discovery of the Dead Sea Scrolls, the term occurred in only four books outside the Old Testament: the *Pss. Sol.* (17.32; 18.5,7), *1 Enoch*, *2 Apoc. Bar.* and *4 Ezra*.

[121] 'Messiah', *ABD* IV. 777. De Jonge's cautions are worth careful consideration; however, arguments from silence, particularly where written sources are concerned, are also difficult. Authors do not necessarily include all or even the most common of their beliefs in any one composition.

recently, the argument in favour of an extreme position which emphasizes radical diversity within the various Judaisms, particularly regarding
the perception of future eschatological deliverers, is increasingly being
put forward. For example, Charlesworth asserts that 'One can no longer
assume that most Jews were looking for the coming of the Messiah.'[122]
R. A. Horsley proposes dropping the concept 'Messiah/messianic' altogether,[123] and W. S. Green contends that 'the primacy of "the messiah"
as a subject of academic study derives not from ancient Jewish preoccupation, but from *early Christian word-choice, theology and apologetics*'
(emphasis mine).[124]

There is good reason, however, to believe that 'the pendulum of scholarly opinion has swung too far'.[125] While there was without doubt considerable diversity of thought, practice and belief within Judaism at this
time, the argument can be made in favour of a common Judaism,[126] which
included an overarching expectation of an eschatological deliverer known

[122] J. H. Charlesworth, 'From Messianology to Christology: Problems and Prospects',
in *The Messiah: Developments in Earliest Judaism and Christianity*, edited by J. H.
Charlesworth, with J. Brownson, M. Davis, S. J. Kraftchick and A. F. Segal. Minneapolis:
Fortress, 1992, p. 35. See also the numerous articles in two recent works: J. H. Charlesworth,
ed., *The Messiah: Developments in Earliest Judaism and Christianity*, with J. Brownson,
M. Davis, S. Kraftchick and A. Segal. Minneapolis: Fortress, 1992; and J. Neusner, W. S.
Green and E. Frerichs, eds., *Judaisms and Their Messiahs at the Turn of the Christian Era*,
Cambridge: Cambridge University Press, 1987.
[123] '"Messianic" Figures and Movements in First-Century Palestine', in *The Messiah:
Developments in Earliest Judaism and Christianity*, edited by Charlesworth, with Brownson,
Davis, Kraftchick and Segal, p. 295. He further contends, 'It is becoming increasingly
evident that there was little interest in a Messiah, Davidic, or otherwise, let alone a standard
messianic expectation, in the diverse Palestinian Jewish literature of late Second Temple
times.'
[124] 'Introduction: Messiah in Judaism: Rethinking the Question', in *Judaisms and Their
Messiahs at the Turn of the Christian Era*, edited by Neusner, Green and Frerichs, p. 4.
Green may be partially correct, but, as is frequently noted, for early Christianity apologetic
to have been effective, it would have had to appeal to concepts which had a correspondence
within Judaism.
[125] J. J. Collins, *The Scepter and the Star: The Messiahs of the Dead Sea Scrolls and
Other Ancient Literature*, ABRL, New York: Doubleday, 1995, p. 4. For an up-to-date
discussion of research, see W. Horbury, *Jewish Messianism and the Cult of Christ*, London:
SCM Press, 1998, pp. 36–63, and the recent superb collection of essays from the Oxford OT
seminar on Davidic messianism in J. Day, ed., *King and Messiah in Israel and the Ancient
Near East: Proceedings of the Oxford Old Testament Seminar*, JSOTSup 270, Sheffield:
Sheffield Academic Press, 1998.
[126] J. Dunn, *The Partings of the Ways between Christianity and Judaism and their Significance for the Character of Christianity*, London: SCM Press, 1991, pp. 18–30; E. P.
Sanders, *Judaism: Practice and Belief 63 BCE–66 CE*, London: SCM Press, 1992, p. 49;
M. Bockmuehl, *This Jesus: Martyr, Lord, Messiah*, Edinburgh: T. & T. Clark, 1994,
pp. 104–5. For example, regarding eschatology, Sanders, *Judaism*, p. 298, opines that 'when
Jews who thought about the future concretely sat down to describe it, they did not have only
one model to follow. They all trusted in God. *That* is common.'

by a cluster of designations best served by the single signifier 'messiah'. Horbury has persuasively argued that by the beginning of the Second Temple period 'the Davidic hope already constituted a relatively fixed core of messianic expectation, both in Palestine and in the Diaspora'.[127] Additionally, the case for broadening the scope beyond the stringent terminological criteria of de Jonge is compelling. De Jonge's contention that the sole criteria for determining a 'messianic' passage be the presence of the term מָשִׁיחַ, while helpful in its caution, is perhaps too severe a limitation and does not reflect the diversity of data. First, a primary weakness in de Jonge's position is that he excludes the messianic kingship exegesis and insertions of Χριστός found in the LXX, particularly in the Psalms and Isaiah.[128] Second, he ignores passages which, although they do not include מָשִׁיחַ, appear to refer to an eschatological figure which may be considered 'messianic'.[129] The interconnection between the Davidic king and 'righteous Branch' in Jer. 23.5 (33.15) introduces provocative imagery which is also employed in Isa. 11.1–5 and Zech. 3.8.[130] These texts link the future Davidic king with the metaphor of 'the Branch' and form a conceptual and linguistic web. Such 'exegetical interconnections' evince a messianic interpretative exercise that was occurring already in the LXX and Dead Sea Scrolls.[131] Thirdly, de Jonge overlooks texts in which מָשִׁיחַ refers to an eschatological figure other than the ideal Davidic

---

[127] 'Messianic Associations', 52; see also his *Jewish Messianism*, pp. 13–35. K. Pomykala, *The Davidic Dynasty Tradition in Early Judaism: Its History and Significance for Messianism*, Atlanta: Scholars, 1995, p. 270, argues that the Davidic expectation was limited to the period spanning from 50 BC (*Ps. Sol.* 17) to AD 100 (4 Ezra), whereas Horbury, *Jewish Messianism*, p. 63, concludes that messianic hopes were widespread in the Persian, Herodian and Hasmonaean periods.

[128] On LXX Psalms, see J. Schaper, *Eschatology in the Greek Psalter*, WUNT 76, Tübingen: Mohr (Paul Siebeck), 1995, pp. 138–64. See also J. Lust, 'Messianism and Septuagint', in *Congress Volume: Salamanca, 1983*, edited by J. A. Emerton, Leiden: Brill, 1985, pp. 174–91; Seeligmann, *Septuagint Version*, pp. 118–20; and Horbury, *Jewish Messianism*, pp. 48–9; 90–6.

[129] Collins, *Scepter and the Star*, p. 12.

[130] See also *Pss. Sol.* 17.32; 18.5, 7. Horbury, 'Messianic Associations', 40, further explores 'messianic associations' between Judah and the lion in Gen. 49.9 (which reappears in Rev. 5.5), along with the designation 'root', which occurs in Isa. 11.1. Thus, Jeremias' argument, 'παῖς θεοῦ', p. 683, that servant is associated with messiah in Ezek. 34.23–24; 37.24–5; Zech. 3.8; and in the later literature of 4 Ezra 7.28; 13.32, 37, 52; 14.9; *Syr. Bar.* 70.9; *Tg. Isa.* 43.10; 52.13; *Tg. Zech.* 3.8; *Tg. Ezek.* 34.23–4; 37.24, if considered in this light, has some validity. The complete absence of the designation 'servant of God' from rabbinic literature is somewhat surprising (so Jeremias, 'παῖς θεοῦ').

[131] Horbury, 'Messianic Associations', 40, additionally observes, 'These exegetical interconnections ... tend to unify and strengthen the complex of messianic texts; and it is noteworthy that they are developed so far, in specifically messianic interpretation, by the period of the Septuagint and the Qumran texts.'

King.[132] These are worth noting simply because they demonstrate that there was a degree of diversity amongst conceptualizations of a messianic personage. In the midst of this diversity, it would be natural for a blending of themes, ideas and expectations to occur, resulting in what many consider 'messianic associations'; indeed, this is what we find.

Thus, given that there appears to have been something of a common eschatological expectation, messianic interconnections within the literature, and a certain fluidity and diversity of messianic personages, the conclusion that one may speak of 'messiah' as a component of early Judaism is probable. Because of the diversity within a general coherence of messianic expectation, the question then arises how one is to define 'messiah'.[133] In his recent book, G. S. Oegema presents a working definition: '*Ein Messias ist eine priesterliche, königliche oder andersartige Gestalt, die eine befreiende Rolle in der Endzeit spielt.*'[134] This effectively epitomizes current conclusions concerning the messiah and maintains an emphasis upon diversity of forms within a central conception of the end-time role of liberator.

The study which follows will be based upon the assumption that a common messianic expectation did exist during Matthew's composition and that exegetical interconnections and messianic associations, which may have involved Isa. 42.1–4, were reflective of it. The exploration of sources which support a messianic reading will begin with the most obvious and frequently cited and then proceed to the more obscure.

The Dead Sea Scrolls

Isa. 42.1–4 is not explicitly cited in a messianic context in the scrolls. While this may seem to rule out a messianic reading of this passage in early Judaism, the text of 1QIsa[a] contains markings at 42.1 and 4 that may hint at the manner in which Isa. 42.1–4 was read by the community. The margins of the manuscript by both verses 1 and 4 are inscribed with

---

[132] Collins, *Scepter and the Star*, pp. 11–14.

[133] J. J. Collins, 'Messiahs in Context: Method in the Study of Messianism in the Dead Sea Scrolls', in *Methods of Investigation of the Dead Sea Scrolls and the Kirbet Qumran site: Present Realities and Future Prospects*, edited by M. Wise, et al., New York: New York Academy of Sciences, 1994, p. 224.

[134] *Der Gesalbte und sein Volk: Untersuchungen zum Konzeptualisierungsproze der messianischen Erwartungen von den Makkabäern bis Bar Koziba*, Schriften des Institutum Judaicum Delitzschianum 2, Göttingen: Vandenhoeck & Ruprecht, 1994, p. 28. Similarly, Collins, *Scepter and the Star*, p. 12, affirms that four specific types of messianic figures existed in the literature during the period; these include kingly, priestly, prophetic and heavenly messiahs.

an X, thereby setting the material apart from the surrounding context and suggesting that the passage was read, or had import, as an individual unit.[135] Although one may not argue from these paragraph markings that the text was read messianically, the fact that it was marked off attests to its early independent use and further indicates that the text was of some significance for the Qumran scribe and/or community.

A probable reference to Isa. 42.3 occurs in 1QH^a 12.25 (= 4.25), which is most provocative due to the fact that its anomalous text appears to be the same as that found in Matthew 12.20b. 1QH^a 12.25 reads, 'You will bring their[136] justice forth to victory and truth unto equity.'[137] This use occurs in a section of the *Hodayot* which extols God as the source and purveyor of justice (12.30, 31, 37, 40) on behalf of the covenant people (12.37). In this passage Isa. 42.3 may not be explicitly messianic; however, its declaration that God will establish justice on behalf of this group, or individual, contributes to the general expectation of God's coming rule, a concept of which Matthew himself may have been aware and upon which he might have drawn.

The Similitudes of Enoch and Psalms of Solomon

Although frequently mentioned in discussions concerning the composition of *Pss. Sol.* 17–18 and *1 Enoch* 37–71, no explicit citation of Isa. 42.1–4 occurs in these two documents. It appears, however, that allusions to and/or echoes of this passage are present, evident on a verbal, theological and/or ideological level. Such possible exegetical interconnections between Isa. 42.1–4 and these passages are worth exploring for the light that they might shed upon the understanding of Isa. 42.1–4 during the period in question.

1 Enoch is a complex composite of several eras and authors,[138] and further complicating matters is the fact that the passages of interest

---

[135] Tov, *Textual Criticism*, p. 216, suggests that the X in the margins is employed to mark 'content divisions'.

[136] F. García Martínez, ed., *The Dead Sea Scrolls Translated: The Qumran Texts in English*, translated by W. Watson, Leiden: Brill, 1994, p. 335, translates the first clause in the singular as 'You will make his right triumph'.

[137] S. Holm-Nielsen, *Hodayot: Psalms from Qumran*, Acta Theologica Danica 2, Aarhus: Universitetsforlaget, 1960, p. 76. See the discussion in chapter 5, n. 68.

[138] E. Isaac, '1 (Ethiopic Apocalypse of) Enoch (Second Century B.C.–First Century A.D.): A New Translation and Introduction', in *The Old Testament Pseudepigrapha*, edited by J. H. Charlesworth, vol. I, Garden City, NY: Doubleday, 1983, pp. 6–7. See also G. W. E. Nickelsburg, *Jewish Literature between the Bible and the Midrash: A Historical and Literary Introduction*, Philadelphia: Fortress, 1981, pp. 150–1, for the implications of the copies of *1 Enoch* in the Dead Sea Scrolls for authorship and date.

happen to occur in the *Similitudes* (chs. 37–71), a section whose date and provenance have been hotly debated. The pendulum of recent scholarship has swung in the direction of Jewish authorship, supporting a date of the late first or early second century AD.[139] Thus, *1 Enoch* presents a text in which the ideas contained therein may be considered generally contemporaneous with Matthew and perhaps reflective of an understanding of the text in at least one strand of Judaism.

The designation the 'Elect One' (ὁ ἐκλεκτός) in LXX Isa. 42.1a is widely considered the source for the use of the 'Chosen/Elect One' in *1 Enoch* 37–71,[140] a figure, it seems, who is identical to the messianic son of man.[141] As Collins notes, 'It is . . . generally agreed that "the Chosen One," who appears in all three parables is the same being, since he exercises the same functions as the "son of man" and the two expressions are interchanged in such a way the identification is not in doubt.'[142] In the composition the author(s) of *1 Enoch* appear(s) to have drawn upon a variety of passages for the description of the Elect One. For example, in 39.6 the statement 'the Elect One of righteousness and faith' seems to append a further ascription to the title elements from Isa. 11.4–5.[143] Nevertheless, greater influence from Isa. 42.1–4 than the mere contribution of the title 'Elect One' appears probable. D. W. Suter raises the prospect that the judicial element found in texts which feature the Elect One and

---

[139] The current consensus is that the *Similitudes* are early and Jewish. See J. C. Greenfield and M. E. Stone, 'The Enochic Pentateuch and the Date of the Similitudes', *HTR* 70 (1977): 51–65, who argue for a first-century date, and M. Knibb, 'The Date of the Parables of Enoch: A Critical Review', *NTS* 25 (1979): 345–59, who posits a date between AD 70 and 135, in part because of the apparent influence of the *Similitudes* on the Gospel of Matthew. For the suggestion of a date prior to AD 70, see F. M. Wilson, 'The Son of Man in Jewish Apocalyptic Literature', *Studia Biblica et Theologica* 8 (1978): 39–40. In addition to these proposals, the members of the SNTS Pseudepigrapha Seminar concluded in 1977 in Tübingen, and again in 1978 in Paris, that the *Similitudes* were of Jewish origin, written at the latest by the first century AD.

[140] M. Black, *The Book of Enoch or I Enoch: A New English Edition with Commentary and Textual Notes*, SVTP, Leiden: E. J. Brill, 1985, p. 197, writes 'the title "Elect One" (בחיר) comes unmistakably from Second Isaiah's term for the "servant of the Lord" (Isa. 41:8,9, 42:1; cf. Luke 23:35)'. Similarly, the designation 'Righteous One' probably finds its source in Isa. 53.11 (so also Jeremias, 'παῖς θεοῦ', p. 687).

[141] So M. Black, 'Servant of the Lord and Son of Man', *SJT* 6 (1953): 10; M. D. Hooker, *The Son of Man in Mark: A Study of the Background of the Term 'Son of Man' and Its Use in St Mark's Gospel*, London: SPCK, 1967, p. 39; C. Colpe, 'ὁ υἱὸς τοῦ ἀνθρώπου', *TDNT* VIII.429; Jeremias, 'παῖς θεοῦ', p. 687. The passages where this title occurs in *1 Enoch* are 39.6; 40.5; 45.3, 4; 49.2, 4; 51.3, 5; 52.6, 9; 53.6; 55.4; 61.5, 8, 10; 62.1. The referent in 46.3, 48.6 and 49.4 is likewise the Elect One.

[142] 'The Heavenly Representative: The "Son of Man" Figure in the Similitudes of Enoch', in *Ideal Figures in Ancient Judaism: Profiles and Paradigms*, edited by J. Collins and G. Nickelsburg, SBLSCS 12, Chico: Scholars, 1980, p. 113.

[143] Black, *I Enoch*, p. 197.

the son of man (based upon Dan 7.9, 13) is derived from Isa. 42.1–4, a text in which מִשְׁפָּט figures prominently.[144] This is an idea worth examining for potential implications regarding the use of Isa. 42.1–4.

The association of the title 'Elect One' with judicial imagery begins in *1 Enoch* 45.3 with the assertion that he will 'sit on the seat of Glory'.[145] From this station, the Elect One dispenses judgment upon the wicked and offers the blessings of the new age to the righteous. The judgment takes many forms throughout the texts: in 49.4 the secret things are judged; 55.4 sees Azazel and his angels judged; 61.8 focuses upon the holy ones whose deeds are scrutinized; and finally in ch. 62, this time with the son of man on the throne, the ruling class is condemned and the righteous blessed.[146] The event of judgment itself transpires during the days of the Elect One, a timeframe which suggests an eschatological judgment at the end of days. While it is ill-advised to be emphatic, the linkage between judgment and the Elect One and a lack of a developed view of Davidic kingship suggest that Isa. 42.1–4 may have indeed influenced this element of *1 Enoch*.

The influence of Isa. 42.1–4 upon the composition of *1 Enoch* may not be limited to the theme of judgment, however; it may also be the source for the themes of 'a light to the gentiles' and compassion upon the brokenhearted in *1 Enoch* 48.2–7, traditionally associated with Isa. 49.2, 6. Isa. 49.2 allows for the pre-existence and naming of the son of man, while the phrase 'a light to the gentiles' occurs in 49.6. There seems little reason to dispute these findings; however, neither the staff imagery nor

---

[144] *Tradition and Composition in the Parables of Enoch*, SBLMS 47, Missoula: Scholars, 1979, pp. 26–7. It is possible that the judicial element derives from Isa. 11.3–4, in which the root of Jesse, the Davidide, will righteously judge, and one would not want to polarize the texts, both of which involve the expectation of the righteous judgment of God at the end of days. Reasons that Isa. 42.1–4 is the more likely source include: (1) ὁ ἐκλεκτός does not occur in Isa. 11.1ff. whereas it does in Isa. 42.1–4 within the context of judgment/justice; and (2) neither the Elect One nor the Son of man appears to possess the traits of the future Davidic ruler, which one might expect if Isa. 11.1ff. were in view.

[145] The phrase 'throne of Glory' appears in 51.3, 55.4 and 62.3, 5. The son of man is seated in 62.5 and 69.27, 29, having been placed there by the Lord of the Spirits in 61.8, 62.2. The 'head of days' sits on the 'throne of Glory' in 47.3. Cf. Matt. 25.31–46, in which the son of man (vv. 31–3) and king (vv. 34ff.) are merged and judgment/justice is dispensed.

[146] The judgment texts include 62.5 and 69.27, 29. See G. W. E. Nickelsburg's study, *Resurrection, Immortality, and Eternal Life in Intertestamental Judaism*, HTS 26, Cambridge, MA: Harvard University Press, 1972, pp. 70–2, which attempted to establish the use of Isa. 52–3 in the composition of *1 Enoch* 62, and as E. Sjöberg confirms (*Der Menschensohn im Äthiopischen Henochbuch*, Lund: C. W. K. Gleerup, 1946, pp. 121–8, followed by Colpe, 'ὁ υἱὸς τοῦ ἀνθρώπου', p. 426), references to the passion statements are absent. Similarly, no linkage appears to exist between the use of Isa. 42.1–4 in these texts and a suffering-servant motif. The judgment scenes are accompanied by a description of the blessed state of the righteous.

the compassionate element found in *1 Enoch* 48.4 can be located in Isa. 49.[147] These motifs may derive from Isa. 42.1–4. The text of *1 Enoch* 48.4 reads as follows:'He will become a staff for the righteous ones in order that they may lean on him and not fall. He is the light of the gentiles and he will become the hope of those who are sick in their hearts.'[148]

W. D. Davies has suggested that this text is a reference to Isa. 9.2, an assertion which, while possible, is doubtful.[149] Instead, this passage appears to be a conflation of the ideas and imagery of the staff/reed found in Isa. 42.3 and 2 Kings 18.21, and serves to further characterize the son of man figure. Several reasons support this claim. First, although Isa. 42.3 does not contain a reference to a staff, it does, however, incorporate the imagery of a bruised reed. Significantly, early rabbinic traditions juxtapose Isa. 42.3 alongside 2 Kings 18.21 by gĕzērâ šawâ, constructing a wordplay on 'reed' and 'reed of a staff'.[150] Second, the phrase 'light to the gentiles', which occurs several times in LXX Isaiah, appears in Isa. 42.6 as well as 49.6.[151] Finally, the phrase 'hope of those who are sick in the hearts', in addition to the obvious reference to Isa. 61.1, 2,[152] bears a conceptual resemblance to the compassionate ministry of the servant in Isa. 42.3, in which he will not crush the bruised nor snuff out the smouldering. The fact that all three images occur in close proximity to one another in Isa. 42.1–6, when combined with the rabbinic usage of the staff/reed imagery in Isa. 42.3, offers adequate verbal and thematic similarities for *1 Enoch* 48.4 to be considered an echo of, if not an allusion to, Isa. 42.3. Thus, from the use of the title Elect One and other possible influences of Isa. 42.1–4 upon *1 Enoch*, one may consider the text messianic in pre-Christian times.

The *Psalms of Solomon* present a similar picture of the messiah to that found in *1 Enoch*, although the presence of Isa. 42.1–4 is neither obvious nor necessary. Brierre-Narbonne surmised that Isa. 42.1–4 may

---

[147] Brierre-Narbonne, *Exégèse apocryphe*, p. 41, also lists Isa. 42.3, 4 as possibly influencing *1 Enoch* 48.4.

[148] Isaac, '1 Enoch', pp. 5–89.

[149] *Paul and Rabbinic Judaism: Some Rabbinic Elements in Pauline Theology*, 4th edn, Philadelphia: Fortress, 1980, p. 279.

[150] Cf. Isa. 36.6. Later rabbinic material contrasts Isa. 42.3 and 2 Kings 18.21. R. Jannai, who received the tradition from R. Ḥiyya, employs Isa. 42.3 in *b. Yebam.* 93a (Strack and Stemberger, *Introduction*, p. 90, date R. Ḥiyya in the fifth generation of the Tannaites (AD 200–250)). Similarly, *b. Ber.* 56b provides a second conflation of Isa. 42.3 and 2 Kings 18.21. The meaning of each passage has been modified from its original context through continued, combined usage, rendering any reference to the servant or messiah non-existent. The sayings appear to have become proverbial by this time. If the reference to R. Ḥiyya *b. Yebam.* is accurate, the combination and use of Isa. 42.3 and 2 Kings 18 was secure by AD 250.

[151] Cf. Isa. 51.4; *Ode Sol.* 13.32. Luke 2.32 reads, φῶς εἰς ἀποκάλυψιν ἐθνῶν.

[152] So Black, *I Enoch*, p. 210.

have influenced elements of the portrait of the ideal Davidic King, the Lord Messiah, presented in *Pss. Sol.* 17–18.[153] If his observation is correct, it could prove significant, particularly if Matthew is at all dependent upon the *Psalms*, as indicated by the possibility that Matt. 13.16 is dependent upon *Ps. Sol.* 17.44 or 18.6.[154] Whether or not Matthew knew and used elements of this text, he has certainly departed from the portrait of the messiah pictured here. The concern of this section is, however, not with the possible influence of the *Psalms of Solomon* upon Matthew, but that of Isa. 42.1–4 upon the portrait of the messiah found in the *Psalms* themselves. Brierre-Narbonne postulates three possible points of contact between Isa. 42.1–4 and *Ps. Sol.* 17.29, 31 and 35, all of which involve the themes of universalism and judgment/justice. 17.29 refers to the king as judge of peoples and nations, which echoes the theme of κρίσις in 42.1, 3, 4. This attention to the nations continues in 17.31, but here the nations are streaming from the ends of the earth to behold the glory of God.[155] Finally, 17.34b–35 exhibits a remarkable element in its focus upon the compassionate rule of the Lord over the nations, a seminal universalism that is certainly evident in Isa. 42.1–4.[156] It must be granted that one cannot be assured that Isa. 42.1–4 contributed to the ideas expressed in these three verses; however, the fact that these ideas were current around the time of Matthew is important in and of itself.

One might also note the parallels between Matthew's presentation of Jesus and the *Psalms'* understanding of messiah. The *Psalms of Solomon* include the bestowal of the spirit upon the messiah in 17.37 and a triumphalistic element inherent in the Lord Messiah's rule. The effects of his reign create a community whose values and orientation oppose those of the present one (17.20); the king and people are righteous and the judge is obedient. The emphasis upon the righteous rule of the messiah, the description that the days will be characterized by mercy (18.9), and the general state of well-being that is brought about by the all-powerful messiah in many ways parallels Matthew's presentation of Jesus and his christology. The difficulty with such an analysis, of course, is that no direct, explicit citation of Isa. 42.1–4 occurs; however, throughout the

---

[153] *Exégèse apocryphe*, p. 41; his purported reference to 17.28 is not straightforward; however, 17.29 with its note of universalism may derive from Isa. 42.1–4. His suggestion that 17.35–6 is influenced by Isa. 42.3, 4, 6 is also plausible.

[154] Whether Matthew would have had access to or used these texts is pure speculation; however, the similarities are striking. R. B. Wright, 'Psalms of Solomon: A New Translation and Introduction', in *The Old Testament Pseudepigrapha*, edited by Charlesworth, vol. II, Garden City, NY: Doubleday, 1985, pp. 640–1, dates them generally within 125 BC and the early first century AD or, more narrowly, 70–45 BC.

[155] The traditional argument that Isa. 66.18–21 is behind this passage seems reasonable.

[156] This provides a significant contrast to the portrait of Isa. 11.1–10.

composition no OT passage is directly quoted, leaving readers to speculate on verbal or thematic echoes. The moments of conceptual continuity are worth mentioning, particularly in documents which are probably
within a century of each other.

Targums

The text most frequently adduced in support of a pre-Christian messianic
interpretation of Isa. 42.1–4 is the Targum to Isaiah.[157] Such an appeal
may not be unwarranted for, as B. D. Chilton observes, 'The Targum
shows us that the term "servant" could be taken as a designation of the
messiah (cf. 43.10). This is particularly the case at 52.13 and 53.10.'[158]
Nevertheless, in the Targum to 42.1–4 it is far from certain whether it is
meant to be interpreted messianically.

The recent critical editions of Stenning and Chilton do not include
the reading אה עבדי משיחא,[159] opting instead to follow the manuscripts
which omit mešiḥa and restrict the reading to 'my servant', the ramifi-
cation of which appears to challenge the frequent uncritical assertions
that the passage is messianic. In spite of this omission and initial appear-
ances, however, it may still be argued that 42.1a was understood messianically. First, the passage contains an individualistic emphasis throughout
42.1–4. Second, the linkage of mešiḥa and servant is undisputed in 43.10,
52.13 and 53.10, passages which are unequivocally messianic. Third, the
overall context of 42.1–7 argues in favour of the position that corporate
Israel is not in view here. This is especially evident in verse 7, in which
the individual of verse 6 is appointed 'to open the eyes of *the house
of Israel* who are as it were blind to the law' (emphasis mine).[160] The
specific distinction between the servant and the 'house of Israel' implies
an individual.[161] Fourth, one could argue that the overall context of the

---

[157] Cope, *Matthew*, pp. 36–7, and Davies and Allison, *Matthew*, II.323–4. Jeremias, 'παῖς
θεοῦ', pp. 692–3, argues that it can be demonstrated that 'the Messianic interpretation of
the servant texts Is. 42.1 and 52.13 in Tg. Is. is old'.

[158] *A Galilean Rabbi and His Bible: Jesus' Own Interpretation of Isaiah*, London: SPCK,
1984, pp. 199–200; see also *Glory*, pp. 86–96.

[159] The reading is found in Prof. P. de Lagarde's edition of the Codex Reuchlinianus
(*Prophetae Chaldaice*), the Ms Jews' College, and the First and Second Rabbinic Bibles.
Str-B I.630, and R. A. Aytoun, 'The Servant of the Lord in the Targum', *JTS* 23 (1922):
177, include it in their translations. Cf. Jeremias, 'παῖς θεοῦ', p. 693 n. 292.

[160] The confusion arises from the MT's use of the second person 'you' found in vv. 6–7.
The text reads that the Lord has given you 'to open the eyes that are blind', and so forth,
which could be read as referring either to corporate Israel or an individual.

[161] Aytoun, 'Servant of the Lord', 177. Chilton, *Glory*, p. 80, observes, 'Although "servant" language has been used in respect of Israel (41:8), the present usage appears messianic.'

passage contains specifically messianic overtones. These all suggest that the messianic identification contained in the variant reading in verse 1, whether present or not in the original, is nevertheless conceptually present throughout. Thus, the conclusion that the Targums do not represent a corporate or collective interpretation of the servant in Isa. 42.1–4, but an individualistic one, appears sound.

Such a messianic affirmation is complicated by the difficulty of establishing the authorship and date of the targumic literature.[162] The current consensus on these issues describes a text that developed over a considerable period of time and constitutes both early and late strata of material.[163] The Targums betray a popular origin and purpose, and more closely resemble a dynamic equivalent than a direct translation.[164] As such, they offer insights into popular ideas after AD 100 and perhaps prior to this date as well. Be that as it may, there remains considerable doubt as to the value of targumic material for NT studies.

In an attempt to determine the dates of the various strata in the Targums, Chilton has suggested that the meturgeman employed an exegetical framework that he attributes to an early date and is evidenced in many of the most frequent terms in the Targum. Three terms central to this exegetical framework are present in Isa. 42.1–4: *memra*, holy spirit, and Law. In the broad usage of *memra*[165] (here in Isa. 42.1 for עַבְדִּי), the reader finds hints

---

[162] See M. McNamara, *The New Testament and the Palestinian Targum to the Pentateuch*. Rome: Pontifical Bible Institute, 1966, pp. 20–33, and B. D. Chilton, *The Isaiah Targum: Introduction, Translation, Apparatus and Notes*, Edinburgh: T. & T. Clark, 1987, pp. xxv–xxviii. Two persons are associated with the Targums. First, the Talmud claims that Jonathan ben Uzziel, student of Hillel, composed the Prophetic Targum aided by Haggai, Zechariah and Malachi (Megillah 3a (quoted in Chilton, *Glory*, p. 1)). If so, then elements within the text could be dated shortly after the time of Hillel. Second, Joseph bar Ḥiyya, fourth-century AD leader of the Babylonian Pumbedita Academy, is also linked with the Targum on the Prophets because of his apparent translation and consolidation of the Targums.

[163] Several authors have taken on this issue with promising results for NT studies. Aytoun, 'Servant of the Lord', 172; McNamara, *New Testament and the Palestinian Targum*, pp. 33–6; 259–61; and Chilton, *Glory*, pp. 1–12.

[164] Aytoun, 'Servant of the Lord', 172, rightly notes this point, but given his late dating of the material he comments, 'Generally speaking, the Targums do not provide much that is of value to any but the textual expert.' In contrast, Chilton, *Glory*, p. 4, concludes that 'a coherent Targum tradition could only evolve out of generations of synagogue practice', and that the Targums are something of a 'bridging document between intertestamental literature on the one hand, and Rabbinica on the other'.

[165] The more traditional and simplistic view maintains that *memra* was simply either a common targumic paraphrase for נְפֵשׁ or evidence of the meturgeman's anti-anthropomorphic attitude (see Aytoun, 'Servant of the Lord', 177 n. 2). For an overview of more recent scholarship concerning *memra*, see A. Chester, *Divine Revelation and Divine Titles in the Pentateuchal Targumim*, Tübingen: Mohr (Paul Siebeck), 1986, pp. 293–313, who concludes that *memra* originated as an exegetical device that developed a more nuanced theological usage.

of the theology of the meturgeman.[166] The term means simply the 'word' or 'voice' of God.[167] While it has been argued that the usage of *memra* appeared and receded 'before classical Rabbinica achieved written form', Chester cautions that this may not necessarily be the case, arguing instead that the reason for the absence of *memra* from rabbinic literature may be due more to its limited development for usage within the synagogue.[168] Offering further support for a possible early date of this section of the Targum is the inclusion of the term 'holy' to modify spirit.[169] 'Holy' was inserted for two probable reasons: first, to emphasize Divine revelation and, second, to edit out anthropomorphisms directed towards God.[170] Moreover, 'holy spirit' was generally understood as 'that which permits a person to act or speak in the LORD's name'[171] and usually had a prophet in view.[172] Thus, 42.1b appears to affirm that the result of the impartation of the holy spirit is the 'revelation' of God's 'judgment/justice to the peoples' through the servant.[173] Finally, if the servant is interpreted as messiah, a distinct linking of messiah with the promulgation of Torah to the nations is evidenced. All three terms may evince an early date for the material in the Targum to Isa. 42.1–4, but this is by no means certain.

Thus, the Targum on Isa. 42.1–4 presents an individual, probably a messianic figure, who proclaims the word of God to the peoples, here a word of justice/judgment.[174] That his vocation is perceived as prophetic is alluded to through the insertion of the terms *memra* and 'holy'. The poor and needy are identified as those who receive compassionate care. Finally,

---

[166] Chilton, *Glory*, p. 65, concludes, 'The inference seems inescapable that memra usage is not merely *ad hoc*, but represents a rather more systematic development of theological thought than might have been expected.'

[167] See Chester, *Divine Revelation and Divine Titles*, p. 312. Chilton, *Glory*, pp. 56–69, delineates eight usages and nuances to the term in the Isaiah Targum: (i) an occasion for rebellion; (ii) an agent of punishment; (iii) a demand for obedience; (iv) an edict; (v) a voice; (vi) divine protection; (vii) an eternal witness; (viii) an intermediary. His suggestion that Isa. 42.1 be included with Isa. 49.5 under the rubric of 'divine protection' is debatable.

[168] Chester, *Divine Revelation and Divine Titles*, p. 312.

[169] One should also note its presence in e.g. 1QH 4.26 (17.26); 8.20 (16.20); and 15.6–7 (7.6–7).

[170] J. F. Stenning, ed. and trans., *The Targum of Isaiah*, Oxford: Oxford University Press, 1949, pp. xii–xiii.

[171] Chilton, *Glory*, p. 49.

[172] Schäfer, *Vorstellung vom heiligen Geist*, p. 52, observes that a congruence exists between targumic and later rabbinic usage of 'holy spirit', rendering determination of the level of development to which this usage conforms difficult.

[173] Cf. the targumic usage of יגלי in place of the MT's יוציא.

[174] Another intriguing element of the Targums duplicates the NT reading 'in whom I am well pleased' which occurs at the baptism, transfiguration and in Matthew's version of Isa. 42.1 in 12.18. The Targum to Isa. 43.10, which is the first explicit messianic reference in the Targum, contains this reading in place of the MT's 'my servant, whom I have chosen'.

the early dating and the populist nature of the Targums argue in favour of a broad dissemination of the concept of a prophetic,[175] messianic servant uniquely endowed with God's spirit. Just how early these ideas became associated with this text, and whether the interpretation found therein is as old as Jeremias would have us believe, remains difficult to determine. The conclusion that the Targums appear to express a messianic understanding of the text that is pre-Christian appears to be sustainable.

Later Judaism

Three later uses, which are difficult to date, are also noteworthy not only because they may provide evidence of early material but also because they demonstrate the continued lines of Jewish interpretation. First, *Midr. Ps.* 2.7 appeals to both Isa. 42.1 and Isa. 52.13, in a text which seems to define 'son' in the phrase 'Thou art My son' as Israel.[176] This text is much disputed due to possible alteration by Jews in reaction to an early Christian messianic interpretation. There is no doubt, however, concerning the identity of the individual presented in the text of *Midr. Ps.* 43.3, in which any hint of a corporate understanding of the servant in Isa. 42.1 is abandoned completely. Commenting on Ps. 43.3, 'O send out your light and truth', the Midrash posits by metonymy that 'the light' is one redeemer and 'the truth' a second. The section reads,

> *Thy truth* being the Messiah, son of David; as it is written 'The Lord hath sworn in truth unto David; He will not turn from it: of the fruit of thy body will I set upon thy throne' (Ps. 132.11). Likewise Scripture says, *Behold, I will send you Elijah the prophet* (Mal. 3.23) who is one redeemer, and speaks of the second redeemer in the verse *Behold My servant whom I uphold* (Isa. 42.1). Hence 'O send out Thy light and Thy truth'.[177]

[175] Koenig, *L'herméneutique analogique*, pp. 355–7, proposes that Isa. 42.1–4 announces a new type of prophecy at the end of the exile accompanied by the Law that would become a permanent theophany, the universalized theophany of the God of Israel.

[176] Because of the antiquity of the method of midrash and the fact that the formal collection of midrash began as early as the second century AD, it is worthy of consideration in the context of NT studies. Strack and Stemberger, *Introduction*, p. 350, report that there have been haggadic collections of the Psalms from quite an early time, citing *Gen. Rab.* 32.3, which tells of an *Aggadah de-Tehillim* of R. Ḥiyya. W. G. Braude, ed., *The Midrash on the Psalms*, 2 vols., New Haven: Yale University Press, 1959, vol. I, p. xi, argues, 'even post-Talmudic Midrashim – which, to be sure, occasionally have local and temporary coloring – are in effect new literary arrangements of old material that goes back to Talmudic times.'

[177] Braude, *Midrash*, I.445.

The linking of the servant with the second redeemer, the son of David, who was to follow Elijah, strikes several chords with the Gospel tradition and Matt. 12.17ff.,[178] in which reference to the servant of Isa. 42.1–4 (12.18–21) occurs in the context of royal messiahship and in close proximity to a son of David reference (12.23).

Finally, a text from *Pesiqta Rabbati*, Pisca 36,[179] focuses upon the Messiah's pre-creational agreement to endure seven years of suffering for the sins of those on earth prior to his revelation. Also discussed is the state of the generation contemporaneous with his advent. This offers another illuminating glimpse into the interpretation of the servant of Isa. 42.

> How dare you bring charges against that generation which will be greatly esteemed for its noble conduct, a generation in which I shall rejoice, and in which I shall take delight, which I shall uphold because of My pleasure in it, as is said *Behold My servant, whom I uphold, Mine elect in whom My soul delighteth; I have put My spirit upon him*, etc. (Isa. 42.1)? How then dare you bring charges against it?[180]

Conclusion

Several conclusions may be drawn from this brief analysis. First, although a striking text, Isa. 42.1–4 was not employed with the same frequency as Isa. 11.1–10 or 61.1–2 in early Judaism. When it was, or seemed to be, used, the emphasis may generally be divided along Jeremias' lines. The Palestinian traditions tend towards a messianic interpretation, and the Diaspora community, here primarily represented by the LXX, understood the text to refer to Israel. There is no indication that the text was employed in a context of weakness or suffering, nor was the text ever associated,

[178] The OT messianic designation 'Son of David' (cf. *Ps. Sol.* 17.21), impregnated with the expectation of a Davidic descendent to inaugurate the time of salvation, is employed in the Synoptics in relation to Jesus (cf. E. Lohse, 'υἱὸς Δαυίδ', *TDNT* VIII.478–88, and F. Hahn, 'Son of David', *EDNT* III.391–2). In Matthew the occurrences are primarily in the context of healing miracles, during which the crowds either question or affirm this designation in regard to Jesus: 9.27; 12.23; 15.22; 20.30ff.; 21.9, 15.

[179] W. G. Braude, trans., *Pesikta Rabbati: Discourses for Feasts, Fasts, and Special Sabbaths*, 2 vols., Yale Judaica Series 18, New Haven and London: Yale University Press, 1968, vol. II, pp. 676–83. The first extant reference to the collection known as *Pesikta Rabbati* comes to us from Rashi (1040–1105). In the first Pisca a temporal reference suggests that 777 years have elapsed since the destruction of the Temple, indicating a compilation date during the seventh century. This dating, however, is unreliable. Pisca 36, which contains a reference to Isa. 42, forms part of the group of Piscas 34–7, which were redacted perhaps as early as the fifth century (Braude, *Pesikta Rabbati*, p. 24).

[180] *Ibid.*, pp. 679–80.

so far as we can tell, with Isa. 53. The LXX, in fact, seems to reverse the weakness evident in 42.4a with reference to Israel.

One may also cautiously assert that the passage under review contributed to the messianic conception, as it does appear to have been considered messianic in some quarters. 1QIsaᵃ, *1 Enoch, Psalms of Solomon* and possibly the Targums indicate that the passage was read messianically prior to Matthew's composition. The passage may have contributed the themes of justice and judgment, the nations, and the spirit to the conception of the messiah and the messianic age. The reasons for its lack of usage may have been due to the manner in which the individual is portrayed therein. Unfortunately, given the few documents from the period, it is difficult to construct a history of interpretation of any passage, never mind one that is used infrequently. Matthew's employment of the text provides a much more extensive usage to explore. That he builds upon existing Jewish interpretation seems reasonable in light of the Jewish usage, but although continuity between Matthew and the Jewish usage exists, Matthew's creativity is also evident in his application of this profound passage to the life and ministry of Jesus, the messiah.

4

ISAIANIC FORMULA QUOTATIONS
IN MATTHEW

In chapter 3 the fluidity and variety of text-forms during the period in which Matthew worked have been illustrated and examined. This chapter will take a sounding in Matthew's use of the Old Testament in order to determine the relationship of his usage to the phenomena of the 'non-aligned' texts, the fluid state of the textual traditions prior to the early second century AD, and the subsequent reform movement away from the 'freedom' of the LXX to translations more closely aligned with the MT. Now it is time to consider the kind of text that Matthew used and how he used it. Moreover, because the particular text I shall be scrutinizing is derived from Isaiah, such an examination must take careful notice of how Matthew appears to use the text of Isaiah.

Although the following analysis will not offer an entirely new perspective, a re-examination of the data affords an opportunity to consider Matthew's text-form in the light of current models of textual transmission. I shall also consider the final form of the text, its rhetorical force and Matthew's purportedly theological usage. As was observed in chapter 2, it is methodologically unsound, particularly bearing in mind the fluid state of the text during the first century, to separate the discussion of text-form from the rhetorical force of the final form. They are interrelated. If the author is involved in editing the text, as seems likely in Matthew, then these alterations help to illuminate the theological and narrative interests of the author.

This chapter will also evaluate the hypothesis that Matthew's appeal to Isaiah in the formula citations, especially in chs. 4–13 (4.15–16; 8.17; 12.18–21; 13.14–15), is the result of a sustained interest in the theme of the salvation of Israel and the role of Jesus in that salvation.[1] As Rothfuchs has suggested,

---

[1] R. H. Gundry, *Matthew: A Commentary on His Handbook for a Mixed Church under Persecution*, 2nd edn, Grand Rapids: Eerdmans, 1994, p. 60. I use the designation of Isaiah here in place of the modern critical construct Deutero-Isaiah because of the anachronism involved. See the recent essay by Leske, 'Isaiah and Matthew', pp. 152–69, who attempts

Vor allem aber bilden diese vier Erfüllungszitate insofern ein 'Corpus' für sich, als sie die Heilsbedeutung des Wirkens Jesu an den Verlorenen vom Hause Israel ausdrücken. Es ist diese Heilsverkündigung des Werkes Jesu an Israel, die der Evangelist mit dem Namen des Propheten Jesaja betont in Verbindung gebracht hat.[2]

Above all, these four fulfilment quotations constitute by themselves a 'corpus' in so far as they express the soteriological meaning of the work of Jesus to the lost of the house of Israel. It is this salvific proclamation of the work of Jesus to Israel that the evangelist has emphatically brought in connection with the name of the propet Isaiah.

Other authors have also echoed Rothfuchs' claims. Van Segbroeck, for example, argues that Matthew's use of Isaiah, whose primary message was salvation to Israel, is meant to further underline the failure of Israel to respond to Jesus messiah.[3] Although not immediately obvious, the conjecture that Matthew's frequent use of Isaiah represents a sustained reading in light of Israel's salvation seems worthy of further testing.

In this chapter, then, an attempt will be made to explore the two topics mentioned above: Matthew's usage of the Old Testament, and his use of Isaiah in the Isaianic citations from the opening section of Matthew. The citations to be considered are Isa. 7.14 in Matt. 1.23, 8.23b–9.1 in 4.15–16 and 53.4a in 8.17. The anticipated result of such an investigation will be to establish whether a pattern of usage of the Isaianic texts is discernible, to trace the possible implications of text-form, location and thematic content for Matthew's narrative, and to determine whether such data may contribute to a more comprehensive understanding of the role of Isa. 42.1–4 in Matt. 11–13. Three issues in particular will be examined. First, an analysis of the text-form will be conducted in an attempt to ascertain whether the variant texts of the citations reveal Matthean emphases. The second level of exploration seeks to determine the usage and meaning of the citations in their Matthean contexts. This will also require excursions into the original context of the citations in order to determine if the original context is significant for Matthew and if Matthew's usage of the wider Isaianic context is theological. Third, when I investigate

to demonstrate that the themes evinced in 2 and 3 Isaiah are further developed in later prophetic tradition and in Matthew.

[2] *Erfüllungszitate*, p. 43.
[3] 'Les citations d'accomplissement', p. 126. Also see Leske, 'Isaiah and Matthew', pp. 152–69.

Matthew's citation of Isa. 42.1–4 in chapter 5, a primary difficulty will be to determine why Matthew includes a large segment of apparently super-fluous content. Thus, special consideration will be devoted to the content in these other Isaianic citations and their possible import in their sur-rounding context and Matthean christology. Finally, a note on language usage: I have consistently used the phrase 'Matthew translates' through-out this study in lieu of the more cumbersome but precise 'Matthew's text is translated as...'

Analysis of Isaianic formula quotations

As in Qumran, Isaiah plays a prominent role in Matthew, who refers to Isaiah more than any other OT text. The Isaianic text-forms employed are somewhat varied and the apparent reasons for inclusion in the Matthean narrative are equally diverse. Although one may, it seems, discern a the-ological agenda, the extent of such an agenda is questionable. The most explicit and indisputable usage occurs in Matthew's quotation of Isa. 7.14 in 1.23. It is here that I begin the analysis.

Matthew 1.23 = Isaiah 7.14

Matthew's citation of Isa. 7.14 occurs in one of the Gospel's more com-plicated and condensed narratives (1.18–25).[4] Deciphering the pericope is difficult on almost every level, whether one wants to consider its redac-tional history, its import within the Matthean narrative as a whole or its links to the surrounding context. In the midst of this demanding pericope Matthew cites Isa. 7.14, which serves as a useful starting point for an analysis of Matthew's use of the Old Testament because of its straight-forward text-form, obvious relationship to its context, and its explicit bi-referentiality.[5]

The text-form

Matthew 1.23	LXX Isaiah 7.14	MT Isaiah 7.14
ἰδοὺ ἡ παρθένος	ἰδοὺ ἡ παρθένος	הִנֵּה הָעַלְמָה
ἐν γαστρὶ ἕξει	ἐν γαστρὶ ἕξει	הָרָה
καὶ τέξεται υἱόν,	καὶ τέξεται υἱόν	וְיֹלֶדֶת בֵּן

---

[4] C. T. Davis, 'Tradition and Redaction in Matthew 1:18–2:23', *JBL* 90 (1971): 412–14, and Pesch, 'Gottessohn', 395–6.

[5] See chapter 1 for a definition of bi-referentiality.

καὶ καλέσουσιν⁶   καὶ καλέσεις⁷   וְקָרָאת
τὸ ὄνομα αὐτοῦ   τὸ ὄνομα αὐτοῦ   שְׁמוֹ
Ἐμμανουήλ,   Ἐμμανουηλ   עִמָּנוּ אֵל:

Aquila, Symmachus and Theodotion

ἰδοὺ ἡ νεᾶνις ἐν γαστρὶ συλλαμβάνει καὶ τίκτει υἱόν,
καὶ καλέσεις ὄνομα αὐτοῦ Ἐμμανουηλ

Matthew's version of Isa. 7.14, the first of the formula citations, is generally septugintal in character, evidenced most clearly in the adoption of
the LXX reading παρθένος for הָעַלְמָה⁸ (later corrected towards the MT in
Aquila, Symmachus and Theodotion with the substitution of νεᾶνις) and
in its agreement with the LXX's ἕξει⁹ to translate the Hebrew adjective
(or participle) הָרָה.¹⁰ In 1.23b, however, Matthew's version diverges from
all known texts when it translates the MT's וְקָרָאת with the third-person
plural καλέσουσιν. The difficulty presented by the MT at this point is also
manifest in the versions of the LXX, in which the translation καλέσεις occurs in LXX A and B and καλέσει in LXX א.¹¹ Finally, it ought to be
noted that the 'translation' of Emmanuel offered by Matthew, μεθ' ἡμῶν
ὁ θεός, is the LXX text from Isa. 8.10, which further supports the LXX
lineage of Matthew's version.

---

⁶ The reading of καλέσεις is supported in D *pc* bo^mss Or and Eus, and is an adjustment
which appears to be made in light of the LXX. See also Justin, *Dial.* 66.2, in which this
reading occurs within a longer citation.
⁷ א reads καλέσει, while καλέσετε is found in Q* Luc sah Tert. Cypr. Ir.^lat and καλέσεις is
found in B A C. Note also the two variant readings in Justin: *Dial.* 66.2 includes καλέσουσι,
while *Dial.* 43.5 reads καλέσεται.
⁸ On this disputed passage see as early as Justin, *Dial.* 43, 77; Irenaeus, *Adv. haer.* 3.21.1
(= Eusebius, *HE* 5.8.10); Origen, *C. Cels.* 1.34–5; Eusebius, *DE* 7.1.
⁹ LXX A Q א Eus., *HE* 5.8.10. See also Matthew's usage of ἕχειν in 1.18, ἐν γαστρὶ
ἔχουσα.
¹⁰ LXX B, it should be noted, uses the more common LXX translation of λήμψεται for
הָרָה while the three later Greek versions (Aquila, Symmachus, Theodotion) use συλλαμβάνει. Cf. Luke 1.31; it reads, συλλήμψῃ ἐν γαστρὶ καὶ τέξῃ υἱὸν καὶ καλέσεις τὸ ὄνομα
αὐτοῦ Ἰησοῦν, which, according to Kilpatrick, *Origins*, p. 53, suggests an early connection
in the tradition.
¹¹ The Hebrew text is troublesome at this point, and much depends upon how one points
the text. The Masoretic pointing suggests a little-used third-person feminine singular (see
GKC § 74g). It should be observed, however, that the same form occurs in Gen. 16.11 in a
line of text which, apart from distinctions in person and tense, closely resembles Isa. 7.14,
and is translated as second-person singular. Observe וְקָרָאת שְׁמוֹ יִשְׁמָעֵאל כִּי־שָׁמַע יְהוָה אֶל־עָנְיֵךְ.
This parallel is quite striking for its verbal correspondence to the MT, although manuscript
evidence indicates a reading of קָרָאת (GKC § 74g). Note also that 1QIsa^a וקרא allows for
either a Pual or impersonal third-person singular form. Although Gundry's suggestion, *Use
of the Old Testament*, p. 90, that 1QIsa^a may represent the original reading is dubious, he
is probably correct that confusion in the Hebrew texts led to disorder in the Greek texts.

While it is not impossible that a divergent Hebrew text lies behind Matthew's version or that he drew upon an as yet unknown Greek translation[12] (and given the diversity of the Greek translations on this text, this is a real possibility), the most probable and simple explanation is that this variant represents a Matthean alteration made in light of contextual concerns[13] to avoid confusion between the naming of Jesus in 1.21 by Joseph, and the corporate ascription of Emmanuel in 1.23b, which was seemingly a confessional designation.[14] As observed in the previous chapter, minor adjustments of tense, person and subject to accommodate the context are common in Jewish texts of this period. One may conclude that Matthew directly or indirectly used LXX A, a text which was widely used in early Jewish-Christian circles due to its reading of παρθένος.[15] To assert direct Matthean dependence upon LXX A may be presumptuous, however, because Matthew could have instead been quoting from memory or from a written source, while consciously or unconsciously adjusting the text in his composition. This eliminates any need to posit that Matthew himself translated the Hebrew 'under the influence of the LXX'.[16]

The relationship of the citation to context and meaning

The question regarding how the citation functions within its context raises provocative issues for this study. Before addressing this puzzle directly, however, several introductory matters should be developed. First, the replacement of the name of Isaiah with the phrase ὑπὸ κυρίου in the formula introducing the citation appears to disclose Matthew's view of Scripture

---

[12] Gundry, *ibid.*, p. 90, contests that Matthew's text 'witnesses to yet another Septuagintal reading'.

[13] *Pace* Strecker, *Weg*, p. 55. Several factors complicate this discussion. For example, the question arises concerning the source of 1.18–25. Was it a source Matthew copied which already contained the citation? This is doubtful if the formula introducing the citation is Matthean, a position which scholarship now universally accepts. The citations, then, may also have been inserted by the author. For discussions concerning the sources used and possible scenarios, see Brown, *Birth*, pp. 96–121, and Soares Prabhu, *Formula Quotations*, pp. 229–53.

[14] So Stendahl, *School*, p. 98; Rothfuchs, *Erfüllungszitate*, pp. 50–60; J. Schniewind, *Das Evangelium nach Matthäus*, NTD 2, Göttingen: Vandenhoeck & Ruprecht, 1964, p. 15. Matthew's plural Greek text may have translated a Semitic impersonal plural, 'one' (cf. the variant in 1QIsaᵃ), a possible, but doubtful explanation.

[15] If Matthew had texts at his disposal which reflected Barthélemy's καιγε recension, we see no evidence of it here as Matthew clearly follows the LXX reading, although this is probably because the LXX version and its reading of παρθένος had already attained an important place in the early Christian tradition.

[16] Stendahl, *School*, p. 99; similarly, Soares Prabhu, *Formula Quotations*, pp. 230–1. The postulate of a translation from the Hebrew at this point is overly complicated, impossible to prove and unnecessary.

and prophecy; it is the Lord who speaks through the prophets (cf. 2.15).[17] On a rhetorical level, the emphasis upon the Divine speaking through the prophet seems to heighten the reader's awareness of the divine origins of the conception and role of Jesus, authorizing the narrative and elevating the discussion above the banal.[18] Second, Isa. 7.14 does not appear to have been widely cited in early Jewish literature and never in connection with a messianic figure; this suggests that the usage in Matthew is primarily an early Christian exegetical phenomenon.[19] Third, the compositional history of 1.18–25 is a very complicated affair.[20] As Kupp observes, whether the passage represents a Matthean composition based upon existing traditions,[21] the coalescing of traditions[22] or the adaptation of an already extant narrative, oral or otherwise,[23] the implication of the verbal and clausal parallels between the citation and the surrounding narrative (particularly 1.21) is that Matthew has made the passage

[17] However, Ἡσαΐου is inserted by D *pc* it sy^s.(c).h sa^ms; Ir^lat pt. Rothfuchs, *Erfüllungszitate*, pp. 40–1, asserts that reasons for the exclusion of the prophet's name here include (1) the frequency of κύριος in the infancy narrative, and (2) the fact that Isa. 7.14 is thematically distinct from the other four Isaianic citations (4.14–16; 8.17; 12.18–21; 13.35) and thus not suited to Matthew's purpose. Pesch, 'Gottessohn', 397–8, however, suggests that the reason for the inclusion of κύριος may be found in the fact that υἱός occurs in 1.23a. He argues that behind this inclusion is a linkage between son and God and a 'Son of God' christology (cf. Gundry, *Matthew*, p. 24). While this proposal is attractive, D. Verseput, 'The Role and Meaning of the "Son of God" Title in Matthew's Gospel', *NTS* 33 (1987): 537–41, is appropriately cautious, and more recently J. Nolland, 'No Son of God Christology in Matthew 1:18–25', *JSNT* 62 (1996): 4–5, argues against a Son of God emphasis in 1.22–3.

[18] This is especially so if one considers 1.22–3 to be included in the angel's pronouncement. Although this position is now generally rejected, J. C. Fenton, 'Matthew and the Divinity of Jesus: Three Questions Regarding Matthew 1:20–23', in *Studia Biblica 1978*, vol. II: *Papers on the Gospels*, edited by E. A. Livingstone, Sheffield: JSOT Press, 1979, pp. 79–80, argues in its favour. Matthew employs a similar strategy when he pits the Pharisees against the 'word of God' in 15.1–9 or in 12.7.

[19] Kupp, *Matthew's Emmanuel*, p. 166. 1QH 3.6–7 (= 1QH11.9–10) is frequently cited as possibly referring to the birth of a messiah. Isa. 7.14 is often associated with Hezekiah in contexts which are not messianic (Justin, *Dial.* 43; *Exod. Rab.* on 12.29 and *Num. Rab.* on 7.48; see Str-B I.75), although it should be noted that Hezekiah was considered messianic in the rabbinic tradition (so Davies and Allison in *Matthew*, I.177, who cite *ARN* 25; *b. Sanh.* 94a; *b. Ber.* 28b).

[20] For discussions of this topic, see Bultmann, *History*, pp. 291–4; Davis, 'Tradition and Redaction', 414–21; Brown, *Birth*, pp. 104–21; Hagner, *Matthew 1–13*, pp. 15–16; Soares Prabhu, *Formula Quotations*, pp. 294–300; and Kupp, *Matthew's Emmanuel*, pp. 159ff.

[21] Kilpatrick, *Origins*, pp. 53–5.

[22] M. Dibelius, *From Tradition to Gospel*, London: Ivor Nicholson & Watson, 1934, pp. 128–9.

[23] Brown, *Birth*, pp. 105–18; Luz, *Matthew*, p. 102; Hagner, *Matthew 1–13*, p. 16. The difficulty of Brown's attempt to determine the tradition/redactional history ought to be noted. See Kilpatrick, *Origins*, p. 53; Hagner, *Matthew 1–13* and Luz, *Matthew*, p. 116 n. 8, for lists of Matthean vocabulary in the section.

his own.[24] Fourth, in comparison with other citations, a more intimate relationship between the citation and the surrounding pericope is perhaps supported by the fact that the formula quotation is located in the middle of the pericope.[25]

How then does it function within the context? At first glance, the conclusion that Matthew's primary reason for including the citation is to validate through Scripture the unusual circumstances of Mary's conception finds substantial support in Matthew's retention and intentional use of the LXX's reading of παρθένος.[26] On a structural level, therefore, the referent of the phrase 'all this took place to fulfil' would be the previous narrative affirming the virginal conception.[27] It needs to be noted, however, that although the miraculous conception figures prominently in this pericope, it plays a minor role in Matthew's overall narrative and does not resurface in the Gospel. As observed in chapter 2, such an explanation accounts for merely one element of the citation and cannot justify the inclusion of the apparently superfluous content in 1.23b, which many rightly argue is of greater significance in the narrative.[28] It seems odd that Matthew would include the second line with its Emmanuel motif, which has no immediately obvious relationship to the conception, if his only intent was simply to validate Jesus' conception. The obvious symmetry

[24] Kupp, *Matthew's Emmanuel*, p. 161. See also Hagner, *Matthew 1–13*, pp. 15–16. Luke 1.31 also offers evidence of the use of Isa. 7.14 (see I. H. Marshall, *The Gospel of Luke: A Commentary on the Greek Text*, NIGTC, Grand Rapids: Eerdmans, 1978, p. 66; Lindars, *New Testament Apologetic*, p. 214).

[25] If one accepts that the formula is Matthean, then there is good evidence to suggest that Matthew himself constructed this text around the citation. It is perhaps easier to argue that the verbal similarities between the citation and context derive from the citation, than to suggest that the pericope existed in its present shape, that Matthew simply inserted the citation into traditional material and that the verbal correspondences are a matter of chance.

[26] F. W. Beare, *The Gospel according to St Matthew: A Commentary*, Oxford: Blackwell, 1981, p. 71. On the possibility of an apologetic motive to counter slanderous comments behind Matthew's use of παρθένος, see McConnell, *Law and Prophecy*, p. 107.

[27] R. T. France, *The Gospel according to Matthew: An Introduction and Commentary*, TNTC, Grand Rapids: Eerdmans, 1985, pp. 79–80, argues that it is the whole account of the origin and naming that is in view (similarly, Luz, *Matthew*, p. 121). Verseput, 'Son of God', 533, argues that both the 'virgin birth and divine election' are encompassed by the fulfilment.

[28] In this sense it is quite similar to the other Isaianic formula citations of 4.15–16 and 12.18–21. Kupp's argument, *Matthew's Emmanuel*, pp. 166–9, that the primary emphasis of the passage may not be the virgin birth but the Emmanuel motif is a provocative one. He does not, however, acknowledge the difficulty of assigning relevance to the material in 1.23b within its present context. See also Luz, *Theology*, p. 31, who indicates its significance, but who also notes its enigmatic character, although he pays scant attention to the difficulty presented by the presence of 1.23b, devoting most of his discussion to this theme.

produced by the placement of the presence motifs in 1.23b and 28.20 indicates, however, that this is an important theme for Matthew, even if there is little reason for this portion of the citation in the immediate context. The inclusion of 1.23b and the explicit recurrence of this theme throughout the Gospel offers a conspicuous example that may be investigated in order to determine how citations with apparently superfluous material function, and may provide clues as to how problems with other similar texts might be resolved (e.g., 4.15–16 and 12.18–21).

In an attempt to address the problem of bi-referentiality, Kupp postulates two levels of meaning. He argues that on the surface level the 'terminological correspondence' with the virginal conception 'provides basic surface congruity', but on a deeper level the 'motif of fulfilment in Emmanuel is found in its translation and association with OT divine presence'.[29] Thus Kupp maintains that the primary reason for citing the text is to justify the unusual circumstances surrounding the child's conception described in the narrative,[30] while the Emmanuel motif is cited for christological reasons.

Stendahl is certainly correct to assert that Matt. 1 is about who Jesus is, and 1.23b contributes to this programme.[31] By translating this designation as μεθ' ἡμῶν ὁ θεός, Emmanuel focuses the reader's attention and provides a prominent theme which is developed throughout the Gospel.[32] At the very least, this designation affirms that in the person of Jesus the OT conception that 'God will be present in the midst of

[29] *Matthew's Emmanuel*, p. 168. Kupp's recent thesis attempts to address this difficult issue by asserting that the conception is a secondary interest, and that Isa. 7.14 is used because (1) 'the meaning of Emmanuel "fulfils", captures best the person and mission of Jesus as narrated in Mt 1.1–21'; (2) the usage of the virgin birth possesses a more profound element, namely, as the Abrahamic and Davidic descendant, 'Jesus fulfils God's preordained plan to save and be "with" his people'; and (3) Χριστός is 'fully summed up' in the 'prophecy of the Emmanuel child as the potent agent of God's presence'. The difficulty with Kupp's proposal here is that it is not immediately obvious that Matthew's 'all this' (1.22) refers to 1.1–21 in its entirety, nor that Emmanuel and the prominence of the theme of presence can bear the contextual weight he supposes.

[30] W. C. van Unnik's observation, 'Dominus Vobiscum', in *New Testament Essays: Studies in Memory of Thomas Walter Manson, 1893–1958*, edited by A. J. B. Higgins, Manchester: Manchester University Press, 1959, p. 302 n. 58, that Justin Martyr only cites the first half of Isa. 7.14 may say more about Justin's own interests and less about his understanding of Matthew's text.

[31] K. Stendahl, 'Quis et Unde? An Analysis of Mt. 1–2' [1964], in *The Interpretation of Matthew*, edited by G. Stanton, 2nd edn, Edinburgh: T. & T. Clark, 1995, pp. 74–6; so also McConnell, *Law and Prophecy*, p. 105 and Pesch, 'Ausführungsformel' (1967), 79–80.

[32] Kupp, *Matthew's Emmanuel*, pp. 169–70; McConnell, *Law and Prophecy*, p. 106; so also Luz, *Theology*, p. 31, who observes, 'the most important aspect is the second half of the verse'.

his people to succour, judge, and save' is fulfilled,[33] or it may be that
Matthew is equating Jesus with God, as Irenaeus and much of the church
have understood it.[34] While Matthew does not explicitly equate Jesus with
God, the theme of the continued presence of Jesus with his people, which
opens the Gospel, cryptically emerges throughout the following chapters
in passages such as 17.17; 18.20; 25.31–46 and 26.29, and finds a particular parallel at the close of the book in 28.20, effectively book-ending
Matthew.[35] The prophetic declaration that 'they (the people of 1.21) will
call him Emmanuel' is recalled in the final words of the book addressed to
the disciples, 'I am with you always, to the end of the age.' Thus, the textual adjustment in 1.23 to the third-person plural (καλέσουσιν) effectively
includes this corporate element and evinces a broader theological agenda,
offering further support to the thesis that the adjustment originates with
the hand of Matthew.[36]

---

[33] D. Hill, *The Gospel of Matthew*, NCBC, London: Marshall, Morgan and Scott, 1972,
p. 80; P. Bonnard, *L'évangile selon Saint Matthieu*, 3rd edn, Commentaire du Nouveau
Testament, Neuchâtel: Delachaux & Niestlé, 1970, p. 22; van Unnik, 'Dominus Vobiscum', pp. 287–8. For an OT background on the divine presence, see now Kupp, *Matthew's
Emmanuel*, pp. 109–56, and van Unnik, 'Dominus Vobiscum', *passim*.

[34] *Adv. haer.* 3.21.4. Fenton, 'Matthew and the Divinity of Jesus', pp. 79–82, and Hagner,
Matthew 1–13, p. 21. As one might suspect, scholars are quite divided on this issue. In favour
of the position that Matthew here equates Jesus with God, the following points have been
made: (1) Matthew seems to have a high christology; (2) Jesus' presence on earth is in
contrast to God's presence in heaven; (3) the parallel with 28.20 suggests that the presence
of Jesus is aligned with that of God (whether the ἐγώ of 28.20 corresponds to the θεός
of 1.23 is difficult to determine). Finally, already by Irenaeus' time the text was read as
affirming Jesus' divinity.

[35] O. Michel, 'The Conclusion of Matthew's Gospel: A Contribution to History of the
Easter Message', in *The Interpretation of Matthew*, translated by R. Morgan, edited by G. N.
Stanton, 2nd edn, Edinburgh: T. & T. Clark, 1995, p. 45; S. C. Barton, *The Spirituality of
the Gospels*, London: SPCK, 1992, p. 11; and B. J. Malina, 'The Literary Structure and
Form of Matt. XXVIII. 16–20', *NTS* 17 (1970): 95–6. The theme of the presence of Jesus
in Matthew is complex. On this topic see J. A. Ziesler, 'Matthew and the Presence of Jesus
(1)', *EpRev* 11 (1984): 55–63; 'Matthew and the Presence of Jesus (2)', *EpRev* 11 (1984):
90–7; L. Keck, 'Matthew and the Spirit', in *The Social World of the First Christians: Essays
in Honor of Wayne A. Meeks*, edited by L. White and O. Yarbrough, Minneapolis: Fortress,
1995, 145–55; and B. Charette, '"Never Has Anything Like This Been Seen in Israel": The
Spirit as Eschatological Sign in Matthew's Gospel', *JPT* 8 (1996): 31–51.

[36] In the double naming of Jesus we learn much about his future role. Joseph is to call
the child 'Jesus', but the people will call him 'Emmanuel'. The referent of the third-person
plural ought to be considered the 'people' of v. 21. In the flow of the narrative, Luz, *Matthew*,
p. 121, may be correct that 'the people' at this point refers to the people of Israel, but surely
a reading within the Christian community would find the statement ironic, with the new
referent the universal people of God (so most commentators). This would be particularly
true upon a second reading of the Gospel. It is the very people who are saved from their sins
who will in turn call his name 'Emmanuel' due to their experience of the saving presence
of God in Jesus. Thus, already at this early point, Matthew's high christology is making an
appearance. It is difficult to determine exactly what is meant by 'sins'. As 9.2, 20.25 and

One is thus compelled to posit two levels of meaning, as Kupp and others have done, in order to account for Matthew's usage.[37] On a descriptive level, therefore, the initial element in the citation (1.23a) validates the surface level of the narrative, Mary's unusual conception, while the second element (1.23b) announces the future response of his people to him, thus serving to adumbrate the child's identity and role. As much as Joseph's naming of the child Jesus at the behest of the Angel of the Lord presages Jesus' future role as saviour, this prophetic announcement of the second naming 'Emmanuel' also contributes to Matthew's portrait of Jesus. Thus, although there are tenuous ties to the immediate context through the textual adjustment in 1.23b, the citation places new data concerning the child before Matthew's intended audience. The effective insertion of a seminal element into the flow of the narrative upon which Matthew later draws may in part explain why this text might read better without the formula citation. Matthew employs this text in a messianic fashion to validate not only the virgin birth but, perhaps more importantly, to define Jesus' identity as one in whom the community experiences the presence of God.[38]

Given that Isa. 7.14 is not employed in Judaism to support a messianic or Davidic redeemer/ruler figure, Matthew's usage is somewhat unusual, evidencing a tension with its original context. Most recently, Weren has explored the continuity and discontinuity between Matthew's usage and the Isaianic context.[39] He argues in favour of greater continuity because (1) both Matthew and Isaiah attribute the words of the prophecy to God; (2) Matthew demonstrates knowledge of the broader context of Isaiah by connecting Isa. 7.14 with 8.8, 10 in Matt. 1.24, and possibly drawing the names in the genealogy in Matt. 1.9 from LXX Isa. 7.1; and (3) the house of David is the concern of Isa. 7.2 and 13, which is also manifest in Matt. 1.1 and 20 with the title 'son of David'.[40] One might also add that both passages associate the child with the presence of God among the people to save and deliver.

26.28 indicate, Matthew appears to have a broad view of sin, which encompasses the entire individual.

[37] So also McConnell, *Law and Prophecy*, p. 108.

[38] Stanton, *Gospel for a New People*, p. 361, argues that Matthew's interests are primarily christological.

[39] 'Quotations from Isaiah', pp. 447–65. The difficulty with Weren's proposal is that he offers no evidence from the period that the passage was understood in the manner he describes. See also Dodd, *According to the Scriptures*, p. 79.

[40] On the question of the Davidic messiah in Matthew's use of the infancy traditions, see W. B. Tatum, '"The Origin of Jesus Messiah" (Matt 1:1,18a): Matthew's Use of the Infancy Traditions', *JBL* 4 (1977): 529–33.

Complicating the discussion concerning continuity and discontinuity is the fact that Isa. 7.10–17 is a notoriously difficult passage in its own right, which should caution against dogmatic assertions.[41] The most frequently observed element of discontinuity is that Matthew's interests are theological and soteriological, whereas Isaiah's concerns were geopolitical, namely, the threat to the Davidic dynasty should Ahaz be overthrown by the newly established political alliance between Rezin and Pekah (Isa. 7.5–6). The birth of the child who was to serve as a sign to that generation appears to have been expected within a few short years after the prophecy.[42] The promised child was to demonstrate God's support, and thereby the survival, of the Davidic dynasty, assuring the well-being of the people through the continuing presence of God.[43] Weren theorizes that a process of 'semantic transformation' lies at the heart of the discontinuity.[44] Liberation from 'political trouble' is transformed by Matthew to refer to liberation from 'sins'; however, this division of political and salvific concerns, popular in today's literature, may be too hasty. Certainly, Matthew does not present Jesus as threatening to overthrow Herod or the Roman Empire;[45] however, Matthew does appear to develop Jesus' role as leader of the people (1.21; 2.3, 6; 9.36), at times in direct conflict with the religious/political elite, namely Herod (2.3–4; 14.1ff.) and the Pharisees and Scribes (2.3; 9.36; 23.1ff.), and employs nationalistic language to describe Jesus' people (21.43; 27.25), all of which suggest that the troubling biblical theological issues of nation, people and land are not distant. Certainly the manner in which these themes are developed in the narrative deserves more careful analysis. It must be observed, however, that Matthew's presentation of Jesus is distinct from that of figures portrayed in other texts, such as Isa. 11.1–5, *Ps. Sol.* 17, *1 Enoch*, and so on, in which the deliverer is charged with overthrowing foreign political oppression and the purging and purification of

---

[41] J. H. Hays and S. A. Irvine, *Isaiah the Eighth-Century Prophet: His Times and His Preaching*, Nashville: Abingdon, 1987, pp. 130–6.

[42] Since Duhm, OT scholars have speculated over the historical identity of this child. It has been posited that he was the son of Ahaz (J. Scullion, 'An Approach to the Understanding of Isa. 7:16–17', *JBL* 87 (1968): 288–300) or the son of Isaiah (H. Wolff, 'A Solution to the Immanuel Prophecy in Isa 7:14–8:22', *JBL* 91 (1972): 449–56). The link for Matthew between the old and the new probably resulted from the LXX reading of παρθένος.

[43] The possible nexus between the foretold child and the Davidic dynasty is found in the declaration of 7.13, 'Hear then, O house of David' and the opening statement of v. 14, 'Therefore the Lord himself will give you a sign'. The recipient of v. 14 is presumably 'the house of David' of v. 13.

[44] 'Quotations from Isaiah', pp. 456–7.   [45] *Ibid.*, p. 456.

Israel.[46] Matthew opens his Gospel with a decided departure from such an emphasis.

If the present analysis is correct, then Matthew cites an OT text that has relevance both to the origins of Jesus, in this case scriptural support for the virginal conception, and to the broader depiction of his story of Jesus. The one who was born of a virgin will also be called Emmanuel by his people. 1.23b includes material that clearly transcends the initial context and articulates a theme that adds a profound element to Matthew's narrative and christology. The textual adjustment, which probably originates from the hand of Matthew, serves to distinguish the double naming, but it also embodies an element which corresponds to the people he would save in 1.21 and to whom he would promise his ongoing presence in 28.20. Additionally, and somewhat surprisingly, Matthew's usage, while theologically interpreted and appropriated, betrays an acquaintance with the original context and suggests a closer reading of this section of Isaiah than he has sometimes been given credit for in the past.

Matthew 4.15–16 = Isaiah 8.23b–9.1

Although Matthew's use of Isa. 7.14 is relatively straightforward and explicit, his employment of Isa. 8.23b-9.1 is not as easily explained. Similar characteristics to those of Matt. 1.23 do, however, reappear: (1) Matthew's text is distinct, possibly reflecting his concerns; and (2) the citation also appears to be bi-referential, although the second level or deeper meaning is not explicitly stated elsewhere in the Gospel. The subsequent investigation will adhere to the above method involving an initial examination of the textual distinctions followed by an analysis of the function of the citation within its context, keeping an open mind to possible Matthean emphases.

The text-form

Matthew 4.15–16	LXX Isaiah 9.1–2	MT Isaiah 8.23b–9.1
γῆ Ζαβουλὼν	χώρα Ζαβουλων	אַרְצָה זְבֻלוּן
καὶ γῆ Νεφθαλίμ,	ἡ γῆ Νεφθαλιμ	וְאַרְצָה נַפְתָּלִי
		וְהָאַחֲרוֹן הִכְבִּיד

---

[46] Several commentators have noted this point; see Hill, *Matthew*, p. 80.

		MT Isaiah
Matthew 4.15–16	LXX Isaiah 9.1–2	8.23b–9.1
ὁδὸν θαλάσσης,	ὁδὸν θαλάσσης[47]	דֶּרֶךְ הַיָּם
	καὶ οἱ λοιποὶ οἱ τὴν	
	παραλίαν κατοικοῦντες	
πέραν τοῦ Ἰορδάνου,	καὶ πέραν τοῦ Ἰορδάνου	עֵבֶר הַיַּרְדֵּן
Γαλιλαία τῶν ἐθνῶν,	Γαλιλαία τῶν ἐθνῶν	גְּלִיל הַגּוֹיִם׃
	τὰ μέρη τῆς Ἰουδαίας	
[16]ὁ λαὸς ὁ καθήμενος	ὁ λαὸς ὁ πορευόμενος[48]	הָעָם הַהֹלְכִים
ἐν σκοτίᾳ[49]	ἐν σκότει	בַּחֹשֶׁךְ
φῶς εἶδεν μέγα,	ἴδετε[50] φῶς μέγα	רָאוּ אוֹר גָּדוֹל
καὶ τοῖς καθημένοις	οἱ κατοικοῦντες	יֹשְׁבֵי
ἐν χώρᾳ καὶ σκιᾷ θανάτου	ἐν χώρᾳ καὶ σκιᾷ θανάτου	בְּאֶרֶץ צַלְמָוֶת
φῶς ἀνέτειλεν αὐτοῖς.	φῶς λάμψει ἐφ᾽ ὑμᾶς.	אוֹר נָגַהּ עֲלֵיהֶם׃

The numerous variants in the LXX translation reflect the difficulty presented by this passage in the Hebrew;[51] thus the translation found in
Matthew with its distinct text-type, frequent lacunae, and linguistic variations comes as no surprise. Because the citation is inserted into Markan
material (Mark 1.14–15), which is expanded by Matthew, the citation
presents an opportunity to analyse Matthew's use of the Old Testament
on a very fundamental level.

Matthew's text evinces contact with both the MT and LXX, and the
excision of material from both of these sources is in apparent support
of the geographical emphasis of 4.12–13. Consider Matthew's opening
line, γῆ Ζαβουλὼν καὶ γῆ Νεφθαλίμ, which is reasonably close to the
MT's אַרְצָה זְבֻלוּן וְאַרְצָה נַפְתָּלִי.[52] Matthew's excision of the MT's 8.23a
warrants his significant grammatical adjustment in this line. The verbs to

[47] Considerable doubt exists whether ὁδὸν θαλάσσης was part of the original LXX.
Absent from the text of LXX B, it is found in LXX A, Aqu and Theo. Ziegler, ed., *Isaias*,
p. 67, is unsure. Given that the phrase καὶ οἱ λοιποὶ οἱ τὴν παραλίαν κατοικοῦντες may
be a loose translation of וְהָאַחֲרוֹן הִכְבִּיד דֶּרֶךְ הַיָּם, there is good reason to doubt its authenticity.
If it was not in the LXX, then Matthew's text represents the MT at this point. See G. I.
Davies, 'Did Matthew know Hebrew?' (unpublished paper).

[48] Ziegler, ed., *Isaias*, p. 27, argues that καθήμενος, which is found in LXX A and several
other less significant texts, is probably a Matthean intrusion.

[49] The reading σκοτίᾳ is attested in א¹ B D W Or^pt. Stendahl, *School*, p. 104; Davies
and Allison, *Matthew*, I.385; and Hagner, *Matthew 1–13*, p. 70, suggest that the reading
adopted by NA²⁷ as found in א* C L Θf¹·¹³ 33 M Or^pt reflects assimilation to the LXX.

[50] The variant reading εἶδεν is found in LXX א* Luc C.

[51] Ziegler, ed., *Isaias*, p. 67, notes the uneven Hebrew in this section.

[52] The Gospel here is closer to the Greek revisions but betrays the redactional emphasis
of its author.

which the two locales serve as accusative objects in the MT have been omitted, and unlike the LXX, in which the locales function as vocatives, Matthew places them in apposition to Galilee.[53] Two further differences exist vis-à-vis the LXX text. First, Matthew consistently translates the two occurrences of אַרְצָה with γῆ whereas the LXX opts for the synonym χώρα in the first phrase.[54] The assertion that 'anarthrous γῆ + proper name is characteristic of our redactor', a proclivity which argues in favour of Matthean adjustment, must be balanced by the fact that the text of Symmachus also translates the MT with a double γῆν.[55] Second, Matthew's καὶ γῆ Νεφθαλίμ provides a careful rendering of the MT, and counters the LXX by introducing καί and omitting the feminine definite article associated with γῆ.[56] But, lest one think it all too straightforward, a point of agreement between Matthew and the LXX against the MT is found in their common spelling of Νεφθαλίμ, the final μ absent in the Hebrew singular נַפְתָּלִי.[57]

In the remainder of verse 15, Matthew's text generally mirrors the LXX; however, one must note that missing from Matthew's text are two sections

[53] Davies and Allison, *Matthew*, I.381. This could explain the reading in the accusative of Symmachus.

[54] LXX Isa. 2.7 and 37.7 also render the double אֶרֶץ with γῆ and χώρα respectively.

[55] Davies and Allison, *Matthew*, I.381, are correct in their observation that this form is unique to Matthew and occurs seven times; see also Gundry, *Matthew*, pp. 60–1, who notes that γῆ occurs in redactional material twenty-one times, six times in material unique to Matthew (cf. Soares Prabhu, *Formula Quotations*, p. 96 n. 201). These observations need to be tempered by the fact that if Matthew employed a revised LXX text, such as Symmachus, his adjustment here may be limited to the grammatical level. See W. Schenk, *Die Sprache des Matthäus: Die Text-Konstituenten in ihren makro- und mikrostrukturellen Relationen*, Göttingen: Vandenhoeck & Ruprecht, 1987, p. 110; Jones, *Matthean Parables*, p. 360 n. 13; F. Neirynck and F. van Segbroeck, *New Testament Vocabulary: A Companion Volume to the Concordance*, with the collaboration of Henri Leclercq, BETL 65, Leuven: Leuven University Press, 1984, p. 226. Previous assertions that the distinctive features in Matthew's text derive from its author are difficult to prove, particularly in light of the geographical emphasis. One possible hint may be found in the term γῆ, which Matthew appears to employ with the more narrow denotation of a geographical or tribal area, a definition not found in the other Synoptics. In addition to this, the citation of Micah 5.1 in 2.6 reads γῆ Ἰούδα against both the MT (אפרתה) and the LXX (Ἐφράθα). The minor adjustments of χώρα to γῆ and the inclusion of a καί, rather than Stendahl's 'semitic monotony', *School*, p. 104, may suggest either variants from another version or, more likely, hints of a Matthean theology of the land.

[56] 1QIsaᵃ includes the article. New, *Old Testament Quotations*, p. 103, adds that 'here Matthew has extensively adapted the LXX to his context', and later, 'There is no evidence that Matthew has translated the Hebrew.' The difficulty with New's position is that such an 'extensively adapted' LXX may in fact be a non-LXX Greek text in circulation, or perhaps Matthew translated the MT and adapted it 'with some reminiscences of the LXX' (so Soares Prabhu, *Formula Quotations*, p. 97). Cf. Rothfuchs, *Erfüllungszitate*, pp. 67–70; and McConnell, *Law and Prophecy*, p. 119.

[57] The form Νεφθάλεις occurs in Jos., *Ant.* 1.305, and Νεφθάλις in 2.181.

of the LXX that correspond to lines not found in the MT.[58] Furthermore, Matthew's rendering of דֶּרֶךְ הַיָּם with ὁδὸν θαλάσσης may follow the LXX, but if this line was originally absent from the LXX then Matthew is once again closer to the MT.[59] If ὁδὸν θαλάσσης is not the original LXX reading, its attestation in Aquila and Theodotion could indicate Matthean reliance upon a revised version, or perhaps its inclusion represents his own translation of the MT. Finally, Matthew's text parallels the LXX with two additional geographical references, πέραν τοῦ Ἰορδάνου and Γαλιλαία τῶν ἐθνῶν. While πέραν τοῦ Ἰορδάνου is a reasonable rendering of the MT, Matthew's use of Γαλιλαία τῶν ἐθνῶν betrays a LXX text,[60] this time at odds with the texts of Aquila (θίνας τῶν ἐθνῶν) and Symmachus (ὅριον τῶν ἐθνῶν).

Although Matthew's text offers a marked departure from both the MT and the LXX in 4.16, it also exhibits intermittent contact with one or the other throughout the verse. Matthew renders both participles which serve as subjects in the MT, הַהֹלְכִים and יֹשְׁבֵי, with varied cases of the participle ὁ καθήμενος rather than the more literal LXX glosses ὁ πορευόμενος and οἱ κατοικοῦντες.[61] A second anomaly occurs in Matthew's third-person

---

[58] There is some doubt whether the LXX's καὶ οἱ λοιποὶ οἱ τὴν παραλίαν κατοικοῦντες is a poor rendering of the MT's וְהָאַחֲרוֹן הִכְבִּיד. Matthew's excision of this text may simply be for contextual concerns. With the omission of τὰ μέρη τῆς Ιουδαίας, Matthew is closer to the MT and one could argue that Matthew is knowledgeable concerning the wording of the MT either 'directly or indirectly' (so G. I. Davies, 'Did Matthew Know Hebrew?'). New's assertion, *Old Testament Quotations*, p. 103, that Matthew has edited the LXX in light of the context must assume that the movement towards the MT is a mere coincidence demanded by context.

[59] See Ziegler, ed., *Isaias*, pp. 66–7, on LXX 9.1 and ὁδὸν θαλάσσης. Rather than labelling it an example of 'careless copying' (so Allen, *Matthew*, p. 34), BDF §161 (1) accounts for the 'poor Greek' by asserting that it is a 'literal translation of Hebr. דֶּרֶךְ', which here functions as a preposition (cf. BAGD, ὁδός, 554.1a).

[60] This is evidenced in the designation 'Galilee' for the MT's גְּלִיל (BDB, 165, defines גְּלִיל as 'circuit' or 'district'). Soares Prabhu's suggestion, *Formula Quotations*, p. 97, that Matthew translated the MT and arrived at the same reading as the LXX at this point is suspect.

[61] Numerous explanations have arisen regarding Matthew's use of καθήμενος in the two lines of v. 16. Rothfuchs, *Erfüllungszitate*, p. 69, suggests that the occurrence in v. 16a has been influenced by its occurrence in v. 16b. A possibility not fully explored concerns the striking similarity of the text to Luke 1.79, which reads, τοῖς ἐν σκότει καὶ σκιᾷ θανάτου καθημένοις. Perhaps both authors had access to the same Greek non-LXX text (cf. *Ode Sol.* 9.79, which has the identical text). Or Matthew may have been influenced by another passage. LXX Isa. 42.7 has the reading καθημένους ἐν σκότει for the MT's יֹשְׁבֵי חֹשֶׁךְ, which parallells Matthew's text here. LXX Ps. 106.10 (107.10) has καθημένους ἐν σκότει καὶ σκιᾷ θανάτου for the Hebrew יֹשְׁבֵי חֹשֶׁךְ וְצַלְמָוֶת (see A. Schlatter, *Der Evangelist Matthäus: Seine Sprache, sein Ziel, seine Selbständigkeit*, Stuttgart: Calwer Verlag, 1982, p. 115). Similarly, Isa. 29.18, a text which contributes to the collage in Matt. 11.5, contains the language of οἱ ἐν τῷ σκότει. Finally, Davies and Allison, *Matthew*, I.385, note *2 Bar.* 59.2, which reads, 'At that time the eternal law shone on all those who sat in darkness. . .'

singular aorist εἶδεν in contrast to the LXX's imperative plural ἴδετε for the MT's רְאוּ אוֹר גָּדוֹל, which may suggest knowledge of Hebrew.[62] Matthew departs from both the MT and LXX with his addition of καί to commence the following line and with his employment of the dative participle τοῖς καθημένοις (καὶ τοῖς καθημένοις) to translate יֹשְׁבֵי, placing Matthew closer to the Hebrew than the LXX's οἱ κατοικοῦντες. Given that יָשַׁב may be translated as either 'sit' or 'dwell',[63] Matthew's text betrays knowledge of the Hebrew. In a reading distinct from the MT, Matthew's text mirrors the LXX's ἐν χώρᾳ καὶ σκιᾷ θανάτου (for בְּאֶרֶץ צַלְמָוֶת). This likewise suggests dependence upon the LXX and it is difficult to contend that Matthew arrived at this reading independently of it.[64] Another Matthean peculiarity occurs in his rendering of the closing verb נָגַהּ with the aorist ἀνέτειλεν, which parallels εἶδεν and counters the LXX's future λάμψει.[65] Contrast is also present in the semantic variation between ἀνατέλλειν, which means 'to rise', and λάμπειν, which simply means 'to shine'.[66] One final distinction between the LXX and Matthew concerns the rendering of עֲלֵיהֶם: the LXX uses ἐφ' ὑμᾶς while Matthew, redundantly, the dative plural αὐτοῖς.

Matthew's version remains at points close to and yet distinct from the MT, the LXX and the early Greek versions. Only two instances provide firm evidence that Matthew may have known Hebrew (the use of εἶδεν and καθημένοις), but it is impossible to know whether Matthew knew

[62] Unfortunately, early non-LXX versions do not exist for this text. On the question of Ur-Lucian, Gundry, *Use of the Old Testament*, p. 107, notes that the several disagreements between Lucian and Matthew make the suggestion that Matthew was working from an Ur-Lucianic text unlikely. The fact that they agree on εἶδεν is probably a coincidence of translational demands.

[63] BDB, pp. 442–3.

[64] In order to present Matthew as a Targumist, Gundry, *Use of the Old Testament*, p. 107, is forced to argue that the MT may be corrupted at this point and that a Hebrew *Vorlage*, which both the LXX and Matthew mirror, lies behind their translations. Another option is that the LXX has been corrupted by Matthew (so Davies and Allison, *Matthew*, I.386). Of note is the fact that Luke 1.79 contains the text ἐν σκότει καὶ σκιᾷ θανάτου, which, apart from σκότει, possesses grammatical and verbal agreement. Perhaps this is evidence of a common source.

[65] Stendahl, *School*, pp. 105–6, proposed a possible link here to the OT Peshitta *denāḥ*, which may in turn 'preserve the text of a Targum lost to us'. But Soares Prabhu, *Formula Quotations*, pp. 99–100, rightly notes that *denāḥ* may mean either 'to rise up' or 'to shine' (so M. Jastrow, *A Dictionary of the Targumim, the Talmud Babli and Yerushalmi, and the Midrashic Literature*, 2 vols., New York: Pardes, 1950).

[66] Matthew's rendering of ἀνατέλλειν for the MT נָגַהּ is quite free; it is never used to translate this verb in the LXX. It is possible that the source of this reading derives from Isa. 58.10, with its context and ideas resembling 8.23–9.1, or perhaps Num. 24.17 or Mal. 4.2 (cf. *T. Sim.* 7.1 and Heb. 7.14); so Lindars, *New Testament Apologetic*, p. 198; Lohmeyer, *Matthäus*, p. 64 n. 1.

the language and used the Hebrew text or whether he simply had access to another non-LXX version.[67] The clear modifications with respect to the LXX raise serious doubts whether the LXX was the base text, although agreement with the LXX against all known versions at two points (Γαλιλαία τῶν ἐθνῶν (v. 15) and ἐν χώρα καί σκιᾷ θανάτου (v. 16)) implies familiarity with the LXX. Such a state of affairs renders Matthew's text very similar to what Tov designated as 'non-aligned' and may very well represent the work of a scribe. The assertion that several of the adjustments to the citation betray Matthew's own hand may only be made, it seems, if the peculiarities are reflected in the surrounding context. Thus, the function of the citation within its context must be considered a key factor when determining whether Matthew simply drew upon an already existing Greek translation that was closer to the MT.

The relationship of the citation to context and meaning

Few reasons exist which would cause one to doubt that on a surface level Isa. 8.23b–9.1 is included to validate Jesus' move to Capernaum[68] or, perhaps more accurately, to demonstrate how Jesus of Nazareth's geographical movements fulfilled Scripture, thereby authorizing him as the one whom the early Christians believed him to be. The emphasis upon geography in Matthew's narrative and in the quotation (Isa. 8.23b) also squares with the detailing of the geographical movements of Jesus' life found thus far in the Gospel.[69] Given the inclusion of Isa. 9.1, however, it would be naive to assert that this fully accounts for the incorporation of the entire citation. Attempts to imbue the citation with greater significance in the Gospel have in part been hampered by the fact that Galilee appears to lack theological import and by Matthew's use of ambiguous

[67] Scholars who posit that Matthew translated directly from the Hebrew include Beare, *Matthew*, p. 116; Rothfuchs, *Erfüllungszitate*, pp. 67–70; McConnell, *Law and Prophecy*, p. 119. Gundry, *Use of the Old Testament*, p. 108, offers a moderating position by noting, 'This quotation, we conclude, shows some contact with the LXX, but is primarily an independent rendering of the Hebrew.' R. R. Ottley, *The Book of Isaiah according to the Septuagint (Codex Alexandrinus)*, vol. II, text and notes, Cambridge: Cambridge University Press, 1906, pp. 152–3, argues that Matthew employed another LXX, which was nearer to the MT than ours. Strecker's argument, *Weg*, pp. 63–6, that Matthew used a Testimony here seems the least likely option given that the changes seem to have been made in light of the surrounding context. New, *Old Testament Quotations*, p. 103, rejects the position that Matthew may have used a version 'akin to that of Aquila, Symmachus, or Theodotion'; however, his reason for doing so is not compelling.

[68] Rothfuchs, *Erfüllungszitate*, p. 67.

[69] So Stendahl, 'Quis et Unde?', pp. 71–4, and Davies and Allison, *Matthew*, II.380. The problem produced by the fact that Capernaum is not mentioned in the Old Testament is resolved by its location in the region of Naphtali and beside the sea.

language and ideas not widely disseminated.[70] One may, however, perceive a greater depth of meaning in the citation without attaching undue
emphasis to Galilee. In a manner resembling those in Matt. 1.23b and
2.6b,[71] the citation in 4.16 may endow a profound element to the narrative. To demonstrate this, three topics will be briefly discussed: the original
historical context of the citation; the emphases of the various versions;
and the function of Matt. 4.12–17 and the poetic imagery present within
the citation itself.[72]

Both continuity and discontinuity exist between Matthew's use of the
citation and its historical and literary context in Isaiah.[73] While investigations remain largely speculative, scholarship has pointed to some curious
correspondences. Although one cannot be certain, it seems that Isaiah's
prophecy addressed the historical situation observed in 2 Kings 15.29 and
1 Chron. 5.26, in which the Israelites from the entire region of Naphtali
were the first to be taken into captivity and suffer physical and political
oppression at the hands of Tiglath-pileser III and the Assyrians during
733–732 BC. Isaiah 9 addresses 'the annexation of the northern part of
Israel c.732 B.C.' and 'his [Tiglath-pileser's] organization of it into three
provinces'.[74] In the MT, Isaiah's proclamation to these northern regions
incorporates the promise of freedom (9.4–5) and of 'endless peace' under
the just and righteous rule of the Davidide (Isa. 9.6–7).[75] The versions
of the LXX and Targum modify this picture somewhat in their translations.
The LXX, through its inclusion of the line τὰ μέρη τῆς Ιουδαίας (a phrase
omitted by Matthew), has essentially abandoned the geographical parameters of the MT of the two northern regions and broadened the text to refer

---

[70] Further complicating this theory is the fact that up to this time no eschatological
expectation from the period has been associated with Galilee (so Davies and Allison,
Matthew, II.381).

[71] Although there is not room to discuss Matt. 2.6 in depth, this text confirms the present
work in the following ways: (1) the textual adjustments reflect the theological emphases of
Matthew; and (2) while a geographical query regarding the messiah's birthplace initially
prompted appeal to the text, the citation makes a much broader statement concerning the
messiah's/Jesus' person and ministry, namely, that his origins derive from the royal tribe of
Judah, and thus he fulfils the anticipated leadership role as the ideal Davidic King.

[72] This text has been most recently addressed by Weren, 'Quotations from Isaiah',
pp. 447–65, and Soares Prabhu, *Formula Quotations*, pp. 88–135.

[73] Isa. 8.23 is a complicated text on both linguistic and historical levels. For a comprehensive discussion of the issues, see J. A. Emerton, 'Some Linguistic and Historical
Problems in Isaiah VIII.23', *JSS* 14 (1969): 151–73, and particularly his conclusions on
p. 171 regarding the crux terms הקל and הָאַחֲרוֹן.

[74] Emerton, *ibid.*, 156.

[75] This interpretation depends, of course, upon how one translates Isa. 8.23. The Hebrew
is quite difficult at this point.

to all Israel.[76] The Targums, by way of comparison, 'historicize' the text, further emphasizing the events of the past.[77]

In contrast to the interpretations of the LXX and Targums, Matthew appears to draw upon the geographical specificity of the MT in support of Jesus' movements and his messianic ministry. As noted above, Matt. 4.12–13 marks Jesus' move from Nazareth to Capernaum, the town that would become his home, documenting a shift that accounts for the geographical focus of the citation in the edited version. More than a mere physical change of location, however, this move to Capernaum/Galilee (in the region of Naphtali) in 4.12–17 also marks the movement in the narrative from John the Baptist to Jesus. This is accomplished by its comment upon the beginning of Jesus' ministry and becomes further clarified in the summary of Jesus' message in 4.17.[78] In order to understand this more fully, the knotty issue concerning the role of Matt. 4.12–17 must be addressed.

The structure of Matthew as a whole is unresolvedly complex, and Matt. 4.12–17, an important moment in the Gospel, provides no relief.[79] Matt. 4.12–17 corresponds to Mark 1.14–15, which Matthew redactionally expands, adjusting 4.12 (= Mark 1.14a) and inserting new material in verse 13, the formula citation in verses 4.14–16 and the redactional summary of Jesus' proclamation in verse 17 (= Mark 1.14b–15).[80] Matt. 4.12–17 offers a highly condensed pericope, which appears to function as a transition in the narrative[81] linking the prior context, 1.1–4.11, which introduces Jesus, with 4.18ff., which focuses upon Jesus' ministry in

[76] Soares Prabhu, *Formula Quotations*, pp. 92–4; Weren, 'Quotations from Isaiah', p. 461. See Seeligmann, *Septuagint Version*, pp. 118–19, who also notes the messianic character of the text in the LXX, with its emphasis upon the announcer and bringer of a peaceful rule characterized by justice and right.

[77] So Soares Prabhu, *Formula Quotations*, pp. 94–5; cf. Chilton, *The Isaiah Targum*, p. 21.

[78] So Hagner, *Matthew 1–13*, p. 74 and Weren, 'Quotations from Isaiah', pp. 461–2.

[79] For example, Gundry, *Matthew*, p. 11, considers Matthew 'structurally mixed'.

[80] While Mark 1.14b contains a summary of Jesus' message, Matthew redacts the text and gives both John (Matt. 3.2) and Jesus (4.17) the same summary message, μετανοεῖτε· ἤγγικεν γὰρ ἡ βασιλεία τῶν οὐρανῶν.

[81] Weren, 'Quotations from Isaiah', p. 462, who labels it a 'hinge narrative', and Hagner, *Matthew 1–13*, p. 74. Kingsbury, *Christology*, p. 51, agrees that 4.12–16 is transitional. J. Gnilka, *Das Matthäusevangelium*, 2 vols., HTKNT, Freiburg: Herder, 1986, p. 99, concurs with Kingsbury that v. 17 ought to be taken with vv. 18ff., but for different reasons. F. Neirynck, ΑΠΟ ΤΟΤΕ ΗΡΞΑΤΟ and the Structure of Matthew', in *Evangelica II 1982–1991*, edited by F. Neirynck and F. van Segbroeck, BETL, Leuven: Leuven University Press, 1991, p. 146, accepting the traditional argument, asserts that '4,12 marks the beginning of Jesus' ministry'.

Galilee.[82] Connected to the preceding material through the inclusion of the news of John's imprisonment (4.12), the section commences with Jesus' resultant 'withdrawal' to Capernaum. With John removed from the scene, the door is open for Jesus to begin his ministry in Galilee.[83] The summary declaration, 'Repent, for the Kingdom of heaven is near', not only continues John's proclamation (3.2), but, for Matthew, marks the dawning of the messianic age.

Key to the structure in this section is the much disputed formula ἀπὸ τότε ἤρξατο in 4.17. Although Kingsbury and others offer a forceful argument that the formula indicates a new section in the Gospel (4.17–16.20), Neirynck's case that 4.12–17 constitutes one pericope remains more convincing.[84] As Neirynck observes, enough connections exist between 4.17 and 4.12–16 to warrant that it be included in the same paragraph.[85] Similarly, the proposed break between 16.20 and 16.21, in which the identical formula occurs, is frustrated by the fact that 16.21–3 is thematically linked to 16.13–20.[86] 4.12–17, because it associates the events of John's imprisonment, Jesus' relocation, and the advent of Jesus' proclamation with the formula citation, signals that the pericope concerns new beginnings and the providence of God.[87] Within this framework, the import of the citation is given greater clarity – Matthew's interests move beyond a purely geographical proof-text.

The citation itself confirms that this reading is plausible. As noted above, the verbal links between verse 15 of the citation and the

[82] The structure of Matthew at this point is disputed. The assertion of E. Krentz, 'The Extent of Matthew's Prologue: Toward the Structure of the First Gospel', *JBL* 83 (1964): 410–11; Kingsbury, *Christology*, p. x; and D. R. Bauer, *The Structure of Matthew's Gospel: A Study in Literary Design*, JSNTSup 31, Sheffield: JSOT Press, 1988, pp. 73–8, that the phrase ἀπὸ τότε ἤρξατο marks a distinct division in 4.17 and again in 16.21 is weak on several levels: (1) it fails to account adequately for the five narrative/discourse blocks; (2) other formulae are more prominent; (3) it also occurs in 26.16 with some import (see extended critique in Neirynck, 'Structure', pp. 153–4).

[83] Both 4.12–17 and 14.14 (cf. 11.7–15) seem to present the relationship and ministries of John and Jesus as somehow connected. Cf. also 11.11, 12; 14.13. For full discussion see the conclusions of J. P. Meier, 'John the Baptist in Matthew's Gospel', *JBL* 90 (1980): 401–5 and especially W. Trilling, 'Die Täufertradition bei Matthäus', *BZ* 3 (1959): 271–89.

[84] Krentz's position, 'Matthew's Prologue', 409–14, that 1.1–4.16 is the opening section of the Gospel has been championed by Kingsbury, *Christology*, pp. 16, 23, and Soares Prabhu, *Formula Quotations*, pp. 120–3. See Neirynck, 'Structure', pp. 141–5, especially p. 142 n. 5, for a history of scholarship on this issue and an extensive bibliography.

[85] Neirynck, 'Structure', p. 152; *pace* Soares Prabhu, *Formula Quotations*, pp. 120–3.

[86] So especially France, *Evangelist and Teacher*, p. 152.

[87] Howell, *Matthew's Inclusive Story*, p. 129, suggests that the ἀπὸ τότε refers to John's arrest, and it is from this point that Jesus 'begins' his ministry; so also Edwards, *Matthew's Story*, p. 18.

surrounding context are well documented and require only a passing mention. The geographical designations Ζαβουλών and Νεφθαλίμ from verse 13 are reproduced in their LXX orthography in the citation. The phrase from the citation ὁδὸν θαλάσσης finds a corresponding term in the *hapax legomenon* παραθαλασσίον (4.13), which describes Capernaum, thus coupling Capernaum with the regions of Zebulun and Naphtali. The significance of these observations is enhanced if, as seems likely, verse 13 is a Matthean composition.[88] Finally, the LXX phrase 'Galilee of the Gentiles', a phrase which Davies and Allison assert provides the reason for the inclusion of this citation,[89] while a historically accurate designation for this region,[90] anticipates statements throughout the Gospel concerning the place of the gentiles in the community of faith. That it has a 'fiktiven Character' and presages the gentile mission is no doubt true;[91] however, one must be cautious of too quickly dismissing any concern for the land and people of Israel in this statement. Matthew's emphasis upon Jesus' move to Capernaum and the mention of Zebulun and Naphtalai may suggest a desire to demonstrate that the messiah went initially to the tribes of Israel who were the first to be taken into captivity (cf. 10.5–6; 15.24).[92] Freyne combines the two concerns in his assertion that 'The importance of Galilee ... is not that Matthew exploits its gentile associations during the ministry as in Mark, but rather that as part of Israel, a ministry that was conducted there once can now be justified as a messianic

---

[88]   See the extended discussion by Soares Prabhu, *Formula Quotations*, pp. 129–34, who asserts that 4.13 is a Matthean creation based upon the citation (also Davies and Allison, *Matthew*, I.376, who label it a 'redactional sentence'). Additionally, Γαλιλαία and the phrase πέραν τοῦ 'Ιορδάνου recur in the summary of Jesus' ministry in 4.25, suggesting their influence upon the broader geographical composition of Matthew.

[89]   *Matthew*, I.383; Garland, *Matthew*, p. 41.

[90]   The topic of Galilee necessitates a complex discussion, due in part to the dearth of evidence from the area. The studies of S. Freyne, *Galilee, Jesus, and the Gospels: Literary Approaches and Historical Investigations*, Philadelphia: Fortress, 1988, pp. 259–334; E. Meyers, 'The Cultural Setting of Galilee: The Case of Regionalism and Early Judaism', in *ANRW* II. 19.1, Berlin and New York: de Gruyter, 1979, pp. 686–702; and R. Horsley, *Archaeology, History, and Society in Galilee: The Social Context of Jesus and the Rabbis*, Valley Forge: Trinity Press International, 1996, offer extended treatments. One thing is clear from recent study: the population of Galilee, like its neighbour to the south, was characterized by diversity and included a devout Jewish population, particularly after the Hasmonean expansion. Thus, Garland's reference to 'the reviled Galilee of the Gentiles (see I Macc 5.15)', *Matthew*, p. 41, seems to reflect an uncritical usage of 1 Maccabees for historical reconstruction. Furthermore, from a Jewish perspective, it was within the boundaries of the Land of Israel.

[91]   Luz, *Matthäus*, I.171.

[92]   Jones, *Matthew*, p. 24. There is not room to explore this in greater detail at this point, but one wonders whether there is in Matthew a greater concern for the Land than is otherwise understood.

visitation to Israel, which is also to encompass all the nations, as the Isaianic prophecies had foretold.'[93]

Matt. 4.16 contains parallel lines of Hebrew poetry, which, because they evidence slight distinctions, probably ought to be considered an example of synthetic or, to use R. Alter's designation, 'semantic' parallelism. Alter urges that 'the characteristic movement of meaning is one of heightening or intensification... of focusing, specification, concretization, even what could be called dramatization'.[94] The passage that Matthew cites and the manner in which he quotes it demonstrate a linkage between the geographical element in verse 15 and the descriptive element of verse 16. Although a semantic shift from land to people occurs, that the people of the land mentioned in verse 15 are the addressees in verse 16 is implied. Two themes are present in verse 16, represented by the imagery of darkness and light. The simple observation of line $16a^1$, 'the people, who are sitting in darkness', is heightened in $16b^1$, 'to those who sat in the region and darkness of death'. Similarly, the predicate in line a^2, 'have seen a great light', is offered greater specificity in b^2, 'a light has risen/dawned'. The elementary representation of light and darkness can communicate release from bondage, death, oppression into freedom and liberty; this is evocative imagery that is perhaps too profound to include in a section that is strictly interested in a shift of house. To determine whether such is the case, the issue concerning the referents of 'the people' and 'light', and the meaning of 'sitting in darkness' needs to be determined.

The identification of λαός in Matthew has been obfuscated by discussions of texts such as 21.43 and 27.25 in connection with the larger issue of Matthew's understanding of Christianity's relationship to Judaism and salvation history.[95] In the introductory section of 1.1–4.11(17), however, in which the term λαός occurs four times (1.21; 2.4, 6; 4.16), determining its referent is not nearly as complex. Immediately following the genealogy, which includes something of a history of the Jewish people, 1.21 implies that those who are to be saved 'from their sins' would most naturally comprise Israel.[96] Two other uses occur in ch. 2. In 2.4, the phrase γραμματεῖς τοῦ λαοῦ identifies the people as Jews. Similarly, the

---

[93] *Galilee, Jesus, and the Gospels*, p. 90; see his helpful treatment on pp. 70–90.

[94] *The Art of Biblical Poetry*, New York: Basic Books, 1985, p. 19.

[95] The term occurs fourteen times in Matthew: 1.21; 2.4, 6; 4.16, 23; 13.15; 15.8; 21.23; 26.3, 5, 47; 27.1, 25, 64. Saldarini, *Matthew's Christian-Jewish Community*, pp. 27–43, argues for a non-theological reading. Those in favour of a theological reading are Frankemölle, *Jahwebund*, pp. 191–220; P. Beauchamp, 'L'évangile de Matthieu et l'héritage d'Israël', *Recherches de science religieuse* 76 (1988): 5–38; and Trilling, *Das wahre Israel*, pp. 61–79.

[96] This is not to say that a second reading would not disclose the irony of the statement and the fact that the Jews had rejected their messiah.

occurrence in 2.6, which arises within the citation of 2 Sam. 5.1 (cf. 1 Chron. 11.2),[97] explicitly identifies the people as Israel in its announcement that the messiah will be 'a leader/shepherd of my people Israel'.[98] One may conclude, then, that on the narrative level, in these initial stages at least, 'the people' are Jews. Once again, however, attention must also be drawn to the fact that the inclusion of 'Galilee of the Gentiles' in 4.15 substantially colours the referent of λαός (4.16) and foreshadows the inclusion of the gentiles into the people of God explicitly stated in 28.18–20.

More difficult, however, is the determination of the meaning of the phrases 'who sit in darkness' and 'those who sit in the region and shadow of death'. Few clues are offered in the context to assist the reader's comprehension, and, if one were to limit the discussion exclusively to Matthew, then it must be acknowledged that this poetic language is difficult to trace. The powerful imagery may simply refer to the eradication of darkness in the presence of light or imply that the people are waiting in 'ignorance'.[99] Perhaps aware of these idioms through exposure to texts such as Ps. 107.10–11, in which rebellion against God is the cause of the state of darkness, an informed reader, one could argue, might think of the spiritual condition of Israel; or they might possibly recall the darkness and blindness in Isa. 42.7, which is more akin to political exile.[100] In the NT realm, the imagery most often refers to moral decay.[101] One Matthean connection frequently evoked is 1.21, in which the assertion 'he will save his people from their sins' assumes a state of sinfulness from which the people needed saving.[102] It is also possible that Matthew may have had in mind the aimlessness evoked in 9.36, in which the people are described as sheep without a shepherd.[103] Thus, Jesus is not only the people's saviour; he is also their new shepherd/king.

---

[97] While it is possible that Micah 5.3 is in mind here, the verbal correspondence of Matthew's text with LXX 2 Sam. 5.1 should be preferred over a text which Matthew would have had to edit.

[98] Schenk, *Sprache*, p. 128.

[99] New, *Old Testament Quotations*, p. 103. Cf. Jones, *Matthew*, p. 24, who argues in favour of the 'new freedom offered by the restitution of God's kingdom'.

[100] Beare, *Matthew*, p. 116, urges that the phrase refers to 'a nation sunk in gloom'. Cf. Hagner, *Matthew 1–13*, p. 174.

[101] Davies and Allison, *Matthew*, I.385; in support they cite Luke 1.79; John 1.5, 3.19; 8.12; Rom. 2.19; 3.12; Eph. 5.8, 11; Col. 1.13; 1 Thess. 5.4–5; 1 Pet. 2.9; 1 John 2.9, 11. Each of the uses of σκότος or σκοτεία provides support for such a usage.

[102] Luke's usage in 1.77–9 is similar, in which he links 'knowledge of salvation' to the 'forgiveness of sins'.

[103] Weren, 'Quotations from Isaiah', p. 463, notes this possible emphasis in addition to a linkage with 1.21 and being trapped in sin.

Matthew's use of the 'light' motif may aid in understanding his utilization of darkness. While it is possible that Matthew may be simply presenting Jesus as a revealer,[104] such an explanation does not fully account for the imagery. Not a major motif in Matthew, 'light' is used sparingly. The rising star in 2.2 illustrates one usage of light, but this is not picked up again in the narrative. Similarly, the uses in 5.14 and 16, which admonish the disciples to be the 'light of the world', remain undeveloped.[105] While the term φῶς may not be especially illuminating, Matthew's redactional inclusion of the aorist ἀνέτειλεν may provide some assistance. ἀνατέλλειν, which means either 'to sprout' or 'to arise',[106] is most conspicuous in its use in LXX Num. 24.17, where it is interpreted messianically (ἀνατελεῖ ἄστρον ἐξ Ιακωβ καὶ ἀναστήσεται ἄνθρωπος ἐξ Ισραηλ).[107] The related noun ἀνατολή in LXX Jer. 23.5, Zech. 3.8 and 6.12 translates צֶמַח, which, as Schlier observes, was equated with messiah, especially in the synagogue.[108] In light of these uses, the reference in Matt. 2.2, 'for we saw his star *at its rising*' (ἐν τῇ ἀνατολῇ),[109] may not be as banal as it first appears and may instead suggest a messianic interpretation.[110] In addition to these texts, passages such as Mal. 4.2, 'the son of his righteousness will rise', or Isa. 42.7, 'a light to the nations', may also have impacted on the language used. Such an idea also finds a parallel in the Gospel of John, in which the theme of Jesus bringing light to a dark world is common.[111] These texts, plus the fact that the light of the messiah seems to have been known in rabbinic literature,[112] present a strong case in favour of the position that in the use of the words 'the light

---

[104] So Stendahl, *School*, pp. 117, 141–2.

[105] Other uses of φῶς occur in 6.23; 10.27; and 17.2.

[106] LSJ, p. 123; H. Schlier, 'ἀνατέλλω, ἀνατολή', *TDNT* I.351–2.

[107] Num. 24.17 is used messianically in CD 7.18–19; 1QM 11.6; 4Q175.12 (4QTest); *T. Levi* 18.3; *T. Jud.* 24.1. Similarly, LXX Ezek. 29.21 seems to employ ἀνατέλλειν with a messianic nuance.

[108] Schlier, 'ἀνατολή', pp. 352–3.

[109] Frequently noted in this regard is that a translation of 'in the east' for ἐν τῇ ἀνατολῇ in Matt. 2.2 is erroneous; instead, the idiom is better rendered 'at its rising', referring to the star followed by the Magi. Cf. Ign., *Eph.* 19.1–3. Passages in the New Testament that refer to Jesus as the Star include Luke 1.78; 2 Pet. 1.19; and Rev. 22.16. See further O. Michel, 'Das Licht des Messias', in *Donum Gentilicium: New Testament Studies in Honour of David Daube*, edited by E. Bammel, C. K. Barrett and W. D. Davies, Oxford: Clarendon, 1978, *passim*.

[110] Schlier, 'ἀνατέλλω', p. 353, observes regarding Justin's exegesis of ἀνατολή in Zech. 6.12, 'Justin always understands the ἀνατολή of Zech. 6.12 (*Dial.*, 100,4; 106,4; 121,2; 126,1) in terms of the ἀνατέλλειν of LXX Num. 24.17, so that for him the advent of Christ is the rising of a star.'

[111] John 1.9; 8.12; 12.35, 46 (as also noted in Davies and Allison, *Matthew*, I.386).

[112] See Str-B I.161–2; also O. Michel, 'Das Licht des Messias', pp. 140–50, whose starting point is the bright light that appeared to Paul on the road to Damascus.

has dawned' Matthew had in mind the arrival of the messianic age and its concomitant blessing. If Matthew had the full context of the citation in view, especially Isa. 9.6–7, then such an understanding seems most likely. The referent may be the historic Jewish population to the north and/or foreshadow the gentile inclusion into the people of God. This explanation has the added benefit of agreeing with Matthew's presentation of Jesus thus far in the narrative and is later confirmed (11.2–6).

The textual distinctiveness of Matthew's citation of 4.15–16 suits his context perhaps too well, suggesting editorial work on some level. Whether he began with the MT and produced a translation or adapted a Greek version is impossible to know. It is curious, however, that there remain strong correspondences to the LXX. The text also betrays a use similar to that of Isa. 7.14 in Matt. 1.23, in which relevance is found on two distinct levels. Here in 4.15–16 not only is Jesus' geographical movement to Capernaum validated through Scripture, but Matthew also corroborates his ministry in Galilee and the future outreach to the gentiles expressed most explicitly in 28.18–20. Through the use of the evocative imagery of light and darkness, Matthew establishes that in Jesus' person and ministry the light of the messianic age has dawned in the north– that is, if the inclusion of ἀνατέλλειν is indeed Matthean, as seems most likely. The MT's emphasis upon geography and release from political and physical oppression may thus be understood as expanded in Matthew to incorporate not only geographical elements but the freedom which accompanies the arrival of the kingdom of God. As Senior observes, 'The summary of Jesus' ministry that follows. . . and the whole narrative of the Gospel will illustrate the meaning of this text. The Matthean Jesus saves both Jew and Gentile from the burden of sin (1.21).'[113] Thus, the text continues Matthew's concerns for the establishment and reconstitution of the people of God through his spirit-endowed messiah.

Matthew 8.17 = Isaiah 53.4a

The substantive issues of intended meaning and broader significance arise once again with the citation of Isa. 53.4a in Matt. 8.17, in what initially appears to be a simple proof-text to validate Jesus' healing ministry. Since the challenge presented by Hooker to the longstanding assumption that

---

[113] D. P. Senior, *Matthew*, ANTC, Nashville: Abingdon, 1998, p. 63. Cf. Weren, 'Quotations from Isaiah', p. 464, who opines that this quotation 'contains the main lines of the entire Gospel in a nutshell'.

espied a reference to a suffering servant,[114] one cannot read 8.17 without
questioning the extent of Matthew's meaning. Is it simply a proof-text
which validates Jesus' acts of healing, or is there more than mere theological exuberance behind claims that a profound theological perception
of Jesus' role is found within? Several converging issues contribute to
the difficulty posed by this quotation. In 8.17 Matthew exercises editorial licence, including Isa. 53.4a while omitting 53.4b. In addition to this
redactional activity, Matthew's text-form is distinct, raising the inevitable
queries concerning its source, relationship to the surrounding context and
rhetorical function within the narrative. Given the general tenor of Isa. 53,
it is curious that Matthew does not explicitly raise the issue of vicarious
suffering, but Hooker may have overstated her case with the assertion
that

> There is no thought in this verse of any expiation of sin; the
> meaning is certainly not that the guilt which caused the suffering
> was transferred in some way to Jesus ... Matthew's purpose
> here is to show that Jesus' work was foreordained by God, and
> foreshadowed in the Old Testament, not to derive evidence from
> the Old Testament for any doctrine concerning the meaning of
> that work.[115]

Before attempting to address these broader, complex issues of context
and meaning, however, a description of the text-form and investigation
into the possible source may contribute to the subsequent discussion.

The text-form

Matthew 8.17	LXX Isaiah 53.4a	MT Isaiah 53.4a
αὐτὸς τὰς ἀσθενείας ἡμῶν ἔλαβεν	οὗτος τὰς ἁμαρτίας ἡμῶν φέρει	אָכֵן חֲלָיֵנוּ הוּא נָשָׂא
καὶ τὰς νόσους ἐβάστασεν	καὶ περὶ ἡμῶν ὀδυνᾶται	וּמַכְאֹבֵינוּ סְבָלָם

Targum

בכין על חובנא הוא יבעי ועויתנא
בדיליה ישתבקן ואנחנא חשיבין
כתישין מחן מן קדם יהוה ומענן

---

[114] *Jesus and the Servant*, p. 3.   [115] *Ibid.*, p. 83.

Aquila, Symmachus[116]

ὄντως αὐτὸς νόσους ἡμῶν ἀνέλαβεν
καὶ τοὺς πολέμους[117] ἡμῶν ὑπέμεινεν.

Regardless of recent assertions to the contrary, it is doubtful that the LXX forms the basis for Matthew's translation of this passage.[118] Matthew's text bears little resemblance to the 'spiritualized' emphasis evidenced within the LXX and Targum, and appears to represent a more physical and literal non-LXX translation which is, upon detailed examination, quite faithful to the MT[119] and close at points to Aquila and Symmachus.

Matthew's first line generally follows the same grammatical structure as the MT, LXX and versions of Aquila and Symmachus: pronoun + object + pronoun + verb. The resemblances, however, end there. Opening with αὐτός for הוּא, in contrast to the LXX's less precise οὗτος, Matthew's text omits אָכֵן.[120] Likewise, in contrast to the LXX's spiritualized τὰς ἁμαρτίας ἡμῶν, Matthew's text renders the Hebrew חֳלָיֵנוּ with the more literal τὰς ἀσθενείας ἡμῶν. Although the two terms ἀσθενεία and חֳלִי are not precise equivalents, they do overlap; חֳלִי, which denotes physical disease or sickness, possesses a more narrow semantic range than ἀσθενεία, which, in addition to physical disease and illness,[121] also encompasses general weakness, moral feebleness or even poverty.[122] Noteworthy is the

---

[116] One should also note Ign., Pol. 1.3, ' "Bear the sicknesses" of all as a perfect athlete' (πάντων τὰς νόσους βάσταζε ὡς τέλειος ἀθλητής). There remains some question as to whether 1 Pet. 2.24 evinces dependence upon Matthew or represents an independent rendering of another source: ὃς τὰς ἁμαρτίας ἡμῶν αὐτὸς ἀνήνεγκεν ἐν τῷ σώματι αὐτοῦ ἐπὶ τὸ ξύλον, ἵνα ταῖς ἁμαρτίαις ἀπογενόμενοι τῇ δικαιοσύνῃ ζήσωμεν, οὗ τῷ μώλωπι ἰάθητε.

[117] Symmachus reads πόνους.

[118] Most recently, New, Old Testament Quotations, pp. 104–5. While New's proposal is possible, the extent of the adaptation could as easily demonstrate that Matthew translated from the Hebrew or used another existing Greek translation. Only a bias towards Matthew using the LXX as the basis for his citations would lead to New's conclusion here.

[119] 1 Clem. 16.4 follows the LXX text rather than Matthew in his lengthy quotation of Isa. 53.

[120] So Menken, 'Isaiah 53:4 in Matthew 8:17', 316–17; pace Rothfuchs, Erfüllungszitate, p. 93, who suggests that αὐτός is the rendering for אָכֵן. Menken's suggestion that ὄντως translates אָכֵן in Aquila and Symmachus makes more sense. The LXX also appears to have omitted אָכֵן, opting instead for οὗτος. What is surprising is that Rothfuchs argues that knowledge of the LXX and its context demonstrates 'daß in Mt 8,17 keine passionstheologische Bedeutung eigetragen werden darf...' ('that there is no sense of the theology of the passion in Matt. 8.17').

[121] G. Stählin, 'ἀσθενεία', TDNT I.490–3.

[122] LSJ, p. 256; Stählin, 'ἀσθενεία', p. 493.

fact that ἀσθενεία only occurs seven times in the LXX and is never used to translate חֳלִי.[123]

Another significant distinction is evident in the translation of the Qal perfective נָשָׂא, which means broadly 'to lift up' or 'to bear/carry'.[124] Instead of the LXX's ambiguous present tense φέρει,[125] Matthew employs the aorist of λαμβάνειν, which essentially means 'to take' or 'to take from' the individual.[126] In the second line, here probably an example of synonymous parallelism, Matthew's translation τὰς νόσους ἐβάστασεν, 'he bore/carried our sickness/infirmities', is much closer to the MT's וּמַכְאֹבֵינוּ סְבָלָם, both structurally and linguistically,[127] than the LXX's περὶ ἡμῶν ὀδυνᾶται,[128] 'felt or suffered pain for us'. Matthew omits the first-person plural suffix and translates מַכְאֹבֵינוּ with τὰς νόσους, although presumably the Hebrew suffix is picked up in the Greek definite article. The LXX, Aquila and Symmachus all include ἡμῶν, and while, as Menken observes, its omission in Matthew may avoid 'unnecessary repetition',[129] its absence disrupts the poetic structure, metre and parallelism which are maintained in these other versions. As with the difference in semantic ranges between ἀσθενεία and חֳלִי, νόσος, which denotes 'sickness, disease (physical or mental), distress, anguish', possesses a broader semantic range than does מַכְאֹב, for which the English gloss 'pain' is sufficient.[130]

---

[123] So also Menken, 'Isaiah 53:4 in Matthew 8:17', 317. Most frequently, ἀρρωστία and μαλακία are used.

[124] BDB, pp. 670–1.

[125] Menken, 'Isaiah 53:4 in Matthew 8:17', 316, notes that φέρειν translates the Qal of נשא twenty-seven times.

[126] λαμβάνειν is used to translate the Qal of נשא some 150 times in the LXX. Davies and Allison, *Matthew*, II.36, argue that 'Removal not contraction' is in view here.

[127] Cf. the Qal of סבל in Gen. 49.15; Isa. 46.4, 7; 53.4, 11; Lam. 5.7; the Pual in Ps. 144.14; and the Hitp. in Qoh. 12.5; in the majority of these contexts סבל means 'to bear'. The meaning of מכאוב is 'pain' in general, both physical and emotional; see Jer. 30.15; 45.3; 51.8; Pss. 32.10; 38.18; 41.4 (phys.); 69.27 (phys.?); Job 33.19; Lam. 1.12, 18; Qoh. 1.18; 2.23; 2 Chron. 6.29 (both?).

[128] Cf. Democr. 159; Hippoc., *Epid.* 4.12, Soph., *El.* 804; Ar., *Vesp.* 283; *Ran.* 650; Pl., *Rep.* 583d; in the passive: 'to feel or suffer pain', and here in our context 'for us'.

[129] 'Isaiah 53:4 in Matthew 8:17', 318. Perhaps Matthew was quoting from memory and simply forgot the ἡμῶν.

[130] BDB, p. 456. Of particular interest is the fact that νόσος is elsewhere never known to translate מכאוב, but frequently translates חֳלִי. So Menken, 'Isaiah 53:4 in Matthew 8:17', 318–19, who cites 2 Chron. 21.19 and Hos. 5.13; Aquila and Symmachus employ it in the first line in Isa. 53.4. G. A. Deissmann's proposal, *Bibelstudien: Beiträge, zumeist aus den Papyri und Inschriften, zur Geschichte des Sprache, des Schrifttums und der Religion des hellenistischen Judentums und des Urchristentums*, Marburg: N. G. Elwert'sche, 1895, pp. 97–100, that νόσος translates חֳלִי and ἀσθενεία is put for מכאוב, although creative, fails to convince. For a critique see L. Rydbeck, *Fachprosa, vermeintliche Volkssprache und Neues Testament. Zur Beurteilung der sprachlichen Niveauunterschiede im nachklassischen Griechisch*,

Although Matthew's text-form presents a distinct translation when compared with the LXX or Targum, it is closer to the MT and thus somewhat resembles the Greek versions of Aquila and Symmachus. Several arguments have been made in favour of a Matthean translation. First, and perhaps most significantly, the text has been altered to incorporate an intentional emphasis upon physical illness, thereby suiting Matthew's context admirably. Second, the vocabulary of the textual adjustments (particularly, βαστάζειν, νόσος and ἀσθενεία) point to Matthew's involvement. Finally, the tone of the citation fits Matthew's presentation of Jesus and his christology rather well. His use of Isa. 53.4a within such an explicitly physical context, while not necessarily unique, is distinct from the spiritualizing of the LXX, Targums, and early Christian usages of the text in passages such as *1 Clem.* 16, which adhere to the LXX rather closely. The fact that Matthew's translation resembles that of Aquila and Symmachus may suggest that Matthew is working with ideas within Judaism. Nevertheless, the translation is peculiar enough for us to conclude tentatively that the text was translated by Matthew from the Hebrew.

The relationship of the citation to context and meaning

Attempts to explain Matthew's apparently 'non-redemptive'[131] use of Isa. 53.4a are divided into two general camps: those who view it as a proof-text to support Jesus' therapeutic ministry,[132] and those who detect reference to the suffering servant of Isa. 53 and thus posit a connection between healing and the atonement.[133] The case against attributing such a degree of theological import to the citation is seemingly a good one. Reasons supporting this position include: (1) the context into which Matthew has inserted the citation concerns healings, not atonement, and, in fact, no mention is made of the atonement;[134] (2) the physical language employed in Matthew's version of the citation and the elements which have been included and excised appear to highlight physical healing;[135] (3) to this

---

Acta Universitatis Upsaliensis, Studia Graeca Upsaliensia 5, Uppsala: Berlingska, 1967, pp. 161–3.

[131] So France, *Matthew*, p. 158.

[132] Hooker, *Jesus and the Servant*, p. 46.

[133] Most recently, Garland, *Matthew*, p. 98; Senior, *Matthew*, p. 100; D. A. Carson, *Matthew*, EBC, Grand Rapids: Zondervan, 1985, pp. 205–6.

[134] The citation follows a summary statement of Jesus' healing ministry in 8.16, which in turn follows three dramatic miracles at the opening of Matt. 8 (the healings of the leper, vv. 1–4; the centurion's servant, vv. 5–13; and Peter's mother-in-law, vv. 14–15).

[135] The text clearly draws upon the physical dimension of the MT; see Gundry, *Use of the Old Testament*, p. 111.

point in the narrative, the first-time reader would have little reason to think of the cross event as having any direct affiliation to Jesus' healing ministry; (4) Matthew does not present Jesus himself as suffering illness, which one might expect if Jesus had taken sickness and disease upon himself.[136] If such is the case, then Luz is justified in his assertion that 'frühchristliche wie damalige jüdische Exegese einzelne Schriftworte manchmal (!) völlig unabhängig von ihrem Kontext zitiert' ('like Jewish exegesis at that time, early Christian exegesis would sometimes (!) cite individual passages without regard to their original context').[137]

These factors may very well prove to point the way forward, but arguments have been presented in favour of the position that a linkage exists between Jesus' healings and the atonement in Matthean thought.[138] First, the fact that Isa. 53 has been cited at all suggests its broader context is in view.[139] Second, central to the case in favour of such a theological/ soteriological interpretation is the fact that Matthew (like much of Judaism at the time) does appear to postulate a nexus between sin and disease in 9.2–6, in which Jesus associates the forgiveness of sins with physical healing.[140] And although an atonement theology is not explicitly developed in the Gospel, this does not mean that one is not assumed. Certainly, 1.21 sets the tone for the Gospel, while 20.28 offers a further clue, as does the redactional addition of εἰς ἄφεσιν ἁμαρτιῶν in 26.28.[141] If Matthew considered the mission of Jesus within soteriological categories, as the statement 'to save his people from their sins' in 1.21 suggests, and held that Jesus' death and resurrection were central to this role, then to view the healing of sickness in light of the cross event seems a reasonable assumption. Matthew's version of Isa. 53.4 could accommodate this point, and, importantly, it is well within the boundaries of the MT.[142] Although

---

[136] France, *Matthew*, p. 159 n. 1. Although Jesus does not physically take the illnesses upon himself, the image of him as a servant of humanity offering freedom to the sick and weak is a vivid one. A similar portrait is found in the rabbinic tradition in *b. Sanh.* 98b of the 'leprous messiah' sitting at the gate amongst the sick and leprous.

[137] *Matthäus*, II.19. Pace Hill, *Matthew*, p. 161.

[138] A good argument against the assumption that this concept forms the background to 8.17 is that it depends upon a sophisticated reader and reading strategy. In the development of the narrative, the first-time reader would probably not catch the subtlety of a theological reading.

[139] H. W. Wolff, *Jesaja 53 im Urchristentum*, 3rd edn, Berlin, 1952, p. 73.

[140] *Pace* Menken, 'Isaiah 53:4 in Matthew 8:17', 324 n. 40; McConnell, *Law and Prophecy*, pp. 120–1.

[141] D. Senior, *The Passion Narrative according to Matthew: A Redactional Study*, BETL 39, Leuven: Leuven University Press, 1982, pp. 80–3. The observation that the cross event is not the climax in the Matthean narrative may help to account for the fact that the atonement is not more fully developed.

[142] See also Soares Prabhu, *Formula Quotations*, p. 166 n. 20, who observes that

it must be granted that Isa. 53.4 speaks only of bearing infirmities and carrying sickness, it is the broader context of Isa. 53 which informs the reader that the method involves vicarious suffering and death.[143] Third, the meaning of the term βαστάζειν, while debatable, seems to imply a bearing or taking upon oneself.[144] Thus, Matthew may have included Jesus' healings of physical illness within his understanding of the life and ministry of Jesus as in some way carrying the sins of humanity.

In a recent article, Menken singled out βαστάζειν as a *crux interpretum* of Matthew's usage of Isa. 53.4a.[145] Attempts to define βαστάζειν in 8.17 have moved in two directions, as either 'carry/bear' or 'take away/remove',[146] with appeals generally made to Matt. 3.11 in defence of the latter. The term occurs three times in Matthew (3.11, 8.17 and 20.12), all without Synoptic parallel. Given that 3.11 and 20.12 are less exposed theologically, it is perhaps a more prudent method to begin with these two references. The usage in 20.12 is the most straightforward, in which it is most commonly defined as 'bear/carry'.[147] Matt. 3.11 is, however, more complicated. BAGD and MM define βαστάζειν in 3.11 as 'remove', assuming that Matthew follows the other Synoptists and John, who are concerned with loosening (λύειν) 'the thong of the sandals'. While 'remove' is well within the semantic domain of βαστάζειν, given the context in Matthew, 'carry/bear' is perhaps the better option.[148] Matthew's text modifies the imagery found in Mark, Luke, John and Acts

Matthew's translation/interpretation is 'philologically legitimate, and even in the spirit of Isaiah's text'.

[143] Carson, *Matthew*, p. 205.

[144] Senior, *Matthew*, p. 100, observes that it is this term that is 'more in the direction of vicarious suffering exemplified in the servant motif'. It may also foreshadow 'the Passion that Jesus will yet endure'. Jones, *Matthew*, p. 54, observes that the term and context commend a 'studied ambiguity' in the translation and that his style of life as servant was a great sacrifice which he endured for the benefit of the poor, marginalized and outcast.

[145] This was made evident in Menken's treatment of the term, 'Isaiah 53:4 in Matthew 8:17', 322, and the implications of his results for his understanding of Matt. 8.17.

[146] Most frequently cited for support is BAGD, p. 137.3a, in which this use of βαστάζειν is defined as 'remove', a definition not advanced by LSJ, p. 310. The definition is based upon (1) *PGM* IV.1058, in which the text βαστάξας τὸ στεφάνιον ἀπὸ τ. κεφαλῆς is cited; and (2) the removal of disease by a physician in Galen, *De compos. medic. per gen.* 2.14, in which a first-century physician is quoted as saying, ψώρας τε θεραπεύει καὶ ὑπώπια βαστάζει. This would suggest that Matthew had a similar thought to Mark's and Luke's, namely, the 'removal' of the sandal. On this issue see especially the study of Rydbeck, *Fachprosa*, pp. 154–66.

[147] In this context, the term simply refers to the 'bearing of a burden', here the burden of a long day's work in the heat. The passage originates from the Matthean *Sondergut*, rendering it virtually impossible to determine whether the term is original to the source or redactional.

[148] W. Wiefel, *Das Evangelium nach Matthäus*, THKNT, Leipzig: Evangelische Verlagsanstalt, 1998, p. 51; Davies and Allison, *Matthew*, I.315; Allen, *Matthew*, p. 25.

from loosing the thong to carrying the sandal, and although it shifts the picture somewhat, both images were well known in antiquity, and thus the theme of humility and subordination remains intact.[149] The quandary arises when one endeavours to establish the denotation in Matthew 8.17. Do the seemingly consistent usages in 3.11 and 20.12 suggest a similar definition? Simply to assert with Menken that in the context of 8.17 the verb clearly means 'the *removal* of sicknesses and diseases' is too bold, due to both the ambiguity of the term and its context.[150] Instead, a more cautious approach ought to be employed which considers the linguistic evidence and the issues raised by the context and Matthew's theology.

Central to the discussion is the translation of the MT's סָבַל with βαστάζειν. A complicating factor, which is often encountered when translating into a receptor language, is the fact that βαστάζειν and סָבַל are not direct translational equivalents. סָבַל (Isa. 53.4) contains a narrow semantic range and simply means to 'bear' a load, be it physically (Gen. 49.6) or metaphorically, as in YHWH carrying Israel (Isa. 46.4, 7), the people bearing iniquities (Lam. 5.7), or the servant bearing pain and disease (Isa. 53.3, 4, 11). Although it is true that the LXX never renders the Hebrew verb סָבַל with βαστάζειν, the translation in Matthew is not wholly without equivalents; for example, Aquila employs βαστάζειν to translate סָבַל in Isa. 53.11 in a context not unlike that of Matthew.[151] Whether Matthew has in view the limited range of the Hebrew or the broader range of the Greek[152] is an issue that only can be decided by examining the context, which unfortunately appears ambiguous.

[149] So Allen, *Matthew*, p. 25; Hagner, *Matthew 1–13*, p. 51; Beare, *Matthew*, p. 96. Davies and Allison, *Matthew*, I.315, observe that τὸν ἱμάντα, found in Mark 1.7, Luke 3.16 and John 1.27, is omitted from Matthew, essentially shifting the imagery from the thongs to the sandal itself. (Cf. Acts 13.25, which, while lacking τὸν ἱμάντα, nevertheless includes λῦσαι.) Additionally, Davies and Allison note that the carrying of clothing, sandals, etc., by a servant was a sign of servanthood (see *b. Sanh.* 62b; *b. B. Meṣiʿa* 41a; *b. ʿErub.* 27b and especially *b. Pesaḥ.* 41). Since τὸν ἱμάντα is common to John, Mark and Luke, and λῦσαι occurs in the traditions found in these Gospels and Acts 13.25, it is more likely that Q (if a Q version of this text ever existed) originally read λύειν instead of βαστάζειν as has been suggested by Luz, *Matthew*, p. 148. Constructing the postulate that Matthew's text in 3.11 represents Q based upon the supposition that a Q text lies behind Matt. 3.7–12//Luke 3.7–9, 16–17 is one speculation too far. Given the agreement between Mark, Luke, John and Acts, there is little reason to assume Q for Matthew's source here. It naturally follows then that if τὸν ἱμάντα and λύειν reflect Q, there is good reason to believe that βαστάζειν is either a Matthean adjustment or derives from another source.

[150] Menken, 'Isaiah 53:4 in Matthew 8:17', 323.

[151] The parallelism of Isa. 53.11 is enlightening: 'the righteous one, my servant will make many righteous, he will bear their iniquities'.

[152] Menken's argument, 'Isaiah 53:4 in Matthew 8:17', 322–4, that Matthew is not only aware of, but exploits, this ambiguity in his use of the broader range of the Greek term, while possible, assumes much.

One wonders, however, whether the divide over this text is not the result of an incorrectly framed inquiry due to preconceived notions, both positive and negative, regarding the *Ebed YHWH* of Isa. 53 and limited linguistic evidence. The emphasis of the quotation upon physical healing is manifest in both the text-form of the quotation and the context into which it has been inserted. Its immediate context is a summary statement of Jesus' healing ministry one evening (8.16).[153] This summary follows hard upon the accounts of three episodes in which individuals who come into contact with Jesus have been healed (8.1–4, 5–13, 14–15).[154] The choice of Isa. 53.4 for use in this context seems an odd one. Certainly if Matthew merely desired a proof-text for healings or the relationship of healings to the messianic age, texts similar to the collage in Matt. 11.5 would have served admirably.

A window into Matthew's usage may be found in the language of the citation itself, that is, 'he took our weaknesses, he carried/removed our diseases'. The text appeals to the posture of Jesus in relation to the broken humanity surrounding him. As Gerhardsson observes, in Matthew's usage of Isa. 53.4a the accent is not upon sovereignty, but upon Jesus' servanthood and humility.[155] Similarly, Hill proposes that Jesus' deeds of power are manifestations of his mercy, obedience and lowliness.[156] In this respect it is fascinating that Jesus heals as servant in Matthew, as the quotation of two servant texts after summaries in both 8.17 and 12.18–21 exhibits. Neither servant text depicts a victorious messianic figure; instead, they present a portrait of one who cares and empathizes with humanity. It is this relational aspect that indicates that present within Matthew's usage is an awareness of the identification of the individual servant with humanity.[157] This interrelationship includes elements of both suffering and justice as Jesus identifies with a broken humanity, offering healing and freedom. Thus, contained within this citation is a vibrant

---

[153] It would be a misnomer to label Jesus a physician–a healer, perhaps, but a healer in the sense of a wonder-worker or messianic figure. This is an important distinction given Matt. 11.2–6, for the healings are meant to point in the direction of Jesus' identity.

[154] This section of Matthew brings to mind the last recorded healing in the Gospel in 21.14, which contains material unique to Matthew (cf. Luke 19.39–40). The probable linkage between healings and purification in this text is hinted at in the background literature (cf. Lev. 21.18; 2 Sam. 5.8; 1QSa; 4QMMT 52–7 (4Q394); *m. Ḥag.* 1.1 and LXX 2 Kings 5.6–8; John 9.1; Acts 3.1–2). See discussion of this passage in chapter 6.

[155] B. Gerhardsson, *The Mighty Acts of Jesus according to Matthew*, Lund: CWK Gleerup, 1979, p. 91. See the much fuller treatment of this issue in his 'Gottes Sohn als Diener Gottes', 73–106.

[156] Hill, 'Son and Servant', 9; so also Barth, 'Matthew's Understanding of the Law', p. 128.

[157] Rogerson, 'Hebrew Conception of Corporate Personality', 15–16.

christology which contributes to Matthew's overall portrait of Jesus, and although the designation 'servant' is omitted, one cannot escape the image of servanthood, a motif which radically alters common perceptions of the Davidide. The problem of the usage of Isa. 52.13–53.12 in Judaism and early Christianity notwithstanding,[158] Matthew's use of the text discloses a significance for the author beyond a mere proof-text for Jesus' healing activities.

In summary, perhaps more than all the texts discussed in this section, this one betrays the hand of Matthew or possibly a translation used within the community, evidenced particularly in the use of νόσος and βαστάζειν. Because of its specific usage for physical healings, it is doubtful that it was derived from a Testimonies source. While it is a fact that the Matthean emphasis upon a bearing of 'physical' weakness/disease runs counter to two known Jewish traditions evidenced in the LXX and Targums, it does not run counter to the later Greek translations of Aquila and Symmachus (cf. Isa. 53.11).[159] On the important question of bi-referentiality, this text is less clear than the previous two. The obvious reason for the citation is to validate Jesus' acts as healer; however, on another level it stresses the character and demeanour of the healer, who as a servant compassionately identifies with a broken humanity and offers wholeness.

Conclusions

Although I have considered only a few of Matthew's formula citations, it is clear that his usage of the Old Testament is distinct and creative, defying easy categorization. The text-form presents one enigma which, unless further texts are unearthed, will probably never be solved. When compared with other texts from the period,[160] however, Matthew's text-form reflects the fluidity and variety that characterized this era. This should caution against overstatements regarding Matthew's use and knowledge of Hebrew, or lack thereof. The fact that the Minor Prophets scroll provides evidence that Greek revisions date back into the first century BC raises legitimate uncertainty concerning whether Matthew did indeed translate directly from the Hebrew.[161] At several points where Matthew is closer to

---

[158] For a summary of the infrequent usage of Isa. 53 in this period, see Page, 'Suffering Servant', 481–97.

[159] Matthew's understanding of the text is, therefore, not unique and may have been part of the conformist movement towards the MT.

[160] See chapter 3.

[161] G. I. Davies, 'Did Matthew Know Hebrew?', cautions 'The existence of this early material surely means that before it is assumed that Matthew created his formula-quotations

the MT only two conclusions are possible: either he (or someone within his community) knew and worked with Hebrew, or he was familiar with a revised Greek version that closely adhered to the MT. Either has to be considered a justifiable option. New's conclusion that Matthew extensively adapted the LXX is problematic in this regard. Additionally, the present study has concluded that Matthew's handling of the texts is not unlike that of his other sources. He appears to have employed those texts best suited to his purposes, as in 1.23 for example, but he also seems to have made adjustments to the text in light of contextual and theological interests. That a source text would coincidentally possess a reading that was perfectly suited to Matthew's concerns in the context might happen once or even twice, but the extent of the adjustments argues strongly against translational serendipity, and as such seriously undermines the contention that the textual adjustments originated in a revised Greek text. Luz's assumption that Matthew's community had a copy of Isaiah in its library is probably correct,[162] but to restrict it to a copy of the LXX perhaps is too severe. A copy of the LXX was no doubt available, but in addition to this there seems to have existed either a Hebrew edition and/or a revised Greek version.

More important, however, has been the observation concerning the bi-referentiality of the citations, which validates the surface or narrative level, as well as recalling and/or presaging ideas concerning or ways of viewing Jesus' person and ministry within the broader message of the Gospel. This confirms Hartman's theory that a citation 'evoke[s] a bundle of ideas connected with its context, and/or its interpretation and usage'.[163] 1.23b is a prime example of this effect. The text clearly is cited to authorize the virginal conception, but more importantly it introduces the 'Emmanuel' motif upon which Matthew later draws. 4.15–16 functions in a similar manner, as it moves beyond the merely geographical (4.12–13//4.15) to interject material which dramatically demonstrates that the messianic light has dawned upon the people of this region. 8.17 is perhaps the most difficult example and resists attempts to demonstrate its significance beyond being a mere proof-text for Jesus' therapeutic activities. There is, however, subtle evidence suggesting that for Matthew, Jesus' function as healer contains within it a sense of identification by the compassionate servant with the broken and marginalized. In this respect

by direct consultation of the Hebrew, the possibility has to be tested that he derived his more accurate knowledge of the Hebrew at second-hand, from one of these revised Greek versions.'

[162] Luz, *Matthew*, p. 157–8.

[163] 'Problem of Communication', 134.

there may even be links between Jesus' healings and the purification of the defective for complete incorporation into the people of God.

Finally, the propositions of Rothfuchs, Gundry and van Segbroeck concerning an overarching use of Isaiah in the formula citations can thus be affirmed and expanded. The Isaiah texts all appear to involve the issues of the messianic age and its concomitant effects. Each functions in a unique manner, linking the person of Jesus to the fulfilment of OT expectations, and each introduces new material into the narrative, demonstrating in some way that Jesus is the long-awaited one. Stanton's observation that Matthew's concerns are 'primarily Christological' in the citations in Matt. 2 may be extended to these three Isaianic citations as well. The question now arises whether this paradigm may account for Matthew's usage of Isa. 42.1–4, the longest quotation in the Gospel.

5

ISAIAH 42.1–4 WITHIN THE CONTEXT
OF MATTHEW 11–13

The historical usage and influence of Isa. 42.1–4, as observed in chapter 3, appears to demonstrate that the passage contributed to the understanding of the character and expectation of the messianic age. In particular, where it is employed to support the messianic ideal, the concepts of spirit, justice and the universal rule of the messiah are also manifest. The primary question of concern here is whether Matthew drew upon such a perception and incorporated it into his presentation of Jesus. Given the manner in which Matthew employed Isa. 7.14, 8.23b–9.1 and 53.4, one might expect his use of the passage to reflect his theological concerns.[1] But this is to anticipate a conclusion without exploring the data. The evidence certainly supports a web of verbal and metaphorical relationships between certain citations and their immediate and remote contexts. Whether this can be maintained for Isa. 42.1–4 in Matt. 12.18–21 is a more difficult matter and is the subject of this chapter.

Two remarks that impinge upon the study may be made at this point regarding Matthean text-form. First, Matthew's redactional treatment of Mark and Q reveals an author who, although creative, is fastidious with these sources, and predisposes one to assume that a similar posture is taken with regard to his other sources.[2] One may thus cautiously affirm the argument that the unique text-form found in these citations reflects his particular theological interests. Second, the results of the analysis of the Isaianic passages in chapter 4 indicate the facile nature of the assumption that Matthew's use of the Old Testament is simplistic proof-texting. Instead, Matthew seems to employ the Old Testament with two

---

[1] E. Schweizer, *The Good News according to Matthew*, Atlanta: John Knox, 1975, pp. 281–2, suggests that the text was employed 'to stimulate reflection' and not to 'prove Jesus was the messiah'.

[2] Commentators are divided on this point. Gundry, *Matthew*, pp. xxiv–xxx, argues for a free hand with the tradition; Luz, *Matthew*, pp. 76–8, is much more cautious. Stanton, 'Creative Interpreter', pp. 326–45, explores several passages that appear to indicate Matthean expansions to the sayings of Jesus, which further demonstrates the hand of an interpreter/redactor.

levels of reference. This may also be the case with Matthew's version of Isa. 42.1–4, the longest and perhaps most distinct of the citations.

With these concerns in mind, the evaluation of the function of Isa. 42.1–4 that follows in this chapter will proceed in several stages. First, a careful analysis of the distinctive text-form will be undertaken, in the hope that possible clues to its function in the context may be unearthed. It must be acknowledged, however, that, although the textual anomalies may reflect Matthean redactional interests, one must also seriously consider the possibility that early Christian traditional usage may lie behind elements of the distinctive text. In addition to the detailed analysis of the text-form, the study will also consider the rhetorical force of the final form of the citation and possible implications that derive from it.[3] Having arrived at possible conclusions from the text itself, I shall undertake an examination of the role of the citation and its themes within its context. The result of this, it is hoped, will not only lead to a more lucid understanding of the function of this substantial quotation in Matthew's Gospel but perhaps point to suitable christological insights, upon which chapter 6 will reflect.

An overview of Matthew's text-form

The subsequent chart displaying the various known texts from which Matthew could have drawn is arranged to indicate textual differences. It will be followed by a brief discussion of the most significant distinctions.

Matthew 12.18–21	LXX Isaiah 42.1–4	MT Isaiah 42.1–4	Targum
[18]ἰδοὺ ὁ παῖς μου	[1]Ιακωβ ὁ παῖς μου	הֵן עַבְדִּי	הא עבדי
ὅν[4] ἡρέτισα,	ἀντιλήμψομαι αὐτοῦ	אֶתְמָךְ־בּוֹ	אקרבניה
ὁ ἀγαπητός μου	Ισραηλ ὁ ἐκλεκτός μου	בְּחִירִי	בחירי
εἰς ὅν[5] εὐδόκησεν	προσεδέξατο αὐτὸν	רָצְתָה	דאתרעי ביה

---

[3] See the discussion in chapter 2, pp. 30–4, chapter 5, pp. 151–2, and chapter 6.

[4] D is unique in its reading of εἰς ὅν.

[5] The determination of Matthew's text is very difficult at this point. The variant text ὅν is found in ℵ* B 892 *pc* ff¹ and was accepted as original by the NA²⁵, Tischendorf, Merk, Westcott and Hort. Least likely is ἐν ᾧ, which occurs in D f¹ 33 1424; Ir^lat. The currently accepted text εἰς ὅν is found in ℵ¹ C^vid L W θ 0106 0233 f¹³ MajT, the UBS⁴ and NA²⁷. εἰς ὅν probably ought to be preferred for the following reasons: (1) it is a rare form which represents the most difficult reading; (2) it is supported by 2 Pet. 1.17, which is probably dependent upon Matt. (*pace* R. Bauckham, *Jude, 2 Peter*, WBC 50, Waco: Word, 1983, p. 209); (3) the tendency would be to correct 12.18 towards the texts of 3.17 and 17.5, which read ἐν ᾧ; (4) ὅν occurs in the previous line of 12.18a (although D inserts εἰς);

		MT Isaiah	
Matthew 12.18–21	LXX Isaiah 42.1–4	42.1–4	Targum
ἡ ψυχή μου·	ἡ ψυχή μου	נַפְשִׁי	מימרי
θήσω	ἔδωκα	נָתַתִּי	אתין
τὸ πνεῦμά μου	τὸ πνεῦμά μου	רוּחִי	רוח קודשי
ἐπ' αὐτόν,	ἐπ' αὐτόν	עָלָיו	עלוהי
καὶ κρίσιν τοῖς ἔθνεσιν	κρίσιν τοῖς ἔθνεσιν	מִשְׁפָּט לַגּוֹיִם	דיני לעממין
ἀπαγγελεῖ.	ἐξοίσει	יוֹצִיא:	יגלי:
¹⁹οὐκ ἐρίσει	²οὐ κεκράξεται	לֹא יִצְעַק	לא יצוח
οὐδὲ κραυγάσει,	οὐδὲ ἀνήσει	וְלֹא יִשָּׂא	ולא יכלי
οὐδὲ ἀκούσει τις	οὐδὲ ἀκουσθήσεται	וְלֹא־יַשְׁמִיעַ	ולא ירים
ἐν ταῖς πλατείαις	ἔξω	בַּחוּץ	בברא
τὴν φωνὴν αὐτοῦ.	ἡ φωνὴ αὐτοῦ	קוֹלוֹ:	קליה:
²⁰κάλαμον	³κάλαμον	קָנֶה	ענותניא דכקני
συντετριμμένον⁶	τεθλασμένον	רָצוּץ	רעיע
οὐ κατεάξει	οὐ συντρίψει	לֹא יִשְׁבּוֹר	לא יתבר
καὶ λίνον τυφόμενον	καὶ λίνον	וּפִשְׁתָּה כֵהָה	וחשיכיא
	καπνιζόμενον		דכבוצין
οὐ σβέσει,	οὐ σβέσει	לֹא יְכַבֶּנָּה	עמי לא יטפי
	ἀλλὰ εἰς ἀλήθειαν	לֶאֱמֶת	לקושטיה יפיק
	ἐξοίσει κρίσιν	יוֹצִיא מִשְׁפָּט:	דינא:
	⁴ἀναλάμψει	לֹא יִכְהֶה	לא יהלי
	καὶ οὐ θραυσθήσεται	וְלֹא יָרוּץ	ולא ילאי
ἕως ἂν ἐκβάλῃ	ἕως ἂν θῇ	עַד־יָשִׂים	עד דיתקן
εἰς νῖκος τὴν κρίσιν.⁷	ἐπὶ τῆς γῆς κρίσιν	בָּאָרֶץ מִשְׁפָּט	בארעא דינא
²¹καὶ τῷ ὀνόματι	καὶ ἐπὶ τῷ ὀνόματι	וּלְתוֹרָתוֹ	ולאורייתיה נגוון
αὐτοῦ	αὐτοῦ		
ἔθνη ἐλπιοῦσιν.	ἔθνη ἐλπιοῦσιν	אִיִּים יְיַחֵילוּ:	יכתרון

Theodotion, Isaiah 42.1a	Aquila, Isaiah 42.1a	Symmachus, Isaiah 42.1a
ἰδοὺ ὁ παῖς⁸ μου ἀντιλήμψομαι αὐτοῦ	ἰδοὺ (ὁ) δοῦλός μου,	ἰδοὺ ὁ δοῦλός μου,

(5) D's insertion of εἰς earlier in 12.18 is better explained by the presence of εἰς ὅν; and (6) perhaps most importantly, Theodotion and Symmachus both include ὅν εὐδόκησεν, which may suggest a scribal tendency to correct the rare reading of εἰς ὅν to ὅν alone.

⁶ Κάλαμον συντετριμμένον is omitted in D*.

⁷ αὐτοῦ is inserted in X 28 1424 *al* syʰ sa mae.

⁸ Qˢʸʰ, Thdt records Theodotion's reading as δοῦλος rather than παῖς.

Theodotion, Isaiah 42.1a	Aquila, Isaiah 42.1a	Symmachus, Isaiah 42.1a
ὁ ἐκλεκτός μου ὃν εὐδόκησεν ἡ ψυχή μου, οὐ σβέσει καὶ τῷ νόμῳ αὐτοῦ	 οὐ σβέσει καὶ τῷ νόμῳ αὐτοῦ	ὁ ἐκλεκτός μου ὃν εὐδόκησεν ἡ ψυχή μου· οὐ σβέσει καὶ τῷ νόμῳ αὐτοῦ

The text-form

The complexity of Matthew's version of Isa. 42.1–4 has challenged scholars for centuries and continues to puzzle. A close examination of the citation reveals hints of Matthean and pre-Matthean translational work as well as reliance upon other traditions, and may assist in determining Matthean concerns in the text of this citation. It is this crucial question of Matthean interest exhibited in the citation that matters here and to which the text-form is a valuable guide. The ensuing section will present only a description of the text-form; comments regarding the significance, if any, of the text-form will emerge in a later discussion.

12.18a

The text of Isa. 42.1a in 12.18a is perhaps the most distinctive of Matthew's version. The fact that Isa. 42.1 appears to have been widely used in early Christian tradition, as evidenced by its inclusion in both the Baptism and Transfiguration narratives of all three Synoptics, may imply that Matthew is drawing upon an already existing tradition, but at key points Matthew seems to make the text his own. Assuming a one-to-one translational correspondence, Matthew's renderings of the Hebrew can be listed as follows:

1.   ἰδοὺ ὁ παῖς μου = הֵן עַבְדִּי
2.   ὃν ἡρέτισα = אֶתְמָךְ־בּוֹ
3.   ὁ ἀγαπητός μου = בְּחִירִי
4.   εἰς ὃν εὐδόκησεν ἡ ψυχή μου = רָצְתָה נַפְשִׁי

The translations evident in numbers 1 and 4 are straightforward and easily accounted for, if not as already existing translations of the LXX, then as those of other Greek versions, with a few minor modifications. Numbers 2 and 3, however, prove baffling to those exponents of the one-to-one correspondence theory. For ease of discussion I shall address the translations in the above order.

1. Matthew's ἰδοὺ ὁ παῖς μου provides a close rendering of the MT's הֵן עַבְדִּי, matching the text of Theodotion. The use of παῖς here agrees with the LXX in contrast to Symmachus' (and Aquila's) use of δοῦλος.[9] Matthew does not, however, follow the LXX in its identification of the servant as Ιακωβ and Ισραηλ.[10]

2. More complicated is Matthew's rendering of אֶתְמָךְ־בּוֹ ('I will uphold/lay hold of him')[11] with ὃν ἡρέτισα ('whom I have chosen'). The LXX, Theodotion and Aquila concur in their usage of the future tense ἀντιλήμψομαι ('lay hold of', 'assist'), which closely resembles the MT. Matthew thus goes against all known versions with his aorist use of the NT *hapax legomenon* αἱρετίζειν,[12] a term which bears slight semantic relationship to ἀντιλαμβάνειν or תמך.[13] As is frequently noted, however, αἱρετίζειν is the normal translation of בחר in the LXX.[14] This led Torrey, for example, to postulate a *Vorlage* of בחרתי בו for Matthew's text possibly derived from Isa. 44.1–2 (cf. 41.8 and 43.10).[15] More likely is Stendahl's position that Matthew may have anticipated ὁ ἐκλεκτός μου (LXX).[16] The fact that αἱρετίζειν translates בחר eliminates recent 'unrewarding attempts'[17] to construe ὁ ἀγαπητός μου as a gloss

---

[9] See the textual note on Theodotion's possible rendering of παῖς as δοῦλος. There is a lengthy, ongoing discussion regarding the meaning of παῖς (see I. H. Marshall, 'Son of God or Servant of Yahweh? A Reconsideration of Mark 1.11', *NTS* 15 (1968): 326–36). There seems little doubt that παῖς usage was being superseded by δοῦλος. On this see P. Katz, 'Das Problem des Urtextes der Septuaginta', *TZ* 5 (1949): 17 (also cited in Gundry, *Use of the Old Testament*, p. 111).

[10] Cf. the texts of Justin (*Dial.* 123 and 135), which include the full version of LXX Isa. 42.1 in support of his thesis that Jesus is Israel, king.

[11] Massebieau, *Examen des citations*, p. 22, suggests a sense of 'to take hold of' or 'to acquire' as in adopt, whereas Allen, *Matthew*, p. 130, translates it as 'adopt'. The Targum's אקרבניה, 'I will bring him near', may carry a similar force.

[12] Used only here in the entire New Testament; it can mean 'to choose' (LXX Gen. 30.20) or, more specifically, 'to adopt' (see LSJ, p. 41; H. Schlier, 'αἱρετίζω', *TDNT* I.184).

[13] Instructive in this regard is the usage of תמך in Isa. 41.10 and 13. In both cases the theme is the sustaining/upholding support of God towards Israel.

[14] αἱρετίζειν occurs twenty-six times in the LXX, twelve of which translate בחר: Judg. 5.8; 1 Chron. 28.4, 6, 10; 29.1; 2 Chron. 29.2; Pss. 24.12; 118.30, 173; Hag. 2.24; Zech. 1.17; 2.12.

[15] *Documents of the Primitive Church*, p. 65. The difficulty with Torrey's solution is that it assumes a Hebrew *Vorlage* of which we have no record, and cannot explain the inclusion of ὁ ἀγαπητός. Gundry, *Use of the Old Testament*, p. 112, adds that 44.2 and 41.8–9 also contain the 'ἀγαπητός-motif', although in neither case is the titular ὁ ἀγαπητός employed; 41.8–9 uses ὃν ἠγάπησα and 44.2, ὁ ἠγαπημένος.

[16] *School*, p. 110. Gundry, *Use of the Old Testament*, p. 112, suggests that Matthew 'brings in בחרתי בו not in place of אתמך בו so much as by omission of the latter in anticipation of בחירי – to make room for ὁ ἀγαπητός μου from the voice at Jesus' baptism and transfiguration, where it stems from the Targum to Ps. 2:7'.

[17] G. Vermes, *Scripture and Tradition in Judaism*, SPB 4, Leiden: Brill, 1961, p. 222.

of בְּחִירִי,[18] and the equally awkward attribution of αἱρετίζειν to תמך.
Additionally, Matthew's clause ὃν ᾑρέτισα captures the sense of the
MT's nominal phrase בְּחִירִי (LXX's ὁ ἐκλεκτός μου) rather well. It may
be that the Matthean text translates the accusative element in אֶתְמָךְ־בּוֹ
with the accusative ὅν, and excludes אֶתְמָךְ by replacing it with the aorist
ᾑρέτισα which anticipates בְּחִירִי. Noticeably absent is the concept of
'upholding, sustaining or taking hold of', thereby creating room for
the affirmation of divine election/choice[19] and the later inclusion of
the messianic designation ὁ ἀγαπητός μου in place of the messianic
title ὁ ἐκλεκτός.[20] In Matthew's new construction, 'the servant', who
is divinely chosen, now parallels 'the Beloved', the source of divine
pleasure, and thus incorporates the overtones of 'sonship' within the
context.

3. If one accepts the above, or a similar, scenario, then strained attempts to demonstrate that ὁ ἀγαπητός translates בְּחִירִי become unnecessary. Only a perspective of translation which assumes a one-to-one
correspondence or demands that every word be accounted for could posit
that 'my Elect' equates 'my Beloved'. The now dated explanation that
the inclusion of ὁ ἀγαπητός μου in 12.18a results from a poor translation of בְּחִירִי should be rejected.[21] A related issue is raised by J. A.
Robinson's assertion that ὁ ἀγαπητός is interchangeable with ὁ ἐκλεκτός.[22] Robinson's argument relies heavily upon Matt. 12.18, which is the
sole extant record of this translation. And while Robinson would seem
to have texts such as *1 Enoch* 37–71 on his side, in which the phrases
'the Elect', 'the Chosen' and 'the Son of Man' all appear as messianic
designations and are used interconnectedly, these associations do not in
themselves argue for linguistic interchangeability, nor that 'the Beloved'

[18] So Grindel, 'Matthew 12,18–21,' 110; although he correctly observes that ἀγαπητός
normally translates יָחִיד or יָדִיד and that it is never used for בְּחִירִי in either the LXX or Hexapla,
he curiously concludes that it is 'probably an exegetical rendering of bᵉhîrî prompted by
early Christian vocabulary'.
[19] So Lindars, *New Testament Apologetic*, p. 147. Note that the sense of 'upholding',
which is also present in MT Isa. 42.4a, is conspicuously absent from Matthew's text.
[20] This adjustment seems to be Matthean and may indicate that Matthew himself is
responsible for the text-form in 12.18a (cf. Matt. 27.40 εἰ υἱὸς εἶ τοῦ θεοῦ and Luke 23.35
εἰ οὗτός ἐστιν ὁ χριστὸς τοῦ θεοῦ ὁ ἐκλεκτός). Does this suggest an aversion in Matthew
to the title ὁ ἐκλεκτός?
[21] Grindel, 'Matthew 12,18–21', 110; Gundry, *Use of the Old Testament*, p. 30.
[22] 'Ascension of Isaiah', *HDB* II.501; Jeremias, 'παῖς θεοῦ', p. 710. Robinson (p. 501)
argues that 'At the period when the Gospels were written "the Beloved" and "the Elect" were
practically interchangeable terms, for Mt writes ὁ ἀγαπητός μου (12¹⁸) in citing Is 42¹,
where the Heb. is בְּחִירִי (LXX ὁ ἐκλεκτός μου); and Luke (9³⁵) substitutes ὁ ἐκλελεγμένος
for ὁ ἀγαπητός in the words spoken at the transfiguration' (emphasis mine).

should be included with this grouping because of its occurrence in Matt. 12.18a.²³

Having tentatively accepted that ὁ ἀγαπητός was used to designate a messianic figure, scholarship remains divided as to its source for the Baptism and Transfiguration narratives.²⁴ Recent studies have postulated that ὁ ἀγαπητός is a Matthean addition to harmonize this citation with the Baptism and Transfiguration voices. This seems the most reasonable option. However, this is not a straightforward decision because it is complicated by the use of an almost identical text in 2 Pet. 1.17 and

---

²³ Additional arguments against Robinson's construct include: (1) Matthew's version of Isa. 42.1a is unique in its inclusion of ὁ ἀγαπητός; (2) the most natural translation, ὁ ἐκλεκτός, occurs in the LXX and later in both Theodotion and Symmachus, suggesting widespread knowledge of the translation and further distinguishing the Matthean anomaly (see Rabin, 'Translation Process', 2–4, for a discussion of the translation process and the problem of 'correlation between source and receptor text'); (3) it is extremely doubtful that Luke 'substituted' ὁ ἐκλελεγμένος for ὁ ἀγαπητός (9.35); instead, he probably worked from the LXX or a different tradition; (4) as mentioned above, Matthew seems to anticipate בְּחִירִי.

²⁴ See J. A. Robinson, *St Paul's Epistle to the Ephesians: A Revised Text and Translation with Exposition and Notes*, 2nd edn, London: Macmillan, 1904, pp. 229–33. The origins of the title ὁ ἀγαπητός must, therefore, be accounted for on other grounds. Bauckham offers a concise and clear summary in *2 Peter*, pp. 205–10. Most popular has been the position that it was derived from the Targum to Ps. 2.7 (D. Plooij, 'The Baptism of Jesus', in *Amicitiae Corolla: A Volume of Essays Presented to James Rendell Harris on the Occasion of His 80th Birthday*, edited by H. G. Wood, London: University of London Press, 1933, p. 248; T. W. Manson, 'The Old Testament in the Teachings of Jesus', *BJRL* 34 (1951–2): 323–4; Gundry, *Use of the Old Testament*, p. 112). This has subsequently been challenged by E. Lohse, 'υἱός', *TDNT* VIII.362, who asserts that the Targum actually downplays the designation and is in fact coloured by its anti-Christian rhetoric. P. G. Bretscher, 'Exodus 4:22–23 and the Voice from Heaven', *JBL* 87 (1968): 301–11, postulates that the title's origins may be found in Exod. 4.22. Key to his position is that πρωτότοκος is the equivalent of ἀγαπητός, an association which is not immediately evident. A third position, already discussed above, suggests that ὁ ἀγαπητός translates בְּחִירִי in Matt. 12.18a. See the works of Jeremias, 'παῖς θεοῦ', pp. 701–2; O. Cullmann, *Baptism in the New Testament*, translated by J. K. S. Reid, SBT 1, London: SCM Press, 1950, p. 17; R. H. Fuller, *The Foundations of New Testament Christology*, London: Collins, 1969, p. 170. C. H. Turner, 'Ο ΥΙΟΣ ΜΟΥ Ο ΑΓΑΠΗΤΟΣ', *JTS* 27 (1926): 113–29, has argued that ἀγαπητός is analogous to μονογενής (only), a common Greek idiom. The uses of ὁ ἀγαπητός in the Akedah (Gen. 22.2, 12, 16) may provide another potential source. Here the Hebrew בִּנְךָ יְחִידְךָ is translated in the LXX as τὸν υἱόν σου τὸν ἀγαπητόν, providing especially fertile ground for speculation, although its weakness is that an Isaac typology is generally lacking in the New Testament (Vermes, *Scripture and Tradition*, pp. 222–3). In addition to these passages, one might also include the possible messianic usage of ὁ ἀγαπητός in LXX Ps. 44.1 (I am indebted to W. Horbury for this reference), LXX Isa. 26.17, and Zech. 12.10, all of which suggest a messianic titular usage prior to Christianity. One may also add those with ὁ ἠγαπημένος as a title for Christ in Eph. 1.6; *Barn.* 3.6; 4.3, 8; *1 Clem.* 59.2, 3; Ign., *Smyrn.* Inscr.; *Acts Paul & Thecla* 1 (cited in J. A. Robinson, 'Ascension', p. 501; Bauckham, *2 Peter*, p. 209); and those which include ἀγαπητός with υἱός or παῖς, i.e. *Herm. Sim.* 5.2.6; *Mart. Polyc.* 14; *Ep. ad Diogn.* 8; *Acts Paul & Thecla* 24.

the apparent influence of Isa. 42.1a upon both the Baptism and Transfiguration narratives (see discussion below).

4. The final distinctive phrase of Matt. 12.18a which bears upon this study is εἰς ὃν εὐδόκησεν for the MT's רָצְתָה and translated προσεδέξατο αὐτόν in the LXX.[25] In a manner similar to Matthew, Symmachus and Theodotion also include ὃν εὐδόκησεν for, as many have noted, εὐδοκεῖν (plus the accusative) was common in biblical and non-biblical Greek.[26] Mark 1.11, generally thought to have been influenced by Isa. 42.1a, contains the reading ἐν σοὶ εὐδόκησα. If, as seems likely, Mark does depend upon Isa. 42.1a, then this may indicate an early Christian use of Isa. 42.1 in a textual format similar to Matthew's and prior to its composition. Additionally, the fact that Symmachus and Theodotion also contain this reading legitimately questions the supposition that Matthew translated this passage from Hebrew; instead, he may have used an already existing Greek translation in use within the early Christian community.[27]

Important in the determination of the degree to which the text of Matt. 12.18a may have been adjusted by Matthew is the consideration of 12.18a in light of other parallel texts, namely, the Baptism (cf. Mark 1.11; Luke 3.22; John 1.34) and Transfiguration (cf. Mark 9.7; Luke 9.35; 2 Pet. 1.17). Several authors are in agreement with Grindel's assertion that a common non-LXX source may reside behind these references, perhaps the same source as that of Matthew.[28] The chart below presents the various texts of the Gospels and other traditions of the Baptism and Transfiguration, a comparison of which demonstrates the manner in which Matthew seems to handle his sources.[29]

---

[25] In the LXX, the verb εὐδοκεῖν is used to translate חפץ, הלצ and רצה. For a summary of positions, see F. L. Lentzen-Deis, *Die Taufe Jesu nach den Synoptikern: Literarkritisch und gattungsgeschichtliche Untersuchungen*, Frankfurt: Joseph Knecht, 1970, pp. 191–2. New, *Old Testament Quotations*, p. 107, suggests that Matthew may be 'hearkening back to the wording' of the Baptism narrative, and neglects to note the similarity to Theodotion and Symmachus, a fact which argues against Matthew's use of the LXX throughout.

[26] Gundry, *Use of the Old Testament*, p. 113.

[27] Gundry's assertion, *ibid.*, p. 112, that Matthew 'renders [the Hebrew] independently' and that the 'agreement with Theodotion is "not significant" ' ignores the early use of the text in Greek in Mark, etc. See Lindars, *New Testament Apologetic*, pp. 144–52, for an attempt to demonstrate early Christian usage. Bauckham, *2 Peter*, p. 210, concludes that the agreement between Matthew and 2 Pet. 1.17 here provides evidence of an independent tradition upon which both authors drew. See R. J. Miller, 'Is There Independent Attestation for the Transfiguration in 2 Peter?' *NTS* 42 (1996): 620–5, for a recent critique of Bauckham's position.

[28] Grindel, 'Matthew 12,18–21', 110, 112.

[29] A chart similar in many respects to this one is located in Bauckham, *2 Peter*, pp. 206–7.

Matt. 12.18aᵃ	ἰδού		ὁ παῖς μου...	ὁ ἀγαπητός μου
Baptism				
Matt. 3.17	οὗτός	ἐστιν	ὁ υἱός μου	ὁ ἀγαπητός
Mark. 1.11	σύ	εἶ	ὁ υἱός μου	ὁ ἀγαπητός
Luke 3.22	σύ	εἶ	ὁ υἱός μου	ὁ ἀγαπητός
Gos. Eb. (cited in	σύ μου εἶ		ὁ υἱός	ὁ ἀγαπητός
Epiph. *Haer.*	οὗτός	ἐστιν	ὁ υἱός μου	ὁ ἀγαπητός
30.13.7–8)				
John 1.34	οὗτός	ἐστιν	ὁ ἐκλεκτός	τοῦ θεοῦ.³⁰
Transfiguration				
Matt. 17.5	οὗτός	ἐστιν	ὁ υἱός μου	ὁ ἀγαπητός
Mark 9.7	οὗτός	ἐστιν	ὁ υἱός μου	ὁ ἀγαπητός
Luke 9.35	οὗτός	ἐστιν	ὁ υἱός μου	ὁ ἐκλελεγμένος³¹
2 Peter 1.17	[οὗτός ἐστιν]		ὁ υἱός μου	ὁ ἀγαπητός μου οὗτός ἐστιν
Clem. *Hom.* 3.53	οὗτός	ἐστίν	μου ὁ υἱός	ὁ ἀγαπητός
Apoc. Pet. E 17	This is		my son	whom I love

Matt. 12.18aᵇ	εἰς ὅν	εὐδόκησεν	ἡ ψυχή μου·
Baptism			
Matt. 3.17	ἐν ᾧ	εὐδόκησα	
Mark 1.11	ἐν σοί	εὐδόκησα	
Luke 3.22	ἐν σοί	εὐδόκησα	
Gos. Eb. (cited in	ἐν σοί	ηὐδόκησα	
Epiph. *Haer.*	ἐφ' ὅν	ηὐδόκησα	
30.13.7–8)			
Transfiguration			
Matt. 17.5	ἐν ᾧ	εὐδόκησα·	ἀκούετε αὐτοῦ
Mark 9.7			ἀκούετε αὐτοῦ
Luke 9.35			αὐτοῦ ἀκούετε
2 Peter 1.17	εἰς ὅν ἐγώ	εὐδόκησα	
Clem. *Hom.* 3.53	εἰς ὅν	εὐδόκησα	τουτοῦ ἀκούετε
Apoc. Pet. E 17	and in whom	I have pleasure	

---

³⁰ Although John's text is difficult at this point, the reading of ὁ ἐκλεκτός ought to be preferred over ὁ υἱός (the reading in NA²⁷). For thorough evaluations of the data, see A. Harnack, 'Zur Textkritik und Christologie der Schriften des John', *SAB* (1915): 552–6; R. E. Brown, *The Gospel according to John (i–xii): Introduction, Translation and Notes*, AB, New York: Doubleday, 1966, pp. 57–8; and G. Fee, 'The Textual Criticism of the New Testament', in *The Expositor's Bible Commentary*, vol. I: *Introductory Articles*, Grand Rapids: Zondervan, 1979, pp. 431–2. As the textual evidence is divided evenly, the decision must seemingly be made on internal grounds (so Fee, p. 431).

³¹ For a thorough discussion of the variant readings in Luke 9.35 for ὁ ἐκλελεγμένος, see Marshall, *Luke* p. 388, and B. Metzger, *A Textual Commentary on the Greek New Testament*,

As is frequently noted, a closer examination of Matthew's Baptism (3.17) and Transfiguration (17.5) passages demonstrates the virtual equivalence of Matthew's texts in contrast with those of Mark and Luke. The most common conclusion is that Matthew harmonized the two scenes.[32] His use of οὗτός ἐστιν in his Baptismal scene parallels his account of the Transfiguration in contrast to Mark, which contains two distinct readings (Luke presumably follows Mark at this point): σὺ εἶ opens the Baptism, whereas οὗτός ἐστιν commences the Transfiguration. Furthermore, Matthew's Transfiguration appears to have been coordinated with the Baptismal scene with the addition of ἐν ᾧ εὐδόκησα,[33] a clause not present in Mark 9.7 or Luke 9.35. Matthew's penchant for stock phrases and formulae throughout the Gospel further buoys this conjecture that Matthew's creative hand is behind this coherence.[34]

If one accepts that the alignment of Matt. 3.17 with 17.5 finds its origin in Matthew, the proposal that he has likewise adjusted 12.18a to agree with these two important texts becomes more supportable. The inclusion of ὁ ἀγαπητός in Mark 1.11 and 9.7 indicates use of the title in connection with both the Baptism and the Transfiguration prior to Matthew.[35] The question, then, is whether Mark, or his tradition, drew upon a text or exegesis similar to that of Matthew's version of 12.18a.[36] Matthew 12.18a is the only extant text of Isa. 42.1a which includes ὁ ἀγαπητός. To base an argument upon this and assert that Isa. 42.1a was the source of ὁ ἀγαπητός or was used in connection with these two events seems implausible. It is the inclusion of ἐν ᾧ εὐδόκησα that indicates that Isa. 42.1a was used in conjunction with the Baptism narrative (cf. Mark 1.11; Luke 3.22).[37] Thus, the assertion that Matthew's version of Isa. 42.1a lies behind the passage seems suspect; nevertheless it does appear that

2nd edn, London: United Bible Societies, 1975, p. 148, both of whom conclude that it should be viewed as the original reading.

[32] If John's text represents the oldest tradition, Matthew may be reliant upon such a text, but one must still explain the inclusion of ὁ ἀγαπητός. Bauckham, *2 Peter*, p. 210, challenges the alignment of Matt. 17.5, suggesting instead that it represents an independent tradition, which along with 2 Pet. 1.17 points to an older textual tradition.

[33] The use of ἐν ᾧ in place of Mark's and Luke's ἐν σοί is probably a further adjustment to align it with the usage of οὗτός ἐστιν.

[34] See J. C. Anderson, *Matthew's Narrative Web*, pp. 226–42.

[35] Lindars, *New Testament Apologetic*, pp. 139–41.

[36] So W. Zimmerli and J. Jeremias, *The Servant of God*, London: SCM Press, 1957, p. 81, who assume that עבדי = παῖς and was later replaced by υἱός.

[37] Plooij, 'Baptism', p. 249. If ὁ ἐκλεκτός is the original reading in John 1.34, as seems likely, it may suggest that the oldest tradition is based primarily upon Isa. 42.1a; Mark's text would then present a further stage in the process and indicate the usage of Ps. 2.7 and/or Gen. 22 in the development (see A. D. A. Moses, *Matthew's Transfiguration Story and Jewish-Christian Controversy*, JSNTSup 122, Sheffield: Sheffield Academic Press, 1996, pp. 135–48).

Isa. 42.1a is used in the Baptism.[38] Additionally, Luke's usage of the distinct form ὁ ἐκλελεγμένος in his Transfiguration (9.35) provides separate evidence of the import of Isa. 42.1a. Thus, it seems that the usage of ὁ ἀγαπητός in Matt. 3.17 does not derive from Matthew 12.18a. Matthew is simply following Mark at this point. Whether the text of Isa. 42.1a reflected in Matt. 12.18a was well known and exerted influence on these traditions at an early date is difficult to ascertain. 2 Pet. 1.17 may offer evidence for such a theory, but it is probably dependent upon Matthew.[39] As for the slight differences between Mark 1.11, 9.7 and Matt. 3.17, 12.18a and 17.5, and so on, the fluidity and variety within the texts from the period render any decision regarding development and dependence tentative at best.

A final point regarding the metre of Matthew's text ought to be mentioned. Despite the adjustments, Matthew's text maintains a poetic structure and metre resembling those of the MT, Theodotion and Symmachus.[40] The retention of a poetic quality in Theodotion, Symmachus and Matthew suggests close attention to the Hebrew text.

12.18b

The latter half of 12.18 provides three noteworthy points of contrast. First, the choice and use of the future tense of τίθημι[41] rather than the aorist form of δίδωμι found in the LXX further distinguishes Matthew; how far Matthew is from the MT's נָתַתִּי may be debated. Stendahl's proposal of contact between Matthew's text and the Targum imperfect אֶתֵּן is tenable, particularly if, as seems likely, the messianic interpretation found in the Targum is earlier than Matthew.[42] A messianic interpretation of this prophetic text may have led to the use of the future tense of both

---

[38] One must note, however, that the variety of forms evidenced (see above chart) and the variants in the text of Matt. 12.18a itself render any arguments regarding dependence tentative at best.

[39] The key issue is whether Matthew's text of Isa. 42.1a represents the author's own work, with 2 Pet. 1.17 copying Matthew, or a separate tradition upon which both authors drew independently. The Achilles' heel in Bauckham's analysis involves his attempt to explain the insertion of ὁ ἀγαπητός into Isa. 42.1. This appears to be a Matthean feature which is difficult to explain on other grounds, particularly when the title ὁ ἐκλεκτός was both linguistically more precise and more conspicuously messianic, as the translations of Symmachus and Theodotion demonstrate.

[40] So Torrey, *Documents of the Primitive Church*, p. 46.

[41] Gundry, *Use of the Old Testament*, p. 113, notes Matthew's agreement with the term and tense of the Targum's אֶתֵּן.

[42] Gundry, *ibid*. One must be cautious of basing a theory of contact with a Targum solely on tense, given the fluidity of the texts and willingness to adjust them in light of contextual concerns. Furthermore, perfective aspect in the MT may be translated by the past, present

τίθημι and ἀπαγγέλλω,[43] whereas the LXX aorist implies accomplished fulfilment.[44]

Second, the final clause in verse 18 opens with καί, which is extant in neither the MT nor LXX but is of interest because it parallels the texts of 1QIsaᵃ and the Bohairic. Finally, Matthew's choice of the future ἀπαγγελεῖ[45] ('he will announce/proclaim') to translate the MT's Hiphil יוֹצִיא, in disagreement with the LXX's future ἐξοίσει ('he will bring forth'), provides a nuanced distinction, the degree of which is debatable.[46] The extent to which Matthew's version has diverged from the MT depends upon how one defines יוֹצִיא, which is used on occasion in the MT with a denotation of 'verbal promulgation'.[47] In Isa. 48.20 the LXX translates the Hiphil הוֹצִיאוּהָ with ἀπαγγείλατε, in a context in which the emphasis resides upon verbal proclamation.[48] The Targum's reading provides a parallel to Matthew's text and their contact at this point may reflect an early Jewish interpretation.

12.19

Further distinctions emerge in Matt. 12.19 between Matthew's text and the MT and LXX, some of which possibly derive their origins from Matthew.[49] Once again the direction of scholarly discussion has been

or future tenses. To use the language of Waltke and O'Connor, *Biblical Hebrew Syntax*, p. 481, 'Perfective aspect may occur in reference to any time period.'

[43] Barth, 'Matthew's Understanding of the Law', p. 126 n. 5.

[44] This criterion is not, however, consistently applied. Cf. Matt. 4.15–16, which contains εἶδεν within a prophetic citation. Arguments based upon a consistent use of tense are tenuous at best.

[45] Matthew redactionally inserts ἀπαγγέλλειν in 28.8 and possibly here. Goulder, *Midrash and Lection*, p. 477, includes the term with others in what he labels 'semi-Matthean'. Lindars, *New Testament Apologetic*, p. 147, argues that Matthew here replaces judgment with 'words of preaching'.

[46] Stendahl, *School*, p. 111, once again postulates possible contact with the Targum, here with the imperfect יוֹבִל (followed by Gundry, *Use of the Old Testament*, p. 113).

[47] BDB, p. 425 § 3k, refers to the bringing forth of words or speech as a definition. In support the editors cite Job 8.10; 15.[1]3 (*sic*); Prov. 10.18; 29.11; Neh. 6.19; and Isa. 48.20 (which is rendered in the LXX with ἀπαγγέλλειν). It is also used with the sense of 'publishing a report' in Num. 14.37 and Deut. 22.14. Scholars are yet again divided as to the quality of Matthew's rendering. Allen, 'Matthew xii.19–Isaiah xlii.2', 141, suggests that ἀπαγγελεῖ is nearer to the Targum than the MT, whereas Torrey, *Documents of the Primitive Church*, p. 65, takes the view that יוֹצִיא is 'well rendered by ἀπαγγελεῖ'.

[48] The translational difference in the LXX may only be due to creativity on the part of the translator, as a perusal of ἐκφέρειν in LSJ or BAGD reveals that connections with 'verbal proclamation' are not to be found. Thus, it appears that interpretative urgencies are evidenced in the language employed here.

[49] Stendahl, *School*, p. 112, considers this text as evidence that 'the form of the text in Matthew is an interpretation of the prophecy in the light of what happened to Jesus'.

focused upon the issue of terminological correspondence in the translation, namely, does ἐρίσει = יְצָע and κραυγάσει = יִשָּׂא? Most contentious
has been the question of possible sources for Matthew's ἐρίζειν. Clearly
distinct from both the MT and LXX, numerous attempts have been made
to explain this 'variant', usually with reference to known texts. Its inclusion has been justified by the lack of a corresponding verb in the Hebrew
text,[50] or alternatively explained either as the result of a 'mistranslation
of the Lewisian Syriac *nrib*',[51] a Matthean correction based upon an Eastern Aramaic Targum read in light of the Western Aramaic nuance,[52] or a
targumization of Matthew. Speculation that a Semitic background lies behind the citation has suffered from a scarcity of textual evidence from the
period. The supposition of an UrMatthew in Syriac, Hebrew or Aramaic
is quite unlikely. Similarly, the hypothesis of an Aramaic selection of
Testimonies, or translation of OT texts, is difficult to prove. Ultimately, it
is almost impossible to precisely determine Matthew's source, especially
now in light of the studies which demonstrate the fluidity of the texts. If
there is a connection between the adjustment (or 'variant') and the context, then the answer regarding its origin probably stems from Matthew
himself and not from an unknown text-form.

The question arises, then, of the meaning of ἐρίζειν and its relationship to the context. On a linguistic level these are difficult to determine.
The passages included in LSJ certainly confirm a definition of 'verbal

[50] So D. T. Zahn, *Das Evangelium des Matthäus*, Kommentar zum Neuen Testament,
Leipzig: Georg Böhme, 1903, p. 451 n. 68, who further argues that κραυγάσει, Matthew's
second verb, corresponds to the first Hebrew verb יְצָע and that the second Hebrew verb
יִשָּׂא was left untranslated, a conjecture rejected by Nestle, 'Matthew xii.19–Isaiah xlii.2',
93. Nestle agrees with Zahn that κραυγάσει corresponds to יְצָע, but avers that Matthew's
first verb (ἐρίσει) corresponds to the second in the MT (יִשָּׂא).

[51] D. S. Margoliouth, 'The Visit to the Tomb', *ExpTim* 38 (1926/7): 278, following
Nestle, describes this passage as possibly 'the foundation-stone of Synoptic criticism'. The
curious correspondence between the Syriac *nrib* and Matthew's text led Nestle, 'Matthew
xii.19–Isaiah xlii.2', 189, to postulate an 'intermediate Aramaic' stage of Matthew between
the Hebrew text and Matthew's Greek text. Nestle, p. 93, posits a Semitic Matthew that used
the root רוב with the sense of 'to be loud' and also 'quarrelsome', which was later translated
into Greek using ἐρίζειν. Thus, we have the order נשׂא (Heb.) = רוב (Syriac) = ἐρίζειν.
Allen, 'Matthew xii.19–Isaiah xlii.2', 140–1, notes that Matthew's κραυγάσει translates
the MT's יִשָּׂא and that דיב 'seems to be peculiar to Syriac, and not to occur in Aramaic'.
He concludes that 'Matthew's clauses are in the order of the Hebrew, and that ἐρίσει is a
rendering *ad sensum* of יְצָע, or of an intermediate Aramaic translation.' On this see also
M. Black, *An Aramaic Approach to the Gospels and Acts*, Oxford: Clarendon, 1946, p. 257.

[52] Stendahl's overly complex view explicated in *School* has been rightly challenged on
numerous fronts. For the most requiring critique see Gärtner, 'Habakkuk Commentary', 20.
Gundry, *Use of the Old Testament*, p. 114, correctly questions whether the proposed distinction between Eastern and Western Aramaic existed at the time of Matthew's composition. In
addition to Gundry's bibliography, see K. Beyer, *The Aramaic Language: Its Distribution
and Subdivisions*, translated by J. F. Healey, Göttingen: Vandenhoeck & Ruprecht, 1986.

wrangling',[53] but these texts generally derive a verbal dimension from their contexts, allowing for the specificity of 'verbal' in the broader definition of 'wrangling', 'strife', and so forth. The primary hindrance in the Matthean citation is that no such context exists apart from its parallel κραυγάζειν.[54] The meaning of ἐρίζειν appears to be constrained by that pairing to signify *verbal* wrangling.

In the final clause of 12.19, the translations are encumbered by the causative element in the Hiphil יַשְׁמִיעַ and the accusative קוֹלוֹ, a key difference between the LXX and Matthew. The LXX renders the phrase with a future passive form, placing 'voice' in the nominative (οὐδὲ ἀκουσθήσεται ἔξω ἡ φωνὴ αὐτοῦ),[55] while Matthew's text employs τις as the subject with a future active verb, thus retaining 'voice' in the accusative. If the unlikely assertion that there is a heightened emphasis in the Matthean version proves accurate, then the stress resides in the addition of τις and the straightforward active construct. Given the semantic range of יחוּץ, both the LXX's ἔξω and Matthew's ἐν ταῖς πλατείαις are appropriate renderings. If Matthew's variant version represents an adjustment by Matthew or early Christian tradition, the change from the more general LXX reading of 'outside' to the specific 'in the streets' would seem a natural translation allowed by the Hebrew.

12.20

Matthew's συντετριμμένον and τυφόμενον of verse 20 are rough equivalents to the LXX's τεθλασμένον and καπνιζόμενον and the MT; however, the LXX's συντρίψει ('crush' or 'rub together') is not as close as Matthew's κατεάξει ('shatter' or 'break into pieces'), which is a good translation of יְשַׁבּוֹר. The texts of Symmachus, Theodotion and Aquila all agree in their use of ἀμαυρόν against both Matthew and the LXX, effectively demonstrating the variety in the Greek translations of the period.

A more serious puzzle emerges with the final line in 12.20, which is entirely distinct from the MT and LXX. It is possible that Matthew has completely excised two lines of text, Isa. 42.3b–4a, substituting the single line ἕως ἂν ἐκβάλῃ εἰς νῖκος τὴν κρίσιν. Or 12.20b may represent a loose

[53] LSJ, p. 688, notes the definitions 'strive, wrangle', citing among others *Il*. 1.6; 12.423; *Od*. 18.277; Soph., *El*. 467; and 'challenge, vie with', *Od*. 8.371; 5.213; *Il*. 3.223; 9.389.

[54] Cf. Polem., *Cyn*. 40; Galen, *De loc. aff.* 8.287K; 2 Esdras 3.13. Gundry, *Use of the Old Testament*, p. 113, observes the import of the poetic parallelism in controlling the establishment of the semantic range of both terms.

[55] Torrey, *Documents of the Primitive Church*, p. 65, postulates that the Niphal (יִשָּׁמַע) is behind Matthew's text.

equivalent of either 42.3b or 4a, or perhaps a combination of the two. The lacuna has been variously explained as dittography, homoioteleuton,[56] or creative targumization. Other suggestions have pointed to the possible influence from another text, perhaps, for example, Hab. 1.4 or an unknown Hebrew *Vorlage* of which 1QHᵃ 12.25 (4.25) may be representative.[57]

Three observations emerge which may help one through the maze. First, ἕως ἄν probably translates עַד in 42.4b[58] rather than לְ in 42.3c.[59] Second, ἐκβάλῃ could translate either יוֹצִיא (42.3c)[60] or יָשִׂים (42.4b), but it is most probable that just as the LXX translates the Hiphil of יצא with ἐκβάλλειν, Matthew does likewise.[61] Third, and perhaps most importantly, it is unlikely that Matthew's εἰς νῖκος translates either לְאֶמֶת (42.3c) or בָּאָרֶץ (42.4b).[62]

Until recently, the common assumption was that εἰς νῖκος derived from Hab. 1.4.[63] There both מִשְׁפָּט and יצא occur in the same clause with לנצח (מִשְׁפָּט וְלֹא־יֵצֵא לָנֶצַח), which, although translated by εἰς τέλος in the LXX, is frequently translated by εἰς νῖκος in Aquila.[64] This theory suggests that Matthew, influenced by Hab. 1.4, substituted לנצח for לאמת or בארץ. In its favour is the fact that נצח means 'victory' in Aramaic and probably has this meaning in Hab. 1.4.[65] Unfortunately, the text of Aquila is missing for both Isa. 42.3b–4a and Hab. 1.4. Although it is possible that Hab. 1.4 has influenced the text of Matt. 12.20, the surrounding context of Habakkuk, which questions God's justice, runs counter to Matthew's positive declaration of the victory of κρίσις. Additionally, the mood of יצא is distinct; in Habakkuk it is a Qal while in Isa. 42.3 it occurs in the

---

[56] Allen, *Matthew*, p. 131, explains it as a jump from the first מִשְׁפָּט to the second. Others have postulated a jump from κρίσις to κρίσις. What these theories cannot explain, however, are the additional unique readings found in Matthew.

[57] De Waard, *Comparative Study*, p. 68.

[58] So confident that this marker is the decisive factor, Gundry, *Use of the Old Testament*, p. 114 n. 5, relegates discussion on this point to a footnote. See also de Waard, *Comparative Study*, p. 69.

[59] Note that the form לְאֶמֶת only occurs here in the Old Testament.

[60] In 12.18 ἀπαγγέλλω was used for יוֹצִיא, and, given that the LXX uses ἐκφέρειν in both v. 18 and v. 20, one might expect Matthew's text to share a similar consistency.

[61] Cf. 2 Chron. 23.14; 29.5, 16; Ezra 10.3. Stendahl, *School*, p. 114, and Grindel, 'Matthew 12, 18–21', 113, both suggest that each of these occurrences appears in the context of violence. Whether it does so in Matthew depends upon how one interprets 'bring forth justice to victory'.

[62] O. Bauernfeind, 'νικάω', *TDNT* IV.944, posits the unlikely idea that εἰς νῖκος translates לְאֶמֶת.

[63] Gundry, *Use of the Old Testament*, pp. 114–15 and Stendahl, *School*, p. 113.

[64] A. Rahlfs, 'Über Theodotion-Lesarten im Neuen Testament und Aquila-Lesarten bei Justin', *ZNW* 20 (1921): 186–9.

[65] Holm-Nielsen, *Hodayot*, p. 84 n. 58, takes נצח to mean 'fortunate advance, victory'; cf. Isa. 26.7, in which נצח has an adverbial sense of 'hindered'.

Hiphil. Finally, Jewish writings do not bring these two texts together. All these factors raise legitimate doubts concerning direct dependence upon or use of Habakkuk by Matthew,[66] unless, of course, there existed an exegetical stage of which we are unaware.

With the discovery of 1QHᵃ 12.25 (= 4.25),[67] ותוצא לנצח משפטם ולמישדים אמת, translated 'And Thou bringest their justice forth to victory and truth unto equity',[68] de Waard optimistically concludes that we need look no further for Matthew's text.[69] All exuberance aside, it is possible that 1QHᵃ 12.25 is somewhat dependent upon Isa. 42.3b: both texts contain a positive tone, both employ the Hiphil of יצא, and the author of 1QHᵃ demonstrates 'special preference for Deutero-Isa'.[70] Despite these similarities, however, one problem remains. The text of 1QHᵃ 12.25 is not an explicit citation of Isa. 42.3, but neither does it appear to be a translation of Hab. 1.4.[71] Additionally, verbal differences exist between the MT of Isa. 42.3 and 1QHᵃ 12.25, not only with reference to לנצח but also to the reading of ולמישדים אמת in the clause which follows. The phrase 'you bring their justice forth to victory', however, is strikingly similar to Matthew's text, and provides proof of the reading's existence in Jewish literature from the period. Merely establishing a reading's existence does not, however, demonstrate the interpretative tradition that led to such a reading, its breadth of dissemination, or why early Christians or Matthew incorporated it into this citation. 1QHᵃ 12 is not an especially sectarian hymn; thus it is difficult to determine its origin or breadth of dissemination. These are insoluble questions given the data available. One thing is certain, however–Matthew's reading here reflects a thoughtful exegetical use of Scripture, possibly Isa. 42.3.

The excised text also deserves scrutiny, as it may provide further insight into Matthew's concerns in the citation. Absent is any reference to suffering or death which 42.4a may have implied. That such a reading

[66] De Waard, *Comparative Study*, p. 68, makes similar points with regard to the differences between 1QHᵃ 12.25 (4.25) and Hab. 1.4.

[67] See Puech, 'Quelques aspects de la restauration du rouleau des Hymnes (1QH)', *JJS* 39 (1988): 38–55, for comments regarding the order of the various psalms.

[68] As translated by Holm-Nielsen, *Hodayot*, p. 76. He further suggests, p. 84 n. 58, that the context for the unique text may depend upon Isa. 42.3. This is certainly possible. Cf. García Martínez, ed., *Dead Sea Scrolls*, pp. 334–5, who offers the translation, 'You will make his right triumph, and truth through justice.' As in Isa. 42.1–4, the difficulty involves how to translate נצח. What is of interest is that this particular hymn further extols the justice of God (12.30–1, 37, 40).

[69] De Waard, *Comparative Study*, p. 69.   [70] *Ibid.*, p. 68.

[71] *Ibid.*; de Waard makes similar observations to those above, noting that יצא occurs in the Qal imperfect, a form distinct from the Hiphil in Isaiah, and that OT critics have not linked Isa. 42.3 with Hab. 1.4.

was possible is evidenced by Maimonides who cites this text as evidence for the death of the Messiah.[72] The 'faithful' manner in which justice is brought forth is also conspicuously absent (42.3b). Finally, the location of justice's establishment 'upon the earth' is salient in its omission.

12.21

Often considered a later interpolation,[73] the inclusion of the LXX line καὶ [ἐπὶ] τῷ ὀνόματι αὐτοῦ ἔθνη ἐλπιοῦσιν marks a clear divergence from the MT and Greek revisions.[74] Matthew's text is identical to the LXX, except for an omitted ἐπί, which is nevertheless picked up in Matthew's dative.[75] The most striking element of Matthew's and the LXX's text is the replacement of 'Torah' with 'name', and 'islands' with 'gentiles/nations'. ὀνόματι is a puzzling reading,[76] which probably ought not to be explained as a Greek corruption due to the fact that all LXX manuscripts and early Latin texts agree on the reading. The revisions of Aquila, Theodotion and Symmachus are, it must be observed, unified in their movement back to the MT's reading of 'law', but this is expected. The broad, early support for the reading may appear to buttress Gundry's speculation that 'we are dealing with lost variants in the Hebrew text', but this is unlikely given the fact that 1QIsaᵃ,ᵇ agree against Matthew and the LXX, suggesting the MT is the original Hebrew reading.[77] The adoption of the LXX reading

---

[72] See p. 1.

[73] Based upon the text-form, Kilpatrick, *Origins*, p. 94, argues that the citation was included in two stages; the non-LXX vv. 18–20 was inserted first, followed by the LXX's v. 21 at a later stage. Kilpatrick is preceded by Bacon, *Studies*, p. 475, who assigned it to 'R's reliance upon the LXX', and Schlatter, *Matthäus*, p. 402, for whom it is the product of a 'second hand' (cf. Manson, 'Old Testament', 323). Although the fact that the verse is omitted in min. 33 may appear to support this position, the mixed text-form of most of the other formula quotations, which include LXX elements, would indicate otherwise.

[74] Ziegler's suggestion, *Isaias*, p. 277, that ὀνόματι is a Greek corruption for νόμῳ suffers from lack of evidence and further neglects to explain the reading of ἔθνη for אִיִּים (Gundry, *Use of the Old Testament*, p. 115 n. 4). New, *Old Testament Quotations*, pp. 106–7, uncritically adopts Ziegler's inclusion of νόμῳ and then surprisingly states that 'no significant variants for this text' exist, when in fact the reverse is true: no textual evidence exists to support the reading νόμῳ.

[75] Gundry, *Use of the Old Testament*, p. 115, oddly suggests that this variant in Matthew argues in favour of independence from the LXX. One should note its similarity to Isa. 11.10 cited in Rom. 15.12 (ἐπ᾽ αὐτῷ ἔθνη ἐλπιοῦσιν). F. J. Matera's suggestion, 'The Plot of Matthew's Gospel', *CBQ* 49 (1987): 250, that 12.21 is a conflation of Isa. 42.4, 9 and 11.10 (LXX) is possible, but 12.21 can also be explained from its own context.

[76] See chapter 3, pp. 58–9.

[77] Gundry, *Use of the Old Testament*, p. 115. Torrey, *Documents of the Primitive Church*, p. 65, is probably correct that this last line was simply 'an ancient, and probably widespread, variant reading'; but Torrey cannot explain whether or not the 'variant' was exegetically

of ἔθνη as a translation for אִיִּם by Matthew certainly serves his universal interests.[78]

Conclusions regarding Matthew's text-form of 12.18–21

Matthew's text has been variously explained as a 'fresh translation from the Hebrew',[79] a text that Matthew copied from a previous source or book of Testimonies, or a Matthean revision of the LXX. Given the textual evidence from the period, it is less possible than ever to make a definitive judgment; however, some tentative conclusions can be put forward as a result of even this brief analysis:

1. Matt. 12.18a evinces signs of pre-Matthean usage in early Christian tradition in connection with the Baptism and Transfiguration. In this earlier stage it seems probable that the text employed was similar to the early Greek revisions of Aquila, Theodotion and Symmachus (ὁ παῖς μου, εὐδόκησεν) rather than the LXX. While it is impossible to demonstrate the various stages of development, two are salient. First, Matthew may have relied on a Greek text that had been revised towards the MT (ὁ παῖς μου, ὃν εὐδόκησεν). Of course it is equally possible that Matthew himself or others within his community made these changes on the basis of their exegesis of the MT. Matthew's personal attention may be in evidence in the modifications manifest in the structure and terms employed (e.g. αἱρετίζειν, ὁ ἀγαπητός) and the close alignment of the text to 3.17 and 17.5. If this is the case, this second point would suggest that Matthew is himself responsible for the adjustments in 12.18a.

2. In those places where Matthew's text corresponds to the LXX, the translation offered is the most obvious translation of the Hebrew. Again, this could be Matthew's own work or could represent his dependence upon an early Greek revision. This

---

motivated. For an insightful discussion, see Koenig, *L'herméneutique analogique*, pp. 355–69.

[78] Similarly translated in LXX 41.5. These are the only two locations in the LXX which translate אי with ἔθνος. Whether it is as poor a translation as Gundry asserts is questionable. In both contexts the reading of the LXX, while a loose translation, may simply be an example of metonymy in which the location of islands is replaced by their residents, the gentiles (cf. Gen. 10.5).

[79] A. H. McNeile, *The Gospel according to St Matthew*, London: Macmillan, 1915, p. 172, asserts, 'The Aramaic collection of *testimonia* from which it was derived was translated from a Heb. recension differing both from that used by the LXX and from the M.T.'

challenges New's assumption that the LXX was the base text for Matthew's translation. The fact that Matthew also employed the LXX in its distinctive reading of Isa. 42.4b (= Matt. 12.21) suggests that he had access to a copy of the LXX and that he was willing to employ it when it suited his theological agenda. This, of course, leads one to the conclusion that Matthew worked with at least two texts, the LXX and either a Hebrew text, an Aramaic text or a Greek revision towards the Hebrew.[80]

3. It is worth noting that the verbs are frequently the point at which Matthew departs from the LXX. Most alterations are possible translations, albeit more nuanced renderings, of the Hebrew. For example, θήσω for נָתַתִּי instead of the LXX's ἔδωκα in 12.18b; ἀπαγγελεῖ for יוֹצִיא in place of the LXX's ἐξοίσει; κατεάξει for יִשְׁבּוֹר in place of the LXX's συντρίψει. In each occurrence, it is debatable which is closer to the MT.

4. Matthew's use of ἐρίσει in verse 19 is a special case in point. While a precise explanation remains problematic, it is perhaps best not understood as a 'mistranslation' of the Syriac Peshitta. Instead, it is possible that either Matthew adjusted the text for contextual or theological reasons or the text was taken over from an earlier tradition. It is difficult, however, to imagine another context for the citation that would necessitate a change of this nature. As a result, it is at this point that Matthew's agenda may be most evident, although the precise basis for the adjustment, whether textual (doubtful) or interpretative (more probable), remains a mystery. If it was interpretative, then one would expect that the context would evince a similar concern.

5. Subtle editorial adjustments made in accordance with Matthew's perception of the life and ministry of Jesus appear to exist. These include the use of ἐρίζειν mentioned above and the shift from ἐκφέρειν in LXX Isa. 42.1 and 3 to ἀπαγγέλλειν in 12.18 (42.1) and ἐκβάλλειν in 12.20 (if it translates 42.3). Similarly, both the excision of the lines of text and the substitution of the foreign line in 12.20b (possibly deriving from 1QH[a] 12.25 or an interpretation of Hab. 1.4), and the inclusion of the LXX in 12.21 seem to demand a theory which encompasses adjustments influenced by theological reflection.

6. In light of these general conclusions, the assertion that the translation of Isa. 42.1–4 as found in Matthew represents a fresh

---

[80] Cf. Menken, 'Isaiah 42,1–4 in Matthew 12,18–21', 52.

translation from the Hebrew by Matthew is too facile.[81] Instead, the text-form bears the marks of continued usage, in which an author (or authors) drew upon elements from Christian traditional usage, known textual interpretations, and possibly even texts from Qumran, and adjusted the text accordingly.

Matthew's unique text-form, it seems, demonstrates his use of either the Hebrew, or more likely a Greek (or Aramaic) text conformed to the Hebrew, which he then altered in the light of his own concerns.[82] Ultimately, the singular challenge to such a theory concerns the question whether the modifications bear any relationship to the surrounding context or Matthew's general theological interests. Surely this is the one crucial test for any hypothesis that postulates a scribe or Targumist as author; it is also the one point that has proved most difficult to pin down.

An analysis of Matthew 12.18–21

When placed over against the other versions, the anomalies that arise in Matthew's text have the potential of indicating Matthew's particular interests. One must be cautious, however, for this method relies upon the ability of the interpreter to determine which changes are truly Matthean, and, given the fluidity of the texts during this period, this is not an elementary task. One might also observe that most readers from the period would not have had several versions of Isaiah to consult, nor the linguistic capabilities to draw comparisons with the Matthean text. Thus, whether those members of Matthew's reading or listening audience would have recognized the adjustments as significant or distinctive is debatable. It does seem, however, that the innovative alterations made on a terminological, grammatical and/or linguistic level effectively create a unique web of relationships, thereby shifting the rhetorical emphasis of the citation. Reader-response critics might argue that the rhetorical force of the final form of Matthew's peculiar text is dissimilar to that of LXX Isa. or even the MT. The audience participating in the reading event would have been moved and challenged in new ways as a result of these novel grammatical and linguistic intra-relationships. With this in mind, a brief

---

[81] *Ibid.*, 52.

[82] Recently, however, the theory that Matthew might have drawn on a book of Testimonies has received a boost from 4QFlor and John Ryl Pap 460. The fact that Matthew's version of Isa. 42.1a recurs in 2 Pet. 1.17 suggests either direct dependence upon Matthew, or an independent source upon which both drew (which, I have argued, is unlikely); or, it is just possible that Matthew's version of Isa. 42.1–4 was included in a Testimony book and made its way into 2 Peter in that fashion.

overview of Matthew's version of the citation, surveying grammatical and linguistic links, should help to determine the meaning and emphases, and may ultimately prove an illuminating exercise.

The two parallel lines in 12.18a serve to limit and define one another (ᵃBehold my servant, whom I have chosen, ᵇmy Beloved, in whom my soul delights). They in turn specify and identify one particular individual.[83] The subject in both lines receives greater elaboration through the addition of a relative clause. Like David or Moses in the Old Testament (cf. Pss. 89.3; 105.26; 106.23), the servant in 12.18aᵃ is the one marked by divine choice. Its parallel clause discloses that the pleasure of God rests upon this individual, this time labelled the Beloved. Reminiscent of the Baptism scene (3.17), in which the sonship of Jesus is made manifest, 12.18aᵇ also alludes to the intimate relationship between Father and Son, an idea marginally developed in 11.25–30.[84] Thus, the designation 'the servant of the Lord', although primarily functional because of its parallel with the Beloved, attains a connotation of greater intimacy and perhaps even plays upon the dual meanings of 'servant/child' inherent in the term παῖς.[85] Furthermore, Matthew's placement of ὁ παῖς μου alongside the messianic designation ὁ ἀγαπητός μου suggests a messianic understanding of the servant in a manner similar to that of Zech. 3.5, in which the phrase 'my servant, the Branch' occurs. One should not go so far as Kingsbury in his diminishment of the import of the servant in Matthew's portrayal of Jesus. As will be demonstrated, Matthew's picture of the intimate servant, who is the son, is crucial to his Gospel and christology. This is especially so in a context like chs. 11–13, in which Jesus' conflict with the Pharisees and separation from Israel, questions involving his identity, and rejection by others all find expression. The affirmation and identification of Jesus as the anticipated one constitutes a significant moment in the Gospel.

Traditionally, 12.18b has been considered a statement concerning the resource provided to the servant for the completion of his mission, namely, the bestowal of the Spirit. There is little doubt that this is in fact true; however, one cannot divorce the bestowal of Spirit from the images of 12.18a, which would indicate both an ethical and a relational basis for

---

[83] What is of special interest is that Matthew's replacement of 'my Elect One' with 'my Beloved' significantly shifts the image from selection to sonship. Kingsbury, *Christology*, p. 95, argues that the accent falls not upon 'Servant' but upon God. The observation concerning the thrice recurring μου reveals this emphasis. Although the servant is the subject of the text, he is described from God's perspective. In this sense the text functions similarly to the Baptism and Transfiguration narratives, in which the voice of God identifies the individual.

[84] Senior, *Matthew*, p. 139.

[85] See D. R. A. Hare, *Matthew*, Interpretation, Louisville: John Knox Press, 1993, p. 136.

the gift of Spirit. In this way, information is supplied as to why the Spirit was bestowed, and moves the reader beyond the Baptism narrative, in which the endowment was simply narrated. As noted in chapter 3, for the first-century reader the Spirit language would have been pivotal and at the very least would have served to mark Jesus as the eschatological deliverer (cf. 12.27–8).[86]

Three points in 12.18b draw the reader's attention. First, the servant is seemingly involved in a mission of proclamation, which, because it is linked to the endowment of the Spirit, could indicate that the mission is somehow prophetic, possibly reminiscent of Deut. 18.15, 18.[87] This popular assertion does not, however, square with Matthew's general portrayal of Jesus. In fact, in 11.2–6 Matthew excises the prophetic element from Q (Luke 7.18)[88] and instead emphasizes a messiahship which is implicitly, if not specifically, royal (cf. 21.1–16).[89] The citation offers no clue concerning the form that the 'proclamation' or 'report' in 12.18b would take or its relationship to κρίσις.[90] Perhaps the report is indirectly related to Jesus' message and deeds, as is implied in Jesus' instructions to John's disciples, 'Go and report (ἀπαγγέλλειν) to John what you see and hear.' Rather than an explicit verbal report of justice, his deeds and message possibly comprise the proclamation of justice; the kingdom of God has arrived and Jesus announces its arrival, but in an indirect, oblique fashion. This will be elaborated upon later in the chapter.

A second, closely related issue is that one must make a clear judgment on the meaning of κρίσις ('judgment' or 'justice') in 12.18b and 20. The

---

[86] Stanton, *Gospel for a New People*, p. 180, notes the import of the Spirit for Matthew's christology.

[87] J. Schniewind, 'ἀπαγγέλλω', *TDNT* I.66–7, mentions the possible link to the prophetic and Deut. 18.15, 18.

[88] Cf. Luke 7.18, which seems to have a prophetic Jesus in view, whereas Matthew adds the phrase τὰ ἔργα τοῦ Χριστοῦ. See the extended discussion in Beaton, 'Messianism, Spirit, and Conflict'.

[89] One should note Williamson's comment, 'Messianic Texts in Isaiah 1–39', in *King and Messiah in Israel and the Ancient Near East: Proceedings of the Oxford Old Testament Seminar*, edited by J. Day, JSOTSup 270, Sheffield: Sheffield Academic Press, 1998, p. 239, that of all the servant songs, Isa. 42.1–4 contains 'the most overtly royal language'. Allison, *The New Moses: A Matthean Typology*, Minneapolis: Fortress, 1993, pp. 233–5, attempts to link the servant of Isa. 42.1–4 with Mosaic typology and has to settle for 'congruence'.

[90] Zahn's assertion, *Matthäus*, pp. 453–4, that it refers to Jesus' proclamation through the church to the gentiles is doubtful given the small amount of evidence that the Matthean church had begun such a mission. A possible link may exist in CD 6.10–11, 'until there will arise one who will teach righteousness/justice at the end of days' (עד עמד יורה הצדק באחרית הימים). Although the text employs צֶדֶק rather than מִשְׁפָּט, the reference to one who will come at the end of times and teach justice/righteousness provides an interesting parallel. Gundry, *Matthew*, p. 230, who does not cite this passage, posits that 12.20b may refer to the 'teaching of justice'.

question surrounding the meaning of κρίσις is an ancient *crux interpretum*,[91] and is perhaps the key element to understanding this servant text.[92] The lack of a consensus by modern commentators on how best to translate κρίσις at this point reflects the difficulty.[93] Despite the numerous and frequent attestations in favour of 'judgment', 'justice' may be preferable for the following reasons:

1. The consensus that the denotation of the usage of κρίσις in 23.23 is 'justice', not 'judgment', offers confirmation that such a meaning lies within the realm of Matthew's semantic range.

2. In contrast to other uses of κρίσις, there is a noticeable lack of formulaic language involving κρίσις in 12.18 and 20.[94] In each text in which κρίσις refers to judgment (10.15; 11.22, 24; and 12.36, 41–2), Matthew uses formulaic language, for example, 'in the day of judgment', ἐν ἡμέρᾳ κρίσεως (10.15; 11.22; 24; 12.36), or 'rising up in judgment against this generation',

---

[91] So Luz, *Matthäus*, II.247 n. 39, who cites Chrysostom 40.2 = 581; Augustine, *De civ. D.* 20.30 = 6.28 1304–5; Hilary 12.10 = SC 254, 276.

[92] Neyrey, 'Thematic Use', 464.

[93] Advocates of 'justice' include M. Davies, *Matthew*, p. 95; J. Schmid, *Das Evangelium nach Matthäus*, Regensburger Neues Testament 1, 3rd edn, Regensburg: Pustet, 1956, p. 209; Beare, *Matthew*, p. 275; W. Grundmann, *Das Evangelium nach Matthäus*, THKNT, Leipzig: Evangelische Verlagsanstalt, 1968, p. 326; Hill, 'Son and Servant', 12; G. Tisera, *Universalism according to the Gospel of Matthew*, European University Studies, Series XXIII, Theology, vol. 482, Frankfurt am Main: Peter Lang, 1993, pp. 174–5. Those who take it as eschatological judgment include B. Weiss, *Das Matthäus-Evangelium*, 9th edn, Göttingen: Vandenhoeck & Ruprecht, 1898, p. 234; Allen, *Matthew*, p. 130; Verseput, *Rejection of the Humble Messianic King*, pp. 197–8; McNeile, *Matthew*, p. 172; Cope, *Matthew*, p. 43 n. 80; and Luz, *Matthäus*, II.247. Neyrey, 'Thematic Use', 464–5, is indicative of the position in favour of judgment when he appeals to the following context in 12.36ff., arguing that there is nothing in the prior context which may explain κρίσις.

[94] An examination of the texts reveals that the forms in which the term κρίσις occurs may also intimate its meaning. The texts of 12.18, 20 and 23.23 lack the formulaic element found in the other texts (e.g. 'in the day of judgment').

Matt. 5.21	ἂν φονεύσῃ, ἔνοχος ἔσται τῇ κρίσει
Matt. 5.22	ἀδελφῷ αὐτοῦ ἔνοχος ἔσται τῇ κρίσει·
Matt. 10.15	γῇ Σοδόμων καὶ Γομόρρων ἐν ἡμέρᾳ κρίσεως ἢ τῇ πόλει ἐκείνῃ.
Matt. 11.22	Σιδῶνι ἀνεκτότερον ἔσται ἐν ἡμέρᾳ κρίσεως ἢ ὑμῖν
Matt. 11.24	Σοδόμων ἀνεκτότερον ἔσται ἐν ἡμέρᾳ κρίσεως ἢ σοί
Matt. 12.36	περὶ αὐτοῦ λόγον ἐν ἡμέρᾳ κρίσεως·
Matt. 12.41	ἄνδρες Νινευῖται ἀναστήσονται ἐν τῇ κρίσει μετὰ τῆς γενεᾶς ταύτης
Matt. 12.42	βασίλισσα νότου ἐγερθήσεται ἐν τῇ κρίσει μετὰ τῆς γενεᾶς ταύτης
Matt. 23.33	ἐχιδνῶν, πῶς φύγητε ἀπὸ τῆς κρίσεως τῆς γεέννης;
Matt. 12.18	πνεῦμά μου ἐπ' αὐτόν, καὶ κρίσιν τοῖς ἔθνεσιν ἀπαγγελεῖ
Matt. 12.20	ἕως ἂν ἐκβάλῃ εἰς νῖκος τὴν κρίσιν.
Matt. 23.23	τὰ βαρύτερα τοῦ νόμου, τὴν κρίσιν καὶ τὸ ἔλεος καὶ τὴν πίστιν

ἐν τῇ κρίσει μετὰ τῆς γενεᾶς ταύτης (12.41–2). Also noteworthy is that with the exception of the phrase πῶς φύγητε ἀπὸ τῆς κρίσεως τῆς γεέννης; ('how will you escape from the condemnation/judgment of hell?') in 23.33, every usage in which judgment is clearly in view is formulaic and in the dative. The two occurrences in 12.18 and 20 are not formulaic and are in the accusative, similar to those in 23.23.

3. There is an increasingly hopeful and positive tone in the text with its mention of the nations.[95] Compare the linkage of κρίσις by a temporal ἕως ἄν in 12.20b to the ministry of compassion in 12.20a, and to the soteriological and universal language in 12.21 via the addition of καί. The proclamation of κρίσις is directed towards the gentiles/nations, who in verse 21 (Isa. 42.4) 'trust in his name', language which is too sanguine for a judgment context.

4. The linkage of κρίσις with πνεῦμα (12.18) and εἰς νῖκος (12.20)[96] is unusual if κρίσις refers to judgment. Instead, the empowering of the Spirit to accomplish the mission, combined with a translation of εἰς νῖκος as 'victory', argues for a victorious establishment of some kind, most probably in conjunction with the anticipated reign of God.

5. OT usage demonstrates that a range of meaning beyond 'judgment' is associated with מִשְׁפָּט, which includes a connotation of behaving in a right manner, particularly towards the oppressed and down-trodden. It is this ethical/religious usage, rather than a strictly legal one, which perhaps best characterizes Matthew's employment in 12.18, 20 and 23.23.

Third and finally, the use of the term ἔθνη, both here and later in verse 21, is curious. Isa. 42.1–4, like Isa. 51.1–8, possesses a striking universalism,

---

[95] Hare, *Matthew*, pp. 137–8, suggests that the *judgment* proclaimed here is hopeful. He argues this by citing 12.41, in which he translates κρίσις as judgment. Jonah's pronoucement of judgment resulted in an act of repentence by the Ninevites. Hare infers that a proclamation of judgment against 'this generation' might have similarly positive results. The difficulty with this position is that rising up in judgment does not appear to possess positive connotations in this context. Reading the successful results of Jonah's prophetic proclamation into the text may be too much, given that the text includes the Queen of the South, who also will rise in judgment. She is not known to have been associated with a prophetic ministry and repentance.

[96] *Pace* R. Kraft, '"εἰς νῖκος": Permanently/Successfully: 1 Cor 15:54; Matt 12:20', in *Septuagintal Lexicography*, edited by R. Kraft, Missoula: Scholars, 1975, pp. 153–6, who attempts to demonstrate that the phrase ought to be translated as 'permanently' or 'successfully'.

which has only been hinted at in the Gospel up to this point.[97] Although it is tempting to translate the term as 'gentiles', it is probably better translated inclusively as 'nations'.[98]

Verses 19–20a mark a shift in the citation from divine approval and the nature of the mission to the demeanour of the servant during his assignment. As noted above, this section evinces subtle but extensive editing and may reveal Matthew's interests most clearly. The use of the ambiguous term ἐρίζειν (to 'quarrel, wrangle'), paralleled with κραυγάζειν and οὐδὲ ἀκούσει τις ἐν ταῖς πλατείαις, depicts the servant's bearing amidst verbal confrontations.[99] On the surface, the reader is presented with a servant who does not himself incite verbal battles. Nothing in this text suggests that the servant is silent; rather, verse 19 describes his demeanour towards his foes. Verse 20a provides a description of his attitude towards the bruised and the faint. With vivid metaphors a compassionate note is struck: 'a broken reed he will not shatter', and similarly, 'a smouldering wick, he will not extinguish'. The difficult task of establishing the referents of wide-ranging metaphors is further compounded by the use of this citation. The Isaiah Targum fills out the translation by equating the poor with the bruised reed and the needy with the smouldering wick.[100] A common assumption among commentators has been that these two metaphors refer to Jesus' compassion extended to the ill of verse 15.[101] Barth, however, suggests that limiting the connection to the sick in verse 15 is too

---

[97] The inclusion, however, of the four women in the genealogy (1.3, 5–6), the magi (2.1–3), 'Galilee of the gentiles' (4.16) and the Centurion (8.5–13) has ensured that the theme is not far beneath the surface of the narrative.

[98] So Schweizer, *Matthew*, p. 282; Trilling, *Das wahre Israel*, p. 103; Tisera, *Universalism*, pp. 182–5. *Pace* D. R. A. Hare and D. J. Harrington, '"Make Disciples of All the Gentiles" (MT 28:19)', *CBQ* 37 (1975): 359–69; K. Bishop, 'St Matthew and the Gentiles', *ExpTim* 59 (1948): 249; J. P. Meier, 'Nations or Gentiles in Matthew 28:19?' *CBQ* 39 (1977): 95. Neyrey, 'Thematic Use', 466, posits an apologetic use of ἔθνη against Jewish particularism and in favour of a mission to the gentiles, notably with reference to believing gentiles in 12.41–2. Tisera, *Universalism*, p. 184, bases part of his argument upon the idea that Jesus has gone 'beyond the limits of the law' (v. 7). This seems problematic on several fronts, but particularly because it is not clear that Jesus has in fact exceeded the boundaries.

[99] Neyrey, 'Thematic Use', 463, postulates that the emphasis does not reside in Jesus' demeanour as such, but upon those who refuse to listen to him. This is certainly possible given the context of chs. 11–13; however, the focus throughout Isa. 42.1–4 is upon the servant himself, not upon those who surround him. Consider the parallelism between 'he will not wrangle, nor cry out' and the final line, 'nor will anyone hear his voice in the street'; the stress seems clearly to rest upon the bearing of the servant.

[100] Chilton, ed., *The Isaiah Targum*, p. 81, translates the key subjects as 'the poor' and 'the needy'. In the place of 'poor', Stenning, ed., *Targum*, p. 140, prefers 'meek'.

[101] Lohmeyer, *Matthäus*, pp. 186–7; A. Sand, *Das Gesetz und die Propheten: Untersuchungen zur Theologie des Evangeliums nach Mätthaus,* Biblische Untersuchungen 11, Regensburg: Pustet, 1974, p. 155.

severe; instead, he proposes that the referent must be the 'comprehensive sense of the work of Jesus the Saviour for the lost, of πτωχοὶ εὐαγγελίζονται (11.5)' (cf. 9.36; 11.28; 23.4).[102] However one decides, a vivid contrast has been created. In the face of conflict, the servant will not fight and may even retreat to the margins, but when confronted with need he exhibits great compassion.

The lines in verses 20b–21 provide an unusual climax to the quotation, to which Matthew's distinctive text substantially contributes. In the LXX, a correlation is drawn between the state of the servant ('he will shine out and not be wearied') and the arrival of justice upon the earth. The MT is more revealing concerning the state of the servant: 'he will not falter or be discouraged until he establishes justice on the earth'. In Matthew, however, his use of ἕως ἄν links verse 20b with the lines which precede (as noted above), thereby establishing a nexus between the compassionate ministry in verse 20a and the victorious bringing forth of justice in verse 20b without reference to a possibly weakened state of the servant. If the linkage is temporal,[103] as seems most likely, then the verse marks a chronological development which incorporates the idea that he will care for the poor and oppressed until the victorious establishment of justice, which will occur at the consummation of the ages.[104]

Finally, 12.21 almost appears tacked on to the end, with negligible relationship to the context; however, joined to the previous line by a connective καί, the verse effectively captures two significant themes for Matthew—the christological ('hope in his name') and the universal (the inclusion of the nations). The use of the term ὄνομα throughout Matthew comprises an important christological motif (cf. 1.21, 23; 7.22; 10.22; 18.5, 20; 19.29; 24.5, 9; 28.19), which occurs here, somewhat surprisingly, in place of the MT's תּוֹרָה.[105] The question arises whether there is embedded in this adoption of the LXX reading a perspective of Jesus and the Law. Koenig's proposition maintaining that a relationship existed between name, Law and remembrance in texts like Exod. 3.15; Pss. 97.12; 119.55; 1QIsa[a] 26.8, is provocative. If this is the case, Matthew's usage of name here may be more than merely copying the LXX; instead, the inclusion of the name of Jesus is an element in Matthew's development

---

[102] 'Matthew's Understanding of the Law', p. 128. Beare, *Matthew*, p. 275, proposes a broad category encompassing the weak.

[103] BDF § 383.

[104] This may allude to the christological assertion of the ongoing presence of Christ (1.21; 18.17; 25.31–46; 28.20).

[105] For an intriguing discussion on a possible scenario explaining the LXX variants for ὄνομα, see Koenig, *L'herméneutique analogique*, p. 232 n. 40.

of a high christology, calling to mind the various titles and names already expressed throughout the Gospel.[106] The citation closes with the assertion that 'the nations' will 'hope' in his name, continuing an optimistic tone within a universalistic frame.

Thus, we find in Matthew's text-form that the citation identifies the servant using the language of sonship from the Baptism and Transfiguration. This filial relationship to God appears to constitute the basis for the affirmation of divine pleasure and the bestowal of the Spirit. Important to the context, however, is the fact that the Spirit undergirds or empowers the servant in his mission of the proclamation of justice. The deportment of the servant is depicted from two angles: he behaves in a non-confrontational manner towards those who oppose him, while at the same time extending compassion to the weak and faint. Finally, linked to verse 20 by a temporal ἕως ἄν are two closing lines. The first line affirms that 'justice will be brought forth to victory', heralding a victorious denouement to the period of pain and injustice. The final line professes a universal openness to the nations, declaring that they will derive hope from the servant.

The relation of text-form to context and meaning

Even a brief examination of the quotation reveals that by citing Isa. 42.1–4 Matthew introduces a thematically expansive text into the narrative. The textual adjustments undertaken by Matthew, and perhaps others associated with him, merely enhance its appeal. In a manner reminiscent of the citations explored in chapter 4, this quotation also appears to be bireferential; however, arriving at a reasonable description of such a level of reference has to this point been elusive.

Like the other formula citations, 12.17–21 opens with a version of the standard formula, ἵνα πληρωθῇ τὸ ῥηθὲν διὰ Ἡσαΐου τοῦ προφήτου λέγοντος. The telic ἵνα limits the referent of the citation to the preceding material. Three primary points of contact between the context and citation have traditionally been proposed. The first two possible bridges are derived from verses 15–16, 'many crowds followed him, and he cured all of them, and he ordered them not make him known'. The fact that verses 15–16 comprise one long sentence connected by καί makes it difficult to arrive at a clear-cut decision; either one or both of the two aorist verbs 'he healed' (ἐθεράπευσεν) and 'he warned' (ἐπετίμησεν) could serve as the referent of ἵνα. The third proposal originates in Jesus' conflict with and withdrawal from the Pharisees in verse 14.

---

[106] Neyrey, 'Thematic Use', 466.

12.15–16 consists of a heavily redacted version of Mark 3.7–12, a central text for Mark's 'messianic secret', in which Jesus' command to the 'unclean spirits' becomes in Matthew merely a command of silence to those healed.[107] This modified secrecy motif is thought to provide a bridge from the context to the citation, particularly to the language of verse 19, 'he will not wrangle nor cry out' and/or 'nor will anyone hear his voice in the streets'.[108] This assumes, of course, that the reason for the charge of silence is to control potential difficulties which an explosion of undesired popularity resulting from Jesus' miracles might create.[109] Although possible, this explanation validates the narrative in a very round-about manner. The citation presents the servant's demeanour in the face of conflict, or verbal wrangling, and Jesus' command to silence does not appear to be an attempt to contain the crowds' spontaneous enthusiasm towards him. Others have instead suggested that the warning confirms Jesus' lowliness,[110] or, as Wrede puts it, is 'proof of his unassuming nature and quiet reserve'.[111] Wrede's portrait of Jesus at this point is questionable, if only because it is at odds with Jesus' comportment in 12.1–14 and 12.22ff. A counter proposal might take into account the re-jection (11.16–24) and conflict (12.1–14; 22ff.) motifs, and the themes of hiddenness and revelation (11.6, 25–30), which predominate in Matt. 11–13.[112] Luz's observation that Israel's rejection begins in Matt. 12 is pertinent at this point.[113] If the secrecy charge is linked to the hidden-ness and disclosure motifs, then the referent of verse 19 also becomes more intelligible. The emphasis resides in the servant's demeanour with

[107] The messianic secret is clearly not as important in Matthew as in Mark. The Matthean texts in which it occurs include 8.4; 9.30; 12.16; 16.20; 17.9.

[108] So Stendahl, *School*, p. 113, who contends that it manifests the 'reluctant attitude of Jesus to publicity'; also Wiefel, *Matthäus*, p. 231; Trilling, *Das wahre Israel*, p. 126. Lindars, *New Testament Apologetic*, p. 151, adds further that 'Mt [was] probably unaware of the real point of the adaptation of the text, to prove that the gentleness of Christ's methods is consistent with the Church's claim about him.'

[109] So Hagner, *Matthew 1–13*, p. 199; France, *Matthew*, pp. 153, 205–6; Y.-E. Yang, *Jesus and the Sabbath in Matthew's Gospel*, JSNTSup 139, Sheffield: Sheffield Academic Press, 1997, p. 216; Schnackenburg, 'Siehe da mein Knecht', p. 220. Cf. Matt. 8.4; 9.30; 16.20. When read in light of 12.14, this may indeed be true; however, it does not mesh with the assumptions in 11.2–6, in which he openly broadcasts his deeds to the followers of John in front of all, implying that knowledge of and insight into his message and deeds are key to understanding his real identity.

[110] So Barth, 'Matthew's Understanding of the Law', pp. 106–7, following W. Wrede, *The Messianic Secret*, translated by J. Greig, London: James Clarke & Co., 1971, p. 156.

[111] *Messianic Secret*, p. 156.

[112] McConnell, *Law and Prophecy*, p. 122.

[113] Luz, *Matthäus*, II.243–4. This theme finds expression in 13.33ff., in which it becomes evident that Jesus employs parables to discriminate between those who can and cannot comprehend, and in 13.36 with Jesus' move indoors. So Davies and Allison, *Matthew*, II.424.

respect to those in Israel who are rejecting or directly opposing him, and presages the hiddenness of revelation which comes to the forefront in Matt. 13 (13.15–16, 34–6).

A second, periodically mentioned option, which relates to the secrecy motif as described above, concerns the withdrawal (ἀναχωρέω) of Jesus on account of the perceived threat posed by Pharisaic scheming.[114] The emphasis is laid upon the non-confrontational bearing of Jesus, who chooses to withdraw rather than directly confront his foes.[115] This demeanour is also evident in verse 19a, 'he will not wrangle, nor cry out'. In connection with this, it may be significant that on three occasions a healing/ministry scene follows the withdrawal of Jesus, forming a sequence of threat, withdrawal, then ministry. In addition to 12.17–21, the other texts depicting this cycle are 4.12–17 and 14.13ff. 4.12–17 presents Jesus' withdrawal to Capernaum after hearing of John's imprisonment, a circumstance which appears to imply a threat against Jesus also.[116] This movement, as noted in chapter 4, is validated by Isa. 8.23–9.1, which is central to the beginning of his ministry (cf. 4.12–24). In a similar manner, 14.13 marks the withdrawal by Jesus to the wilderness due to the perceived jeopardy echoed in Herod's execution of John the Baptist. This is subsequently followed by another healing scene in 14.14, prompted by Jesus' compassion towards the crowds. These three episodes present a picture of Jesus as one who, if possible, avoids open conflict and conducts his ministry away from the centres of power in Israel.[117]

---

[114] McConnell, *Law and Prophecy*, p. 122.

[115] McNeile, *Matthew*, p. 173, opines that the referent of v. 19 is the refusal on Jesus' part of an 'open quarrel' with the Pharisees, and of his 'self-advertisement as the Messiah'. Cf. Weiss, *Matthäus*, p. 234; Grundmann, *Matthäus*, p. 325.

[116] F. Filson, *A Commentary on the Gospel according to St Matthew*, BNTC, A. & C. Black: London, 1960, p. 72, questions whether ἀναχωρέω means here 'withdrawal' in the face of a perceived threat. Instead, he observes that both Nazareth and Capernaum were ruled by Herod, the Galilean Tetrarch, who had John arrested. Thus, he proposes that Jesus' move is a challenge to Herod rather than a retreat. Similarly, see also Soares Prabhu, *Formula Quotations*, pp. 124–5, and Luz, *Matthew*, p. 94 n. 14. Luz further suggests that a comparison of 4.12 with 2.22 reveals that the element of flight found in 2.22 is missing in 4.12. The issue of the geographic boundaries of Herod's jurisdiction is problematic; however, one wonders whether it must be either/or. Not all rulers exercise the same level of control within their domains (so H. Swete, *The Gospel according to St Mark: The Greek Text with Introduction and Indices,* London: MacMillan & Co., 1909, p. 12). In Matthew's narrative it is the situation of John's imprisonment that prompts the move by Jesus, which, combined with the verb ἀναχωρέω, suggests, at the very least, a concern for his own welfare or, more likely, an awareness of the political situation in Judah (McNeile, *Matthew*, p. 43). Nor is it necessary to accept Chrysostom's position that ἀναχωρέω means 'flight' (14.1 = 226–7).

[117] An approach which is non-confrontational in nature does not necessarily imply weakness or lowliness in and of itself. Jerusalem with its leaders appears in Matthew as the centre

A third attempt to explain the citation's inclusion appeals to a possible link between the summary nature of the healings which precede the citation (12.15) and the compassion expressed in verse 20, 'the bruised reed he will not break . . .'[118] As Rothfuchs and others have noted, 12.18–21 follows what is the fourth summary passage of Jesus' ministry in Matthew; these include 4.23–4, 8.16, 9.35 and 12.15–16.[119] In these digests, Jesus' ministry is categorized as 'teaching', 'healing', or both. Such an observation downplays the significance of the miracles of healing in the Gospel, cautioning against simplistic conceptions of the use of the Old Testament to validate only the healing element, as has already been noted with regard to 8.16–17. The summary in 12.15–16, strikingly similar to that of 8.16, offers an abstract of Jesus' healing ministry and is also followed by the textually mixed formula citation excised from an Isaianic servant text.

On a narrative level, these three related aspects, the secrecy motif, the Pharisaic threat and the focus upon healing in the summary of 12.15–16, all provide reasonable bridges between the citation and its immediate context and confirm our understanding of Matthew's portrayal of the character and disposition of Jesus. The question regarding the apparently superfluous content in verses 18 and 20b–21, however, remains unanswered. Davies and Allison suggest that 'nothing is superfluous, everything fits';[120] others such as Strecker and Lindars are not so optimistic.[121]

Theological usage

As in the passages examined in the previous chapter, Matthew's use of 12.18–21 appears to have broader christological import both within the context of chs. 11–13 and beyond. It will be demonstrated that the citation suits the concerns of the section as Matthew heightens his focus upon the true identity of Jesus as the ideal Davidide, who brings with him the Kingdom of God and the justice and mercy that were traditionally thought

---

of power (2.3), the place where the prophets were killed (23.34–9). It may be that Matthew was concerned to demonstrate that Jesus was aware of the threat against his life, a frequent motif throughout the birth narrative, or that Jesus was unwilling to challenge forms of government and leadership in a revolutionary manner.

[118] M. Davies, *Matthew*, p. 95, suggests that both the healing summary and the command to silence are in view.

[119] Rothfuchs, *Erfüllungszitate*, pp. 70, 72. One must exercise caution as to the extent of the 'summary' nature of these passages. They do not present summaries of Jesus' ministry as a whole but only summaries of the day's or evening's events, which are representative of his ministry.

[120] *Matthew*, II.324.

[121] Strecker, *Weg*, pp. 82–5; Lindars, *New Testament Apologetic*, pp. 24–31.

to accompany its arrival. The broader context of Matt. 11–13 reveals such an emphasis and suggests that the citation of Isa. 42.1–4 also plays an important rhetorical role which richly enhances the narrative movement beyond mere atomistic proof-texting.

That one of Matthew's primary interests in the Gospel involves the true identity of Jesus is manifest from the opening refrain, Βίβλος γενέσεως Ἰησοῦ Χριστοῦ υἱοῦ Δαυὶδ υἱοῦ Ἀβραάμ (1.1).[122] Throughout the first ten chapters the reader confronts a host of OT citations, miracles, teachings and narrative asides which serve to frame Jesus and identify him. John's query 'Are you the one to come or should we expect another?' (11.2) surprises the reader and marks a significant shift in the tone of the Gospel from the heady days of successful ministry and widespread acceptance of Jesus' ministry in chs. 5–10. An obtuse section in the Gospel, chs. 11–13 creatively interject various reactions to Jesus, scattering cryptic explanations for the responses throughout (e.g. 11.25–6 and the parables of ch. 13).[123] Chapters 14–16 continue the theme of diverse responses to Jesus, culminating in Peter's insightful 'You are the Christ, the son of the living God' in 16.16. Thus, throughout the varied situations, dialogues, parables and narratives in 11.2–16.20, the recurring antithetical motifs of hiddenness and revelation are sounded. Some people hear but do not understand, see but do not perceive. These conceptions are incorporated on a fundamental level in the narrative, creating thematic cohesion where disparity would seem pre-eminent. One final key element which emerges concerns the intensifying conflict between Jesus and the Jewish leaders, and the polemic which surrounds this conflict.[124] It is into a

---

[122] The question of the import of opening segments of the Gospel narratives has been raised in earnest in studies concerning Mark. See, for example, R. E. Watts, *Isaiah's New Exodus*, pp. 53–6; Marcus, *Way of the Lord*, pp. 12–47 (cf. the review of Marcus by B. Longenecker, 'The Wilderness and Revolutionary Ferment in First-Century Palestine: A Response to D. R. Schwarz and J. Marcus', *JSJ* 29 (1998): 322–36).

[123] C. Deutsch, *Hidden Wisdom and the Easy Yoke: Wisdom, Torah and Discipleship in Matthew 11.25–30,* JSNTSup 18, Sheffield: JSOT Press 1987, p. 23.

[124] This point alone would seem to argue against Verseput's assertion that 11.25–12.21 is a parenthesis in which the author explores Jesus as the humble messianic servant (*Rejection of the Humble Messianic King*, pp. 205–6). That there are serious christological misconceptions associated with this perspective will become evident throughout this chapter and particularly in chapter 6. On the conflict between Jesus and the Jewish leadership see G. Baumbach, *Das Verständnis des Bösen in den Synoptischen Evangelien,* Theologische Arbeiten 19, Berlin: Evangelische Verlagsanstalt, 1963, pp. 53–121; J. D. Kingsbury, 'The Developing Conflict between Jesus and the Jewish Leaders in Matthew's Gospel: A Literary-Critical Study', *CBQ* 49 (1987): 57–73; M. A. Powell, 'The Religious Leaders in Matthew: A Literary-critical Approach', unpublished PhD thesis, Union Theological Seminary in Virginia 1988, pp. 74–88; and B. R. Doyle, 'A Concern of the Evangelist: Pharisees in Matthew 12', *AusBR* 34 (1986): 17–34.

narrative which explores the themes of the acceptance and rejection of Israel's messianic king and the true character of his person and ministry that the broader theological content of Isa. 42.1–4 fits securely.

The enigmatic messiah described and identified

The striking statement in 11.27 that 'no one knows the Son except the Father' assumes the counter assertion that the Father reveals the Son. This is made manifest in 16.17, in which Jesus affirms Peter's earlier declaration, 'Flesh and blood have not revealed this to you, but my Father in heaven.'[125] In less explicit terms, the themes of revelation and hiddeness are portrayed in the contrasting episodes in Jesus' home town (13.54–8), where he is considered merely a local boy, and in Gennesaret (14.34–6), where he is 'recognized' (v. 35) and performs remarkable miracles. Inserted into such a context, 12.18a, which, I have argued, owes its distinctiveness to Matthew's ingenuity, affords the reader a lucid glimpse on Jesus' true identity, an authoritative statement from the Father concerning the identification of Jesus, paralleling the prominent scenes of the Baptism (3.17) and Transfiguration (17.5). In 12.18a the 'evaluative point of view' provided by the OT citation belongs to God himself, if one will grant with Matthew that the divine voice may be heard through the Scriptures (cf. 1.23, 2.15).[126]

Isa. 42.4 further contributes to Matthew's thoughts on who Jesus is. Theologically, the variant reading in the LXX adopted by Matthew coordinates well in his broader concerns, a point which argues against its being a later interpolation.[127] First, although the designation 'name' is a simple example of metonymy, in this context it refers to the servant, who is the Beloved. But surely the use of ὄνομα here is also meant to conjure up its earlier uses in 1.21 and 23. As Jesus ('he will save his people from their sins') and Emmanuel ('God with us') are the only names explicitly given to Jesus in Matthew, an alert reader should have remembered these names from early on. And it is in this person that the nations will

---

[125] Luz, *Theology*, p. 36. Observe that this motif of God's disclosure of Jesus' identity occurs also in the Baptism (3.17), Transfiguration (17.5) and servant (12.18a) texts.

[126] Kingsbury, 'Figure of Jesus', 6. As Kingsbury also observes, *Christology*, p. 95, the three occurrences of μου reflect this (so also Rothfuchs, *Erfüllungszitate*, pp. 123–4). He is '*my* servant', '*my* beloved', in whom '*my* soul delights'. Surprisingly, Kingsbury does not include an analysis of 12.18a, which could support his argument against Hill. As Hill, 'A Response', 38–9, notes, the weakness of Kingsbury's argument is that he places too great an emphasis upon this element. Jesus remains the focus of the text.

[127] Schlatter, *Matthäus*, p. 402; Kilpatrick, *Origins*, p. 94; Schweizer, *Matthew*, p. 281; Jeremias, 'παῖς θεοῦ', p. 701.

trust/hope. The inclusion of ἔθνη expands upon Matthew's earlier hints at gentile inclusion.[128] Furthermore, although one may only speculate concerning the omission of 'law'—whether Matthew deliberately chose the LXX reading over the MT, or whether it was less intentional—there does appear to be a theological agenda behind Matthew's usage. For example, the uses in 1.21 and 23 have christological, soteriological and ecclesiological implications. Similarly, the uses in 7.22, 28.19[129] and 18.20,[130] which link Jesus' name to the presence motif, suggest an elevated reverence for Jesus and a high christology. Thus, the assertion that 'nations will hope in his name' fits well within Matthew's broader christological pursuits.

That acquiring an accurate perspective on Jesus is not a straightforward process, however, is acknowledged by Jesus himself in 11.6 in his statement, 'Blessed are those who do not stumble (σκανδαλίζειν) on account of me.' In fact, the section of 11.2–16.20 opens on a rather ominous note with the expression of doubt by John the Baptist concerning Jesus' identity (11.2–3). John's query 'Are you the one to come?' encapsulates the overarching theme of the section[131] as Matthew explores various reactions to Jesus. The difficulty of comprehending who Jesus is, is subsequently given greater explication in the rejection texts of 11.16–19, in which the generation has not 'played along with' either John or Jesus and has misunderstood both. Consider also 11.20–4, in which the cities, having failed to link the wonderful works done in their midst with the one who was expected and to respond with repentance, reject Jesus and incur judgment. Similarly, the genuine enquiry of the crowds (12.23),[132] the vitriolic condemnation by the Pharisees (12.14, 24), the rejection by the Nazarenes (13.54–5) and Herod (14.2), the 'recognition' by Gennesaret (14.34–6) and the disciples (14.33; 16.13–14), and Peter's climactic declaration in 16.16, all explore in one way or another this central motif.[133] The mini-climax in 11.25–6, in which Jesus extols the

---

[128] Both references in 12.18b and 12.21 probably ought to be read in an inclusive sense as 'nations' (so Tisera, *Universalism*, pp. 182–5; *contra* Meier, 'Nations or Gentiles', 95, and Hare and Harrington, 'Make Disciples', 363).

[129] See L. Hartman, 'Into the Name of Jesus: A Suggestion concerning the Earliest Meaning of the Phrase', *NTS* 20 (1974): 432–40.

[130] *m. Abot* 3.2 attributes a similar saying to R. Simeon ben Yohai (AD 70–100); *m. Abot* 3.3, to R. Hananiah b. Teradion (died in the Bar Kokba war (AD 132?)); *m. Abot* 3.6, to R. Hlafta b. Dosa; and see also the Mekilta on Exod. 20.24. For a discussion of the circumstances of various rabbis, see Strack and Stemberger, *Introduction*, pp. 56–100.

[131] Barth, 'Matthew's Understanding of the Law', p. 251, and Garland, *Matthew*, p. 124.

[132] μήτι may be used in 'questions in which the questioner is in doubt concerning the answer *perhaps*', BAGD, p. 520. See also BDF § 427 (2).

[133] Neyrey, 'Thematic Use', 459–70, and Cope, *Matthew*, pp. 34–46, have described the relationship of the citation to its broader context in great detail. Certainly the perspective

Father, who is here identified as 'Lord of heaven and earth' and thus the God of all humanity (cf. Rom. 3.27–31), for hiding these things from the 'wise and intelligent' (σοφῶν καὶ συνετῶν) and revealing them to 'babes' (νήπιοι), intensifies the roles that attitude, posture and revelation play in the comprehension of Jesus' true identity, and serves to establish an extraordinary norm to distinguish *bona fide* insiders from outsiders. In this broader context, the divine perspective provided in 12.18a contributes a meaningful component to the narrative's development. Thus, the one whom the people are in danger of rejecting is none other than God's chosen one, the Beloved (messiah). Furthermore, appeal to such an exalted authority serves to confirm Jesus' own statement in 11.27 concerning the intimacy of the relationship between the Father and the Son.[134] Matthew draws the reader's attention to the enigma of who Jesus is, demonstrating an awareness on Jesus' part, and the author's, that he does not meet populist expectations of messiah or the coming one.

The Spirit, justice and the final age

A second motif in the citation, crucial to the context and Matthew's presentation of Jesus, is the bestowal of Spirit and its relationship to the announcement of justice to the gentiles/nations in 12.18b. Given the close proximity and relationship in the quotation of the two uses of κρίσις, it is unwise to discuss 12.18b apart from 12.20b, 'until he brings forth justice/judgment to victory'. As noted in the previous section, commentators are vague about the exact meaning of ἀπαγγέλλειν in this context. No doubt part of the difficulty rests in the ambiguity of the poetic language. ἀπαγγέλλειν simply means 'report' or 'announce'; whether it refers to a prophetic proclamation here in 12.18b is open to question.[135] Furthermore, there is no record in Matthew of a verbal announcement of justice on Jesus' part.[136] Of interest to the question of the relationship between the Spirit and the proclamation of κρίσις is the attention drawn to healing (exorcism), the work of the Spirit, and the coming of the Kingdom of

---

of God as represented in the citation provides a fitting contrast to those of the Pharisees (12.24–6) and the crowds (12.23).

[134] Perhaps the ambiguity of the term παῖς is played upon in 12.18a in light of the Son of God christology evidenced in 11.27 and the use of ὁ ἀγαπητός.

[135] Until this point Matthew has shown little, if any, interest in a prophetic Jesus. He excised the prophetic reference from Q in 11.2 (Luke 7.16–19), inserting the term 'messiah', which he appears to develop in a kingship/sonship motif throughout chs. 11–13.

[136] It is possible, if one translates κρίσις as judgment, that the line may refer to texts such as 11.20–4; 12.36, 41–2. The difficulty with this scenario is that κρίσις does not seem to mean judgment in the context of the citation.

God in 12.22–30. The fact that Jesus would base his argument for the significance of his healings upon the eschatological bestowal of the Spirit suggests that the deeds themselves were evocative of a symbolic world. Similarly, his retort to John in 11.5 is founded upon essentially the same premise. John ought to have recognized Jesus' identity and the arrival of the messianic age through Jesus' message and deeds.[137] The condemnation of the cities was due to their failure to respond with repentance after exposure to Jesus' ministry. Finally, the grammatical connection (ἕως ἄν) between 12.20a and b also suggests a linkage between the compassionate ministry and κρίσις. Thus, it may be that the 'announcement' of the arrival of κρίσις is found in the deeds and message of Jesus rather than in a verbal promulgation in the strict sense. As Barth writes concerning κρίσις,

> In 12.20 the vocation of the servant of God is named: to bring judgment to victory … It is … a matter of carrying out of the judgment of God with regard to men, to the world … It is clear in the context of 12.18–21 that this is the proper and decisive vocation of the servant of God; all other statements are subordinated to this statement.[138]

Matthew, therefore, links the compassionate deeds and message of Jesus to the arrival of the justice of God. Of equal importance, however, is that Matthew appears to relate the element of justice to his development and presentation of Jesus as the ideal leader/King of Israel, or royal messiah.[139] This is particularly evident in the association of the Son of David designation with healing (9.27; 12.23; 15.22; 20.30; 21.15),[140] and in the emphasis upon mercy and compassion (σπλαγχνίζομαι) in these same pericopes.[141] The convergence of miracles, messiahship and kingship in

---

[137] Matthew is clearer on this than Luke, due to his redactional creation of the block of teaching in chs. 5–7 and healings in chs. 8–9.

[138] 'Matthew's Understanding of the Law', p. 141.

[139] For discussions concerning the development of Davidic messiahship in Matthew, see Verseput, 'Son of God', 533–7; Stanton, *Gospel for a New People*, pp. 180–5; C. Burger, *Jesus als Davidssohn: Eine traditions-geschichtliche Untersuchung*, FRLANT 98, Göttingen: Vandenhoeck & Ruprecht, 1970, pp. 72–106.

[140] As D. Duling, 'The Therapeutic Son of David: An Element in Matthew's Christological Apologetic', *NTS* 24 (1978): 399, observes, Matthew expands Mark's three scenes (Mark 10.47, 48; 12.35) to nine. See also Garland, *Matthew*, p. 213, on the importance of justice in 21.14.

[141] Duling, 'Therapeutic Son', 403–4, notes that 'every use of σπλαγχνίζομαι is found in a healing story, or directly adjacent to one of Matthew's generalizing healing summaries'. See also Kingsbury, 'The Title "Son of David" in Matthew's Gospel', *JBL* 95 (1976): 598–9; Burger, *Davidssohn*, pp. 72–3. On the relation of mercy to miracles, see H. J. Held,

Matthew has remained something of a puzzle simply because no evidence exists in other literature in Judaism, either prior to or contemporaneous with Matthew, that connects miracles to a messiah or idealized royal figure.[142] It is curious that both Son of David and servant passages (8.17; 12.18–21) are associated with healing in the Gospel. Another unexpected correspondence between the Son of David and the servant in 12.20a is the emphasis upon compassion. One suspects that Matthew's view of the Son of David has been shaped in part by his reflection upon the servant, who is in some way representative of the people and compassionately undertakes their salvation (cf. 20.24–34). As noted above, the citation in 12.20 appears to link the benevolent ministry (v. 20a) to the final establishment of κρίσις (v. 20b), which is a necessary component in Israel's conception of the monarchy. If the healings in view in 12.15–16 are understood more broadly by Matthew as deeds which accompany God's visitation of his people in the final age (cf. 11.5; 12.22–4), this would locate the healings within a broader scheme than has been traditionally espoused. While raising numerous questions, this position opens up the possibility that the English gloss of 'justice' for κρίσις is central to Matthew's concerns in 12.18b and 20b. Here κρίσις would then be interpreted as the justice of God evidenced in the liberation of the oppressed and the renewal of the burdened.[143] Such a rendering forms a more comprehensive conceptual bridge between the citation and its preceding context than those previously constructed.[144] Before moving too far in this particular direction, however, a more nuanced definition of κρίσις is necessary, in addition to an exploration of a possible background to Jewish usage in order to establish more firmly whether a nexus indeed exists between justice, kingship and the messianic age.

κρίσις *defined*

It is interesting that justice rather than judgment is the translation of choice for most English translations of Isa. 42.1–4. Similarly, OT scholars have asserted that the theme of justice is key to understanding not only Isa. 42.1–4 but the thematic movement of the book from Isa.

'Matthew as Interpreter of the Miracle Stories', in *Tradition and Interpretation in Matthew*, edited by G. Bornkamm, et al., London: SCM Press, 1963, pp. 257–9.

[142] This issue will be addressed in greater detail below.

[143] Hill, 'Son and Servant', 12; M. Davies, *Matthew*, p. 95; Powell, *God with Us: A Pastoral Theology of Matthew's Gospel*, Minneapolis: Fortress, 1995, pp. 113–48.

[144] E.g. Tisera, *Universalism*, pp. 174–5, who observes the theme of justice without fully exploring its significance in the surrounding context.

40 onwards.[145] Both justice and judgment, however, possess broad semantic ranges that overlap at key points, demanding precise definition
and usage. In English, for example, judgment may be employed in a
broad sense to encompass both the verdict of the judge and the punish-
ment/reward.[146] More narrowly, it may be employed for either the decree
or its resulting effects. Justice also possesses a broad semantic range requiring greater specificity. The term may be defined either morally, as a
quality of just conduct or dealing, or judicially, in which the maintenance
of the right and the assignment of reward or punishment are in view.
Thus conceived, justice is the cardinal virtue which undergirds judgment,
or, as Rawls puts it, 'the first virtue of social institutions, as truth is of
systems of thought'.[147] The complexity and scope of the discussion of
justice is evidenced as early as Plato's *Republic*, and the Jewish world
was no exception (e.g. Hab. 1–4; Ezek. 34; Ps. 72.1–4; etc.).

As is frequently observed in most discussions on this topic, in Judaism
מִשְׁפָּט was fundamentally rooted in the concept of ethical monotheism,
in which God, as king and judge of humanity, was the dispenser and
guardian of justice.[148] The familiar OT refrain 'your throne is established
in righteousness and justice' points to the foundational place justice had
within God's character and reign.[149] Oppressive rulers or structures which
propagated injustice caused the Jewish people to rely upon their God as
their advocate for vindication and justice (Isa. 40.27; Hab. 1.1–4). It was
this point of tension between the reality of injustice and the theological affirmation of judgment for the oppressors that appears to have contributed
to the development of an eschatological perspective which viewed 'God's
punishing judgment . . . as a final act of vengeance to end history'.[150] This

---

[145]   W. Beuken, 'MISPAT: The First Servant Song and Its Context', *VT* 22 (1972): 8–9.
For studies which discuss the issue of justice in Deutero-Isaiah, see K. Elliger, *Deuterojesaja*,
BKAT II, Neukirchen-Vluyn: Neukirchener Verlag, 1978, pp. 206–10; D. W. van Winkle,
'The Relationship of the Nations to Yahweh and to Israel in Isaiah XL-LV', *VT* 35 (1985):
446–58; M. C. Lind, 'Monotheism, Power, and Justice: A Study in Isaiah 40–55', *CBQ* 46
(1984): 432–46; D. Kendall, 'Use of Mišpaṭ in Isaiah 59', *ZAW* 96 (1984): 391–405; and
H. Gossai, *Justice, Righteousness and the Social Critique of the Eighth-Century Prophets*,
American University Studies 7.141, New York: Peter Lang, 1993, *passim*.

[146]   Barth's quotation above seems to entail a broad definition. A passage such as Matt.
11.24, 'it will be better for the land of Sodom on the day of judgment', seems to reflect the
whole process, with particular emphasis upon the resultant punishment.

[147]   *A Theory of Justice*, Cambridge, MA: Harvard University Press, 1971, p. 3 (also cited
in R. L. Cohen, *Justice: View from the Social Sciences*, New York: Plenum Press, 1986,
p. 1).

[148]   See, for example, T. L. J. Mafico, 'Justice', *ABD* III.1127–9.

[149]   Pss. 9.4, 7; 45.6; 89.14; 93.2; 97.2; Prov. 16.12; 20.28; 25.5; 29.44.

[150]   D. W. Kuck, *Judgment and Community Conflict: Paul's Use of Apocalyptic Judgment
Language in 1 Corinthians 3:5–4:5*, NovTSup 66, Leiden: Brill, 1992, p. 61.

point is germane to the discussion because in Jewish and early Christian literature 'judgment' was not limited to the divine decree but had taken on the primarily negative connotation of final judgment upon the ungodly.[151] To use the term 'judgment' with the breadth that Barth employs it, while no doubt correct, can be misleading.

An emphasis upon 'judgment', however, does not represent all the OT data, for κρίσις/ מִשְׁפָּט also denotes 'justice'. In the LXX κρίσις frequently parallells terms which are associated with soteriological rather than condemnatory motifs. For example, in texts such as Isa. 1.17, 21; Jer. 22.3; Zech. 7.9; Micah 6.8; and Hos. 6.6, positive concepts such as seeking the right, defending the fatherless, delivering the oppressed, and caring for widows, all parallel κρίσις, indicating an ethically based definition of 'justice' rather than 'judgment'.[152]

Perhaps most significant in this regard is the connection of κρίσις with צֶדֶק / δικαιοσύνη.[153] Isa. 51.4–6 provides a clear example in which the themes of righteousness, compassion upon the ruined state of Zion, and universal justice for the nations are all interrelated.[154] Note in particular how the language of verse 4 in the MT, 'the law will go out from me; my justice will become a light to the nations', is juxtaposed with verse 5, 'I will bring my deliverance/righteousness speedily, my salvation has gone out, and my arms will rule the peoples; the coastlands wait for me, and for my arm they hope.'[155]

⁴כִּי תוֹרָה מֵאִתִּי תֵצֵא וּמִשְׁפָּטִי לְאוֹר עַמִּים אַרְגִּיעַ׃

⁵קָרוֹב צִדְקִי יָצָא יִשְׁעִי וּזְרֹעַי עַמִּים יִשְׁפֹּטוּ

אֵלַי אִיִּים יְקַוּוּ וְאֶל־זְרֹעִי יְיַחֵלוּן׃

The LXX version of the same text aligns κρίσις with terms such νόμος, δικαιοσύνη and σωτήριον, creating a complex of images which 'have

---

[151] Kuck, *ibid.*, p. 94, further observes that 'a belief in God's judgment can serve to define one group over against another group or provide identity and encouragement in the face of threat'.

[152] See also Hos. 12.7 and Micah 6.8 (cf. Jer. 22.15–16). Examples from the LXX might also be noted: κρίσις parallels ἔλεος in Ps. 100(101).1, ἔλεος καὶ κρίσιν ᾄσομαι; it is combined with ἐλεημοσύνη in Ps. 32(33).5, ἀγαπᾷ ἐλεημοσύνην καὶ κρίσιν, and with ἀλήθεια in Ps. 110(111).7, ἔργα χειρῶν αὐτοῦ ἀλήθεια καὶ κρίσις.

[153] Powell, *God with Us*, pp. 115–17, rightly includes a discussion of δικαιοσύνη in his chapter on social justice.

[154] Lind, 'Monotheism, Power, and Justice', 445.

[155] Cf. 1QIsaᵃ of 51.5, which reads, 'My salvation has gone forth, and *his* arms will rule the peoples; the coastlands wait for *him* and for *his* arm they hope'. Brownlee, *Meaning of the Qumrân Scrolls*, 197, and Barthélemy, 'Le grand rouleau d'Isaïe', 548–9, both argue that the variant suffixes should read third-person singular ו and not first-person singular י. *Pace* Brown, 'Qumran Scrolls', p. 204.

positive connotations from the nations' point of view'[156] due to the universal nature of the salvation motif.

⁴ὅτι νόμος παρ' ἐμοῦ ἐξελεύσεται καὶ ἡ κρίσις μου εἰς φῶς ἐθνῶν. ⁵ἐγγίζει ταχὺ ἡ δικαιοσύνη μου καὶ ἐξελεύσεται ὡς φῶς τὸ σωτήριόν μου καὶ εἰς τὸν βραχίονά μου ἔθνη ἐλπιοῦσιν· ἐμὲ νῆσοι ὑπομενοῦσιν καὶ εἰς τὸν βραχίονά μου ἐλπιοῦσιν

In this context, the clause ἡ κρίσις μου (ἐξελεύσεται) εἰς φῶς ἐθνῶν in 51.4 is obviously to be understood in a salvific, sanguine tone. Old Testament scholars have long noted the relationship between Isa. 51.4–6 and 42.1–4, texts which present a universal offer of justice and salvation to the nations.[157] Thus, these factors, the usage of κρίσις with terms such as νόμος, δικαιοσύνη, σωτήριον, ἔλεος and the phrase εἰς φῶς ἐθνῶν in passages like Isa. 51.4–6,[158] indicate that restricting the definition of κρίσις to final eschatological 'judgment' in Matt. 12.18 and 20 may be overly rigid. If one reads Isa. 42.1–4 messianically, as Matthew and others prior to him have done, a nexus is created between the expectation of justice and the one through whom justice will be established. Thus it happens that justice is an important virtue which plays a substantial role in discussions concerning the messianic or anticipated age to come.

With respect to מִשְׁפָּט in Isaiah 42.1–4, Beuken proposes that the term contains two nuances, each determined by the verb to which it serves as object. In 42.1 it occurs with the Hiphil יוֹצִיא and denotes 'to establish justice' or 'enforce righteousness', thus placing an emphasis upon 'a state of being' or 'a situation to be realized'.[159] The assumption in such a usage is that 'the present situation is devoid of justice' and thus the servant is thought to usher in such a state.[160] The second usage occurs in Isa. 42.4 with יָשִׂים, and Beuken suggests the term is better defined here as 'an ordinance, a law to be proclaimed' or 'the juridical statutes of the new situation of justice'.[161] The possible distinction drawn between 'the

---

[156] Van Winkle, 'Relationship of the Nations', 448.

[157] The issue of nationalism versus universalism in Isa. 40–55 is a complex and controversial topic. For a helpful overview and discussion of relevant texts, see van Winkle, 'Relationship of the Nations', *passim*.

[158] The phrase εἰς φῶς ἐθνῶν occurs only four times in the LXX, each in the context of a salvation motif: *Ode Sol.* 13.32; Isa. 42.6; 49.6; and 51.4.

[159] Beuken, 'MIŠPĀṬ', 6. Cf. Jer. 48.21; 51.9f.; Isa. 40.17, 27; 51.4; Zeph. 3.15; Ps. 94.15; Job 27.2; 34.5.

[160] Cf. texts such as Hab. 1.1–4; CD 1.13–21.

[161] 'MIŠPĀṬ', 7. Cf. Exod. 15.25; 21.1; Josh. 24.5; 1 Sam. 30.5. Occurrences of this verb with other objects with the same meaning of the setting of laws occur in Exod. 19.7; Deut. 4.44; Ps. 78.5; Jer. 33.25; etc.

realisation of a state of justice' and 'the juridical statutes in a new state of justice' may prove significant in the Matthean context.

Justice, messiah and the messianic age

Messianic texts which address the issues of judgment and justice demonstrate that a sharp division between the two may be artificial.[162] While it is true that the linkage of judgment to an eschatological worldview shifted the focus from this present state to future consummation, the arrival of messiah and the resulting messianic age were thought to be characterized by judgment upon the ungodly[163] and the establishment of justice for the righteous. This is evident in *1 Enoch* 1.8–9, which presents an overview contending that all will be judged: the righteous will receive peace and blessing while the wicked will be destroyed. Similarly, Isa. 11.4 juxtaposes the justice offered to the poor and needy with the 'slaying of wicked' by 'the breath of his lips'. After assessing several texts, Collins concludes, '[The messiah] is the scepter who will smite the nations, slay the wicked with the breath of his lips, and restore the Davidic dynasty...He is also the messiah of righteousness, who will usher in an era of peace and justice.'[164] *Ps. Sol.* 17 is likewise instructive in this regard. The messiah's rule, in contrast to the dearth of righteousness and justice in prior times (17.19), is characterized by a general state of justice and righteousness, the compassionate treatment of the nations (34b), exposure of corrupt officials (36), empowerment by the holy spirit (37), faithful and righteous shepherding of the Lord's flock (40c) and abolishment of oppression (41).

In the above texts, the anticipation of a just society established by a righteous ruler contrasts with the unfortunate reality of a flawed society in which oppression and injustice prevail. The prophetic pronouncements poignantly capture the centrality of the virtue of justice to Israel's Law. The explosion of present-day discussions concerning justice have noted the interrelationships of 'sociological, political and economic ideas' and serve to reinforce the complexity and expansiveness of the concept in

---

[162] Whether one may speak of 'The Messiah' or simply a messiah has consumed much scholarly debate. See the early article of de Jonge, 'Use of the Word "Anointed"', 132–48, and Charlesworth, 'From Jewish Messianology to Christian Christology: Some Caveats and Perspectives', in *Judaisms and Their Messiahs at the Turn of the Christian Era,* edited by J. Neusner, W. S. Green and E. Frerichs, Cambridge: Cambridge University Press, 1987, pp. 225–64. See Horbury, 'Messianic Associations', 34–55, for a moderating position.

[163] E.g. Isa. 11.1–4; *1 Enoch* 45–55; *Ps. Sol.* 17; 4Q285. See Overman's survey in *Matthew's Gospel and Formative Judaism*, pp. 19–23, for a discussion concerning the 'ungodly' Jewish leadership in pre- and post-AD 70 literature.

[164] Collins, *Scepter and Star*, p. 67.

Jewish literature.[165] Commenting on Ezek. 34, M. Greenberg urges that
the text presents the 'restoration in Israel of a just social order, peace and
prosperity', an achievement which is explicitly attributed to the handi-
work of the ideal Davidide (34.23; cf. Jer. 23.5).[166] Ezek. 34, in which
the condemnation of the irresponsible shepherds and the elevation of the
ideal shepherd motifs are developed, presents a wonderful account of
the restoration and healing of the people of God which was thought to
accompany the arrival of the Shepherd, the servant David (34.23).

Such a conception of the messiah's rule is evident in messianically
interpreted texts that include justice within their delineation of the character and extent of the future king's reign under God:[167] for example,
1 Sam. 7.5–6, 20; Isa. 9.6; 11.1–5; 51.4–6; Jer. 21.12; 22.3, 15; 23.5; Ps.
72.1–4;[168] *1 Enoch* 96–105;[169] *Ps. Sol.* 17; and CD 6.11a. The petition for
justice in verses 1–4 which opens Ps. 72 is particularly instructive. It captures the cry of an embattled people seeking the utopian kingdom of the
ideal Davidide, under whose rule righteousness and justice in defence of
the poor and disenfranchised would predominate, thereby effecting peace
and prosperity in the land. Similarly, the relationship of the ideal Davidide to a just rule is explored in Jer. 21.12; 22.3, 15; and 23.5,[170] in which
are recorded prophetic hopes for a future ruler who would govern his
kingdom with justice manifest in care for the poor, the oppressed and the
alien. A similar idea may also exist in CD 6.11a, which reads, 'until there
arises he who teaches justice at the end of days'.[171] This passage appears

---

[165] C. Kelbley, ed., *The Value of Justice: Essays on the Theory and Practice of Social
Virtue,* New York: Fordham University Press, 1979, p. 3.

[166] *Ezekiel 21–37: A New Translation with Introduction and Commentary,* AB 22A, New
York: Doubleday, 1997, p. 707. The influence of the shepherd/leader imagery drawn from
Ezek. 34 and possibly even Jer. 23 upon Matthew has been explored by J. P. Heil in 'Ezekiel
34 and the Narrative Strategy of the Shepherd and Sheep Metaphor in Matthew', *CBQ* 55
(1993): 698–708.

[167] One may also view Isa. 42.1–4 in this regard. Beuken, 'MIŠPĀṬ', 3, emphasizes the
royal traits identified in the servant text, suggesting that מִשְׁפָּט is 'the characteristic task of
the royal figure (1 Sam. vii 5f, 20; Isa. ix 6; Jer. xxi 11 [*sic*]; xxii 3, 15; xxiii 5; Ps. lxxii
1,2,4) [*sic*] Only once, *mišpāṭ* is used in connection with classical prophecy: Mich. iii 8.'

[168] See K. Heim, 'The Perfect King of Psalm 72: An "Intertextual" Inquiry', in *The Lord's
Anointed: Interpretation of Old Testament Messianic Texts,* edited by P. Satterthwaite, R.
Hess and G. Wenham, Grand Rapids: Baker, 1995, pp. 223–48.

[169] See particularly chs. 102–4.

[170] Jer. 23.5 is perhaps one of the more well-known messianic texts due to the language
'when I raise up to David a righteous Branch, a King who will reign wisely . . .' The concate-
nation of the phrase 'I will raise up' with 'David, a righteous Branch' and 'a King who will
reign' presents a fluid conceptualization of the identity and function of the eschatological
figure of the end of times.

[171] García Martínez, ed., *Dead Sea Scrolls,* p. 37. The language of CD 6.11 is probably
drawn from Hos. 10.12 (so J. J. Collins, 'Teacher and Messiah? The One who will Teach

to anticipate a messianic teacher of righteousness/justice. The days which precede this expected teacher are labelled 'the time of wickedness', which aligns well with the community's thoughts on the sinful state of Israel. Knibb,[172] based upon CD, has convincingly argued that the Qumran community viewed themselves as the generation finally to be released from spiritual exile (cf. CD 1.3–12; 3.9b–17a; 5.20–6.5).[173] CD 6.11a, which seems to be based upon Hos. 10.12, thus provides another piece of evidence suggesting that the ill-defined expectation of a messianic age would be founded upon justice.

The possible references to healing in Ezek. 34.4 and 16 have prompted some to cite Ezek. 34 in support of the concept of a miracle-working messiah.[174] While this attempt strains the semantic boundaries of the passage, the text may offer assistance on a different level.[175] Ezek. 34 links the ideal shepherd with the themes of the gathering together, feeding, healing of and providing rest for God's people. Justice is central to this formulation. Throughout the description God is the primary actor, that is, until 34.23–4, in which he introduces a mediatorial figure described as 'my servant David' who 'will be a prince among them'. Similar in many respects to this passage is 4Q521, the Qumran text which has most frequently been associated with Matt. 11.5 in attempts to account for a miracle-working messiah. 4Q521 fragment 2, column 2[176] speaks directly about miracles; the blind receive their sight, the twisted are straightened (line 8), the dead

Righteousness at the End of Days', in *The Community of the Renewed Covenant: The Notre Dame Symposium on the Dead Sea Scrolls,* edited by E. Ulrich and J. VanderKam, Christianity and Judaism in Antiquity Series 10, Notre Dame, University of Notre Dame Press, 1994, p. 206). Collins, pp.193–210, argues, based in part on a definition of the last days, that the figure involved is eschatological and thus messianic, defined as either prophetic or priestly. P. R. Davies, *The Damascus Covenant: An Interpretation of the 'Damascus Document'*, JSOTSup 25, Sheffield: JSOT Press, 1983, pp. 122–4, however, argues that the figure refers to the Teacher of Righteousness in Qumran.

[172] M. A. Knibb, 'Exile in the Damascus Document', *JSOT* 25 (1983): 99–117; see also his *The Qumran Community*, Cambridge: Cambridge University Press, 1987, p. 50, for a description of these texts. If J. Murphy-O'Connor, 'The Essenes and Their History', *RB* 81 (1974): 219–21, is correct that CD was written in Babylon and brought at a later date to Palestine, then Knibb's point loses its substance.

[173] Their liturgy, confession, cleansing rites, and obedience to Torah all reflect a community attempting to atone for the misdeeds of previous generations. One might also consider Ps. 126, which expresses the pain of the unfulfilled expectations of the returned.

[174] So P. M. Head, *Christology and the Synoptic Problem: An Argument for Markan Priority*, SNTSMS 94, Cambridge: Cambridge University Press, 1997, p. 183, who follows D. E. Aune, 'The Problem with the Messianic Secret', *NovT* 11 (1969): 29–30.

[175] The text merely refers to the healing/mending of the sheep by the shepherd. To read miracles of healing into this text is to move beyond the semantic categories. I have been unable to locate any usage of this text in the Second Temple or rabbinic literature to support such a contention.

[176] For the translation see García Martínez, ed., *Dead Sea Scrolls*, p. 394.

are raised, good news is proclaimed to the poor and the badly wounded are healed (line 12). The much debated subject of lines 8–13 seems almost certainly to be the Lord (cf. line 9, 'the Lord will perform marvellous acts'); however, the possibility lingers that the Lord may work through a mediator, namely, his messiah mentioned in line 1. Similarly, 4Q504 fragments 1–2, column 2, lines 14–15, in addition to forgiveness of sin, also speaks of God's healing the people of 'madness, blindness and confusion'. What all these texts appear to share is a conception that the healing and renewal of God's people are included in the promise of the future age of YHWH's kingdom.[177] Kvalbein opines that 'Die konkreten Einzelwunder Jesu sind Zeichen für die endzeitliche Restitution des ganzen Volkes Gottes'('The concrete, individual miracles of Jesus are signs of the end-time restitution of the people of God').[178]

It can be concluded that an extensive body of evidence appears to associate a royal messianic figure with the establishment of justice, which is particularly manifest in his care for the poor, the needy and the alien. In each case, the practical implications of a just rule involve the restoration of balance and wholeness to society through the renewal (and perhaps healing) of those who have been exploited and damaged, and the infliction of judgment upon those who have propagated and benefited from the widespread injustice. Texts such as Isa. 51.4–6 and Isa. 42.1–4 (cf. Isa. 2.1–4) contribute a robust universal dimension to the concept of the just rule, implying that the fruits of the future age would not belong exclusively to Israel but would be extended to benefit the nations.

Justice, Law observance and God's people

The narrow view that Matthew presents a 'humble messianic king' needs to be expanded, it would seem, to include within his rule the ethical effects of the reign of God within society, with particular emphasis upon the renewal and reconstitution of the people of God. Concomitant with such a position is the postulate that a dynamic ethical component undergirds Matthew's christology.[179] Presumably, it would be inconceivable to assert that the messianic age and the ideal Davidic King had arrived without

---

[177] H. Kvalbein, 'Die Wunder der Endzeit: Beobachtungen zu 4Q521 und Matth 11,5', *ZNW* 88 (1997): 111–25; he includes Ps. 146.7–8; Isa. 29.18; 35.5; 42.7; 4Q504; and 4Q521 in his analysis. See also R. E. Watts, *Isaiah's New Exodus*, pp. 169–82, on the relationship between healings and the people of God in Isaiah.

[178] 'Die Wunder der Endzeit', 124.

[179] See Gerhardsson, 'Gottes Sohn als Diener Gottes', 73–106, and, more recently, Powell, *God with Us*, pp. 113–48.

including evidence of his just rule. The inclusion of Isa. 42.1–4 provides a step in the right direction; it offers a scriptural basis for the counter-cultural perspective of Jesus' messiahship and kingship (11.6). In addition to depicting a compassionate servant who identifies with and aids broken humanity, it links these deeds with justice. As we will see, Matthew's Jesus, in a non-confrontational manner, offers justice to the poor, sick and lame and to the harassed crowds burdened with the weight and oppression of the legal interpretations of the Jewish establishment (cf. 9.36; 15.1–20; 23.4, 24). Matthew addresses these concerns through his christology, which, as Bornkamm and Barth observe, is related to his understanding of Law.[180] This portrayal provides a striking contrast with the Jewish leadership in 23.23, who have 'forgotten the weightier matters of the law, justice, mercy and faith',[181] themes which seem to be implicit in 11.28–12.16 and likewise in Matthew's subtly creative version of the citation. Such is the present thesis; it only remains to demonstrate that it is the case.

Leadership, Law and oppression

Matthew's primary theological interest in the citation revolves around the establishment of justice for a universal people of God. That Jesus is perceived by Matthew as the agent for effecting such a task is evident in the fact that the ministry of Jesus is presented as the fulfilment of the citation. He is the servant of the Lord who will accomplish the agenda delineated in the citation. Further confirming that justice may be at the centre of Matthew's concerns are the established links between christology, Law and ethics throughout the Gospel. The tendency among scholars to place the element of judgment or justice into the future ought thus to be re-examined. Certainly 12.20b has the future consummation in view, but the initial announcement in 12.18b seems to have implications for the ministry of Jesus. If so, then the final state in which justice is brought forth victoriously refers to a time when justice, inaugurated in verse 18, becomes realized. This is demonstrated in 11.28–12.14, a section in which the issues of Law, christology, mercy and justice all converge, and in which Matthew presents a non-confrontational Jesus concerned with the setting forth of justice evidenced in the liberation of the oppressed and in the demeanour and manner in which he carries this out. The themes

---

[180] Bornkamm, 'End Expectation', 32–8, and Barth, 'Matthew's Understanding of the Law', pp. 125–59.

[181] Doyle, 'Pharisees in Matthew 12', posits that this may be the case in ch. 12.

of justice and injustice, innocence and guilt, and burden and freedom are all present, as are statements concerning the character of Jesus and his ministry.

Chapter 12 builds upon 11.28–30 and Jesus' often recited offer of rest for the burdened and an easy yoke.[182] Despite a plethora of interpretations and implications thereof, something of a consensus has been reached among modern commentators that the audience at the end of ch. 11 consists of the crowds and the burdensome yoke refers to Pharisaic halakhah.[183] Of special interest to the present discussion is the emotive element inherent in the language of 'tiredness', 'weariness' and 'rest for your souls'. These empathic expressions are crucial for understanding 12.1–21, as they adumbrate the care for the down-trodden in 12.20//Isa. 42.3, effectively framing the material in between.[184] One assumes that the offer of the light yoke of Jesus is meant to counter the heaviness produced by pulling a heavy, onerous Pharisaic yoke (cf. 23.4). The invitations 'come to me', 'learn of me' and 'take my yoke upon you' all assume the high christology of 11.27 and are especially powerful in this context.[185] The term 'yoke' probably should be understood to refer to discipleship, which includes both demand and relationship, as particularly expressed in the Beatitudes.[186] Thus, the material of 11.27–30 sets up the narrative of 12.1–14, which focuses upon the contrasting yokes of the Pharisees and of Jesus, and issues of christology.

The material in 12.1–13 regarding Sabbath observance and the resultant reaction by the Pharisees depicted in 12.14 appear to confirm this reading of 11.28–30 and inform the reader that the controversies are meant in part to 'define the character of the messianic yoke'.[187] Central to both 12.1–8 and 9.13 is the question of what is permissible on the Sabbath; this involves the application of Law, or halakhah. Like its Markan counterpart (2.23–8), 12.1–8 revolves around possible breaches of Sabbath by the disciples who have been eating grain on the Sabbath.[188] Matthew,

---

[182] See Stanton, *Gospel for a New People*, pp. 364–66, for early uses of this text.

[183] For an overview of critical issues involved in 11.25–30, see especially A. M. Hunter, 'Crux Criticorum – Matt. XI. 25–30 – A Re-appraisal', *NTS* 8 (1962): 241–9, and Deutsch, *Wisdom*, pp. 21–53.

[184] Hunter, 'Crux Criticorum', 248, links 'I am gentle and lowly in heart' with the servant in Isa. 42.2–3; 53.1ff.; and 2 Cor. 10.1.

[185] See H. D. Betz, 'The Logion of the Easy Yoke and of Rest (Matt 11:28–30)', *JBL* 86 (1967): 24, on the possible relationship of 11.27–30 to 28.18–20.

[186] So Betz, *ibid.*, 24. For explanation of the yoke imagery, see Deutsch, *Wisdom*, p. 135; Stanton, *Gospel for a New People*, pp. 375–6; Yang, *Jesus and the Sabbath*, p. 159.

[187] Verseput, *Rejection of the Humble Messianic King*, p. 153.

[188] On questions which relate to the historical circumstances and literary history of the pericope, see H. Aichinger, 'Quellenkritische Untersuchung der Perikope vom Ährenraufen

however, adds a twist to Mark's account by including unique material in verses 5–8.[189] Although numerous issues are raised by this pericope, it seems that the two principal concerns are halakhah and christology.[190] The additional material explicitly states that the Pharisees have wrongly judged (καταδικάζειν) and condemned the innocent (ἀναίτιος) through their misunderstanding of God and misapplication of his Law. This is an important qualification for the pericope, for it establishes the parameters of the conflict. On a foundational level the conflict arises from divergent perceptions of religion and God.[191]

A brief overview of the material unique to Matthew in this pericope will bear this out. In verse 6, after asserting that in Scripture the priests who serve in the Temple on the Sabbath do so without incurring guilt, Jesus utters the controversial statement that 'something greater than the temple is here'.[192] The implication is that, by virtue of their service to Jesus and his ministry, the disciples are likewise innocent of wrong-doing.[193]

am Sabbat Mk 2,23–28 par Mt 12,1–8 par Lk 6,15', in *Jesus in der Verkündigung der Kirche*, edited by A. Fuchs, SNTU A 1, Freistadt: Plöchl, 1976, pp. 110–53; F. W. Beare, 'The Sabbath Was Made for Man', *JBL* 79 (1960): 130–6; M. Casey, 'Culture and Historicity: The Plucking of the Grain (Mark 2:23–28)', *NTS* 34 (1988): 1–23; B. Cohen, 'The Rabbinic Law Presupposed by Matthew XII. 1, and Luke VI. 1', *HTR* 23 (1930): 91–2; D. M. Cohn-Sherbok, 'An Analysis of Jesus' Arguments concerning the Plucking of Grain on the Sabbath', *JSNT* 2 (1979): 31–41; J. D. M. Derrett, 'Christ and the Power of Choice (Mark 3,6)', *Bib* 65 (1984): 168–88; J. D. G. Dunn, 'Mark 2.1–3.6: A Bridge between Jesus and Paul on the Question of the Law', *NTS* 30 (1984): 395–415; J. A. Grassi, 'The Five Loaves of the High Priest (Mt xii, 1–8; Mk ii, 23–28; Lk vi, 1–5; I Sam xxi, 1–6)', *NovT* 7 (1964): 119–22; J. M. Hicks, 'The Sabbath Controversy in Matthew: An Exegesis of Matthew 12:1–14', *ResQ* 27 (1984): 79–91; and E. Levine, 'The Sabbath Controversy according to Matthew', *NTS* 22 (1976): 480–3.

[189] The question of Matthew's sources for vv. 5–8 is very complicated. R. Hummel, *Die Auseinandersetzung zwischen Kirche und Judentum im Matthäusevangelium*, 2nd edn, BEvT 33, Munich: Chr. Kaiser Verlag, 1966, p. 44, stresses the unity of vv. 5–7. D. Hill, 'On the Use and Meaning of Hosea VI. 6 in Matthew's Gospel', *NTS* 24 (1977): 115, suggests that the verses were 'conceived of and composed by' Matthew.

[190] L. Lybaek, 'Hosea 6,6', pp. 491–9, introduces thought-provoking material into the discussion of this passage; however, her emphasis upon christology to the apparent diminishment of Law suggests an imbalanced approach. Sigal, *Halakah of Jesus*, p. 134, takes the opposite position, arguing that christological concerns are not present in the text; rather, the concern is purely halakhic.

[191] Ellis, 'Biblical Exegesis ', pp. 707ff.

[192] Much debate surrounds this text, primarily revolving around the neuter gender of μεῖζον. The options for the referent include the kingdom, love, Jesus' interpretation of the Law, the disciples, and so forth. Gundry, *Matthew*, p. 223, opines that 'neuter gender . . . stresses the quality of superior greatness rather than Jesus' personal identity'. Luz, *Matthäus*, II.242, maintains that it is the mercy of God which is greater, while Hagner, *Matthew 1–13*, p. 330, argues that it refers 'more generally to the phenomenon of the ministry of Jesus'. . .'the wonderful things the Gospel has been describing to this point'.

[193] Hicks, 'Sabbath Controversy', 87; Saldarini, *Matthew's Christian-Jewish Community*, pp. 130–1. Yang, *Jesus and the Sabbath*, pp. 185–7, offers a christological explanation,

Although the halakhic issues central to Sabbath observance are disputed,[194] the manner in which Matthew has framed the situation focuses
upon the questionable condemnation of the disciples by the Pharisees.
That the issue in 12.1–8 concerns the judgmental attitude of the Pharisees towards the disciples through the former's insistence upon strict
adherence to halakhah is confirmed in the second occurrence of the quotation of Hos. 6.6 in Matthew, here in 12.7. Jesus' reproof that the Pharisees would not have condemned the innocent if they had known that
God 'desires mercy and not sacrifice' is provocative, especially when
read in the light of 11.28–30 and Isa. 42.1–4. Hill is probably correct
that 'ἔλεος contains the connotations of חֶסֶד',[195] but in this context the
point may be that the extension of mercy does not abrogate sacrifice but
is greater than it.[196] As noted in the discussion concerning justice, the
association of the virtue of mercy with justice and salvation concepts in
the Old Testament challenges attempts to separate ethical demand from
ecclesiological and soteriological concerns in the Matthean context.[197] In
Matthew the disengagement of the so-called imperative from the indicative is difficult; they are interlinked. That mercy and justice are two of the
three weightier matters of the Law, which the Pharisees have neglected
(23.23), contributes to their import in the context. Thus, strict adherence
to their halakhah misses the mark because it is based upon a faulty understanding of God and his ways. This is congruent with the manner in
which Matthew frames his rhetoric throughout the divorce texts in 5.31–2;
15.1–14; 19.3–12; and so on; when compared with God's expectations,

'Jesus, who is greater than the temple, now, as the merciful one, allows the disciples to act
under his authority.' This and other theories are inadequate to the degree that they fail to
account for the centrality of the halakhic dispute in the section. The practice of Sabbath-
keeping has not been rescinded; it is merely being considered within the framework of
mercy rather than according to the overly harsh Pharisaic stipulation.

[194] Sigal, *Halakah of Jesus*, pp. 128–36, places Jesus with the proto-rabbis against the
pietistic group of Pharisees.

[195] Hill, 'Hosea VI. 6', 109–10. As Jones, *Matthean Parables*, pp. 365–6, observes, ἔλεος
occurs only three times in Matthew (9.13; 12.7; 23.23), each within the context of conflict
with the Pharisees. He suggests, p. 366, that 9.13 'presents an exegetical debate with ἔλεος
at its center'. B. Przybylski, *Righteousness in Matthew and His World of Thought*, SNTSMS
41, Cambridge: Cambridge University Press, 1980, pp. 100–1, notes that none of the three
instances refer to God's saving activity; instead, they all focus upon God's ethical demand
toward humanity. So also Frankemölle, *Jahwebund*, pp. 301–4.

[196] So M. Davies, *Matthew*, p. 95. Cf. 23.23.

[197] J. Donahue, *The Gospel in Parable: Metaphor, Narrative, and Theology in the Synoptic Gospels*, Philadelphia: Fortress, 1988, pp. 72–86, argues that the elements of justice and
mercy are also central to the parables of the Unmerciful Servant (18.23–35) and the Labour-
ers in the Vineyard (20.1–16). He argues, p. 72, that in Matthew the 'pursuit of the justice
of the Kingdom flows from the experience of unmerited forgiveness from God . . . with the
realization that God's justice is always joined to mercy and with surprising lovingkindness'.

Pharisaic halakhah has got it wrong.[198] Important to Matthew is how this error of the Pharisees has led to the condemnation of the innocent, here the disciples.[199] It is in this nexus between an erroneous tradition and the insistence that people live according to the error that the burdensome yoke becomes evident (cf. 15.4–6, 14; 18.23–35). The Pharisaic yoke needlessly contributes to and increases the severity and pain of the people's earthly existence. It seems reasonable, therefore, to assert that in our context the disciples are representative of the oppressed and down-trodden.

A similar point is made in 9.13, in which Hos. 6.6 is also cited, this time following the Pharisees' query regarding the propriety of Jesus' choice of dining companions, namely, tax collectors and sinners. Here the tax collectors and sinners are the marginalized, the outcasts, and Jesus' concern for them reflects the care for the lost and aimless sheep of Israel (cf. Ezek. 34; Matt. 9.36; 21.31–2; 22.8–10). The fact that such outcasts are hearing the good news will be echoed in 11.5 and in the accusations made in 11.18–19 that Jesus is a drunkard and a glutton, a friend of tax collectors and sinners. Tragic from Matthew's point of view is the Pharisees' misperception of the Law and its relation to mercy, justice and faith, resulting in their insistence upon upholding the 'traditions of men' and culminating in the condemnation, exclusion and marginalization of the innocent, and, ultimately, in widespread injustice.[200] One could argue that from Matthew's perspective Jesus' ministry, his teaching and deeds, were founded upon the principles of mercy and justice; thus he sought out all manner of humanity, inviting them to a feast (cf. 22.9). As such, the dining event was established upon an ethical foundation within Jesus' perception of God's mercy and justice, and his own ministry to humanity (cf. 3.15; 5.17–20).

We are also on familiar ground with the second passage in the immediate context: the healing of the man with the withered hand in 12.9–13.

---

[198] See M. Bockmuehl, 'Matthew 5:32', 291–5, for the possible background of the Matthean halakhah provided in the divorce texts.

[199] So S. van Tilborg, *The Jewish Leaders in Matthew,* Leiden: Brill, 1972, pp. 114–15 and Yang, *Jesus and the Sabbath,* p. 187.

[200] In addition to the thematic emphases, the unusual terms Matthew uses at this point may also point in this direction. The adjective ἀναίτιος, used only here in the New Testament (vv. 5, 7), is never used for an animate being in the LXX or other literature. (See Deut. 19.10, 13; 21.8–9; Sus. 1.60–2. The formulation τὸ αἷμα τὸ ἀναίτιον occurs twice and αἷμα ἀναίτιον occurs four times.) In fact, it only occurs in the LXX in definite and indefinite formulations of 'innocent blood'. This is unusual given the fact that in the LXX the normal term for human innocence is ἀθῷος (cf. Matt. 27.4 (with αἷμα), 24). Likewise, the verb καταδικάζειν is also obscure; one would have instead expected κατακρίνειν.

This pericope continues the theme of regulations for Sabbath observance. The controversy is explored by contrasting the legality of rescuing animals with the healing of an individual on the Sabbath.[201] Incidentally, in these two passages Jesus is not presented as having abandoned Law observance, nor is the question raised whether Sabbath should be maintained. Instead, the Pharisees are painted in a bad light for having more compassion towards animals than humans. The refusal to allow a crippled man's healing, while no doubt a worthy point of discussion among the academy, was viewed by Matthew as essentially unjust. The serious implications of this heavy-handed wielding of the Law are evidenced in the following verses. Once again the material unique to Matthew is our guide into the emphases of the passage. In 12.11–12, Matthew includes a *mashal* to illustrate Jesus' point. The Pharisees are presented as valuing a sheep over a person bound by the effects of physical deformity. If the Law, or God, requires that one wait until after the Sabbath for healing, so be it. If, however, mere human tradition stands in the man's way, while similar traditions allow for an animal to be removed from a ditch, one cannot but conclude that the ruling is not only unjust, but essentially cruel. Jesus' healing of the man's arm, then, is paramount to the liberation of an individual from the oppression of an unjust decision by leadership.

Thus, mercy and the contrast between justice and injustice are integral to these two stories as presented in Matthew. Both parties, although innocent, were condemned by the Pharisees: the disciples for eating grain and the crippled man for having the bad fortune of having Jesus arrive on the Sabbath. That Jesus allowed the disciples to eat in the field and healed the man's arm suggests that, in contrast to the unjust proscriptions propagated by the Pharisees, Jesus' rule is a just one. Thus, Doyle's contention that the point at issue in the citation of Isa. 42.1–4 and Matt. 12 is conflict with the Pharisees is correct as far as it goes.[202] The conflict results from the threat that Jesus posed to Pharisaic control of society through halakhah. Jesus was perceived as one who subverted their world.

---

[201] On the rescuing of animals on the Sabbath, Jewish interpretation was divided. CD 11.13–14 appears to prohibit activities while *b. Sabb.* 128b; *b. B. Meṣiʿa* 32b and *m. Beṣah* 3.6 are more lenient in concern for the animal's welfare (see other references in Str-B I.629–30).

[202] Doyle, 'Pharisees in Matthew 12', 17, argues that the point at issue in Matt. 12 and the citation of Isa. 42.1–4 concerns conflict with the Pharisees. His suggestion, however, that the contrast is drawn between Jesus 'as Son, Servant and Wisdom of God and his adversaries' is overstated and misses the point of the contrast and conflict.

The failure of Pharisaic leadership

Studies concerning characterization in Matthew are uniform in their assertion that Matthew presents the Pharisees as thoroughly evil.[203] In fact, there is not a single example of a good Jewish leader, neither political nor religious, in the Gospel. Simply affirming that the Pharisees were scoundrels, however, lacks precision. In what manner were they poor leaders from Matthew's perspective? The frequently cited classic text in this regard is found in Jesus' critique of the Pharisees in 23.23, 'you have forgotten the weightier matters of the law, mercy, justice and faith'. The link between the weightier matters of the Law and ἔλεος, κρίσις and πίστις implies ultimate failure with regard to their personal observance of the Law and their interaction with the people. The terms 'mercy' and 'justice', while possessing a vertical dimension, imply ethical demand. The critique in 23.4 provides further evidence that a failure has occurred with regard to Law observance, 'You bind heavy burdens to the shoulders of people and do not move a finger to help them.'[204] This text, however, takes the critique one step further by coupling their role as spiritual leaders with the outworking of their harsh and unmerciful administration.

A reading of Matthew reveals several situations in which the Pharisees are presented as treating people in an unjust, heartless manner. The narrative in 15.1–14 focuses on precisely this issue. The pericope opens with the Pharisees' critique of the disciples for not washing their hands before they eat.[205] Here we are confronted by the Pharisees' concern for obedience to their traditions. Several lines in Jesus' dialogue reveal his opinion of the Pharisees and their customs. The retort in verse 3 is telling, 'why do you break the command of God for the sake of your tradition?', as is that in verse 6, 'So for the sake of your tradition you make void the word of God.' The citation from Isa. 29.13, 'teaching the

---

[203] See particularly the Matthean Passion narrative, in which the Jewish leaders are presented in an especially bad light. D. Senior, *The Passion of Jesus in the Gospel of Matthew*, Wilmington: Michael Glazier, 1985, pp. 33–40, and J. P. Heil, *The Death and Resurrection of Jesus: A Narrative-Critical Reading of Matthew 26–28*, Minneapolis: Fortress, 1991, pp. 16–17.

[204] The language of heavy burdens has posed a problem for Christian interpretation. In Matthew the issue cannot be rules versus no rules. As Davies and Allison, *Matthew*, III. 272, observe, the Sermon on the Mount 'blasts that notion'. Certainly passages such as 5.20, 12.1–14, and ch. 15 are concerned with halakhic observance. The Pharisees are critiqued because of the severity of their halakhah (cf. 11.29–30) and the fact that mercy, justice and faith are not in evidence.

[205] Just how widespread the 'washing of hands' was is open to debate. The Aaronic priesthood in Exod. 30.17–20 was instructed to wash their hands. Lev. 15.11 demanded hand-washing after contact with a bodily discharge. See especially 1QS 3.8–9; 5.13; CD 10.10–13, where complete immersion was required before eating.

commandments and doctrines of men', further confirms this estimation, as does Jesus' final statement of the passage in verse 14 that the Pharisees are 'Blind guides leading the blind ... both will fall into the pit.' This sense of directional blindness echoes the statement in 9.36, 'seeing the crowds he had compassion for them, for they were harassed and helpless, like sheep without a shepherd'. Thus, it appears that their utter failure has, in Matthew's opinion, led to the abuse of the people of God. It is not an exaggeration, then, to argue that Matthew presents the Pharisees as having treated the people unjustly as a result of their insistence upon meeting the requirements of halakhah. This is in contrast to Jesus, who, as God's servant, champions mercy and justice by the power of the Spirit, thereby promoting a compassionate renewal of God's people.

Conclusion

The conclusion that Isa. 42.1–4 as employed by Matthew presents more than a mere proof-text now appears sound. This study has reaffirmed the idea that a central concern of Matthew, which contributes substantially to his narrative, is the portrait of the compassionate, humble servant of the Lord, who offers healing and renewal to the oppressed, damaged, poor and marginalized. Verse 20 accords well with this depiction and is drawn upon at key points throughout the Gospel. The quotation also resonates with the portrait of a non-confrontational Jesus who avoids unnecessary conflict with the Jewish leadership.

It is striking, therefore, that in addition to these traditional themes of meekness and humility, language properly associated with this text, a concern with the motif of ethical justice is conspicuous. This is particularly the case as it relates to the Gospel's presentation of the religious leaders, who have tyrannized the people under their care through their demand for strict halakhic observance. If my understanding of this scenario is accurate, Cope's and Neyrey's argument that the citation has no contact with the preceding context cannot be sustained. Connections have been observed between the citation and its preceding and subsequent context, traceable in the themes of Jesus' identity, ethical christology and the establishment of the Kingdom of God. Both in the here and now with the announcement of justice for the nations, and in the anticipated victorious establishment of justice, the quotation endorses a servant of God whose mission is the institution of the universal just rule of God. The ministry of Jesus inaugurates this reign of justice, concomitantly effecting the renewal or re-creation of the people of God (cf. 21.43).

Within this framework, the servant of Isa. 42.1–4 not only provides essential substance to the title Son of God, but contributes vitally to Matthew's understanding of Jesus' identity and demeanour towards both opponent and friend, and, perhaps most significantly, to the ethical substratum of the christology he develops. By establishing justice for the down and out, however, Jesus' just rule would naturally confront the unjust regime of the present leadership. The implications for a potentially aggressive, polemical edge to Matthew's christology is an important theme which the Gospel alludes to and which brings together Matthew's high christology and the meekness of the earthly Jesus. This christological ambiguity forms the topic of discussion in the following chapter.

6

THE CHRISTOLOGICAL CONTRIBUTION OF ISAIAH 42.1–4

If the role of Isa. 42.1–4 in Matthew is initially unclear and difficult to trace, its perceived contribution to Matthean christology is even more so. Kingsbury, for example, diminishes its import by asserting that '[Matthew] develops no "Servant christology" as such', arguing instead that he 'subsume[s] the title of Servant under the broader category of Son of God'.[1] Gerhardsson and Hill elevate the servant texts, contesting that they provide substance for the otherwise vacuous Son of God title.[2] The line of inquiry by Gerhardsson and Hill is widely supported and appears promising; however, the suggestion that Isa. 42.1–4 'fills out' the Son of God title cannot account for the breadth of the citation's content within Matthew's 'multi-faceted' and diverse christology.[3] No doubt one contributing factor to this state of affairs is the current transitional state of christological inquiry into the Synoptics. Thorough investigation of titles remains the predominant, if difficult, entry point,[4] and NT scholars are indebted to the comprehensive studies by Hahn,[5] Cullmann[6] and Kingsbury.[7] The frequently cited article by Keck[8] seems to have given voice to scholarly disquiet concerning a purely titles-based approach to christological inquiry, and since Keck several studies have moved beyond this

---

[1] See particularly *Christology*, p. 94. For a critique of Kingsbury, see D. C. Allison, 'The Son of God as Israel: A Note on Matthean Christology', *IBS* 9 (1987): 78–9, who argues that Son of God is typologically equated with Israel.

[2] Gerhardsson, *Mighty Acts*, pp. 88–91; followed by Hill, 'Son and Servant', 8–15, and 'A Response', 51.

[3] Gerhardsson, *Mighty Acts*, p. 82.

[4] See the helpful introduction by Brown, *Introduction to New Testament Christology*, New York: Paulist, 1994, pp. 71–102.

[5] F. Hahn, *The Titles of Jesus in Christology: Their History in Early Christianity*, translated by H. Knight and G. Ogg, New York: World Publishing Co., 1969, *passim*.

[6] O. Cullmann, *The Christology of the New Testament*, revised edn, translated by S. Guthrie and C. Hall, Philadelphia: Westminster Press, 1959, *passim*.

[7] *Christology*, pp. 40–127.

[8] L. E. Keck, 'Toward the Renewal of New Testament Christology', *NTS* 32 (1986): 362–77. See also the recent article of J. F. McGrath, 'Change in Christology: New Testament Models and the Contemporary Task', *ITQ* 65 (1998): 39–50.

limitation to explore the interrelationship between the titles and the narratives in which they are encased. Now 'titular Christological categories' are perceived as being 'subordinate to narrative ones',[9] and some would go so far as to argue that a form of synergism occurs in which the portrait of Jesus created by the narrative and titles is greater than the sum of the individual titles. As Hill asserts, 'Because he [Matthew] portrays Jesus by means of a story no one category – teacher, healer, Wisdom Incarnate, triumphant Son of man, not even Kyrios or Son of God – is adequate to contain that Jesus reverenced by the Church.'[10] Additionally, it should be noted that the erratic usage and juxtaposition of the titles in Matthew suggest a degree of fluidity in Matthew's conception, similar in many respects to texts such as the *Psalms of Solomon* and *1 Enoch*. The conclusion that the definitions of the individual titles are impacted on by their narrative context seems reasonable.[11] One must be cautious, therefore, in postulating a wooden theory of title usage that merely imports usage and definition from the surviving Jewish literature. Instead, the literature from the period should merely inform and set boundaries for usage.

As has no doubt become obvious throughout this work, I am not convinced that the designation 'servant' functions as a christological title in Matthew. Rather, it seems that the two explicit servant texts (Isa. 42.1–4; 53.4) attend to a more descriptive task. In addition to providing an OT basis that validates the life setting of Jesus, they furnish crucial information which, upon further reflection, explores in great depth the character, bearing and ministry of this enigmatic individual. The illuminating proposal by Gerhardsson,[12] Hill[13] and Schnackenburg[14] that the servant is not subsumed under the Son of God title but rather fleshes it out, concurs with the redaction which the quotation of Isa. 42.1a has undergone in Matt. 12.18a and with its use in the Baptism (3.17) and Transfiguration (17.5) narratives. It also coheres well with Luz's assertion that Matthew has added a horizontal dimension to the already existing vertical dimension of Mark's usage of Son of God, thereby stressing the obedience of

---

[9] Luz, *Theology*, p. 32.

[10] D. Hill, 'In Quest of Matthean Christology', *IBS* 9 (1986): 140.

[11] This is particularly the case with the Son of man. Many have noted that although Kingsbury's claim that the Son of man is a public, non-confessional title (*Christology*, pp. 121–2) is generally correct, it fails to account for a scene such as 25.31–46, which seems to be a clear allusion to Dan. 7. See Hill, 'A Response', 48–50, for a critique of Kingsbury's position.

[12] 'Gottes Sohn als Diener Gottes', 73–106.

[13] 'Son and Servant', 2–16; 'A Response', 37–52; 'In Quest of Matthean Christology', 135–42.

[14] 'Siehe da mein Knecht', 203–22.

the Son to the father's will.[15] The vertical is well documented in frequent discussions, particularly in the numerous pieces by Kingsbury (cf. 3.17; 11.27). The horizontal level, however, is less frequently explored. The earliest text in Matthew that betrays a concern with the horizontal plane is 3.15, in which Jesus and John 'fulfill all righteousness'.[16] The reference here is probably not to the fulfilment of the Law specifically, as there is no command to be baptized, but is instead a primarily ethical reference, with 'all' possessing a quantitative sense.[17] Jesus, therefore, through humility becomes the example of obedience to the will of God (cf. 5.20) for his followers. The inclusion of Isa. 42.1a ('in whom I am well pleased') with the declaration of sonship in 3.17 further confirms that a primary characteristic of this Son is his obedience to the Father; he is servant of God.[18]

Two of the most provocative ideas recently put forward regarding the servant have been those of Gerhardsson, who asserts that Matthew's christology is essentially an ethical one,[19] and Neyrey, who argues that the severe apologetic strain which exists in ch. 12 is fundamentally related to Matthew's presentation of Jesus and is also to be found in Matthew's version of Isa. 42.1–4.[20] Both of these ideas are interrelated and do account for much of the diverse material in the narrative. They lead us, however, along a less travelled path to a portrayal of the 'servant' in Isa. 42.1–4 that is distinct from the one traditionally presented. If Gerhardsson and Neyrey are correct, then the conventional understanding of the christology behind the use of the servant in Isa. 42.1–4 may be called into question. There are several reasons why this passage has been misunderstood.

One crucial factor that has contributed to a misreading of Isa. 42.1–4 is the uncritically accepted view that it should be read through the lens of Isa. 53 and the 'suffering servant' motif.[21] Although Mettinger may have overstated his case at points, he has effectively demonstrated that Duhm's merging of the four songs was erroneous and anachronistic.[22] More

[15] Luz, *Theology*, pp. 35–6. This is a frequent theme in Matthew, evidenced primarily in his use of δικαιοσύνη (3.15).

[16] Barth, 'Matthew's Understanding of the Law', p. 138; Meier, 'John the Baptist', 391.

[17] So Gundry, *Matthew*, pp. 50–1; Luz, *Matthew*, pp. 178–9. On the quantitative sense of πᾶσαν, see BDF § 275.

[18] While Luz, *Matthew*, pp. 175–6, is perhaps too dismissive of the idea that the Passion may be seen here in the reference to the servant, Barth, 'Matthew's Understanding of the Law', pp. 140–1, citing Bornkamm on p. 140, is overly optimistic. The link to the Passion, if it exists at all, is an indirect one.

[19] 'Gottes Sohn als Diener Gottes', 73–106.

[20] 'Thematic Use', 470.

[21] Cf. Cullmann, *Christology*, p. 56.

[22] *Farewell to the Servant Songs, passim.*

importantly, the reading of all servant texts through Isa. 53 has had the effect of minimizing the otherwise diverse content of the four servant songs to a single soteriological theme. As I have demonstrated, Isa. 42.1–4 exceeds the limitations of a narrowly conceived perspective of soteriology. While Isa. 53 appears to have been a key passage in early Christianity,[23] it would be a mistake to subsume all under its vivid imagery, particularly when Matthew evinces no explicit element of suffering in his usage of Isa. 42.1–4, or even Isa. 53.4. At least this much must be acknowledged. In addition to concerns over eisegesis, a second factor contributing to a possible misreading of Isa. 42.1–4 involves the tension created by the juxtaposition of high and low christologies in Matthew. As is frequently noted, the aggressive dialogues and demonstrations in the Temple (21.12–13) and the confrontations of 12.22ff. do not fully cohere with the traditional conception of Jesus as a meek and lowly person. Neyrey's suggestion that 'Matthew's intention is to present Jesus as vocally and aggressively apologetic',[24] as evidenced in the redaction of ch. 12, seems a fair representation of the material and leads one to the heart of Matthew's complex portrait of Jesus. He is at once the heavenly Son of man, who is judge of the world (25.31–46), and also the humble and meek one (cf. 11.28–30), who is present with his people (1.23; 18.20; 25.40, 45).

If the thesis is sound that Matthew presents Jesus as the final eschatological figure, to whom he assigns the labels of messiah, the one to come, the Son of David, Son of God, servant, and so forth, and whose goal is the restoration and renewal of the people of God (1.21, 23; 23.36–9), then these apparently dissonant chords may find resolution within Matthew's broader christological programme. The present analysis of Matthew 12.18–21 confirms an extensive breadth but also demonstrates that a greater coherence undergirds his understanding of Jesus than is otherwise assumed, particularly with regard to the polemical aspect of Jesus which recurs throughout the Gospel (cf. especially 12.22ff.; 21–3; 25). Contrary to popular opinion, in the use of Isa. 42.1–4 Matthew appears to integrate a dynamic ethical component and a high christology. Thus, the compassionate servant is also the agent of universal justice for the nations. Furthermore, this elevated christology, evidenced in the inclusion of sonship language in the title 'my Beloved' and the LXX reading

---

[23] Hooker's argumentation in *Jesus and the Servant* has tempered the excesses found in the discussion concerning the 'suffering servant' in early Christianity. See also Page, 'Suffering Servant', 481–97; W. D. Davies, *Paul and Rabbinic Judaism*, pp. 247ff.; Bellinger and Farmer, *Suffering Servant*; and Janowski and Stuhlmacher, *Leidende Gottesknecht*, for examinations of the servant of the Lord.

[24] 'Thematic Use', 470.

of 'the nations will trust in his "name"', provides a basis for the mission of the servant and establishes Jesus' identity as central to Matthew's understanding of the divine mandate.

This chapter, then, seeks to explore these apparently contradictory elements in Matthew's presentation of Jesus in an attempt to reflect more fully upon the import of Isa. 42.1–4 within Matthew's christology. The underlying question that will be addressed concerns whether the compassionate servant is complemented by the aggressive polemicist motif, or, as is sometimes promulgated, whether a sharp disjunction exists between the portraits in 12.17–21 and 12.22ff.[25] Two passages outside the context of Matt. 12 that are particularly relevant to this exchange are Matt. 21.14–16 and 25.31–46. In these pericopae one confronts a surprisingly complex portrait of Jesus, in which Matthew's theological 'view from above' permeates his historical presentation. In this respect, however, the reader encounters what may be the most difficult component of Matthew's christology, which, although immensely rich and textured or, as Gerhardsson suggests, 'multi-faceted', renders comprehensive statements woefully inadequate. In an attempt to address the aforementioned paradox, the chapter will first define in greater detail what is meant by the phrase 'apologetic Jesus'. This will be followed by a brief examination of three passages from Matthew that may illuminate the issues framed above, namely, 12.22ff.; 21.13–16 and 25.31–46. The chapter will conclude with a further consideration of the rhetorical force of Matt. 12.18–21 and its implications for Matthew's christology. The study will incorporate an analysis sensitive to exegetical and narrative components in an attempt to unravel the intertwined christological, ethical and eschatological themes in which the paradox of the humble/apologetic Jesus is manifest.

The apologetic Jesus defined

Neyrey contests that Matthew presents 'a portrait of Jesus and a description of the church's situation quite different from the popular impression of Jesus as "meek servant"',[26] and that the Jesus of this portrait 'is the very center of controversy and judgment'.[27] Central to Neyrey's postulate is the narrative of Matt. 12.22ff., to which the quotation in 12.18–21 is crucial. He plots the contact points with the citation found in 12.18–21 and the material in 12.22ff. as follows: (1) the disputed authority of Jesus; (2) the character of spirit; (3) the 'scandal' of being ignored; (4) 'judgment on unbelievers'; (5) 'extension of the gospel to all nations';

---

[25] Cope, *Matthew*, p. 34; Verseput, *Rejection of the Humble Messianic King*, pp. 206–7.
[26] 'Thematic Use', 471.   [27] *Ibid.*

(6) the acknowledgment of trust in his name. Additionally, both he and Cope have demonstrated that these numerous terminological and thematic links between the citation and following context imply an interrelationship between the citation and its context during Matthew's composition.[28] Thus conceived, Neyrey's assumption that the quotation serves a pivotal role in this 'extended polemical context' seems warranted.[29] Given this correspondence between 12.18–21 and 12.22ff., the postulate of a strong disjunction between the two passages is somewhat puzzling in its supposition that the aggressive polemic element in Jesus' response to the Pharisees exposes an inconsistency in Matthew's presentation of Jesus. The contradiction between the traditional understanding of 12.18–21 and its surrounding context is a real one, as the so-called 'humble, messianic king' becomes a powerful, regal figure in 12.22ff.

Through judicious use of sociological and redactional methods, Stanton traces the background of the conflict to the parting of the ways between Christianity and Judaism and the resultant 'name-calling'.[30] Two stock jibes directed at the person of Jesus label him a magician and deceiver.[31] What is perhaps most perplexing is the association of these jibes with the Son of David title and healing episodes (9.34; 12.23–4). This particular development has yet to be fully explained.[32] A clue to their usage may be found in the fact that these associations appear to be the result of Matthean redaction, which suggests that they are of special interest to the Evangelist.[33] Thus, the *Sitz im Leben* becomes crucial for understanding

---

[28] Cope, *Matthew*, p. 46; he notes, for example, the frequent occurrence of the terms ἐκβάλλειν (12.20, 24, 26, 27(2), 28, 35(2) (cf. 13.52)) and πνεῦμα (12.18, 28, 31, 32) within the citation and in the section following.

[29] *Ibid.* Neyrey follows Hummel, *Auseinandersetzung*, pp. 125–8, concerning the character of this section. Neyrey's extrapolation of the conflict to 'a bitter controversy between Matthew's church and unbelieving hostile Pharisees' is less obvious.

[30] *Gospel for a New People*, pp. 169–91. Stanton's position is not unlike Neyrey's on this point; see Neyrey, 'Thematic Use', 470–1.

[31] One charge in the Gospel against Jesus is that his exorcisms are accomplished through the power of 'the prince of demons' (9.34; 10.25; 12.24, 27). Stanton, *Gospel for a New People*, p. 179, observes that the charge 'that deceiver' (ἐκεῖνος ὁ πλάνος) occurs in 27.63–4, a passage which is thoroughly Matthean and reveals his own interests. For a sociological analysis of Matt. 12.22ff., see B. J. Malina and J. Neyrey, *Calling Jesus Names: The Sociological Value of Labels in Matthew*, Sonoma: Polebridge, 1988, pp. 1–67.

[32] Baumbach, *Das Verständnis des Bösen*, pp. 120–1, argues that the fundamental conflict in Matthew is between God and Satan, which is manifest in various forms throughout the narrative (see also Powell, 'Religious Leaders in Matthew', pp. 82–4).

[33] It seems impossible to date Matthew solely on this basis due to the infrequent and varied conflicts, both early and late, between Judaism and the church (see most recently Hagner, '*Sitz im Leben*', pp. 60–4; D. R. A. Hare, *The Theme of Jewish Persecution of Christians in the Gospel according to St Matthew*, SNTSMS 6, Cambridge: Cambridge University Press, 1967, pp. 125–7). Stanton, *Gospel for a New People*, pp. 154–7 (see also Neyrey, 'Thematic Use', 140), is probably correct that the conflict depicted in Matthew

this element within Matthew's Gospel.[34] There seems little doubt that these early conflicts between the early Christianity and Judaism are reflected in Matthew's presentation of the clashes between Jesus and the Pharisees; the question remains whether the clashes were currently ongoing (*intra muros*)[35] or the separation of Matthew's communities from Judaism was a *fait accompli* (*extra muros*).[36] As has already been concluded concerning the Son of David title and the possible reason for its relationship to healings,[37] the challenge is fundamentally against Jesus' legitimacy as king or leader of the people of God and against their renewal, which was believed to accompany the arrival of the Kingdom of God. The conflict reveals the struggle between God's chosen king/leader and the rejected Jewish leaders, who, although they continue to manipulate the strings of power, are poor elders from Matthew's and God's perspective (9.36; 23).[38]

The discord between Jesus and the Pharisees seems to arise in three areas: questions over Jesus' identity (cf. 9.34; 12.23, 38), halakhic disputes (12.1–13; 15.1–20), and the positive response of the crowd to healings (9.33; 12.23).[39] This would suggest that Matthew is not presenting merely a disagreement over ontological elements of christology; rather, he is more concerned with the horizontal plane, with issues of ethics and praxis.[40] When examined in this light, it seems that lying behind

finds its origin in the schism between the early church and Judaism; however, as Stanton willingly concedes, the differentiation between the actual narrative of the life of Jesus in Matthew and the concomitant christology and community concerns underlying it is difficult to distinguish. See R. J. Bauckham, 'For Whom Were the Gospels Written?', in *The Gospels for All Christians: Rethinking the Gospel Audiences*, Grand Rapids: Eerdmans, 1998, pp. 30–4, for a thoughtful critique of the postulate of an isolated local community behind the Gospels.

[34] See particularly Overman, *Matthew's Gospel and Formative Judaism*, pp. 1–5; 141–7 (*contra* Bauckham, 'For Whom Were the Gospels Written?', p. 31 n. 35); Stanton, *Gospel for a New People*, pp. 157–68.

[35] So Overman, *Matthew's Gospel and Formative Judaism*, p. 5; however, I am uncomfortable with Overman's assertion that Matthew's community did not 'understand themselves as "Christians". On the contrary they were Jews.' This begs many questions and demands a careful definition of 'Christian', something Overman does not provide.

[36] So Stanton, *Gospel for a New People*, pp. 113–45. Stanton's view is that Matthew's church has recently separated from the synagogue. See also Luz, *Matthew*, pp. 88–9. The least probable position is that Matthew's community has been separated for some time.

[37] See above, pp. 161–4.

[38] The potential for conflict with current leadership has already been alluded to in 2.3, in which Herod and all Jerusalem are troubled (ἐταράχθη; see H. Balz, 'ταράσσω', *EDNT* III.335–6) at Jesus' birth.

[39] Kingsbury, 'Developing Conflict', 195, notes three characteristics of the dispute: (1) it is intensely confrontational; (2) it 'involves the Mosaic law'; and (3) it leads to plotting to kill Jesus.

[40] This is not to suggest that questions of ontology may be separated from ethical

Matthew's portrayals of Jesus and the Pharisees is an attempt to contrast leadership styles in order to demonstrate that Jesus is the ideal leader, the servant of God *par excellence*. Moreover, Matthew appears very careful not to depict Jesus as the initiator of the conflict with the Pharisees; in Matthew's eyes at least, Jesus is not a revolutionary. In each situation of controversy, the Pharisees precipitate the conflict.[41] But neither does Jesus back down from the controversy, unless there is a threat to his existence.[42] This de-politicized element in Jesus' ministry may partly explain the tensions created by the apparent support for the Pharisees in 23.3 and the harsh critique that follows.[43] A brief examination of Matt. 12.22–50 and the issues central to the text may assist in determining Matthew's christological programme more clearly.

The Son of David, the Spirit and the Kingdom of God

Two primary issues arise in 12.22–50. The first concerns the erroneous determination of the source of the S/spirit behind Jesus' ministry of healing (θεραπεύω) (12.25–30) and of his identity (12.23), and forms the basis for his condemnation (12.24). The second involves the Pharisaic rejection of Jesus' ministry and person, from which derives the indictment upon the Pharisees and their generation (12.25–45). It is here in ch. 12 that the theme of Israel's rejection of its messiah gains a more prominent place in the narrative structure. The linkage between the healing, the presence of the Spirit[44] and the arrival of the Kingdom of God (12.28) comprises

concerns, or that the vertical may be disjoined from the horizontal. In Matthew, they are inextricably intertwined. Underlying the challenge to Jesus' leadership is the issue of his authority, which for many is the way into this discussion (Schnackenburg, 'Siehe da mein Knecht', 204–7); however, authority is primarily a concern of ontology, or the vertical, and less so of the horizontal.

[41] The Pharisees are generally depicted as approaching Jesus (e.g., 12.1–8, 9–13, 22ff.) or appearing amongst the crowds (12.24; 15.1ff.).

[42] As noted in chapter 5, the withdrawal motif (12.15a) possibly evident in 12.19 need not in and of itself exclude verbal confrontation, particularly if the reference is to a more severe attack with possibly murderous intent (12.14; 14.13). 16.21 suggests an awareness on Jesus' part that he will die in Jerusalem at the hands of the leadership, as intimated, for example, in the parallel of John's and Jesus' lives throughout the Gospel. See Meier, 'John the Baptist', 399–400.

[43] *Pace* K. G. C. Newport, *The Sources and Sitz im Leben of Matthew 23,* JSNTSup 117, Sheffield: Sheffield Academic Press, 1995, pp. 127–9, who argues that the two statements in 23.3 and 4 represent a poor seam in Matthew's redaction of two traditions. On this see D. E. Garland, *The Intention of Matthew 23,* NovTSup 52, Leiden: Brill, 1979, pp. 46–55.

[44] If πνεῦμα (12.28) represents a Matthean redaction of Q (Luke 11.20, ἐν δακτύλῳ θεοῦ), an emphasis upon Spirit and alignment with 12.18 is probably present. The arguments strongly favour the position that Luke's text represents Q. Those who support this include C. K. Barrett, *The Holy Spirit and the Gospel Tradition,* London: SPCK, 1966, p. 63; Davies

a forceful christological text, which exposes not only Jesus' identity, but also the seriousness of the Pharisaic rejection. While the conflict, which is essentially a continuation of 9.34, may ultimately be between God and Satan[45] and their kingdoms (12.22–30), it is here manifest on the human level between the Pharisees and the Son of David.[46]

Through these events it becomes clear that the very essence of Jesus and his ministry to Israel is challenged; thus it is no surprise to find christology a prominent feature.[47] The healing in verse 22 provides the jumping off point for the conflict; in it the work of the Spirit of God is manifest, revealing the significance of Jesus' identity and the arrival of the Kingdom, which here is manifest in the very deeds of Jesus, his care for the oppressed (here demonically oppressed), and the outcasts (cf. 12.20). The serious nature of the Pharisaic accusation that the source of Jesus' power is Beelzebul is something the narrative explores quite fully;[48] however, in contrast to 9.34, Jesus answers their vitriolic aspersions in a comprehensive manner. The charge has not simply been levelled at him, but also at the Spirit's work through him towards the oppressed, which is ultimately a challenge against the Kingdom of God.[49] This point is further enhanced if the 'healing' scene in verse 22 is figurative or parabolic of Jesus' ministry to Israel.[50] Thus, the Pharisaic challenge and rejection acquires national significance, presaging the final rejection in 27.25. The parable of 12.43–5,

and Allison, *Matthew*, II.340; Beare, *Matthew*, p. 279; Gnilka, *Matthäus*, 1.456. J. M. van Cangh, '"Par l'esprit de Dieu – par le doigt de Dieu" Mt 12.28 par. Lc 11.20', in *Logia: les paroles de Jésus – The Sayings of Jesus,* edited by J. Delobel, BETL 59, Leuven: Leuven University Press, 1992, pp. 337–42, argues that Matt. and 'spirit' best represent Q.

[45] See n. 32.

[46] I understand the title Son of David, cautiously affirmed by the crowds here, to be a legitimate reference for Matthew. For uses of μήτι which anticipate a positive response, see BDF 427 § 2.

[47] J. D. G. Dunn, *Jesus and the Spirit: A Study of the Religious and Charismatic Experience of Jesus and the First Christians as Reflected in the New Testament*, Philadelphia: Westminster, 1975, pp. 48–9, downplays the christology of this passage, emphasizing the Spirit and the eschatological implications found therein.

[48] Whether Neyrey, 'Thematic Use', 470–1, is correct in reading a church situation behind this text is difficult to ascertain.

[49] Is this a precursor to the element of violence against the Kingdom of God mentioned in 11.12ff.? On the issue of violence against the Kingdom, see Andrew J. Overman, *Church and Community in Crisis: The Gospel according to Matthew,* Valley Forge: Trinity Press International, 1996, pp. 166–9.

[50] A. Suhl, 'Der Davidssohn im Matthäus-Evangelium', *ZNW* 59 (1968): 80; J. M. Gibbs, 'Purpose and Pattern in Matthew's Use of the Title "Son of David" ', *NTS* 10 (1963–4): 451–2; W. R. G. Loader, 'Son of David, Blindness, Possession, and Duality in Matthew', *CBQ* 44 (1982): 577–8; 'Matthew 12:28/Luke 11:20 – A Word of Jesus?', in *Eschatology and the New Testament: Essays in Honor of G. R. Beasley-Murray,* edited by H. Gloer, Peabody: Hendrickson, 1988, pp. 39, 43; *pace* Verseput, *Rejection of the Humble Messianic King*, p. 213.

with its closing statement, 'so shall it be with this generation', implies this broader context as it hints at future failure to recognize Jesus' import for the generation that has experienced the cleansing, healing ministry.

The Pharisees, then, are not merely aligned against a man; they have set themselves against the power of God (Spirit) and the revealed Kingdom of God, and, thus, they stand in opposition to the very will of God on earth. They fail to understand that the healings of Jesus, here the Son of David, signpost the arrival of the Kingdom of God. The tensions in Matthew's christology are prominent at this point. Although the chapter is ultimately about larger issues, the opposition to Jesus' compassionate ministry provides further evidence that the Jewish religious leadership have lost their way. Moreover, they do not affirm the care for the lowly or the wounded and broken, a negligence on their part which is indicative of their leadership (9.36; 23.4). The aggressive nature of Jesus' polemic becomes an authoritative pronouncement against the failure of both the Jewish religious leadership and the current generation to recognize in Jesus' life and ministry the coming of God. The narrative concern revolves around the Pharisaic rejection of Jesus' ministry and their inability to comprehend the relationship between the presence of the Spirit and Jesus' identity.[51] The broader theological issues concern the just treatment and healing of humanity, and eschatology. The establishment of justice in the ethical treatment of humanity is linked to Jesus' identity and to eschatology, namely, the arrival of the Kingdom of God.

The restoration of God's people in the Temple

The evocative image of Jesus standing in the Temple as king, healing the blind and the lame, is a climactic moment in the Gospel.[52] Matthew's redacted story-line in 21.1–16 is straightforward. Immediately upon entering Jerusalem as its 'humble' king (Isa. 62.11/Zech. 9.9),[53] Jesus advances on the Temple, which he cleanses in a bold fashion (21.12–13).[54] This dramatic event is followed by the healing of 'the blind and the

---

[51] The full import of the Spirit to Matthew's christology has not yet been fully explored, as Stanton, *Gospel for a New People*, p. 180, has observed.

[52] The source of 21.14–16 is, like that of many passages in Matthew, difficult to trace. In 21.1–10, Matthew reshapes Mark 11.1–17 by moving the Temple scene (Mark 11.15–17//Matt. 21.12–13) forward to the same day as the triumphal entry (Mark 11.1–11) and adds his own material in Matt. 21.14–16.

[53] Garland, *Matthew*, pp. 210–11, helpfully observes that the entry is royal, not triumphal. His further suggestion that the two animals represent two elements of Jesus' identity, one royal and the other humble, is less convincing.

[54] However one views Jesus' activity in the Temple historically, for Matthew it is a significant theological moment. See N. T. Wright, 'Jerusalem in the New Testament', in

lame' in the Temple precincts (v. 14), and the praise offered to the Son of David by the children (v. 15), all to the great chagrin of the chief priests and scribes (v. 16). The paradox created by the two scenes, a humble king riding on an ass, juxtaposed with a Temple scene in which he overturns tables and chairs, stretches the boundaries of coherence and traditional portraits of weakness and lowliness. Most often this aggressive, polemical edge exhibited by Jesus is accounted for simply as his prophetic character,[55] and given the pluriformity and fluidity of messianism in the Second Temple period and of the titles and portraits in Matthew's presentation of Jesus, this is certainly possible. Yet although the crowd's affirmation that Jesus is the prophet from Nazareth captures an element of his life and ministry and may presage a prophetic outburst in the Temple, the designation appears in the narrative in a most subtle way. The three proclamations that Jesus is Son of David (20.30; 21.9; 21.14–15) and the royal symbolism found in the entry on an ass, however, suggest that the kingly image may predominate here.[56] Furthermore, demonstrative behaviour was not solely limited to prophets; some of the kings in Israel functioned in powerful ways. For example, Hezekiah, in the first year of his reign, restored and cleansed the Temple (2 Chron. 29.3–7). In another more robust narrative, the Son of David in *Ps. Sol.* 17.30 purges Jerusalem. Finally, that the city of Jerusalem is shaken (σείω) upon Jesus' arrival (21.10) echoes the turmoil in Jerusalem caused by his birth (2.3) and the earthquake at his death (27.51), possibly denoting an eschatological event.

If the emphasis does reside in Jesus as the ideal Davidic King throughout 21.1–17, several elements of this pericope are of significance. First, Matthew appears to exalt Jesus' status with respect to the Temple. When this scene is read in light of 12.6 ('one greater than the temple'), and is combined with the possibility that the Temple may have been destroyed

---

Jerusalem Past and Present in the Purposes of God, edited by P. Walker, Cambridge: Tyndale House, 1992, pp. 56–64, whose position that Jesus came to Jerusalem as a replacement of the Temple is difficult to substantiate.

[55] Gundry, *Matthew*, p. 412; Davies and Allison, *Matthew*, III.132–46, entitle the section, 'The Prophet-King'. The most frequently made point in favour of the prophetic is the crowd's reply in v. 11, 'this is Jesus, the prophet from Nazareth of Galilee', which Schlatter, *Matthäus*, p. 611, argues is probably a reference to the eschatological prophet of Deut. 18.15. This may be the case, but one must question if the element of kingship is completely lost.

[56] This seems to be one instance where the crowd's declarations are not to be taken as either Matthew's or God's point of view. It is perhaps better understood as a statement of what they actually, but erroneously, thought (cf. 14.1–2; 16.14). One must be cautious in asserting a uniform perspective of the crowd's responses to Jesus. In this context, the numerous pronouncements of Jesus as Son of David and the authority of Scripture in Matt. 21.5 (from Isa. 62.11 and Zech. 9.9) and Matt. 21.9 (= Ps. 118.25) would seem to take precedence.

when Matthew was composed, Jesus' relationship to the Temple and the presence of God is given expression. Second, both the cleansing of the Temple and the healings therein appear to contain motifs of purification[57] and wholeness. The healing of the blind and the lame within the Temple precincts, a scene unique to Matthew, contributes an element potentially critical to this thought, particularly when one considers the fact that these healings in the Temple are the last recorded in Matthew's narrative. In chapters 4 and 5 of this study, it was shown that the healings in Matthew appear to be linked to a broader concern for justice and the renewal/reconstitution of the people of God. Central to this theme is Jesus' role as ideal Davidic King/leader/messianic ruler, which Matthew articulates throughout the narrative. Thus, in Matthew's narrative at least, the scene appears to reflect the twin elements of humility and exalted status that were confronted in Matt. 12. The humble messianic king simultaneously expresses the will of God in an aggressive manner purifying the Temple and compassionately offers healing and restoration in the Temple space.

There has been some doubt whether the blind and lame were excluded from the Temple precints because of questions concerning their purity. Although some have argued that this is the case, there seems to be little evidence that explicitly supports the contention that they were in fact excluded.[58] The Dead Sea Scrolls offer a somewhat different position. The references to the 'blind' and the 'lame' in 4QMMT and 1QSa 2.8–9 suggest that at the very least they were excluded from the congregation because of their deformity or illness and, therefore, were considered unclean or impure.[59] Of particular interest is 1QSa 2.8–9, which applies purity restrictions to those present at the assembly and banquet with the messiah. Matthew presents the exact opposite portrait. His account places

---

[57] Davies and Allison, *Matthew*, III.139, suggest that in Jesus' actions one may find a general eschatological fulfilment that 'the temple and/or its staff will be purified'. In support of this thesis they cite Zech. 14.21; Mal. 3.2–4; *Ps. Sol.* 17.30(33).

[58] *Pace* Davies and Allison, *Matthew*, III.141. Luz, *Matthäus*, III.188–9, is appropriately cautious about the frequently cited evidence concerning the exclusion of the blind and lame from the Temple precincts. He rightly notes that Lev. 21.18 refers to the priesthood, and that 2 Sam. 5.6, 8 is only a historical reference. The frequently referenced *m. Ḥag* 1.1 merely excuses the blind and lame from the obligation of attending festivals (I am grateful to R. Bauckham for his comments on this topic). Texts from Qumran are more difficult. 1QSa 2.8–9 forbids the blind and lame from joining in the messianic banquet, an important communal event; 4QMMT 52–7 excludes the blind and deaf for reasons of purity (cf. also LXX 2 Kings 5.6–8). The New Testament provides indirect evidence in John 9.1 and Acts 3.1–5, which both record encounters with lame people just outside the Temple gates, but still, it appears, within the broader Temple enclosure.

[59] This theme was first brought to my attention by Professor P. Stuhlmacher.

the messiah in the Temple, healing and purifying 'the blind and lame' (cf. Matt. 11.5; Isa. 35.5–6), thus offering them a place among the people of God. If this is an accurate portrayal, then the issue is more grave than modern conceptions of 'discrimination';[60] rather, Matthew is addressing a system which 'promoted social injustice by stigmatizing [the blind and lame] and excluding them according to purity classifications'.[61] Matt. 21.14 presents the arrival of a king who brings with him an offer of renewal and reconstitution to the people of God.[62] He may even be considered a political liberator of sorts.[63]

Thus, we find that the concerns in this text are primarily eschatological and ethical, the core of which are justice and mercy.[64] This picture matches very well with the one presented in Matt. 12.18–21, in which the meek, compassionate one restores the weak and burdened. It appears that Matthew's portrait of Jesus as meek and humble does not mean weak or feeble. Rather, with regard to the weak, oppressed and broken, he is compassionate and eager to extend mercy and justice. Justice served, however, can often indirectly challenge unjust structures within a society and those who affirm, propagate or benefit by fractured societal structures. Perhaps the phrase in 12.20b, 'until he brings justice forth to victory', is meant to be taken in a continuous sense, one in which the people of God are marked by the presence of the Kingdom and of the risen Christ, who continues to offer justice through his community to all humanity.

Matthew 25.31–46 and the ethical king

An important text throughout the history of Christianity, the uniquely Matthean parable of *The Sheep and the Goats* (25.31–46)[65] is not only

---

[60] Tentatively, Davies and Allison, *Matthew*, III.140.

[61] Garland, *Matthew*, p. 213. One wonders if a similar idea is not expressed in the rending of the veil in 27.51, which marks either judgment upon the Temple itself or the opening of the presence of God to all.

[62] Luz, *Matthäus*, III.188, cautiously; less tentative is Garland, *Matthew*, p. 213; Kvalbein, 'Wunder der Endzeit', 123–4; Schnackenburg, 'Siehe da mein Knecht', 221.

[63] Schnackenburg, 'Siehe da mein Knecht', 221.

[64] One must also consider the fact that Matthew cites Hos. 6.6 twice (9.13; 12.7) with an emphasis upon mercy.

[65] The passage enjoys a complicated and lengthy tradition history and *Wirkungsgeschichte*, which, although fascinating, are beyond the analysis here. For a thorough discussion of the textual and tradition histories, see most recently Jones, *Matthean Parables*, pp. 226–65, and also D. R. Catchpole, 'The Poor on Earth and the Son of Man in Heaven: A Reappraisal of Matthew xxv. 31–46', *BJRL* 61 (1979): 355–97. U. Luz, 'The Final Judgment (Matt 25:31–46): An Exercise in "History of Influence" Exegesis', in *Treasures Old And New: Recent Contributions to Matthean Studies,* edited by D. R. Bauer and M. A. Powell, SBL Symposium Series, Atlanta: Scholars, 1996, pp. 271–310, notes its import in the history of Christianity and offers a superb presentation of its *Wirkungsgeschichte*.

central to the Gospel's christology but may even contribute to an understanding of the christology which underlies the use of Isa. 42.1–4. As the final parable, it possesses a prominent position in the Gospel and provides a conclusion to the eschatological discourse.[66] Of particular interest for this study is the high christology contained in the parable and the relationship demonstrated between christology and ethics.[67] The Son of man, later the king (25.34), is given an exalted status, a similar scenario to that of 19.28,[68] in which the Son of man, surrounded by angels, sits on the throne of glory and gathers the nations for judgment (25.31–2).[69] Such imagery depicts a universal, exalted figure directly influenced by the ideas found in Dan. 7 and probably *1 Enoch*.[70]

On a narrative level, Jesus' awareness of and teaching concerning the role of the Son of man in the final judgment suggests, in Matthew's narrative at least, an awareness that he is this exalted figure. It is surprising, therefore, that only two verses later (26.2) Jesus predicts that this exalted Son of man, who will at a future time judge the nations (25.31–2), is himself to be handed over to be crucified (26.2),[71] having been unjustly condemned by those ignorant not only of the significance of their actions but also of the true identity of the one upon whom they have executed judgment.[72] This fact colours the entire Passion narrative and serves to heighten the irony of Israel's rejection of Jesus.

In Matthew's scheme the Son of man is intimately related to the fortunes of the marginalized (the hungry, thirsty, naked, prisoners, etc.), which, as C. C. Rowland points out, parallels Jesus' union with the outcasts throughout his ministry.[73] Regardless of whether one views these

[66] Jones, *Matthean Parables*, p. 226.

[67] Jones, *ibid.*, p. 260, observes that Matthew evinces both a theological basis for ethics (5.45) and a christological one, suggesting that the issue was not clearly defined in this period.

[68] On the relationship between 19.28 and 25.31, see J. Friedrich, *Gott im Bruder? Eine methodenkritische Untersuchung von Redaktion, Überlieferung und Traditionen in Mt. 25, 31–46*, Stuttgart: Calwer, 1977, pp. 54–66, and, most recently, Jones, *Matthean Parables*, pp. 228–39.

[69] That Matthew has here drawn upon Dan. 7.9–14 and possibly *1 Enoch* 37–71 seems the best choice, although the switch to the language of kingship in 25.34 poses some problems. That Jesus is to be viewed as king and judge is perhaps most evident in the phrase 'Come, blessed of my Father', in which there is a clear distinction between the king and the Father. This language possibly alludes to 11.27.

[70] This, of course, depends upon how late one dates *1 Enoch*. See the discussion on dating in chapter 3.

[71] W. L. Kynes, *A Christology of Solidarity: Jesus as the Representative of His People in Matthew*, New York: University of America Press, 1991, pp. 154–5.

[72] Jones, *Matthean Parables*, p. 265.

[73] 'Apocalyptic, the Poor, and the Gospel of Matthew', *JTS* 45 (1994): 514–18.

oppressed ones as the church[74] or a larger group,[75] the Son of man's identification with broken humanity demonstrates Jesus' concern and care for
those less fortunate. Close identification with the lowly and disenfranchised is unexpected from such an exalted person. This contrast of high
and low christologies offers another explicit statement regarding Jesus'
identity. The fact that we have a future event brought into the present
serves not only to offer a glimpse of future judgment; the temporal incon-
gruity serves to provide a christological basis for ethical behaviour in the
present and further confirms that after 'his death and resurrection...he is
Lord and Judge of all nations'.[76] Furthermore, his solidarity with his dis-
ciples/family[77] (cf. Matt. 12.46–50), expressed in his continued presence
with these poor, afflicted ones, affirms not only his humility but also his
representative identification, apparently based upon the recurring theme
of the presence of Jesus, Emmanuel, with his people (cf. 10.40).[78] Thus,
the apocalyptic view extends beyond time, revealing a universal code by
which the nations will be judged.[79] Additionally, in an indirect manner,
the parable offers consolation to the marginalized, affirms that not only
has their plight not gone unnoticed by the divine judge, but he is and
will be present with them and will ultimately judge all nations. He is the
one who is with them in the present, suffers and dies on their behalf and
accompanies them on their mission to the nations (28.18–20).

Beyond this representative identification, in which the righteous
through service of the 'family' members of the Son of man unknowingly
serve and align themselves with him, lies the moral and ethical virtue of
social justice: the needs provided for the 'brethren' are basic to human
existence, involving food, drink, clothing, and care for prisoners and the
alien. The fact that 'brethren' in 25.31–46 refers to the followers of Jesus
should not deter one from noting Jesus' treatment of the marginalized
throughout his ministry. By touching and healing lepers (8.3), dining
with tax collectors and sinners (9.9–13; 11.19), healing the blind, lame,

---

[74] The definition of the marginalized is notoriously difficult. I understand them to be
the persecuted church (Luz, 'Final Judgment', pp. 304–8). Rowland, 'Apocalyptic, the
Poor', 504–18, offers a provocative discussion concerning the possible links between these
passages in Matthew, apocalyptic literature and Jewish mysticism.

[75] D. O. Via, 'Ethical Responsibility and Human Wholeness in Matthew 25:31–46', *HTR*
80 (1987): 79–100.

[76] Jones, *Matthean Parables*, p. 250 n. 249, citing Bornkamm.

[77] Matthew's view of the church is a brotherhood/family (cf. 12.46–50; 18.15, 21, 35;
23.8–12; 25.40; 28.10). Van Tilborg, *Jewish Leaders*, p. 137.

[78] Kupp, *Matthew's Emmanuel*, p. 96; Gerhardsson, 'Gottes Sohn als Diener Gottes',
87; Garland, *Matthew*, p. 244.

[79] See Catchpole, 'Matthew xxv. 31–46', 389ff., and, most recently, Jones, *Matthean
Parables*, pp. 257–9, for texts which refer to this listing of a code of conduct.

deaf and demonized, and proclaiming good news to the poor (11.5//Isa. 61.1), Jesus fulfils OT expectations and models the values of the Kingdom of God for his disciples.

The presence of this heavenly judge with his people mirrors the relationship of the compassionate servant to the people in Matthew's two usages of servant texts, in which the servant identifies with humanity in their plight through tender care (12.20) and offering healing to the ill (8.17). Although the categories of corporate personality have rightly been dispensed with,[80] and the soteriological element is not immediately obvious, there is a sense in which the judge, who is present with his people in 25.31–46, and the king, who heals and purifies the broken and marginalized in the Temple (21.14), intimately identify with all levels of humanity. Even in what may be one of the most exalted, heavenly moments in Matthew's christological conception, a concern for the earthly, involving the ethical protection of human dignity and value, is manifest. In this final vision, the virtue of justice is vital to Matthew's christology and the eschatological justification of ethics.

Isaiah 42.1–4 and Matthew's ethical christology

The rhetorical import of Isa. 42.1–4 within Matthew's narrative and presentation of Jesus is substantial and accords well with this understanding of Matthew's christology. The study has uncovered a more pronounced ethical component than otherwise anticipated, particularly in the two servant citations (Isa. 42.1–4; 53.4).[81] In the case of Isa. 42.1–4, it becomes especially prominent when one considers the force of the final form of the quotation. In addition to the fact that it provides the viewpoint of God, its length and content serve to frame Jesus for the audience in a particular manner and to interject evocative imagery and concepts into the narrative.

The tensions exhibited elsewhere in Matthew's christology also exist in Matthew's version of Isa. 42.1–4, in which the introduction of the title 'Beloved' incorporates into the citation the element of sonship, indicative of a high christology (cf. 28.19). This evocative language summons images of the future hope that was relatively common stock in Judaism. Yet at the same time the text presents a humble, compassionate servant who cares for those already damaged (the crushed reed and smouldering wick), offering encouragement and care. As noted previously in the last chapter, while 12.20a may refer to the healings of 12.15, it seems that

---

[80] Rogerson, 'Hebrew Conception of Corporate Personality', 14–15.
[81] Gerhardsson, 'Sacrificial Service', pp. 29–31.

upon further reflection the referent encompasses an assessment of Jesus' ministry to the down and out, the impure, the poor, the marginalized. This servant passage seemingly affirms the identification of the exalted Son of man with broken humanity (25.31–46), a compassionate note which resonates with numerous passages throughout Matthew. 9.36 presents Jesus' concern for the people under aimless leadership. 11.28–30 offers an invitation to the tired and weary which is based upon the intimate relationship between the Son and Father in 11.27. In a similar vein, Jesus' vision and desire for Israel and the pain of their rejection are evident in his emotive cry over Jerusalem in 23.37. As important as the compassionate, humble element is to Matthew's christology, other currents exist as well.

In his use of Isa. 42.1–4 Matthew associates a high christology with the empowering of the Spirit for a mission (v. 18b) which is universal in scope (v. 21) and the goal of which is the victorious establishment of justice (v. 20b). As alluded to in chapter 5,[82] two stages appear to exist in Matthew's thoughts on the matter of justice, perhaps similar to Stanton's suggestion of a two-parousia scheme.[83] In Jesus' first coming, the arrival of the Kingdom of God is a present, experienced reality (12.28), which also awaits a future denouement. But, as 11.11–12 suggests, it has not been greeted with open arms; instead, it has suffered violence. Similarly, Matthew's ideal King has not been accepted by the current leadership who perceive in Jesus a threat to their position as leaders of the people. Through his presentation of Jesus' deeds and message, Matthew appears to challenge the current establishment. This is particularly evident in Jesus' relationship to the Law,[84] in which the concern is not to advocate the setting aside of Law observance, but rather that halakhic stipulations be based in mercy and justice. In Jesus' deeds and message the will of the Father is expressed, which cuts directly across Pharisaic rule. Naturally one would expect conflict.

An allusion to such conflict is inherent in the line 'until he brings forth justice to victory'. Jesus' concerns regarding strict Pharisaic halakhah, his proclamation of good news to the poor, healing of the blind, lame, unclean, and even gentiles, and universalism suggest an opening of the doors of the Kingdom to all humanity, affirming their dignity and equality. Yet such acts of mercy are also viewed by Matthew as acts of justice. That this is the case is evident in the aggressive behaviour of the Pharisees in response to Jesus' deeds and message. It seems, from Matthew's

---

[82] See pp. 147–8.
[83] *Gospel for a New People*, pp. 185–9.
[84] See Snodgrass, 'Matthew and the Law', pp. 125–7.

point of view, that Jesus is effectively challenging the foundation of their rule, which had led to oppression and elitism. Jesus' mission inaugurates the renewal of the people of God, who follow but one Master (23.8–12). Jesus' aggressive apologetic surfaces in the confrontation with the Jewish leadership, whom the Son of man will one day judge. Although Matthew does not present Jesus as a revolutionary or political insurrectionist, his message is profoundly political in the sense that the emphasis upon justice, mercy and faith challenges the very foundations of the Jewish leadership. This inevitably brings confrontations and conflict, as the Jewish leaders expose their corrupt ways in their rejection of God's servant and in demanding his execution. Yet however proleptic, Matthew's version of Isa. 42.1–4 promises that the servant shall one day bring forth the justice that was commenced in Jesus' ministry to Israel into victory for all nations who put their hope in him.

7

CONCLUSION

This study began with a somewhat modest goal, namely, to explore the function and possible import of Isa. 42.1–4 within Matthew's narrative and christology. In so doing, however, I have arrived at several unexpected conclusions while at the same time confirming the conclusions of numerous recent studies on Matthew's use of the Old Testament which contend that, for many of the formula quotations at least, Matthew's employment of the Old Testament is fundamentally theological and best described as complex. With regard to Isa. 42.1–4, it seems that the quotation was employed by Matthew to validate a particular view of Jesus as royal messiah, namely, that he was the Spirit-endowed, compassionate servant of the Lord whose words and deeds evinced the justice anticipated with the advent of the messiah and the inauguration of the Kingdom of God. That such is the case became evident on the level of the citation's text-form, its role within the surrounding context, and the rhetorical thrust of its final form.

For a considerable period of time, the primary avenue into the topic of Matthew's OT usage in the formula quotations has been through proposed relationships between the anomalous text-form and Matthew's own interests, assuming that Matthew, or his school, produced a type of Targum or version of the passage. The text-form was thought to provide a clear view of Matthew's theological interests. The results of this study have both modified and further supported this approach.

Although there is evidence in the text-form of 12.18–21 that Matthew's creative genius was at work in specific textual adjustments apposite to his narrative and christological concerns, several conclusions concerning text-form caution against over-exuberance on this point. Contemporaneous texts found in Naḥal Ḥever, Masada, Wadi Murrabaʿat and Khirbet Qumran demonstrate that there was both fluidity and variety in the biblical texts during the period and provide evidence that Matthew's anomalous quotations are not as unique as has sometimes been thought. Similarly, the Greek texts from Naḥal Ḥever confirm that the process of modification of the text-form towards the MT had already begun in the latter half of the first century BC. Furthermore, the existence of texts that evince similar idiosyncrasies to those found in Matthew (resembling and yet distinct from both the MT and LXX) should caution against bold assertions that Matthew translated directly from the Hebrew or that the LXX was his base text. It remains a possibility that Matthew may have had before him a Greek manuscript that had already been conformed to the MT. But it also remains possible, perhaps even probable, that Matthew presents us with a scribe who treated the text in the same manner that these sources seem to have been treated. Such an argument is entirely appropriate, if difficult to defend. Additionally, even though Lindars' work has not met with universal assent, Isa. 42.1–4 was associated with the Baptism and Transfiguration prior to Matthew (cf. Mark 1.11; 9.7//Luke 9.35) and thus the text-form may be the result of the work of Christian scribes. The extent to which Matthew drew upon text-forms from early Christendom is, unfortunately, difficult to trace.

Nevertheless, one must also note that the citations appear to support and expand Matthew's theological interests. Furthermore, the adjustments made to the quotations also seem to support Matthew's theological interests. This would suggest that Matthew is the source of many of the modifications. Such a conclusion would fit with Matthew's use and modification of the Mark and Q material, and the OT quotations included from these sources. Thus, it seems that in Matthew's use of the formula quotations we have an example of early Christian exegesis of the Old Testament designed to support the life and ministry of Jesus. What remains in doubt is the exact form of the base text that Matthew worked from and the extent of the modifications to that text. A more definitive description of Matthew's text-form would require a more comprehensive study than is found in these pages.

Matthew's source for Isa. 42.1–4, then, may have been M, early Christian tradition of which we have no record, possibly even a Testimony, or he may have simply employed a text known to him from its messianic use within Judaism. While not overwhelming, there is evidence that suggests that Isa. 42.1–4 contributed to messianic and eschatological perceptions. Contained within it are ideas of Spirit, justice, mercy, the restoration of the people of God and the salvation of the nations. The fact that these concepts were frequently present in prophetic and apocalyptic writings may indicate why Isa. 42.1–4 was read in a messianic fashion and may divulge its attraction to Matthew. Matthew's subtle adjustments intensify these themes in light of his theological and contextual concerns.

Nevertheless, there is a high degree of continuity exhibited between Matthew and early Judaism.

Beyond the issues of text-form and source, the conclusion that Matthew's usage of the Old Testament is complex is central to this study. With respect to the Isaianic formula quotations, it appears that they are essentially bi-referential. This is explicitly demonstrated in the usage of Isa. 7.14a cited in Matt. 1.23. On the narrative level, the primary reason for the quotation, the passage is cited to validate the virginal conception, a theme nowhere else explored in Matthew. But on a theological level, the arguably more consequential theme of Emmanuel, through whom God is present with his people, frequently recurs throughout Matthew's narrative (cf. 18.20; 25.31–46; 28.18–20). Similarly, the other Isaianic quotations in Matt. 4.15–16 (Isa. 8.23b–9.1) and 8.17 (Isa. 53.4a) demonstrate, although in a less explicit manner, these two levels of reference. Bi-referentiality is also present in Matthew's use of Isa. 42.1–4. On a linear, or narrative, level the citation seems to validate Jesus' withdrawal, command to secrecy and/or the healings, all of which occur in the preceding narrative of Matt. 12.14–16. As was observed, however, this level of reference cannot account for the copious amount of superfluous content in this extended quotation. As in the previous quotations of Isaiah, the proposed theological content of the citation is centred in this extraneous material. Matthew, a careful but creative redactor/author, appears to have intentionally included the extra content to buttress his portrait of Jesus.

The quotation of Isa. 42.1–4 incorporates numerous themes found not only in the surrounding context but throughout the Gospel. In contrast to Neyrey and Cope, who both assert that there is little or no contact between the citation and the previous context, I have argued that the primary contextual link is the theme of justice/injustice apparent in the halakhic disputes (12.1–13) and healings (12.8–13) of the preceding context. Beyond the immediate context, this theme, particularly as it relates to the oppressed and marginalized, is evident throughout the Matthean narrative in the emphasis upon purity (9.10–13; 11.5; 21.12–17) and halakhic observance (12.1–13; 15.1–20; 23.2–4, 23). In addition to the motif of justice, the crucial christological feature of the bestowal of the Spirit found in 12.18 also finds expression in both prior (3.16) and subsequent (12.28) contexts. Similarly, one may also observe the theological import of the proleptic universalism depicted in 12.21 (cf. 28.18–20) and trust in the servant's name (1.21, 23) within Matthew's broader presentation of Jesus of Nazareth.

One could devote substantial space to tracing out the themes of justice, universalism, the Spirit, and name within the Gospel, but more significant is the rhetorical force of the entire quotation. This study has sought to tentatively explore the role that the final form of the citation has within the Gospel. This is one step beyond the redactional method which, in an attempt to explicate Matthew's interests, marks the possible adjustments made to the quotation by both earlier tradition and Matthew. The supposition is that the rhetorical force of the final form of the quotation, given that it is peculiarly distinct from other known versions, produces a unique meaning. For example, the fact that 12.21 reads 'the nations will hope in his name' rather than 'the coastlands wait for his law' (MT) substantially alters the meaning of the passage, re-orientates the referents and places the servant rather than Torah at the centre of this universalistic text. When considered as a unit the extended quotation imports a distinct summary or portrait of Jesus into the narrative. The result is such that when Matthew's version is read, the quotation possesses the force of a divine pronouncement on the person of Jesus, offering not only the divine point of view but also a comprehensive description of the person of Jesus as the Spirit-endowed servant, whose mission is to compassionately establish justice for the nations. It is this portrait which underlies Matthew's christology and which appears to be manifest within the peculiar elements of the text-form itself, suggesting a Matthean origin.

The portrayal of the servant found in the citation makes a provocative and distinctive contribution to current proposals regarding Matthean christology and seems to reconcile the apparent paradox of the polemical and compassionate. The compassionate element is manifest in the servant's treatment of the bruised reed and smouldering wick (v. 20), however one unpacks these evocative metaphors. Similarly, the frequently noted quiet, non-confrontational demeanour of the servant evidenced in Jesus' withdrawal (12.14) and command to silence (12.16) seems to be attested in the distinctive text of verse 19. As authors such as Neyrey have observed, however, a counterweight to this meeker side of the servant resides within the citation, for embedded within the affirmation that the servant's mission concerns the announcement and victorious establishment of justice are the seeds of an aggressive, polemical motif. The words spoken and deeds performed by Jesus on behalf of the marginalized, outcast, sick and disenfranchised are tangible manifestations of the justice of God concomitant with the arrival of the Kingdom of God. Moreover, Matthew appears concerned to demonstrate that Jesus, despite the ambiguity that surrounds messianism during this period, is the royal messiah whose task is the establishment and renewal of the people of God.

It is at this point that the tension between the Pharisees and Jesus develops. As was observed earlier, conflict forms a notable theme in Matthew's narrative and presentation of the life of Jesus. Although generally initiated by the Pharisees, Jesus' occasionally aggressive response reflects the fundamental conflict between God and Satan as the Pharisees challenge and ultimately reject the Kingdom of God and its inbreaking. Significantly, the altercation concerns halakhic and purity issues and the ethical implications of Pharisaic interpretation of the Scriptures. It is here that the eschatological elements of Matthew's depiction of Jesus also impinge upon this discussion. Matthew's emphasis does not merely rest upon Jesus' humanity; instead, the theological view from above seeps into the present to heighten the contrast. At the heart of Matthew's presentation lie the ethical implications of the outworking of the justice of God in relation to christology. Matthew attempts to demonstrate that Jesus is indeed the servant of Isa. 42.1–4. Compassion and lowliness, while manifest, are not the sole focus; instead, the status of Jesus as God's Son and the centrality of justice to his mission warrant conflict with the established religious and political elite. Jesus' worldview and identity serve to subvert the establishment in those areas in which they no longer exhibit care for the people under them. The arrival of Israel's king, however humble, can only spark conflict. Thus, the image of the servant transcends categories of humility as Jesus is presented as servant *par excellence,* a figure who in Matthew's account incorporates both the lowly and exalted through the accomplishment of the will of God. Here one finds Matthew's high and low christologies in tension: Jesus is both compassionate and aggressive.

If the conclusions of this study are valid, then several avenues for further enquiry come into view. First, the supposition that justice is instantiated in the person of Jesus may prove a key element in Matthew's christology. The citation appears to contain within it a temporal development— the justice inaugurated in Jesus will finally be brought to victory by Jesus. Additionally, Matthew's apparent emphasis upon the perpetuation of justice in the lives of the disciples (3.15–17) should also be considered in this framework. The parable of 25.31–46 is particularly instructive at this point, for in it one finds the moral, ethical stance of the earthly Jesus and his followers vindicated at the end of time. Thus there is a justification of justice in Matthew's final vision. Re-examining Matthew's christology in light of this substantial emphasis should afford a more accurate understanding of the role of justice throughout the Gospel.

A second subject of study that may prove fruitful in future work is the further examination of the rhetorical force of the formula quotations' final form within the narrative. Once the citations are liberated from the perception that they are somehow foreign objects to the narrative, their value as interjections that contribute to Matthew's portrayal of the life of

Jesus becomes apparent. The evaluation of Isa. 42.1–4 in Matthew has demonstrated that this is the case. While the quotation may not proffer any crucial 'new' material to Matthew, its rhetorical impact at its point in the narrative and the fact that themes from the quotation are evidenced elsewhere in Matthew suggest that the content of the citation transcends the constrictions imposed upon it by the boundaries of such categories as proof-text or authorial aside. This implies that Matthew's use of the Old Testament is closer to what Chatman has labelled general commentary and, as such, contributes significantly to the narrative development. It is the extent of the contribution that remains to be fully explored, the results of which may more thoroughly illuminate aspects of Matthew's rich and textured portrait of Jesus.

BIBLIOGRAPHY

Primary sources

Ante-Nicene Christian Library: Translations of the Writings of the Fathers down to A.D. 325. Edited by A. Roberts and J. Donaldson. 24 vols. Edinburgh: T. & T. Clark, 1867–72.

The Apocrypha of the Old Testament: Revised Standard Version. The Oxford Annotated Apocrypha. Edited by B. M. Metzger. New York: Oxford University Press, 1977.

The Apostolic Fathers. Translated by K. Lake. LCL. 2 vols. Cambridge, MA: Harvard University Press; London: Heinemann, c. 1912–13.

Baillet, M., J. T. Milik, et al. Discoveries in the Judaean Desert. Vols. 1–7. Oxford: Clarendon, 1955–82.

Biblia Hebraica Stuttgartensia. Edited by K. Elliger and W. Rudolph. New edn. Stuttgart: Deutsche Bibelgesellschaft, 1977.

Brown, Francis, S. R. Driver and C. A. Briggs. A Hebrew and English Lexicon of the Old Testament. Oxford: Clarendon, 1977.

The Dead Sea Scrolls in English. Edited and translated by G. Vermes. 3rd edn. Harmondsworth: Penguin, 1987.

The Dead Sea Scrolls Translated: The Qumran Texts in English. Edited by Florentino García Martínez. Translated by W. Watson. Leiden: Brill, 1994.

Eusebius: The Ecclesiastical History. Translated by K. Lake and J. E. L. Oulton. 2 vols. LCL. Cambridge, MA: Harvard University Press, 1926–32.

The Great Isaiah Scroll (1QIsaᵃ): A New Edition. Edited by Donald W. Parry and Elisha Qimron. STDJ 32. Leiden: Brill, 1999.

Hebrew–English Edition of the Babylonian Talmud. Edited by I. Epstein. 20 vols. London: Soncino, 1972–84.

Hennecke, E. New Testament Apocrypha. Edited by W. Schneemelcher. Translation edited by R. McL. Wilson. 2 vols. London: Lutterworth, 1963–5.

Isaac, E., trans. '1 (Ethiopic Apocalypse of) Enoch (Second Century B.C.–First Century A.D.): A New Translation and Introduction'. In The Old Testament Pseudepigrapha. Edited by J. H. Charlesworth. Vol. I, pp. 5–89. Garden City, NY: Doubleday, 1983.

Isaias: Septuaginta Vetus Testamentum Graecum. Vol. XIV. Edited by J. Ziegler. Göttingen, 1939.

Josephus. Translated by H. St. J. Thackeray (vols. I–V), Ralph Marcus (vols. V–VIII) with Allen Wikgren (vol. VIII), and Louis H. Feldman (vols. IX–X). LCL. Cambridge, MA: Harvard University Press, 1926–65.

Klijn, A. '2 Baruch'. In *The Old Testament Pseudepigrapha*. Edited by J. H. Charlesworth. Vol. I, pp. 615–52. Garden City, NY: Doubleday, 1983.

Knibb, Michael A. *The Book of Enoch: A New Edition in Light of the Aramaic Dead Sea Fragments*. 2 vols. Oxford: Clarendon, 1978.

Midrasch Tehillim (Schocher Tob). Edited by S. Buber. Wilna: Romm, 1891.

Midrash Rabbah. Edited by H. Freedman and M. Simon. 10 vols. London: Soncino, 1939.

The Midrash on the Psalms. Edited by W. G. Braude. 2 vols. New Haven: Yale University Press, 1959.

Milik, J. T. *The Books of Enoch: Aramaic Fragments of Qumran Cave 4*. Oxford: Clarendon, 1976.

The Mishnah. Translated by H. Danby. Oxford: Oxford University Press, 1933.

The Odes of Solomon: The Syriac Texts. Edited and translated by J. H. Charlesworth. SBL Texts and Translations 13 (PS 7). Missoula: Scholars, 1977.

The Old Testament Pseudepigrapha. Edited by J. H. Charlesworth. 2 vols. Garden City, NY: Doubleday, 1983–5.

Pesikta Rabbati: Discourses for Feasts, Fasts, and Special Sabbaths. Translated by W. G. Braude. 2 vols. Yale Judaica Series 18. New Haven and London: Yale University Press, 1968.

Rosner, Fred, trans. *Maimonides' Commentary on the Mishnah Tractate Sanhedrin*. New York: Sepher-Hermon Press, 1981.

Septuaginta: Id est Vetus Testamentum graece iuxta LXX interpretes. Edited by A Rahlfs. Two vols. in one. Stuttgart: Deutsche Bibelgesellschaft, c. 1935.

Talmud. *Berakoth: Translated into English with Notes, Glossary and Indices*. Translated by Maurice Simon. In The Babylonian Talmud: Seder Zeraim. London: Soncino Press, 1948.

Talmud. *Sanhedrin: Translated into English with Notes, Glossary and Indices*. Translated by Jacob Shachter. In The Babylonian Talmud: Seder Nezikin. Vol. III. London: Soncino Press, 1935.

Talmud. *Yebamoth: Translated into English with Notes, Glossary and Indices*. Translated by Israel W. Slotki. In The Babylonian Talmud: Seder Nashim. Vol. I. London: Soncino Press, 1936.

The Targum of Isaiah. Edited and translated by J. F. Stenning. Oxford: Oxford University Press, 1949.

The Isaiah Targum: Introduction, Translation, Apparatus and Notes. Translated by B. D. Chilton. Edinburgh: T. & T. Clark, 1987.

Tischendorf, Constantinus. *Novum Testamentum Graece*. 3 vols. Leipzig: Giesecke & Devrient/Hinrichs, 1869–94.

Tov, Emanuel, ed. *The Greek Minor Prophets Scroll from Nahal Hever (8Hev XIIgr)*. DJD VIII. Oxford: Clarendon, 1990.

Wright, R. B. 'Psalms of Solomon: A New Translation and Introduction'. In *The Old Testament Pseudepigrapha*. Edited by J. H. Charlesworth. Vol. II, pp. 639–70. Garden City, NY: Doubleday, 1983.

Commentaries on the Gospel of Matthew

Albright, W. F. and C. S. Mann. *Matthew: Introduction, Translation, and Notes*. AB 26. Garden City, NY: Doubleday, 1971.

Allen, W. C. *A Critical and Exegetical Commentary on the Gospel according to St Matthew.* 3rd edn. ICC. Edinburgh: T. & T. Clark, 1912.

Argyle, A. W. *The Gospel according to Matthew.* Cambridge: Cambridge University Press, 1963.

Beare, F. W. *The Gospel according to St Matthew: A Commentary.* Oxford: Blackwell, 1981.

Benoit, P. *L'évangile selon Saint Matthieu* (trans. of *Gnomon Novi Testamenti,* 1742). Paris, 1961.

Blomberg, C. L. *Matthew.* New American Commentary. Nashville: Broadman, 1992.

Bonnard, P. *L'évangile selon Saint Matthieu.* 3rd edn. Commentaire du Nouveau Testament. Neuchâtel: Delachaux & Niestlé, 1970.

Carson, D. A. *Matthew.* EBC. Grand Rapids: Zondervan, 1985.

Carter, Warren. *Matthew: Storyteller, Interpreter, Evangelist.* Peabody: Hendrickson, 1996.

Davies, Margaret. *Matthew. Readings: A New Biblical Commentary.* Sheffield: JSOT Press, 1992.

Davies, W. D. and Dale C. Allison. *A Critical and Exegetical Commentary on the Gospel according to Saint Matthew.* 3 vols. ICC. Edinburgh: T. & T. Clark, 1988, 1991, 1997.

Fenton, J. C. *Saint Matthew.* Pelican New Testament Commentaries. Baltimore: Penguin, 1964.

Filson, F. V. *A Commentary on the Gospel according to St Matthew.* BNTC. A. & C. Black: London, 1960.

France, R. T. *The Gospel according to Matthew: An Introduction and Commentary.* TNTC. Grand Rapids: Eerdmans, 1985.

Gaechter, P. *Das Matthäus-Evangelium.* Innsbruck: Tyrolia, 1963.

Garland, D. E. *Reading Matthew: A Literary and Theological Commentary on the First Gospel.* New York: Crossroad, 1993.

Gnilka, J. *Das Matthäusevangelium.* 2 vols. HTKNT. Freiburg: Herder, 1986, 1988.

Green, H. B. *The Gospel according to Matthew.* New Century Bible. Oxford: Clarendon, 1975.

Grundmann, Walter. *Das Evangelium nach Matthäus.* THKNT. Leipzig: Evangelische Verlagsanstalt, 1968.

Gundry, R. H. *Matthew: A Commentary on His Handbook for a Mixed Church under Persecution.* 2nd edn. Grand Rapids: Eerdmans, 1994.

Hagner, Donald A. *Matthew 1–13.* WBC 33a. Dallas: Word Books, 1993.
    Matthew 14–28. WBC 33b. Dallas: Word Books, 1995.

Hare, Douglas R. A. *Matthew.* Interpretation. Louisville: John Knox Press, 1993.

Harrington, D. J. *The Gospel of Matthew.* Sacra Pagina. Collegeville, MN: Liturgical, 1991.

Hendriksen, W. *Exposition of the Gospel according to Matthew.* New Testament Commentary. Grand Rapids: Baker Book House, 1973.

Hill, David. *The Gospel of Matthew.* NCBC. London: Marshall, Morgan and Scott, 1972.

Jones, Ivor H. *A Commentary on the Gospel of St Matthew.* Epworth Commentaries. London: Epworth, 1994.

Klostermann, Erich. *Das Matthäusevangelium*. 4th edn. Handbuch zum Neuen Testament. Tübingen: J. C. B. Mohr (Paul Siebeck), 1971.

Lagrange, M.-J. *Evangile selon Saint Matthieu*. Etudes bibliques. Paris: Gabalda, 1923.

Lenski, R. C. H. *The Interpretation of St Matthew's Gospel*. Columbus, OH: Wartburg, 1943.

Limbeck, M. *Matthäus-Evangelium*. Stuttgarter Kleiner Kommentar, Neues Testament. Stuttgart: Katholisches Bibelwerk, 1986.

Lohmeyer, E. *Das Evangelium des Matthäus*. Revised by W. Schmauch. 4th edn. MeyerK. Göttingen: Vandenhoeck & Ruprecht, 1967.

Luz, Ulrich. *Das Evangelium nach Matthäus*. Vol. I: *Mt 1–7*; vol. II: *Mt 8–17*; vol. III: *Mt 18–25*. EKKNT. Neukirchen-Vluyn: Benzinger & Neukirchener, 1985–98.

  Matthew 1–7: A Commentary. Translated by W. C. Linss. Continental Commentaries. Minneapolis: Augsburg, 1989.

McNeile, A. H. *The Gospel according to St Matthew*. London: Macmillan, 1915.

Robinson, Theodore H. *The Gospel of Matthew*. Moffatt New Testament Commentary. London: Hodder & Stoughton, 1928.

Sand, Alexander. *Das Matthäus-Evangelium*. ErFor 275. Darmstadt: Wissenschaftliche Buchgesellschaft, 1991.

Schlatter, A. *Der Evangelist Matthäus: Seine Sprache, sein Ziel, seine Selbständigkeit*. Stuttgart: Calwer Verlag, 1982.

Schmid, Josef. *Das Evangelium nach Matthäus*. Regensburger Neues Testament 1. 3rd edn. Regensburg: Pustet, 1956.

Schniewind, J. *Das Evangelium nach Matthäus*. NTD 2. Göttingen: Vandenhoeck & Ruprecht, 1964.

Schweizer, E. *The Good News according to Matthew*. Atlanta: John Knox, 1975.

Senior, Donald P. *Matthew*. ANTC. Nashville: Abingdon, 1998.

Trilling, Wolfgang. *Das Evangelium nach Matthäus*. 2 vols. Düsseldorf: Patmos-Verlag, 1965.

Weiss, B. *Das Matthäus-Evangelium*. 9th edn. Göttingen: Vandenhoeck & Ruprecht, 1898.

Wiefel, Wolfgang. *Das Evangelium nach Matthäus*. THKNT. Leipzig: Evangelische Verlagsanstalt, 1998.

Zahn, D. T. *Das Evangelium des Matthäus*. Kommentar zum Neuen Testament. Leipzig: Georg Böhme, 1903.

Secondary works

Aichinger, Hermann. 'Quellenkritische Untersuchung der Perikope vom Ährenraufen am Sabbat Mk 2,23–28 par Mt 12,1–8 par Lk 6,15'. In *Jesus in der Verkündigung der Kirche*, pp. 110–53. Edited by A. Fuchs. SNTU A 1. Freistadt: Plöchl, 1976.

Albl, Martin C. *'And Scripture Cannot Be Broken'. The Form and Function of the Early Christian Testimonia Collections*. NovTSup 96. Leiden: Brill, 1999.

Albright, W. F. 'New Light on Early Recensions of the Hebrew Bible'. *BASOR* 140 (1955): 27–33.

Alexander, Philip S. 'Rabbinic Judaism and the New Testament'. *ZNW* 74 (1983): 237–45.

'The King Messiah in Rabbinic Judaism'. In *King and Messiah in Israel and the Ancient Near East: Proceedings of the Oxford Old Testament Seminar*, pp. 456–73. Edited by J. Day. JSOTSup 270. Sheffield: Sheffield Academic Press, 1998.

Alford, H. *The Greek Testament: With a Critically Revised Text, a Digest of Various Readings, Marginal References to Verbal and Idiomatic Usage, Prolegomena, and a Critical and Exegetical Commentary*. 6th edn. London: Rivingtons, 1865.

Allegro, J. M. 'Further Messianic References in Qumran Literature'. *JBL* 75 (1956): 174–87.

Allen, W. C. 'The Old Testament Quotations in St Matthew and St Mark'. *ExpTim* 12 (1900–1): 281–3.

'Matthew xii. 19–Isaiah xlii. 2'. *ExpTim* 20 (1908–9): 140–1.

Allison, Dale C., Jr. 'The Son of God as Israel: A Note on Matthean Christology'. *IBS* 9 (1987): 74–81.

The New Moses: A Matthean Typology. Minneapolis: Fortress, 1993.

Alter, Robert. *The Art of Biblical Poetry*. New York: Basic Books, 1985.

Anderson, A. A. 'The Use of "Ruah" in IQS, IQH, and IQM'. *JSS* 7 (1962): 293–303.

Anderson, J. C. *Matthew's Narrative Web: Over, and Over, and Over Again*. JSNTSup 91. Sheffield: JSOT, 1994.

Augustine. *De Consensu Evangelistarum Libri 4*. English trans. NPNF First Series. Vol. VI, pp. 77–263. CSEL 43. Vienna, 1904.

Aune, David E. 'The Problem with the Messianic Secret'. *NovT* 11 (1969): 1–31.

Aytoun, Robert A. 'The Servant of the Lord in the Targum'. *JTS* 23 (1922): 172–80.

Bacon, B. W. *Studies in Matthew*. London: Constable, 1930.

Baer, David A. 'Stumbling towards Eloquence: The Translator of Septuagint Isaiah'. Unpublished paper presented at the Old Testament Seminar, University of Cambridge, 1995.

When We All Go Home: Translation and Theology in LXX Isaiah 56–66. The Hebrew Bible and Its Versions, vol. I. JSOTSup 318. Sheffield: Sheffield Academic Press, 2001.

Balz, H. 'ταράσσω'. *EDNT* III.335–6.

Barrett, C. K. *The Holy Spirit and the Gospel Tradition*. London: SPCK, 1966.

Barth, Gerhard. 'Matthew's Understanding of the Law'. In *Tradition and Interpretation in Matthew,* pp. 58–164. Edited by G. Bornkamm, G. Barth and H. J. Held. London: SCM Press, 1963.

Barthélemy, Dominique. 'Le grand rouleau d'Isaïe trouvé près de la mer morte'. *RB* 57 (1950): 530–49.

Les devanciers d'Aquila: première publication intégrale du texte des fragments du dodécaprophéton. VTSup X. Leiden: Brill, 1963.

Barton, Stephen C. *The Spirituality of the Gospels*. London: SPCK, 1992.

Bauckham, Richard J. *Jude, 2 Peter*. WBC 50. Waco: Word, 1983.

'For Whom Were the Gospels Written?' In *The Gospels for All Christians: Rethinking the Gospel Audiences*, pp. 9–48. Grand Rapids: Eerdmans, 1998.

Bauckham, Richard J., ed. *The Gospels for All Christians: Rethinking the Gospel Audiences*. Grand Rapids: Eerdmans, 1998.

Bauer, D. R. *The Structure of Matthew's Gospel: A Study in Literary Design.* JSNTSup 31. Sheffield: JSOT Press, 1988.

Bauernfeind, O. 'νικάω'. *TDNT* IV.942–5.

Baumbach, Gunter. *Das Verständnis des Bösen in den Synoptischen Evangelien.* Theologische Arbeiten 19. Berlin: Evangelische Verlagsanstalt, 1963.

Baumstark, A. 'Die Zitate des Matthäus-Evangeliums aus dem Zwölfprophetenbuch'. *Bib* 37 (1956): 296–313.

Beale, G. K., ed. *The Right Doctrine from the Wrong Texts? Essays on the Use of the Old Testament in the New.* Grand Rapids: Baker, 1994.

Beare, F. W. 'The Sabbath Was Made for Man'. *JBL* 79 (1960): 130–6.

Beaton, Richard. 'Messianism, Spirit, and Conflict: The Eschatological Jesus in Mt 11–12'. Unpublished paper presented at the British New Testament Conference. Aberdeen, 1996.

'Justice and Messiah: A Key to Matthew's Use of Isa 42:1–4?' *JSNT* 75 (1999): 5–23.

Beauchamp, P. 'L'évangile de Matthieu et l'héritage d'Israèl'. *Recherches de science religieuse* 76 (1988): 5–38.

Bellinger, W. and W. R. Farmer, eds. *Jesus and the Suffering Servant: Isaiah 53 and Christian Origins.* Harrisburg: Trinity Press International, 1998.

Betz, H. D. 'The Logion of the Easy Yoke and of Rest (Matt 11:28–30)'. *JBL* 86 (1967): 10–24.

Beuken, W. A. M. 'MIŠPĀṬ: The First Servant Song and Its Context'. *VT* 22 (1972): 1–30.

Beyer, Klaus. *The Aramaic Language: Its Distribution and Subdivisions.* Translated by J. F. Healey. Göttingen: Vandenhoeck & Ruprecht, 1986.

Birnbaum, A. 'The Qumrân (Dead Sea) Scrolls and Paleography'. *BASOR* Supplementary Studies, 13–14. New Haven, 1952.

Bishop, K. 'St Matthew and the Gentiles'. *ExpTim* 59 (1948): 249.

Black, Matthew. *An Aramaic Approach to the Gospels and Acts.* Oxford: Clarendon, 1946.

'Servant of the Lord and Son of Man'. *SJT* 6 (1953): 1–11.

The Book of Enoch or I Enoch: A New English Edition with Commentary and Textual Notes. SVTP. Leiden: E. J. Brill, 1985.

'The Theological Appropriation of the Old Testament by the New Testament'. *SJT* 39 (1986): 1–17.

Bockmuehl, Markus. 'Matthew 5:32; 19:9 in the Light of Pre-Rabbinic Halakhah'. *NTS* 35 (1989): 291–5.

This Jesus: Martyr, Lord, Messiah. Edinburgh: T. & T. Clark, 1994.

Bonsirven, Joseph. *Exégèse rabbinique et exégèse paulinienne.* Paris: Beauchesne et ses fils, 1938.

Borgen, P. 'Philo of Alexandria'. In *Jewish Writings of the Second Temple Period: Apocrypha, Pseudepigrapha, Qumran Sectarian Writings, Philo, Josephus,* pp. 233–41. Edited by M. E. Stone. CRINT 2.2. Assen: Van Gorcum; Philadelphia: Fortress, 1984.

Bornkamm, Günther. 'End Expectation and the Church in Matthew'. In *Tradition and Interpretation in Matthew,* pp. 58–164. Edited by G. Bornkamm, G. Barth, and H. J. Held. London: SCM Press, 1963.

Bornkamm, Günther, G. Barth and H. J. Held, eds. *Tradition and Interpretation in Matthew.* NTL. London: SCM Press, 1963.

Bretscher, Paul G. 'Exodus 4:22–23 and the Voice from Heaven'. *JBL* 87 (1968): 301–11.

Brierre-Narbonne, Jean. *Exégèse apocryphe des prophéties messianiques*. Paris: Librairie Orientaliste Paul Geuthner, 1937.

Brockington, L. H. 'Septuagint and Targum'. *ZAW* 66 (1954): 80–6.

Brooke, George J. *Exegesis at Qumran: 4Florilegium in Its Jewish Context*. JSOT-Sup 29. Sheffield: JSOT Press, 1985.

'The Biblical Texts in the Qumran Commentaries: Scribal Errors or Exegetical Variants?' In *Early Judaism and Christian Exegesis: Studies in Memory of William Hugh Brownlee*, pp. 85–100. Edited by C. Evans and W. Stinespring. Atlanta: Scholars, 1987.

'Kingship and Messianism in the Dead Sea Scrolls'. In *King and Messiah in Israel and the Ancient Near East: Proceedings of the Oxford Old Testament Seminar*, pp. 434–55. Edited by J. Day. JSOTSup 270. Sheffield: Sheffield Academic Press, 1998.

Brown, Raymond E. 'The Qumran Scrolls and the Johannine Gospel and Epistles'. In *The Scrolls and the New Testament*, pp. 183–207. Edited by K. Stendahl. London: SCM Press, 1958.

The Gospel according to John (i-xii): Introduction, Translation and Notes. AB. New York: Doubleday, 1966.

The Birth of the Messiah: A Commentary on the Infancy Narratives in Matthew and Luke. New York: Doubleday, 1977.

Introduction to New Testament Christology. New York: Paulist, 1994.

Brownlee, W. H. *The Meaning of the Qumran Scrolls for the Bible*. New York: Oxford University Press, 1964.

'The Background of Biblical Interpretation at Qumran'. In *Qumran: Sa piété, sa théologie et son milieu*, pp. 183–93. Edited by M. Delcor. BETL 46. Paris: Gembloux, 1978.

Bruce, F. F. *Biblical Exegesis in the Qumran Texts*. London: Tyndale Press, 1960.

Bultmann, Rudolf. *History of the Synoptic Tradition*. Translated by J. Marsh. New York: Harper and Row, 1963.

Burger, Christoph. *Jesus als Davidssohn: Eine traditions-geschichtliche Unter-suchung*. FRLANT 98. Göttingen: Vandenhoeck & Ruprecht, 1970.

Burkitt, F. C. *The Gospel History and Its Transmission*. 3rd edn. Edinburgh: T. & T. Clark, 1911.

Cadwallader, Alan H. 'The Correction of the Text of Hebrews towards the LXX'. *NovT* 34 (1992): 257–92.

Calvin, J. *Commentary on a Harmony of the Gospels*. Reprint. 3 vols. Grand Rapids: Eerdmans, 1956–7.

Casey, Maurice. 'Culture and Historicity: The Plucking of the Grain (Mark 2:23–28)'. *NTS* 34 (1988): 1–23.

Catchpole, David R. 'The Poor on Earth and the Son of Man in Heaven: A Reappraisal of Matthew xxv. 31–46'. *BJRL* 61 (1979): 355–97.

Charette, Blaine. *The Theme of Recompense in Matthew's Gospel*. JSNTSup 79. Sheffield: JSOT, 1992.

' "Never Has Anything Like This Been Seen in Israel": The Spirit as Eschato-logical Sign in Matthew's Gospel'. *JPT* 8 (1996): 31–51.

Charles, R. H. *The Book of Enoch or 1 Enoch: Translated from the Editor's Ethiopic Text*. 2nd edn. Oxford: Clarendon, 1912.

Charlesworth, James H. 'From Jewish Messianology to Christian Christology: Some Caveats and Perspectives'. In *Judaisms and Their Messiahs at the Turn of the Christian Era*, pp. 225–64. Edited by J. Neusner, W. S. Green and E. Frerichs. Cambridge: Cambridge University Press, 1987.

'The Pseudepigrapha as Biblical Exegesis'. In *Early Jewish and Christian Exegesis: Studies in Memory of William Hugh Brownlee*, pp. 139–52. Edited by C. A. Evans and W. F. Stinespring. Atlanta: Scholars, 1987.

'From Messianology to Christology: Problems and Prospects'. In *The Messiah: Developments in Earliest Judaism and Christianity*, pp. 3–35. Edited by J. H. Charlesworth, with J. Brownson, M. Davis, S. J. Kraftchick and A. F. Segal. Minneapolis: Fortress, 1992.

Charlesworth, James H., ed. *The Messiah: Developments in Earliest Judaism and Christianity*. With J. Brownson, M. Davis, S. Kraftchick and A. Segal. Minneapolis: Fortress, 1992.

Chatman, Seymour. *Story and Discourse: Narrative Structure in Fiction and Film*. Ithaca and London: Cornell University Press, 1978.

Chester, Andrew. *Divine Revelation and Divine Titles in the Pentateuchal Targumim*. Tübingen: Mohr (Paul Siebeck), 1986.

'Jewish Messianic Expectations and Mediatorial Figures and Pauline Christology'. In *Paulus und Das Antike Judentum*, pp. 17–89. Edited by M. Hengel and U. Heckel. Tübingen: Mohr, 1991.

'The Parting of the Ways: Eschatology and Messianic Hope'. In *Jews and Christians: The Parting of the Ways, A.D. 70 to 135: The Second Durham Tübingen Research Symposium on Earliest Christianity and Judaism (Durham, September, 1989)*, pp. 239–313. Edited by J. Dunn. WUNT 66. Tübingen: Mohr, 1992.

Chilton, Bruce D. *The Glory of Israel: The Theology and Provenience of the Isaiah Targum*. JSOTSup 23. Sheffield: JSOT Press, 1982.

A Galilean Rabbi and His Bible: Jesus' Own Interpretation of Isaiah. London: SPCK, 1984.

Churgin, Pinkhos. 'The Targum and the Septuagint'. *AJSL* 50 (1933–4): 41–65.

Clark, K. W. 'The Gentile Bias in Matthew'. *JBL* 66 (1947): 165–72.

Cohen, B. 'The Rabbinic Law Presupposed by Matthew XII. 1, and Luke VI. 1'. *HTR* 23 (1930): 91–2.

Cohen, Ronald L. *Justice: View from the Social Sciences*. New York: Plenum Press, 1986.

Cohn-Sherbok, D. M. 'An Analysis of Jesus' Arguments concerning the Plucking of Grain on the Sabbath'. *JSNT* 2 (1979): 31–41.

Coleman, R. O. 'Matthew's Use of the Old Testament'. *Southwestern Journal of Theology* 5 (1962): 29–39.

Collins, John J. 'The Heavenly Representative: The "Son of Man" Figure in the Similitudes of Enoch'. In *Ideal Figures in Ancient Judaism: Profiles and Paradigms*, pp. 111–33. Edited by J. Collins and G. Nickelsburg. SBLSCS 12. Chico: Scholars, 1980.

'Patterns of Eschatology at Qumran'. In *Traditions in Transformation: Turning Points in Biblical Faith*, pp. 351–73. Edited by B. Halpern and J. Levenson. Winona Lake: Eisenbrauns, 1981.

'Messiahs in Context: Method in the Study of Messianism in the Dead Sea Scrolls'. In *Methods of Investigation of the Dead Sea Scrolls and the Kirbet*

Qumran Site: Present Realities and Future Prospects, pp. 213–29. Edited by M. Wise, et al. New York: New York Academy of Sciences, 1994.

'Teacher and Messiah? The One Who Will Teach Righteousness at the End of Days'. In *The Community of the Renewed Covenant: The Notre Dame Symposium on the Dead Sea Scrolls*, pp. 193–210. Edited by E. Ulrich and J. VanderKam. Christianity and Judaism in Antiquity Series 10. Notre Dame, University of Notre Dame Press, 1994.

'The Works of the Messiah'. *Dead Sea Discoveries* 1 (1994): 98–112.

The Scepter and the Star: The Messiahs of the Dead Sea Scrolls and Other Ancient Literature. ABRL. New York: Doubleday, 1995.

Colpe, Carsten. 'ὁ υἱὸς τοῦ ἀνθρώπου'. *TDNT* VIII.400–77.

Cope, O. Lamar. *Matthew: A Scribe Trained for the Kingdom of Heaven*. CBQMS 5. Washington: The Catholic Biblical Association of America, 1976.

Cross, Frank Moore. 'The Oldest Manuscripts from Qumran'. *JBL* 74 (1955): 147–72.

'The Evolution of a Theory of Local Texts'. In *Qumran and the History of the Biblical Text*, pp. 306–20. Edited by F. Cross and S. Talmon. Cambridge, MA: Harvard University Press, 1975.

'The History of the Biblical Text in the Light of the Discoveries in the Judean Desert'. In *Qumran and the History of the Biblical Text*, pp. 177–95. Edited by F. Cross and S. Talmon. Cambridge, MA: Harvard University Press, 1975.

The Ancient Library of Qumran. 3rd edn. Sheffield: Sheffield Academic Press, 1995.

Cross, Frank Moore and S. Talmon, eds. *Qumran and the History of the Biblical Text*. Cambridge, MA: Harvard University Press, 1975.

Culler, J. *The Pursuit of Signs: Semiotics, Literature, Deconstruction*. London: Routledge & Kegan Paul, 1981.

Cullmann, Oscar. *Baptism in the New Testament*. Translated by J. K. S. Reid. SBT 1. London: SCM Press, 1950.

The Christology of the New Testament. Revised edn. Translated by S. Guthrie and C. Hall. Philadelphia: Westminster Press, 1959.

Davenport, Gene L. 'The "Anointed of the Lord" in Psalms of Solomon 17'. In *Ideal Figures in Ancient Judaism: Profiles and Paradigms*, pp. 67–92. Edited by J. Collins and G. Nickelsburg. SBLSCS 12. Chico: Scholars, 1980.

Davies, Graham I. 'Did Matthew Know Hebrew?' Unpublished paper presented at New Testament Seminar, University of Cambridge, 1994.

Davies, Philip R. *The Damascus Covenant: An Interpretation of the 'Damascus Document'*. JSOTSup 25. Sheffield: JSOT Press, 1983.

'Eschatology at Qumran'. *JBL* 104 (1985): 39–55.

Davies, W. D. *Paul and Rabbinic Judaism: Some Rabbinic Elements in Pauline Theology*. 4th edn. Philadelphia: Fortress, 1980.

Davis, Charles Thomas. 'Tradition and Redaction in Matthew 1:18–2:23'. *JBL* 90 (1971): 404–21.

Day, John, ed. *King and Messiah in Israel and the Ancient Near East: Proceedings of the Oxford Old Testament Seminar*. JSOTSup 270. Sheffield: Sheffield Academic Press, 1998.

De Jonge, Marinus. 'The Use of the Word "Anointed" in the Time of Jesus'. *NovT* 8 (1966): 132–48.

'The Earliest Christian Use of Christos: Some Suggestions'. In *Jewish*

Eschatology, Early Christian Christology and the Testaments of the Twelve Patriarchs. Collected Essays of Marinus de Jonge, pp. 102–24. Leiden: Brill, 1991.

'Jesus, Son of David and Son of God'. In *Jewish Eschatology, Early Christian Christology and the Testaments of the Twelve Patriarchs. Collected Essays of Marinus de Jonge*, pp. 135–44. Leiden: Brill, 1991.

'Messiah'. *ABD* IV.777–8.

De Waard, J. *A Comparative Study of the Old Testament Text in the Dead Sea Scrolls and in the New Testament*. STDJ 4. Leiden: Brill, 1965.

Deissmann, G. Adolf. *Bibelstudien: Beiträge, zumeist aus den Papyri und Inschriften, zur Geschichte des Sprache, des Schrifttums und der Religion des hellenistischen Judentums und des Urchristentums*. Marburg: N. G. Elwert'sche, 1895.

Delcor, M. *Les hymnes de Qumran (Hodayot)*. Paris: Letouzey et Ané, 1962.

Delling, Gerhard. 'πληρόω'. *TDNT* VI.286–98.

Derrett, J. D. M. 'Christ and the Power of Choice (Mark 3,6)'. *Bib* 65 (1984): 168–88.

Deutsch, Celia. *Hidden Wisdom and the Easy Yoke: Wisdom, Torah and Discipleship in Matthew 11.25–30*. JSNTSup 18. Sheffield: JSOT Press, 1987.

Dibelius, Martin. *From Tradition to Gospel*. London: Ivor Nicholson & Watson, 1934.

Dodd, C. H. *According to the Scriptures: The Substructure of New Testament Theology*. London: Nisbet & Co., 1952.

Donahue, John R. *The Gospel in Parable: Metaphor, Narrative, and Theology in the Synoptic Gospels*. Philadelphia: Fortress, 1988.

Donaldson, Terence L. 'The Law That Hangs (Matthew 22:40): Rabbinic Formulation and the Matthean Social World'. *CBQ* 57 (1995): 689–709.

Doyle, B. R. 'A Concern of the Evangelist: Pharisees in Matthew 12'. *AusBR* 34 (1986): 17–34.

Duhm, Bernard. *Das Buch Jesaia: Übersetzt und Erklärt von Bernhard Duhm*. HKAT III/1. Göttingen: Vandenhoeck & Ruprecht, 1922. Originally published 1892.

Duling, D. C. 'Solomon, Exorcism, and the Son of David'. *HTR* 68 (1975): 235–52.

'The Therapeutic Son of David: An Element in Matthew's Christological Apologetic'. *NTS* 24 (1978): 392–410.

Dunn, James D. G. 'Spirit and Kingdom'. *ExpTim* 82 (1970–1): 36–40.

Jesus and the Spirit: A Study of the Religious and Charismatic Experience of Jesus and the First Christians as Reflected in the New Testament. Philadelphia: Westminster, 1975.

Christology in the Making: A New Testament Inquiry into the Origins of the Doctrine of the Incarnation. Philadelphia: Westminster, 1980.

'Mark 2.1–3.6: A Bridge between Jesus and Paul on the Question of the Law'. *NTS* 30 (1984): 395–415.

'Matthew 12:28/Luke 11:20 – A Word of Jesus?' In *Eschatology and the New Testament: Essays in Honor of G. R. Beasley-Murray*, pp. 29–49. Edited by H. Gloer. Peabody: Hendrickson, 1988.

The Partings of the Ways between Christianity and Judaism and their Significance for the Character of Christianity. London: SCM Press, 1991.

'Messianic Ideas and Their Influence on the Jesus of History'. In *The Messiah: Developments in Earliest Judaism and Christianity*, pp. 365–81. Edited by J. Charlesworth. Philadelphia: Fortress, 1992.

Eco, Umberto. *Interpretation and Overinterpretation. With Richard Rorty, Jonathan Culler and Christine Brooke-Rose.* Edited by Stefan Collini. Cambridge: Cambridge University Press, 1992.

Edgar, S. L. 'New Testament and Rabbinic Messianic Interpretation'. *NTS* 5 (1958): 47–54.

'Respect for Context in Quotations from the Old Testament'. *NTS* 9 (1962): 55–62.

Edwards, R. A. *Matthew's Story of Jesus*. Philadelphia: Fortress, 1985.

Elliger, Karl. *Studien zum Habakuk-Kommentar vom Toten Meer.* BHT 15. Tübingen: Mohr (Paul Siebeck), 1953.

Deuterojesaja. BKAT II. Neukirchen-Vluyn: Neukirchener Verlag, 1978.

Ellis, E. Earle. 'Biblical Exegesis in the New Testament Church'. In *Mikra: Text, Translation, and Reading and Interpretation of the Hebrew Bible in Ancient Judaism and Early Christianity*, pp. 691–725. Edited by M. J. Mulder. CRINT 2.1. Assen and Maastricht: Van Gorcum and Philadephia: Fortress, 1988.

The Old Testament in Early Christianity: Canon and Interpretation in the Light of Modern Research. WUNT 54. Tübingen: Mohr (Paul Siebeck), 1991.

Emerton, J. A. 'Some Linguistic and Historical Problems in Isaiah VIII.23'. *JSS* 14 (1969): 151–75.

Evans, Craig. '1 Q Isaiah[a] and the Absence of Prophetic Critique at Qumran'. *RevQ* 11 (1984): 537–44.

Farmer, William R. *The Synoptic Problem: A Critical Analysis*. Dillsboro: North Carolina Press, 1976.

Fee, Gordon D. 'The Textual Criticism of the New Testament'. In *Introductory Articles*, pp. 419–33. EBC 1. Grand Rapids: Zondervan, 1979.

Fenton, J. C. 'Matthew and the Divinity of Jesus: Three Questions Regarding Matthew 1:20–23'. In *Studia Biblica 1978.* Vol. II: *Papers on the Gospels*, pp. 79–82. Edited by E. A. Livingstone. Sheffield: JSOT Press, 1979.

Fishbane, Michael. *Biblical Interpretation in Ancient Israel.* Oxford: Clarendon, 1985.

'Use, Authority and Interpretation of Mikra at Qumran'. In *Mikra: Text Translation, Reading and Interpretation of the Hebrew Bible in Ancient Judaism and Early Christianity*, pp. 339–77. Edited by M. J. Mulder. CRINT 2.1. Assen and Maastricht: Van Gorcum; Philadelphia: Fortress, 1988.

Fisher, E. 'Hebrew Bible or Old Testament: A Response to Christopher Seitz'. *Pro Ecclesia* 6 (1997): 133–6.

Fitzmyer, Joseph. 'The Use of Explicit Old Testament Quotations in Qumran Literature and in the New Testament'. *NTS* 7 (1960–1): 297–333.

France, R. T. *Jesus and the Old Testament: His Application of the Old Testament Passages to Himself and His Mission.* London: Tyndale Press, 1971.

'The Formula-Quotations of Matthew 2 and the Problem of Communication'. *NTS* 27 (1980): 233–51.

Matthew: Evangelist and Teacher. London: Paternoster, 1989.

Frankemölle, H. *Jahwebund und Kirche Christi.* NTAbh, n.F. 10. 2nd edn. Münster: Aschendorf, 1984.

Freedman, David N. 'The Masoretic Text and the Qumran Scrolls: A Study in Orthography'. In *Qumran and the History of the Biblical Text*, pp. 196–211. Edited by F. Cross and S. Talmon. Cambridge, MA: Harvard University Press, 1975 (originally published in *Textus* 2 (1963): 87–102).

Freyne, Sean. *Galilee from Alexander the Great to Hadrian (323 B.C.E. to 135 C.E.)*. Notre Dame: University of Notre Dame Press/Michael Glazier, 1980.

Galilee, Jesus, and the Gospels: Literary Approaches and Historical Investigations. Philadelphia: Fortress, 1988.

Friedrich, J. *Gott im Bruder? Eine methodenkritische Untersuchung von Redaktion, Überlieferung und Traditionen in Mt. 25, 31–46*. Stuttgart: Calwer, 1977.

Fuller, R. H. *The Foundations of New Testament Christology*. London: Collins, 1969.

Garland, David E. *The Intention of Matthew 23*. NovTSup 52. Leiden: Brill, 1979.

'Matthew's Understanding of the Temple Tax'. In *Treasures Old And New: Recent Contributions to Matthean Studies*, pp. 69–98. Edited by D. R. Bauer and M. A. Powell. SBL Symposium Series. Atlanta: Scholars, 1996.

Gärtner, Bertil. 'The Habakkuk Commentary (DSH) and the Gospel of Matthew'. *ST* 8 (1954): 1–24.

Gerhardsson, Birger. 'Gottes Sohn als Diener Gottes: Messias, Agape und Himmelsherrschaft nach dem Matthäusevangelium'. *ST* (1973): 73–106.

'Sacrificial Service and Atonement in the Gospel of Matthew'. In *Reconciliation and Hope: New Testament Essays on Atonement and Eschatology Presented to L. L. Morris on his 60th Birthday*, pp. 25–35. Edited by Robert Banks. Exeter: Paternoster, 1974.

The Mighty Acts of Jesus according to Matthew. Lund: CWK Gleerup, 1979.

Gibbs, James M. 'Purpose and Pattern in Matthew's Use of the Title "Son of David"'. *NTS* 10 (1963–4): 446–64.

Gossai, H. *Justice, Righteousness and the Social Critique of the Eighth-Century Prophets*. American University Studies 7.141. New York: Peter Lang, 1993.

Goulder, M. D. *Midrash and Lection in Matthew*. London: SPCK, 1974.

Graham, S. 'A Strange Salvation: Intertextual Allusion in Mt 27,39–43'. In *The Scriptures in the Gospels*, pp. 501–11. Edited by C. M. Tuckett. BETL 131. Leuven: Leuven University Press, 1997.

Grassi, Joseph A. 'The Five Loaves of the High Priest (Mt xii, 1–8; Mk ii, 23–28; Lk vi, 1–5; I Sam xxi, 1–6)'. *NovT* 7 (1964): 119–22.

Grech, Prosper. 'The "Testimonia" and Modern Hermeneutics'. *NTS* 19 (1972): 318–24.

Green, W. S. 'Introduction: Messiah in Judaism: Rethinking the Question'. In *Judaisms and Their Messiahs at the Turn of the Christian Era*, pp. 1–13. Edited by J. Neusner, W. S. Green and E. Frerichs. Cambridge: Cambridge University Press, 1987.

Greenberg, Moshe. *Ezekiel 21–37: A New Translation with Introduction and Commentary*. AB 22A. New York: Doubleday, 1997.

Greenfield, J. C. and M. E. Stone. 'The Enochic Pentateuch and the Date of the Similitudes'. *HTR* 70 (1977): 51–65.

Greer, Rowan A. 'The Christian Bible and Its Interpretation'. In *Early Biblical Interpretation*, pp. 107–203. Edited by J. Kugel and R. Greer. Philadelphia: Westminster, 1986.

Grimm, Werner. *Das Trostbuch Gottes: Jesaja 40–55*. Stuttgart: Calwer Verlag, 1990.

Grindel, J. 'Matthew 12,18–21'. *CBQ* 29 (1967): 110–15.

Gundry, R. H. *The Use of the Old Testament in St Matthew's Gospel: With Special Reference to the Messianic Hope*. NovTSup 18. Leiden: Brill, 1967.

Hagner, Donald A. 'The *Sitz im Leben* of the Gospel of Matthew'. In *Treasures Old and New: Recent Contributions to Matthean Studies*, pp. 27–68. Edited by D. R. Bauer and M. A. Powell. SBL Symposium Series. Atlanta: Scholars, 1996.

Hahn, F. *The Titles of Jesus in Christology: Their History in Early Christianity*. Translated by H. Knight and G. Ogg. New York: World Publishing Co., 1969.

'Son of David'. *EDNT* III.391–2.

Hare, D. R. A. and D. J. Harrington. ' "Make Disciples of All the Gentiles" (MT 28:19)'. *CBQ* 37 (1975): 359–69.

Hare, Douglas R. A. *The Theme of Jewish Persecution of Christians in the Gospel according to St Matthew*. SNTSMS 6. Cambridge: Cambridge University Press, 1967.

Harnack, Adolf (von). 'Zur Textkritik und Christologie der Schriften des John.' *SAB* (1915): 552–6.

Harris, J. R. *Testimonies*. With the assistance of Vacher Burch. 2 vols. Cambridge: Cambridge University Press, 1916–20.

Hartman, L. 'Scriptural Exegesis in the Gospel of St Matthew and the Problem of Communication'. In *L'évangile selon Matthieu: rédaction et théologie*. Edited by M. Didier, BETL 29, pp. 131–52. Gembloux: Duculot, 1972.

'Into the Name of Jesus: A Suggestion concerning the Earliest Meaning of the Phrase'. *NTS* 20 (1974): 432–40.

Hasitschka, M. 'Die Verwendung der Schrift in Mt 4,1–11'. In *The Scriptures in the Gospels*, pp. 487–90. Edited by C. M. Tuckett. BETL 131. Leuven: Leuven University Press, 1997.

Hatch, Edwin. *Essays in Biblical Greek*. Oxford: Clarendon, 1889.

Hatch, Edwin and Henry A. Redpath. *A Concordance to the Septuagint and the other Greek Versions of the Old Testament (including the Apocryphal Books)*. 3 vols. Oxford: Clarendon, 1897–1906.

Haupt, E. 'Zur Würdigung der Alttestamentlichen Citationen Ev. Matth. 8,17. 13,35. 27,9. 2,23'. In *Programm des Bugenhagenschen Gymnasiums zu Treptow A. R. Zu der am 11 und 12 April 1870 stattfinden öffentlichen Prüfung*, pp. 1–18. Treptow, 1870.

Hawkins, J. C. *Horae Synopticae: Contributions to the Study of the Synoptic Problem*. Oxford: Clarendon, 1909.

Hayes, John H. and Stuart A. Irvine. *Isaiah the Eighth-Century Prophet: His Times and His Preaching*. Nashville: Abingdon, 1987.

Hays, Richard B. *Echoes of Scripture in the Letters of Paul*. New Haven: Yale University Press, 1989.

Head, Peter M. *Christology and the Synoptic Problem: An Argument for Markan Priority*. SNTSMS 94. Cambridge: Cambridge University Press, 1997.

Heil, John Paul. *The Death and Resurrection of Jesus: A Narrative-Critical Reading of Matthew 26–28*. Minneapolis: Fortress, 1991.

'Ezekiel 34 and the Narrative Strategy of the Shepherd and Sheep Metaphor in Matthew'. *CBQ* 55 (1993): 698–708.

Heim, K. 'The Perfect King of Psalm 72: An "Intertextual" Inquiry'. In *The Lord's Anointed: Interpretation of Old Testament Messianic Texts*, pp. 223–48. Edited by P. Satterthwaite, R. Hess and G. Wenham. Grand Rapids: Baker, 1995.

Held, Heinz Joachim. 'Matthew as Interpreter of the Miracle Stories'. In *Tradition and Interpretation in Matthew*, pp. 165–299. Edited by G. Bornkamm, et al. London: SCM Press, 1963.

Hengel, Martin. *Judaism and Hellenism: Studies in Their Encounter in Palestine during the Early Hellenistic Period*. Translated by J. Bowden. London: SCM Press, 1974.

Hicks, John Mark. 'The Sabbath Controversy in Matthew: An Exegesis of Matthew 12:1–14'. *ResQ* 27 (1984): 79–91.

Hill, David. 'False Prophets and Charismatics: Structure and Interpretation in Matthew 7:15–23'. *Bib* 57 (1976): 327–48.

'On the Use and Meaning of Hosea VI. 6 in Matthew's Gospel'. *NTS* 24 (1977): 107–19.

'Son and Servant: An Essay on Matthean Christology'. *JSNT* 6 (1980): 2–16.

'The Figure of Jesus in Matthew's Story: A Response to Professor Kingsbury's Literary-Critical Probe'. *JSNT* 21 (1984): 37–52.

'In Quest of Matthean Christology'. *IBS* 9 (1986): 135–42.

Hillyer, Norman. 'Matthew's Use of the Old Testament'. *EvQ* 36 (1964): 12–26.

Holm-Nielsen, Svend. *Hodayot: Psalms from Qumran*. Acta Theologica Danica 2. Aarhus: Universitetsforlaget, 1960.

Holtzmann, H. J. *Hand-Commentar zum Neuen Testament: Die Synoptiker*. Freiburg, 1889–91.

Hooker, Morna D. *Jesus and the Servant: The Influence of the Servant Concept of Deutero-Isaiah in the New Testament*. London: SPCK, 1959.

The Son of Man in Mark: A Study of the Background of the Term 'Son of Man' and Its Use in St Mark's Gospel. London: SPCK, 1967.

Horbury, William. 'The Messianic Associations of the "Son of Man"'. *JTS* 36 (1985): 34–55.

Jewish Messianism and the Cult of Christ. London: SCM Press, 1998.

'Messianism in the Old Testament Apocrypha and Pseudepigrapha'. In *King and Messiah in Israel and the Ancient Near East: Proceedings of the Oxford Old Testament Seminar*, pp. 420–33. Edited by J. Day. JSOTSup 270. Sheffield: Sheffield Academic Press, 1998.

Horsley, Richard A. ' "Messianic" Figures and Movements in First-Century Palestine'. In *The Messiah: Developments in Earliest Judaism and Christianity*, pp. 276–95. Edited by J. H. Charlesworth, with J. Brownson, M. Davis, S. J. Kraftchick and A. F. Segal. Minneapolis: Fortress, 1992.

Archaeology, History, and Society in Galilee: The Social Context of Jesus and the Rabbis. Valley Forge: Trinity Press International, 1996.

Horton, Fred L. 'Formulas of Introduction in the Qumran Literature'. *RevQ* 7 (1971): 505–14.

Howell, David B. *Matthew's Inclusive Story: A Study in the Narrative Rhetoric of the First Gospel*. JSNTSup 42. Sheffield: JSOT Press, 1990.

Hultgard, Anders. *L'eschatologie des Testaments des douze Patriarches*. Vol. I:

Interprétation des textes. Acta Universitatis Upsaliensis Historia Religionum 6. Uppsala: Almqvist & Wiksell, 1977.

Hultgren, Arland J. 'The Formation of the Sabbath Pericope in Mark 2:23–28'. *JBL* 91 (1972): 38–43.

Hummel, R. *Die Auseinandersetzung zwischen Kirche und Judentum im Matthäusevangelium*. 2nd edn. BEvT 33. Munich: Chr. Kaiser Verlag, 1966.

Hunter, A. M. 'Crux Criticorum – Matt. XI. 25–30 – A Re-appraisal'. *NTS* 8 (1962): 241–9.

Instone-Brewer, David. *Techniques and Assumptions in Jewish Exegesis before 70 CE*. TSAJ 30. Tübingen: Mohr (Paul Siebeck), 1992.

Janowski B. and P. Stuhlmacher. *Der Leidende Gottesknecht: Jesaja 53 und seine Wirkungsgeschichte mit einer Bibliographie zu Jes 53*. Forschungen zum Alten Testament 14. Tübingen: Mohr (Paul Siebeck), 1996.

Jastrow, Marcus. *A Dictionary of the Targumim, the Talmud Babli and Yerushalmi, and the Midrashic Literature*. 2 vols. New York: Pardes, 1950.

Jeremias, J. 'παῖς θεοῦ'. *TDNT* V.677–717.

Johnson, Sherman E. 'The Biblical Quotations in Matthew'. *HTR* 36 (1943): 135–53.

Jones, Ivor H. *The Matthean Parables: A Literary and Historical Commentary*. NovTSup 80. Leiden: Brill, 1995.

Juel, D. H. *Messianic Exegesis: Christological Interpretations of the Old Testament in Early Christianity*. Philadelphia: Fortress, 1988.

Kahle, P. *The Cairo Geniza*. 2nd edn. Oxford: Clarendon, 1959.

Katz, P. 'Das Problem des Urtextes der Septuaginta'. *TZ* 5 (1949): 1–24.

Keck, Leander E. 'Toward the Renewal of New Testament Christology'. *NTS* 32 (1986): 362–77.

'Matthew and the Spirit'. In *The Social World of the First Christians: Essays in Honor of Wayne A. Meeks*, pp. 145–55. Edited by L. White and O. Yarbrough. Minneapolis: Fortress, 1995.

Keegan, Terence J. 'Introductory Formulae for Matthean Discourses'. *CBQ* 44 (1982): 415–30.

Kelbley, Charles A., ed. *The Value of Justice: Essays on the Theory and Practice of Social Virtue*. New York: Fordham University Press, 1979.

Kendall, D. 'Use of Mišpaṭ in Isaiah 59'. *ZAW* 96 (1984): 391–405.

Kent, H. A. 'Matthew's Use of the Old Testament: A Study in Hermeneutics'. *Bibliotheca Sacra* 121 (1964): 34–43.

Kilpatrick, G. D. *The Origins of the Gospel according to St Matthew*. Oxford: Oxford University Press, 1946.

Kingsbury, Jack D. *Matthew: Structure, Christology, Kingdom*. Philadelphia: Fortress, 1975.

'The Title "Son of David" in Matthew's Gospel'. *JBL* 95 (1976): 591–602.

'The Figure of Jesus in Matthew's Story: A Literary-Critical Probe'. *JSNT* 21 (1984): 3–36.

'The Developing Conflict between Jesus and the Jewish Leaders in Matthew's Gospel: A Literary-Critical Study'. *CBQ* 49 (1987): 57–73.

Matthew as Story. 2nd edn. Philadelphia: Fortress, 1988.

Knibb, Michael A. 'The Date of the Parables of Enoch: A Critical Review'. *NTS* 25 (1979): 345–59.

'Exile in the Damascus Document'. *JSOT* 25 (1983): 99–117.

The Qumran Community. Cambridge: Cambridge University Press, 1987.

Knowles, Michael. *Jeremiah in Matthew's Gospel: The Rejected Prophet Motif in Matthean Redaction*. JSNTSup 68. Sheffield: Sheffield Academic Press, 1993.

Koch, D. A. *Die Schrift als Zeuge des Evangeliums*. Tübingen: Mohr (Paul Siebeck), 1984.

Koehler, Ludwig and Walter Baumgartner. *Hebräisches und Aramäisches Lexikon zum Alten Testament*. 3rd edn. Revised by W. Baumgartner. Edited by B. Hartmann, et al. 3 vols. Leiden: Brill, 1967–83.

Koenig, J. *L'herméneutique analogique du Judaïsme antique d'après les témoins textuels d'Isaïe*. VTSup 33. Leiden: Brill, 1982.

Köhler, Wolf-Dietrich. *Die Rezeption des Matthäusevangeliums in der Zeit vor Irenäus*. WUNT 24. Tübingen: Mohr (Paul Siebeck), 1987.

Kraft, R. '"εἰς νῖκος": Permanently/Successfully: 1 Cor 15:54; Matt 12:20'. In *Septuagintal Lexicography*, pp. 153–6. Edited by R. Kraft. Missoula: Scholars, 1975.

Krentz, Edgar. 'The Extent of Matthew's Prologue: Toward the Structure of the First Gospel'. *JBL* 83 (1964): 409–14.

Kuck, David W. *Judgment and Community Conflict: Paul's Use of Apocalyptic Judgment Language in 1 Corinthians 3:5–4:5*. NovTSup 66. Leiden: Brill, 1992.

Kuhn, Karl Georg, ed. *Konkordanz zu den Qumrantexten*. Göttingen: Vandenhoeck & Ruprecht, 1960.

Kupp, David D. *Matthew's Emmanuel: Divine Presence and God's People in the First Gospel*. SNTSMS 90. Cambridge: Cambridge University Press, 1996.

Kutscher, E. Y. *The Language and Linguistic Background of the Isaiah Scroll (1QIsaᵃ)*. STDJ 6. Leiden: Brill, 1974.

Kvalbein, H. 'Die Wunder der Endzeit: Beobachtungen zu 4Q521 und Matth 11,5'. *ZNW* 88 (1997): 111–25.

Kynes, William L. *A Christology of Solidarity: Jesus as the Representative of His People in Matthew*. New York: University of America Press, 1991.

Leitch, James W. 'Lord Also of the Sabbath'. *SJT* 19 (1966): 426–33.

Lentzen-Deis, Fritz Leo. *Die Taufe Jesu nach den Synoptikern: Literarkritisch und gattungsgeschichtliche Untersuchungen*. Frankfurt: Joseph Knecht, 1970.

Leske, Adrian M. 'Isaiah and Matthew: The Prophetic Influence in the First Gospel; A Report on Current Research'. In *Jesus and the Suffering Servant: Isaiah 53 and Christian Origins*, pp. 152–69. Edited by W. Bellinger and W. Farmer. Harrisburg: Trinity Press International, 1998.

Levine, Etan. 'The Sabbath Controversy according to Matthew'. *NTS* 22 (1976): 480–3.

Lim, Timothy H. *Holy Scripture in the Qumran Commentaries and Pauline Letters*. Oxford: Clarendon, 1997.

Lind, M. C. 'Monotheism, Power, and Justice: A Study in Isaiah 40–55'. *CBQ* 46 (1984): 432–46.

Lindars, Barnabus. *New Testament Apologetic: The Doctrinal Significance of the Old Testament Quotations*. London: SCM Press, 1961.

Loader, W. R. G. 'Son of David, Blindness, Possession, and Duality in Matthew'. *CBQ* 44 (1982): 570–85.

Lohmeyer, Ernst. *Gottesknecht und Davidssohn*. 2nd edn. FRLANT. Göttingen: Vandenhoeck & Ruprecht, 1953.

Lohse, E. 'υἱὸς Δαυίδ'. *TDNT* VIII.478–88.

'υἱὸς κτλ'. *TDNT* VIII.340–62.

Longenecker, Bruce. 'The Wilderness and Revolutionary Ferment in First-Century Palestine: A Response to D. R. Schwarz and J. Marcus'. *JSJ* 29 (1998): 322–36.

Longenecker, Richard N. *The Christology of Early Jewish Christianity*. SBT Second Series 17. London: SCM Press, 1970.

Biblical Exegesis in the Apostolic Period. Grand Rapids: Eerdmans, 1975.

Lövestam, E. *Son and Saviour*. Lund: Gleerup, 1961.

Luomanen, Petri. '*Corpus Mixtum* – An Appropriate Description of Matthew's Community?' *JBL* 117 (1998): 469–80.

Lust, J. 'Messianism and Septuagint'. In *Congress Volume: Salamanca, 1983*, pp. 174–91. Edited by J. A. Emerton. Leiden: Brill, 1985.

Luz, Ulrich. 'Die Erfüllung des Gesetzes bei Matthäus (5,17–20)'. *Zeitschrift für Theologie und Kirche* 75 (1978): 398–435.

'The Son of Man in Matthew: Heavenly Judge or Human Christ'. *JSNT* 48 (1992): 3–21.

Matthew in History: Interpretation, Influence and Effects. Minneapolis: Fortress, 1994.

The Theology of the Gospel of Matthew. Translated by J. B. Robinson. New Testament Theology. Cambridge: Cambridge University Press, 1995.

'The Disciples in the Gospel according to Matthew'. In *The Interpretation of Matthew*, pp. 115–48. Edited by G. N. Stanton. 2nd edn. Edinburgh: T. & T. Clark, 1995.

'The Final Judgment (Matt 25:31–46): An Exercise in "History of Influence" Exegesis'. In *Treasures Old And New: Recent Contributions to Matthean Studies*, pp. 271–310. Edited by D. R. Bauer and M. A. Powell. SBL Symposium Series. Atlanta: Scholars, 1996.

Lybaek, L. 'Matthew's Use of Hosea 6,6'. In *The Scriptures in the Gospels*, pp. 491–9. Edited by C. M. Tuckett. BETL 131. Leuven: Leuven University Press, 1997.

Lyons, John. *Introduction to Theoretical Linguistics*. London: Cambridge University Press, 1972.

Semantics. 2 vols. Cambridge: Cambridge University Press, 1977.

Mafico, Trembla L. J. 'Justice'. *ABD* III.1127–9.

Malina, Bruce J. 'The Literary Structure and Form of Matt. XXVIII. 16–20'. *NTS* 17 (1970): 87–103.

Malina, Bruce J. and J. Neyrey. *Calling Jesus Names: The Sociological Value of Labels in Matthew*. Sonoma: Polebridge, 1988.

Manson, T. W. 'The Old Testament in the Teachings of Jesus'. *BJRL* 34 (1951–2): 312–32.

The Servant-Messiah: A Study of the Public Ministry of Jesus. Cambridge: Cambridge University Press, 1953.

Marcus, Joel. *The Way of the Lord: Christological Exegesis of the Old Testament in the Gospel of Mark*. Louisville: Westminster/John Knox Press, 1992.

'Mark and Isaiah'. In *Fortunate the Eyes that See: Essays in Honor of David*

Noel Freedman in Celebration of His Seventieth Birthday, pp. 449–66. Edited by A. Beck, et al. Grand Rapids: Eerdmans, 1995.

Marcus, R. 'The "Plain Meaning" of Isaiah 42:1–4'. *HTR* 30 (1937): 249–59.

Margoliouth, D. S. 'The Visit to the Tomb'. *ExpTim* 38 (1926/7): 278–80.

Marshall, I. Howard. 'Son of God or Servant of Yahweh? A Reconsideration of Mark 1.11'. *NTS* 15 (1968): 326–36.

   The Gospel of Luke: A Commentary on the Greek Text. NIGTC. Grand Rapids: Eerdmans, 1978.

Massebieau, E. *Examen des citations de l'Ancien Testament dans l'évangile selon Saint Matthieu.* Paris, 1885.

Matera, Frank J. 'The Plot of Matthew's Gospel'. *CBQ* 49 (1987): 233–53.

McConnell, Richard S. *Law and Prophecy in Matthew's Gospel: The Authority and Use of the Old Testament in the Gospel of St Matthew.* Basel: Friedrich Reinhardt, 1969.

McGrath, James F. 'Change in Christology: New Testament Models and the Contemporary Task'. *ITQ* 65 (1998): 39–50.

McKenzie, J. L. *Second Isaiah.* AB. Garden City, New York: Doubleday, 1968.

McNamara, Martin. *The New Testament and the Palestinian Targum to the Pentateuch.* Rome: Pontifical Bible Institute, 1966.

   'The Language Situation in First Century Palestine: Aramaic and Greek'. *Proceedings of the Irish Biblical Association* 15 (1992): 7–36.

Meier, John P. *Law and History in Matthew's Gospel: A Redactional Study of Mt. 5:17–48.* AnBib 71. Rome: Biblical Institute Press, 1976.

   'Nations or Gentiles in Matthew 28:19?' *CBQ* 39 (1977): 94–102.

   'John the Baptist in Matthew's Gospel'. *JBL* 90 (1980): 383–405.

Ménard, J.-E. 'Pais Theou as Messianic Title in the Book of Acts'. *CBQ* 19 (1957): 83–92.

Menken, Maarten J. J. 'The Source of the Quotation from Isaiah 53:4 in Matthew 8:17'. *NovT* 39 (1997): 313–27.

   'The Quotation from Isaiah 42,1–4 in Matthew 12,18–21: Its Text Form'. *ETL* 75 (1999): 32–52.

Mettinger, Tryggve N. D. *A Farewell to the Servant Songs: A Critical Examination of an Exegetical Axiom.* Translated by F. H. Cryer. Lund: CWK Gleerup, 1983.

Metzger, Bruce. 'The Formulas Introducing Quotations of Scripture in the NT and the Mishnah'. *JBL* 70 (1951): 297–307.

   A Textual Commentary on the Greek New Testament. 2nd edn. London: United Bible Societies, 1975.

Meyers, E. 'The Cultural Setting of Galilee: The Case of Regionalism and Early Judaism'. In *ANRW* II.19.1, pp. 686–702. Edited by H. Temporini and W. Haase. Berlin and New York: de Gruyter, 1979.

Michel, O. 'Das Licht des Messias'. In *Donum Gentilicium: New Testament Studies in Honour of David Daube*, pp. 140–50. Edited by E. Bammel, C. K. Barrett and W. D. Davies. Oxford: Clarendon, 1978.

   'The Conclusion of Matthew's Gospel: A Contribution to History of the Easter Message'. In *The Interpretation of Matthew*, pp. 39–51. Translated by R. Morgan. Edited by G. N. Stanton. 2nd edn. Edinburgh: T. & T. Clark, 1995.

Miler, Jean. *Les citations d'accomplissement dans l'évangile de Matthieu: quand Dieu se rend présent en toute humanité.* AnBib 140. Roma: Editrice Pontificio Istituto Biblico, 1999.

Miller, M. P. 'Targum, Midrash and the Use of the Old Testament in the New Testament'. *JSJ* 2 (1971): 29–82.

Miller, Robert J. 'Is There Independent Attestation for the Transfiguration in 2 Peter?' *NTS* 42 (1996): 620–5.

Moo, Douglas J. *The Old Testament in the Gospel Passion Narratives.* Sheffield: Almond, 1983.

Moore, George Foot. *Judaism in the First Centuries of the Christian Era.* 2 vols. New York: Schocken, 1971 (originally published 1927).

Morrow, F. J. 'The Text of Isaiah at Qumran'. Unpublished PhD dissertation. The Catholic University of America, 1973. Ann Arbor, Michigan: University Microfilms, 1977.

Moses, A. D. A. *Matthew's Transfiguration Story and Jewish-Christian Controversy.* JSNTSup 122. Sheffield: Sheffield Academic Press, 1996.

Moule, C. F. D. 'Fulfilment-Words in the New Testament: Use and Abuse'. NTS 14 (1967–8): 293-320.

Mowinckel, S. *He That Cometh: The Messianic Concept in the Old Testament and Later Judaism.* Nashville: Abingdon, 1955.

Mulder, M. J., ed. *Mikra: Text, Translation, and Reading and Interpretation of the Hebrew Bible in Ancient Judaism and Early Christianity.* CRINT 2.1. Assen and Maastricht: Van Gorcum; Philadephia: Fortress, 1988.

Murphy-O'Connor, J. 'The Essenes and Their History'. *RB* 81 (1974): 215–44.

Neirynck, F. 'ΑΠΟ ΤΟΤΕ ΗΡΞΑΤΟ and the Structure of Matthew'. In *Evangelica II. 1982–1991.* pp. 141–82. Edited by F. Neirynck and F. van Segbroeck. BETL. Leuven: Leuven University Press, 1991 (originally published in *ETL* 64 (1988): 21–59).

Neirynck, Frans and F. van Segbroeck. *New Testament Vocabulary: A Companion Volume to the Concordance.* With the collaboration of Henri Leclercq. BETL 65. Leuven: Leuven University Press, 1984.

Nepper-Christensen, P. *Das Matthäusevangelium – ein jüdenchristliches Evangelium?* Acta Theologica Danica 1. Aarhus: Universitetsforlaget, 1958.

Nestle, E. 'Matthew xii.19–Isaiah xlii.2'. *ExpTim* 20 (1908–9): 92–3.
————— 'Matthew xii.19–Isaiah xlii.2'. *ExpTim* 20 (1908–9): 189.

Neusner, Jacob, W. S. Green and E. Frerichs, eds. *Judaisms and Their Messiahs at the Turn of the Christian Era.* Cambridge: Cambridge University Press, 1987.

New, David S. *Old Testament Quotations in the Synoptic Gospels and the Two-Document Hypothesis.* SBLSCS 37. Atlanta: Scholars, 1993.

Newport, Kenneth G. C. *The Sources and Sitz im Leben of Matthew 23.* JSNTSup 117. Sheffield: Sheffield Academic Press, 1995.

Neyrey, Jerome H. 'The Thematic Use of Isaiah 42,1–4 in Matthew 12'. *Bib* 63 (1982): 457–73.

Nickelsburg, George W. E., Jr. *Resurrection, Immortality, and Eternal Life in Intertestamental Judaism.* HTS 26. Cambridge, MA: Harvard University Press, 1972.
————— *Jewish Literature between the Bible and the Midrash: A Historical and Literary Introduction.* Philadelphia: Fortress, 1981.

Nickelsburg, George W. E., Jr. and J. J. Collins, eds. *Ideal Figures in Ancient Judaism*. Septuagint and Cognate Studies 12. Chico: Scholars, 1980.

Nolan, B. M. *The Royal Son of God: The Christology of Mt 1–2*. Orbis biblicus et orientalis 23. Göttingen: Vandenhoeck & Ruprecht, 1979.

Nolland, John. 'No Son of God Christology in Matthew 1:18–25'. *JSNT* 62 (1996): 3–12.

Oegema, Gerbern S. *Der Gesalbte und sein Volk: Untersuchungen zum Konzeptualisierungsprozess der messianischen Erwartungen von den Makkabäern bis Bar Koziba*. Schriften des Institutum Judaicum Delitzschianum 2. Göttingen: Vandenhoeck & Ruprecht, 1994.

Orton, David E. *The Understanding Scribe: Matthew and the Apocalyptic Ideal*. JSNTSup 25. Sheffield: JSOT Press, 1989.

Ottley, R. R. *The Book of Isaiah according to the Septuagint (Codex Alexandrinus)*. Vol. II. Text and notes. Cambridge: Cambridge University Press, 1906.

Overman, J. A. *Matthew's Gospel and Formative Judaism: The Social World of the Matthean Community*. Minneapolis: Fortress, 1990.

Church and Community in Crisis: The Gospel according to Matthew. Valley Forge: Trinity Press International, 1996.

Page, Sydney H. T. 'The Suffering Servant between the Testaments'. *NTS* 31 (1985): 481–97.

Patte, Daniel. *Early Jewish Hermeneutic in Palestine*. SBLDS 22. Missoula: Scholars, 1975.

Perrin, Norman. *What Is Redaction Criticism?* Philadelphia: Fortress, 1969.

Pesch, Rudolf. 'Eine alttestamentliche Ausführungsformel im Matthäus-Evangelium: Redaktionsgeschichtliche und exegetische Beobachtungen'. *BZ* 10 (1966): 220–45.

'Eine alttestamentliche Ausführungsformel im Matthäus-Evangelium (Schlub)'. *BZ* 11 (1967): 79–95.

'Der Gottessohn im matthäischen Evangelienprolog (Mt 1–2). Beobachtungen zu den Zitationsformeln der Reflexionszitate'. *Bib* 48 (1967): 395–420.

Plooij, D. 'The Baptism of Jesus'. In *Amicitiae Corolla: A Volume of Essays Presented to James Rendel Harris on the Occasion of His 80th Birthday*, pp. 239–52. Edited by H. G. Wood. London: University of London Press, 1933.

Pomykala, K. E. *The Davidic Dynasty Tradition in Early Judaism: Its History and Significance for Messianism*. Atlanta: Scholars, 1995.

Porter, J. R. 'The Legal Aspects of the Concept of "Corporate Personality" in the Old Testament'. *VT* 15 (1965): 361–80.

Powell, Mark Alan. 'The Religious Leaders in Matthew: A Literary-critical Approach'. Unpublished PhD thesis. Union Theological Seminary in Virginia, 1988.

God with Us: A Pastoral Theology of Matthew's Gospel. Minneapolis: Fortress, 1995.

Prinsloo, W. S. 'Isaiah 42,10–12: "Sing to the Lord a New Song..."'. In *Studies in the Book of Isaiah: Festschrift Willem A. M. Beuken*, pp. 289–301. Edited by J. van Ruiten and M. Vervenne, BETL 132. Leuven: Leuven University Press, 1997.

Przybylski, B. *Righteousness in Matthew and His World of Thought.* SNTSMS 41. Cambridge: Cambridge University Press, 1980.

Puech, Emile. 'Quelques aspects de la restauration du rouleau des Hymnes (1QH)'. *JJS* 39 (1988): 38–55.

'Une Apocalypse messianique (4Q521)'. *RevQ* 15 (1992): 475–519.

'Messianism, Resurrection, and Eschatology at Qumran and in the New Testament'. In *The Community of the Renewed Covenant: The Notre Dame Symposium on the Dead Sea Scrolls*, pp. 235–56. Edited by E. Ulrich and J. VanderKam. Christianity and Judaism in Antiquity Series 10. Notre Dame, University of Notre Dame Press, 1994.

Rabin, Chaim. 'The Translation Process and the Character of the Septuagint'. *Textus* 6 (1968): 1–26.

Rahlfs, A. 'Über Theodotion-Lesarten im Neuen Testament und Aquila-Lesarten bei Justin'. *ZNW* 20 (1921): 182–99.

Rawls, J. *A Theory of Justice.* Cambridge, MA: Harvard University Press, 1971.

Rengstorf, Karl Heinrich, ed. *A Complete Concordance to Flavius Josephus.* 4 vols. and supplement. Leiden: Brill, 1968–83.

Ringgren, Helmer. *The Faith of Qumran: Theology of the Dead Sea Scrolls.* Expanded edn. Edited with a new introduction by James H. Charlesworth. New York: Crossroad, 1995.

Roberts, C. H. *Two Biblical Papyri in the John Rylands Library Manchester.* Manchester: The University of Manchester Press, 1936.

Robinson, H. Wheeler. *The Christian Doctrine of Man.* Edinburgh: T. & T. Clark, 1911.

Robinson, J. A. 'Ascension of Isaiah'. *HDB* II.500–1.

St Paul's Epistle to the Ephesians: A Revised Text and Translation with Exposition and Notes. 2nd edn. London: Macmillan, 1904.

Rogerson, J. W. 'The Hebrew Conception of Corporate Personality: A Re-Examination'. *JTS* 21 (1970): 1–16.

Rothfuchs, W. *Die Erfüllungszitate des Matthäus-Evangeliums: Eine biblisch-theologische Untersuchung.* BWANT 88. Stuttgart: Kohlhammer, 1969.

Rowland, C. C. 'Apocalyptic, the Poor, and the Gospel of Matthew'. *JTS* 45 (1994): 504–18.

Ruprecht, E. 'Die Auslegungsgeschichte zu den sogenannten Gottesknecht liedern im Buch Deuterojesaja unter methodischen Gesichtspunkten bis zu Bernard Duhm'. Unpublished dissertation, Heidelberg, 1972.

Rutgers, L. V., P. W. van der Horst, H. W. Havelaar and T. Teugels, eds. *The Use of Sacred Books in the Ancient World.* Biblical Exegesis and Theology 22. Leuven: Peters, 1998.

Rydbeck, L. *Fachprosa, vermeintliche Volkssprache und Neues Testament. Zur Beurteilung der sprachlichen Niveauunterschiede im nachklassischen Griechisch.* Acta Universitatis Upsaliensis. Studia Graeca Upsaliensia 5. Uppsala: Berlingska, 1967.

Saebo, Magne, ed. *Hebrew Bible/Old Testament: The History of Its Interpretation.* Vol. I: *From the Beginnings to the Middle Ages (until 1300). Part I: Antiquity.* Göttingen: Vandenhoeck & Ruprecht, 1996.

Saldarini, Anthony J. *Matthew's Christian-Jewish Community.* Chicago: University of Chicago Press, 1994.

Sand, A. *Das Gesetz und die Propheten: Untersuchungen zur Theologie des*

Evangeliums nach Mätthaus. Biblische Untersuchungen 11. Regensburg: Pustet, 1974.

Sanders, E. P. *Judaism: Practice and Belief 63 BCE–66 CE*. London: SCM Press, 1992.

Sanders, James A. 'From Isaiah 61 to Luke 4'. In *Christianity, Judiasm and Other Greco-Roman Cults: Studies for Morton Smith at Sixty. Part One: New Testament*, pp. 75–106. Edited by J. Neusner. SJLA 12. Leiden: Brill, 1975.

Sandmel, Samuel. 'Parallelomania'. *JBL* 81 (1962): 1–13.

Satterthwaite, P., R. Hess and G. Wenham. *The Lord's Anointed: Interpretation of Old Testament Messianic Texts*. Carlisle: Paternoster, 1995.

Sawyer, John F. A. *The Fifth Gospel: Isaiah in the History of Christianity*. Cambridge: Cambridge University Press, 1996.

Schäfer, Peter. *Die Vorstellung vom heiligen Geist in der rabbinischen Literatur*. SANT 28. Munich: Kösel, 1972.

Schaper, Joachim. *Eschatology in the Greek Psalter*. WUNT 76. Tübingen: Mohr (Paul Siebeck), 1995.

Schenk, Wolfgang. *Die Sprache des Matthäus: Die Text-Konstituenten in ihren makro- und mikrostrukturellen Relationen*. Göttingen: Vandenhoeck & Ruprecht, 1987.

Schiffman, Lawrence H. *Sectarian Law in the Dead Sea Scrolls: Courts, Testimony, and the Penal Code*. Chico: Scholars, 1983.

'Messianic Figures and Ideas in the Qumran Scrolls'. In *The Messiah: Developments in Earliest Judaism and Christianity*, pp. 116–29. Edited by J. H. Charlesworth. Minneapolis: Fortress, 1992.

Schille, Gottfried. 'Bemerkungen zur Formgeschichte des Evangeliums II. Das Evangelium des Matthäus als Katechismus'. *NTS* 4 (1957): 101–14.

Schlier, Heinrich. 'αἱρετίζω'. *TDNT* I.184.

'ἀνατέλλω, ἀνατολή'. *TDNT* I.351–53.

Schnackenburg, Rudolf. ' "Siehe da mein Knecht, den ich erwählt habe..." (Mt 12,18): Zur Heiltätigkeit Jesu im Matthäusevangelium'. In *Salz der Erde–Licht der Welt: Exegetische Studien zum Matthäusevangelium Festschrift für Anton Vögtle zum 80. Geburtstag*, pp. 203–22. Edited by L. Oberlinner and P. Fiedler. Stuttgart: Katholisches Bibelwerk, 1991.

'Matthew's Gospel as a Test Case for Hermeneutical Reflection'. In *Treasures Old And New: Recent Contributions to Matthean Studies*, pp. 251–69. Edited by D. R. Bauer and M. A. Powell. SBL Symposium Series. Atlanta: Scholars, 1996.

Schniewind, J. 'ἀπαγγέλλω'. *TDNT* I.66–7.

Schürer, Emil. *The History of the Jewish People in the Age of Jesus Christ*. Revised and edited by G. Vermes, F. Millar and M. Black. 3 vols. Edinburgh: T. & T. Clark, 1973–87.

Scullion, J. 'An Approach to the Understanding of Isa. 7:16–17'. *JBL* 87 (1968): 288–300.

Seeligmann, I. L. *The Septuagint Version of Isaiah*. MVEOL 9. Leiden: Brill, 1948.

Seitz, Christopher R. 'Old Testament or Hebrew Bible? Some Theological Considerations'. *Pro Ecclesia* 5 (1996): 292–303.

Sekki, A. E. *The Meaning of* Ruaḥ *at Qumran.* SBLDS 110. Atlanta: Scholars, 1987.

Senior, Donald P. 'A Case Study in Matthean Creativity: Matthew 27:3–10'. *BR* 19 (1974): 23–36.

  The Passion Narrative according to Matthew: A Redactional Study. BETL 39. Leuven: Leuven University Press, 1982.

  The Passion of Jesus in the Gospel of Matthew. Wilmington: Michael Glazier, 1985.

  'The Lure of the Formula Quotations: Re-Assessing Matthew's Use of the Old Testament with the Passion Narrative as a Test Case'. In *The Scriptures in the Gospels*, pp. 89–115. Edited by C. M. Tuckett. BETL 131. Leuven: Leuven University Press, 1997.

Sigal, Phillip. *The Halakah of Jesus of Nazareth according to the Gospel of Matthew.* Lanham, MD: University Press of America, 1986.

Sim, David C. *Apocalyptic Eschatology in the Gospel of Matthew.* SNTSMS 88. Cambridge: Cambridge University Press, 1996.

  The Gospel of Matthew and Christian Judaism: The Historical Setting of the Matthean Community. Edinburgh: T. & T. Clark, 1998.

Sjöberg, Erik. *Der Menschensohn im Äthiopischen Henochbuch.* Lund: C. W. K. Gleerup, 1946.

Skehan, Patrick W. 'The Text of Isaias at Qumran'. *CBQ* 17 (1955): 38–43.

  'The Qumran Manuscripts and Textual Criticism'. In *Volume du Congrès Strasbourg, 1956*, pp. 148–58. Society for Old Testament Study. VTSup 4. Leiden: Brill, 1957.

Slomovic, E. 'Toward an Understanding of the Exegesis in the Dead Sea Scrolls'. *RevQ* 7 (1969–71): 3–15.

Smith, D. M. 'The Use of the Old Testament in the New'. In *The Use of the Old Testament in the New and Other Essays: Studies in Honor of William Franklin Stinespring*, pp. 3–65. Edited by J. Efird. Durham, NC: Duke University Press, 1972.

Smith, Morton. 'What Is Implied by the Variety of Messianic Figures?' *JBL* 78 (1959): 66–72.

Smith, P. *Thesaurus Syriacus.* 2 vols. Oxford: Clarendon, 1901.

Snodgrass, Klyne. 'Matthew and the Law'. In *Treasures Old And New: Recent Contributions to Matthean Studies*, pp. 99–128. Edited by D. R. Bauer and M. A. Powell. SBL Symposium Series. Atlanta: Scholars, 1996.

Soares Prabhu, George M. *The Formula Quotations in the Infancy Narrative of Matthew: An Enquiry into the Tradition History of Mt 1–2.* AnBib 63. Rome: Biblica Institute Press, 1976.

Soltau, W. 'Zur Entstehung Des I. Evangeliums'. *ZNW* 1 (1900): 219–48.

Sperber, A. 'The New Testament and the Septuagint'. *Tarbis* 6 (1934): 1–29.

  'New Testament and Septuagint'. *JBL* 59 (1940): 193–293.

Stählin, G. 'ἀσθενεία'. *TDNT* I.490–3.

Stanley, C. D. *Paul and the Language of Scripture: Citation Technique in the Pauline Epistles and Contemporary Literature.* SNTSMS 74. Cambridge: Cambridge University Press, 1992.

Stanton, Graham N. 'Matthew as a Creative Interpreter of the Sayings of Jesus'. In *Das Evangelium und die Evangelien*, pp. 273–87. Edited by P. Stuhlmacher. Tübingen: J. C. B. Mohr, 1983.

'The Origin and Purpose of Matthew's Gospel: Matthean Scholarship from 1945–1980'. In *ANRW* II.25.3, pp. 1889–1951. Edited by H. Temporini and W. Haase. Berlin: de Gruyter, 1983.

'Aspects of Early Christian-Jewish Polemic and Apologetic'. *NTS* 31 (1985): 377–392.

'Matthew'. In *It Is Written: Scripture Citing Scripture. Essays in Honour of Barnabus Lindars*, pp. 205–19. Edited by D. A. Carson and H. G. M. Williamson. Cambridge: Cambridge University Press, 1988.

A Gospel for a New People: Studies in Matthew. Louisville, KY: Westminster/ John Knox, 1993.

'The Fourfold Gospel.' *NTS* 43 (1997): 317–46.

Review of *The Matthean Parables: A Literary and Historical Commentary* by Ivor H. Jones. *EpRev* 25 (1998): 100–1.

Stanton, Graham N., ed. *The Interpretation of Matthew*. 2nd edn. Studies in New Testament Interpretation 3. Edinburgh: T. & T. Clark, 1995.

Stanton, V. H. *The Gospels as Historical Documents*. Vol. II: *The Synoptic Gospels*. Cambridge: The University Press, 1909.

Stendahl, Krister. *The School of St Matthew and Its Use of the Old Testament*. 1st Sigler Press edn. Ramsey: Sigler, 1991.

'Quis et Unde? An Analysis of Mt. 1–2'. In *The Interpretation of Matthew*, 69–80. Edited by G. Stanton. 2nd edn. Edinburgh: T. & T. Clark, 1995 (originally published in *Judentum, Urchristentum, Kirche: FS J. Jeremias*, pp. 97–105. Edited by Eltester. Beihefte zur ZNW 26. Berlin: Töpelmann, 1964).

Stephenson, T. 'The Old Testament Quotations Peculiar to Matthew'. *JTS* 20 (1918): 227–9.

Strack, H. L. and G. Stemberger. *Introduction to the Talmud and Midrash*. Translated and edited by M. Bockmuehl. Edinburgh: T. & T. Clark, 1992.

Strecker, Georg. *Der Weg der Gerichtigkeit: Untersuchung zur Theologie des Matthäus*. FRLANT 82. Göttingen: Vandenhoeck & Ruprecht, 1962.

'The Concept of History in Matthew'. In *The Interpretation of Matthew*, pp. 81–100. 2nd edn. Edited by G. N. Stanton. Studies in New Testament Interpretation. Edinburgh: T. & T. Clark, 1995.

Suggs, M. J. *Wisdom, Christology, and Law in Matthew's Gospel*. Cambridge, MA: Harvard University Press, 1970.

Suhl, A. 'Der Davidssohn im Matthäus-Evangelium'. *ZNW* 59 (1968): 57–81.

Suter, David W. *Tradition and Composition in the Parables of Enoch*. SBLMS 47. Missoula: Scholars, 1979.

Swete, H. *The Gospel according to St Mark: The Greek Text with Introduction and Indices*. London: MacMillan & Co., 1909.

Talmon, Shemaryahu. 'The Old Testament Text'. In *The Cambridge History of the Bible*. Vol. I: *From the Beginnings to Jerome*, pp. 159–99. Edited by P. R. Ackroyd and C. F. Evans. Cambridge: Cambridge University Press, 1970.

'Aspects of the Textual Transmission of the Bible in Light of Qumran Manuscripts'. In *Qumran and the History of the Biblical Text*, pp. 226–63. Edited by F. M. Cross and S. Talmon. Cambridge, MA: Harvard University Press, 1975.

'DSIa as a Witness to Ancient Exegesis of the Book of Isaiah'. In *Qumran and the History of the Biblical Text*, pp. 116–26. Edited by F. M. Cross and S. Talmon. Cambridge, MA: Harvard University Press, 1975.

Tatum, W. Barnes. ' "The Origin of Jesus Messiah" (Matt 1:1,18a): Matthew's Use of the Infancy Traditions'. *JBL* 4 (1977): 523–35.

Theisohn, Johannes. *Der auserwählte Richter: Untersuchen zum traditions-geschichtlichen Ort der Menschsohngestalt der Bilderreden das Äthiopschen Henoch.* SUNT 12. Göttingen: Vandenhoeck & Ruprecht, 1975.

Tisera, Guido. *Universalism according to the Gospel of Matthew.* European University Studies, Series 23, Theology, vol. 482. Frankfurt am Main: Peter Lang, 1993.

Torrey, Charles C. *Documents of the Primitive Church.* New York: Harper & Brothers Publishers, 1941.

Tov, Emanuel. 'A Modern Textual Outlook Based on the Qumran Scrolls'. *HUCA* 53 (1982): 11–27.

'The Orthography and Language of the Hebrew Scrolls Found at Qumran and the Origins of these Scrolls'. *Textus* 13 (1986): 31–57.

Textual Criticism of the Hebrew Bible. Minneapolis: Fortress, 1988.

'Hebrew Biblical Manuscripts from the Judaean Desert: Their Contribution to Textual Criticism'. *JJS* 39 (1988): 19–37.

Trilling, Wolfgang. 'Die Täufertradition bei Matthäus'. *BZ* 3 (1959): 271–89.

Das wahre Israel: Studien zur Theologie des Matthäus-Evangeliums. Munich: Kösel, 1964.

Tuckett, Christopher M. 'The Use of the Scriptures in Q'. In *The Scriptures in the Gospels*, pp. 3–26. Edited by C. M. Tuckett. BETL 131. Leuven: Leuven University Press, 1997.

Tuckett, Christopher M., ed. *The Scriptures in the Gospels.* BETL 131. Leuven: Leuven University Press, 1997.

Turner, C. H. 'Ο ΥΙΟΣ ΜΟΥ Ο ΑΓΑΠΗΤΟΣ'. *JTS* 27 (1926): 113–29.

Ulrich, Eugene. 'Multiple Literary Editions: Reflections toward a Theory of the History of the Biblical Text'. In *Current Research and Technological Developments on the Dead Sea Scrolls: Conference on the Texts from the Judean Desert, Jerusalem, 30 April 1995*, pp. 78–105. Edited by D. W. Parrey and S. D. Ricks. Leiden: Brill, 1996.

Vaganay, L. *Le problème synoptique: une hypothèse de travail.* Paris: Desclée et Co., 1954.

Van Cangh, J. M. 'La bible de Matthieu: les citations d'accomplissement'. *ETL* 6 (1975): 205–11.

' "Par l'esprit de Dieu – par le doigt de Dieu" Mt 12.28 par. Lc 11.20'. In *Logia: les paroles de Jésus – The Sayings of Jesus*, pp. 337–42. Edited by J. Delobel. BETL 59. Leuven: Leuven University Press, 1992.

Van der Kooij, Aire. 'The Old Greek of Isaiah in Relation to the Qumran Texts of Isaiah: Some General Comments'. In *Septuagint, Scrolls and Cognate Writings*, pp. 195–213. Edited by G. J. Brooke and B. Lindars. SBLSCS 33. Atlanta: Scholars, 1992.

' "The Servant of the Lord": A Particular Group of Jews in Egypt according to the Old Greek of Isaiah: Some Comments on LXX Isa 49,1–6 and Related Passages'. In *Studies in the Book of Isaiah: Festschrift Willem A. M. Beuken*, pp. 383–96. Edited by J. van Ruiten and M. Vervenne. BETL 132. Leuven: Leuven University Press, 1997.

The Oracle of Tyre: The Septuagint of Isaiah XXIII as Version and Vision. Leiden: Brill, 1998.

Van Ruiten, J. and M. Vervenne, eds. *Studies in the Book of Isaiah: Festschrift Willem A. M. Beuken.* BETL 132. Leuven: Leuven University Press, 1997.

Van Segbroeck, F. 'Les citations d'accomplissement dans l'évangile selon Saint Matthieu d'après trois ouvrages récents.' In *L'évangile selon Matthieu: rédaction et théologie*, pp. 107–30. Edited by M. Didier. BETL 29. Gembloux: Duculot, 1972.

Van Tilborg, S. *The Jewish Leaders in Matthew.* Leiden: Brill, 1972.

Van Unnik, W. C. 'Dominus Vobiscum'. In *New Testament Essays: Studies in Memory of Thomas Walter Manson, 1893–1958*, pp. 270–305. Edited by A. J. B. Higgins. Manchester: Manchester University Press, 1959.

Van Winkle, D. W. 'The Relationship of the Nations to Yahweh and to Israel in Isaiah XL-LV'. *VT* 35 (1985): 446–58.

Van Zijl, J. B. *A Concordance to the Targum of Isaiah.* SBL Aramaic Studies 3. Missoula: Scholars, 1979.

VanderKam, James C. *The Dead Sea Scrolls Today.* Grand Rapids: Eerdmans, 1994.

Vaux, R. de. *Archaeology and the Dead Sea Scrolls.* The Schweich Lectures of the British Academy. London : Oxford University Press, 1973.

Vermes, Geza. *Scripture and Tradition in Judaism.* SPB 4. Leiden: Brill, 1961.

'Bible and Midrash: Early Old Testament Exegesis'. In *Cambridge History of the Bible.* Vol. I: *From the Beginnings to Jerome*, 199–231. Edited by P. C. Ackroyd and C. F. Evans. Cambridge: Cambridge University Press, 1970.

Jesus the Jew: A Historian's Reading of the Gospels. London: SCM Press, 1973.

The Dead Sea Scrolls: Qumran in Perspective. London: SCM Press, 1994.

Verseput, D. J. *The Rejection of the Humble Messianic King: A Study of the Composition of Matthew 11–12.* Frankfurt: Peter Lang, 1986.

'The Role and Meaning of the "Son of God" Title in Matthew's Gospel'. *NTS* 33 (1987): 532–56.

Via, D. O. 'Ethical Responsibility and Human Wholeness in Matthew 25:31–46'. *HTR* 80 (1987): 79–100.

Von Dobschütz, Ernst. 'Rabbi and Catechist'. In *The Interpretation of Matthew*, pp. 27–38. Translated by R. Morgan. Edited by G. N. Stanton. 2nd edn. Edinburgh: T. & T. Clark, 1995.

Wacholder, B. Z. *The Dawn of Qumran: The Sectarian Torah and the Teacher of Righteousness.* Monographs of the Hebrew Union College no. 8. Cincinnati: Hebrew Union College Press, 1983.

Wainwright, Elaine Mary. *Toward a Feminist Critical Reading of the Gospel according to Matthew.* BZNW 60. Berlin: de Gruyter, 1991.

Walker, R. *Die Heilsgeschichte im ersten Evangelium.* FRLANT 91. Göttingen: Vandenhoeck & Ruprecht, 1967.

Waltke, B. K. and M. O'Connor. *An Introduction to Biblical Hebrew Syntax.* Winona Lake: Eisenbrauns, 1990.

Watson, Francis. *Text and Truth: Redefining Biblical Theology.* Grand Rapids: Eerdmans, 1997.

Watts, John D. *Isaiah 34–66.* WBC. Dallas: Word, 1987.

Watts, Rikki E. *Isaiah's New Exodus and Mark*. WUNT 88. Tübingen: Mohr (Paul Siebeck), 1997.

Weren, Wim. 'Jesus' Entry into Jerusalem: Mt 21,1–17 in the Light of the Hebrew Bible and the Septuagint'. In *The Scriptures in the Gospels*, pp. 117–41. Edited by C. M. Tuckett. BETL 131. Leuven: Leuven University Press, 1997.

'Quotations from Isaiah and Matthew's Christology (Mt 1,23 and 4,15–16)'. In *Studies in the Book of Isaiah: Festschrift Willem A. M. Beuken*, pp. 447–65. Edited by J. van Ruiten and M. Vervenne, 447–65. BETL 132. Leuven: Leuven University Press, 1997.

'The Use of Isaiah 5,1–7 in the Parable of the Tenants (Mark 12,1–12; Matthew 21,33–46)'. *Bib* 79 (1998): 1–26.

Westcott, B. F. *An Introduction to the Study of the Gospels*. 8th edn. London: Macmillan and Co., 1895.

Whitelocke, Lester T. *An Analytical Concordance of the Books of the Apocrypha*. 2 vols. Washington: University Press of America, 1978.

Williamson, H. G. M. 'Messianic Texts in Isaiah 1–39'. In *King and Messiah in Israel and the Ancient Near East: Proceedings of the Oxford Old Testament Seminar*, pp. 238–70. Edited by J. Day. JSOTSup 270. Sheffield: Sheffield Academic Press, 1998.

Wilson, F. M. 'The Son of Man in Jewish Apocalyptic Literature'. *Studia Biblica et Theologica* 8 (1978): 39–40.

Wise, M. O. and J. D. Tabor. 'The Messiah at Qumran'. *Biblical Archaeology Review* Nov/Dec (1992): 60–65.

Wolff, Hans Walter. *Jesaja 53 im Urchristentum*. 3rd edn. Berlin, 1952.

'A Solution to the Immanuel Prophecy in Isa 7:14–8:22'. *JBL* 91 (1972): 449–56.

Worton, M. and J. Still, eds. *Intertextuality: Theories and Practices*. Manchester: Manchester University Press, 1990.

Wrede, William. *The Messianic Secret*. Translated by J. Greig. London: James Clarke & Co., 1971.

Wright, N. T. 'Jerusalem in the New Testament'. In *Jerusalem Past and Present in the Purposes of God*, pp. 53–77. Edited by P. Walker. Cambridge: Tyndale House, 1992.

Yang, Yong-Eui. *Jesus and the Sabbath in Matthew's Gospel*. JSNTSup 139. Sheffield: Sheffield Academic Press, 1997.

Ziegler, Joseph. *Untersuchungen zur Septuaginta des Buches Isaias*. Alttestamentliche Abhandlungen, XII. Münster: Verlag der Aschendorffschen Verlagsbuchhandlung, 1934.

'Die Vorlage der Isaias-Septuaginta (LXX) und die erste Isaias-Rolle von Qumran (1QIsa^a)'. In *Qumran and the History of the Biblical Text*, pp. 90–115. Edited by F. M. Cross and S. Talmon. Cambridge, MA: Harvard University Press, 1975.

Ziesler, J. A. 'Matthew and the Presence of Jesus (1)'. *EpRev* 11 (1984): 55–63.

'Matthew and the Presence of Jesus (2)'. *EpRev* 11 (1984): 90–7.

Zimmerli, W. and J. Jeremias. *The Servant of God*. London: SCM Press, 1957.

INDEX OF PASSAGES

Early Jewish literature

INDEX OF MODERN AUTHORS

INDEX OF SUBJECTS

241